STUDIES IN MEDIEVAL AND RENAISSANCE HISTORY

Volume XII
(Old Series, Volume XXII)

STUDIES IN
Medieval and Renaissance History

Volume XII
(Old Series, Volume XXII)

EDITORS:

J. A. S. EVANS

R. W. UNGER

AMS PRESS
New York

AMS PRESS INC.
56 EAST 13TH STREET
NEW YORK, NY 10003

ISSN 0081-8224
ISBN 0-404-62850-8 (Set)
ISBN 0-404-62862-1 (Vol. XII)

Library of Congress Catalog Card Number 63-22098

All AMS books are printed on acid-free paper that meets the guidelines
for performance and durability of the Committee on Production
Guidelines for Book Longevity of the Council on Library Resources.

Manufactured in the United States of America

CONTENTS

INTRODUCTION   vi

The Slight of Honor: Slander and
Wrongful Prosecution in Five English
Medieval Villages.

         Patricia Hogan   3

On Claude Dupuy (1545–1594)

         William McCuaig   45

The Tournament of Power: Public Combat
and Social Inferiority in Late Medieval
England.

         Victor R. Sherb   105

Hunger, Flemish Participation and the
Flight of Philip VI: Contemporary
Accounts of the Siege of Calais, 1346–47.

         Kelly R. DeVries   129

The Family of Dynasties in Medieval
Europe: Dynasties, Kingdoms and
Tochterstämme.

         Armin Wolf   183

Children in Medieval German Jewry: A perspective on Ariès from Jewish Sources.

         Israel Ta-Shma   261

Review Essay: The Gothic Idol and Medieval
Art

         Carol Knicely   283

Book Reviews   299

Books Received   318

Index   325

INTRODUCTION

Studies in Medieval and Renaissance History is a series designed for original major articles in all fields of medieval and renaissance history. Volumes will appear approximately once a year.

Studies in Medieval and Renaissance History was formerly published by the University of Nebraska Press, and the impetus for the creation of the series came from the belief that there was a need for a publication that would accommodate the study that was too long to be included regularly in scholarly journals, but too short to appear as a book. The editors will consider articles in all areas of history from approximately the third to the sixteenth centuries — economic, social and demographic, political, intellectual and cultural, and studies that do not fit neatly into a single traditional category of historical investigation.

While the series is devoted primarily to the publication of major studies, it contains occasional bibliographic essays, and briefer articles dealing with unpublished archival and manuscript resources. The *Studies* also makes available in translation original articles by scholars who do not write in English or French.

Studies in Medieval and Renaissance History is published by AMS Press for the Committee for Medieval Studies at the University of British Columbia, and the editors welcome submissions from all scholars doing research in medieval and renaissance fields, including those whose interests are not strictly historical.

J. A. S. Evans

THE SLIGHT TO HONOR — SLANDER AND WRONGFUL PROSECUTION IN FIVE ENGLISH MEDIEVAL VILLAGES

M. Patricia Hogan

St. Francis Xavier University
Antigonish, Nova Scotia

The Slight to Honor — Slander and Wrongful Prosecution in Five English Medieval Villages

Introduction

Together with all manner of ethnographers, historians now probe the most deep-seated social and psychological factors influencing human behaviour. As one example, we might note recent investigations of *charivari,* the raucous shame rituals conspicuous throughout Europe in the later middle ages and early modern centuries. They were an accepted outlet for the exuberance of adolescent males, allowing them to skewer the hypocrisy and privileges of their elders, especially with regard to remarriage, the youth serving as the conscience of courtship and domestic relations generally.[1] Since the 1960s, French historians have used the term *mentalité* to denote the impulses and psychological states (mental assumptions) giving place to such actions and there are now several studies depicting popular attitudes to plague, magic, childhood, social status, money, and much else.[2]

Long regarded as one of the most powerful influences on human conduct is the individual's sense of honor, with wilful attack on it ranking among the most emotionally-charged and serious of legal offenses. As various social anthropologists, J. K. Campbell, J. G. Peristiany, Julian Pitt-Rivers among others, have shown, such studies offer unrivalled glimpses into the values of sexual prowess, sexual modesty, wealth, authority, bravery, hospitality, secrecy, one's lineage and its obligations, and the pressures exerted on the individual in the name of these.[3] The means of assailing honor, especially the various techniques and objectives of gossip, are just as intriguing. Max Gluckman, for

instance, has seen gossip as essentially a collective activity: it is the property of a group, regulated by it; it crystallizes and reinforces common
values, hence making for the greater solidarity of the group.[4] By contrast, Robert Paine views gossip as fundamentally an individual activity,
for the sake of self-interest. "It is the individual and not the community
that gossips. What he gossips about are his own and others' aspirations,
and only indirectly the values of the community."[5] Peter J. Wilson has
recently seen the two interpretations as not necessarily excluding each
other.[6]

Only since the 1980s have historians, other than the legal contingent, considered this vital prospect, J. A. Sharpe's sifting of sixteenth-century slander cases in York church court records constituting
a major initiative.[7] Innumerable defamation materials await scrutiny, litigation occurring in various common law courts as well as local and
ecclesiastical tribunals.[8] In selecting a focus for the present study, we
might usefully recall a number of complexities relating to the definition of honor, and their resolution.

Scholars today refer to honor as an evaluation of self (values,
sentiments, actions) as others might be imagined to judge one.[9] During
the classical and medieval eras, however, the term related more to private intentions (conscience) with these committing a man to certain
duties (virtues) civic and/or religious. Yet, civic virtue, as Aristotle
noted, invariably becomes defined not by conscience alone but public
acclaim, possible conflict arising between these two standards.[10] Still
later writers, such as Thomas Hobbes, identified honor with power,
whatever means a man has — strength, form, eloquence — to obtain
some future apparent good, and gain recognition by others of his superiority over them.[11] Even approximately similar societies of the same era
have had quite different views of honor. While modern Sarakatsani
shepherds reckon a man's worth as rooted in his flocks and grazing
land, his manpower and the quality of his inherited relations, the
power of his patrons, as well as certain moral attributes, especially
"manliness" — the courage and strength of purpose of males — and
the sexual purity of women,[12] French Valloire villagers see reputation as
resting almost exclusively with the individual's moral character, all else
really being subject to chance.[13] Clearly, public opinion largely decides
what honor is,[14] but this varies not only with the community but, as J.
Davis has decisively shown, with various subgroups and activities within
it.[15] Hence, it becomes a function of the law to establish the criteria of
honor and to impose consensus. This is not to espouse an analytical or

Austinian view of law over the so-called historical view.[16] As Harold J. Berman notes, law involves not only reason and will, the ingredients so decisive for the analytical school, but emotion, intuition and faith, i.e., a total social commitment.[17] The turning point referred to here is that when members of society cannot agree on essentials, they will put their rules and relationships into writing and make formal institutions for themselves.[18]

In England from the seventh century, questions of honor, especially the prejudice of a man's reputation through words, were closely bound up with law codes. The laws exacted strict compensation as well as fines, *bot* and *wite*,[19] and for centuries these cases were handled in local and ecclesiastical courts alone, defamation itself being a term of church law.[20] Only in the sixteenth century did the Common Law really enter the field.[21]

Gossip could definitely involve damaging words as well, more than one *communis garrulatrix* being hailed before medieval village courts.[22] Studies show a fairly clear line between good exchanges and otherwise,[23] Paul Adams noting an extreme form of *mauvaise langue* (*envidia*) among Spanish Pyrenean villagers of Hogar that constitutes outright calumny.[24] Similarly, Juliet Du Boulay notes the villagers of Ambéli as engaging in a type of slanderous innuendo which they prefer to call gossip rather than slander.[25] The speaker is often extremely sophisticated,[26] deviously alluding to failures in office, failures in truth, intemperateness, wealth and the style of life made possible by it, the failure to remain equal, relatives, etc.[27]

Under *diffamatio*, the legal historians Pollock and Maitland also insert the offence of wrongful prosecution (*pro falso clamore suo*), initially accusations of murder and the other felonies, then debt, trespass, and breach of covenant. They were an aggravated form of defamation. The legislation eventually embraced every malicious appeal and even appeals that simply ended in acquittal. There was a "strong feeling" that men should not make charges which they knew to be a lie; these individuals were morally blameworthy.[28]

In selecting a *locus* for our study, we might bear in mind this further truth. The greater the stage on which one acts (and wields authority), obviously the greater the scope for honor; yet, the smaller and more closely interwoven a society, the more likelihood there is of being slandered and possibly the more destructive the blow when it falls. Villages have been uniformly viewed as "face-to-face" societies with multiplex rather than "single-interest" ties.[29] Medieval villagers, for example, were bound to each other by their interspersed lands (open-field arrangements) and collective by-law activities, their self-policing and local court systems which included tithing groups of ten to twelve individuals, juror service, and personal pledging. Finally, the village has also been seen as a moral community, a shared pattern of norms and expectations against which personal behavior is constantly measured and by which it is constrained.[30] Whether the individual likes it or not, he is viewed very much "in the round," as a whole person and in personal ways, and it is difficult to mask behavior.[31] It is for these several reasons that defamation jurisdiction was "naturally" left to village courts for so long — "they alone could secure amends before the same community that had witnessed the affront."[32] Pollock and Maitland note that until adequate investigation has been made of these records, we shall know little of the medieval law of defamation generally.[33]

Some of the richest court-roll collections survive for the villages of Ramsey Abbey, those for Broughton, Warboys, and Wistow being particularly noteworthy. The records begin in the 1270s and for the pre-Black Death years alone, 1270–1350, there are thirty-five to thirty-seven rolls for each of these vills, ten to eighteen being a normal tally.[34] Upwood and Abbots Ripton have been added to this survey[35] as they complete a cluster of settlements immediately adjacent to Ramsey, holdings which its abbots had early and eagerly acquired.[36] There are both similarities and contrasts in the vills. All were essentially arable properties, the Domesday Inquest noting land for fifteen to twenty-three ploughs in each.[37] Yet Abbots Ripton and Upwood were located further upland and retained sizeable reserves of wood well beyond the Middle Ages.[38] The latter additionally enjoyed a more exclusive use of its fen, i.e., less inter commoning.[39] The vills converged and diverged in terms of population too, Abbots Ripton again proving distinctive with only 690 individuals for 1270–1350 as contrasted with 1,000 to 1,200 elsewhere.[40] We might expect these geographic and demographic fundamentals to have influenced residence patterns and work routines. But did they affect behavior otherwise, the tendency to slander or wrongly accuse, for example?

The present study initially examines defamation — the perpetrators, the infamy alleged, the impact of the cases, and the means of social control — as closely as possible within the confines of a single village, Broughton having been randomly selected. We shall then pursue three of the most prominent themes emerging for the five villages, namely (a) women and defamation, (b) property and defamation, and

(c) social status (officials, tradesmen, and families), and defamation. Finally, the major contrasts in the data will be considered under the heading "geography and defamation."

A principal concern of students of legal records is the grey statistic, the percentage of unreported cases. Given the close quarters of village life and the readiness of the human tongue, one suspects that the incidence was high, considerably higher than for other major crimes. Yet, this only makes the extant evidence all the more valuable. As to whether plaintiffs were telling the truth, that is, had defendants in fact used defamatory language, the highly public nature of most incidents (i.e., the presumption of witnesses) serves as one check. A more difficult issue is whether charges of wrongful prosecution were themselves wrongful prosecutions. The lone and not insubstantial safeguard here is subsequent court presentments and it has been used. With these considerations in mind, we shall proceed.

Broughton

Broughton, today, is still a picturesque village, well maintained,[41] and inhabitants from of 1288 to 1350 were similarly quite vigorous towards its 2,372 acres, annual works statements indicating a mustering of 60–70% of customary and wage labour.[42] Residents further mingled to seek marriage partners, land, credit and sureties, to exchange goods and exploit commons rights, and to execute various public services — ale-tasting, the reeveship, capital-pledging, warding marshes, fields, and woodlands.[43] We might expect antagonisms and are not disappointed. They spoke opprobriously *(opprobriosa)* of each other, with foul words *(turpibus verbis)*, slandered each other as thieves, receivers of thieves, infidels, seducers, and whores.

Twenty-two defamations are recorded and were confined to the years 1288–1316 alone; wrongful prosecutions numbered thirty and were spread much more evenly over the seventy years under study.[44] The latter are enrolled with extreme brevity, basic jurisprudence holding that such claims were simply a lie, heinous for it and requiring little further elaboration.[45] Hence, only eight specify a debt, trespass, or breach of covenant.[46] The slanders may furnish a comment on the early fourteenth-century generally, especially the so-called Malthusian crisis, Warboys entries ceasing in 1316 too. These events were highly sensational, occurring before the complete parish assembly, in the midst of a harvest ritual, or in a villager courtyard. In other words, they required a certain intensity, apart from all else, and following 1316 this energy seems to have been noticeably rechannelled. These were well known as years of rain, famine, and a possible widespread subsistence crisis, considerable tempering influences on society generally.[47]

The relationship of offender and victim would seem a foremost consideration, and court rolls readily identify five major groups of villagers: main families; intermediate and often isolated residents (Inter); tradesmen (Trade); officials (Off); and outsiders (Out). Families further divide into: those demographically and economically secure and discharging a number of public responsibilities (A); those disappearing (B); those newly appearing in the records (C); and those continuing in a minor role, assuming juror, pledging, and tasting obligations only once or twice in a generation (D).[48]

In four defamations and nine false claims, members of main families beset each other, the aggressor most often being from a substantial A household. Honor is most contentious among those comprising the broad middle ranges of agrarian and pastoral societies, say seasoned observers.[49] Within these ranks there are those tending to slip from grace and those solidly maintaining themselves. Detraction is often the recourse of the former as they fear becoming moral debtors of former equals.[50] Yet, detraction is also the tool of the dominant, Max Gluckman noting that it is "one of the chief weapons which those who consider themselves higher in status use to put those whom they consider lower in their place".[51] Interestingly, five of the above defendants came from families who were clearly maintaining their influence, another four from households with rising fortunes, and one was from a declining household. Similar details for the plaintiffs, especially the rising status of at least five of them, add notably to impressions of the competitiveness of life among these middle-rank families. The following Table summarizes these data.

Table 1

The Social Status of Main Family Defamers and Victims
1270 – 1350

Key: — maintaining status; ↑ Rising in status; ↓ falling in status

Year	Defendant	Slander Status	Plaintiff	Status
1288	Crane (A)	—	Beneyt (D)	↓

1290	Crane (A)	—	Gore (A)	↓
1297	Mohaut (A)	—	⌈ Randolf (A)	—
			⌊ Carpenter (D)	↓
1306	Ad Portam (A)	—	Hobbe (A)	—

False Prosecutions

1294 (Jan.)	Aleyn (B)	—	John (B)	—
1301	Kyng	↑	Hobbe (A)	—
1306	Randolf (A) (Debt)	—	Kyng (B)	↑
	Gore (A)	↓	Broughton (A)	↑
1316	Hanecok (D)	—	Edward (D)	↓
			Abbot (A)	↑
			Fysshere (A)	↑
1334	Attegate (C) (Debt)	—	Outy (A)	↑
1337	Outy (A) (Breach of covenant)	↑	Clericus (B)	↓
			Parson (D)	↓
1340	Ad Pontem (A) (Debt)	↑	Ad Portam (A)	—
	Gore (A) (Debt)	↓	Hanecok (D)	—

These details are taken from Britton, Community of the Vill, pp. 222–33.

Another six males defamed or false claimed against women, Ralph Everard (B), for instance, alleging that the wife of John Le Bon (A) had stolen wheat from the lord's fields (1294), and John Beneyt (D) defaming Katerine Bele (Inter) as a thief who had wrongly taken bread and money from her sister's house (1294).[52] The entries confirm a commonplace, viz., that women are the principal victims of gossip.[53] The unique feature is the male aggressor, men commonly confining their allegations to their own sex.[54] Given the social equality of several of the defendants and plaintiffs, it would seem that village males simply saw women as stout rivals in the daily round, rather than assuming an extreme gender antipathy. Women, for their part, fear gossip more than men, largely because their contacts with their communities are closer and more continuous.[55] Still, they clearly met fire with fire: four women either defamed or false claimed against a male[56] and another three slandered one of their own sex. Margaret, wife of Hugh Knyt (Inter) called the daughter of Ralph, the butcher, a receiver of thieves

before the whole parish (1291); Agnes, wife of John Pege (Inter)
defamed Christina of London (Inter) as a whore(1307), and seven
years later similarly maligned Christina Couper (Trade). They were certainly the keenest critics with regard to sexual matters.[57]

Throughout history, women have been reckoned the main
agent, the true purveyors of gossip and scandal. The suspicion is that
being by nature "weaker of mind," and lacking public occupation and
good education they are prone to talk about people, not news and
opinions. They are interested in private lives, hidden and secret affairs,
and more attentive to small manifestations of personality.[58] Yet, this is
not really the testimony of these particular entries. In fact, the most
intriguing factor is the number of property offenses wrongly charged
against them. Almost half (five) of the total eleven theft and debt prosecutions saw a woman as victim.

Tradesmen and officials also figure conspicuously in the
entries. In 1288, Simon le Bon (A) defamed the ale of Robert Curtys;[59]
in 1307, William Pege (Inter) slandered Roger, the Miller of
Houghton, as a thief who stole the lord's fowl. All told, smiths, brewers,
coopers, and millers were defendants in three suits and plaintiffs in
two.[60] Village officers who appeared before the court included the
bailiff, woodward, reeve, bedel, and marshall. They were uniformly victims in a total of six presentments. In 1297, Simon le Bon and his wife
(A) spoke maliciously of the Bailiff, Geoffrey of Swynford, as did
Richard of Hyrst (Inter), the latter having been indicted for a faulty
work performance, *male falcavit*.[61] Especially bitter were the charges
hurled at them by tradesmen, the actions of Robert the Swineherd in
1311 being extremely revealing. In one clash, he defamed the bedel,
woodward, and reeve as treacherous and seducers, also false claiming
against the latter two. He had forestalled the three officers, waylaying a
horse which they had seized as rent, and was eventually placed in
stocks. The herd appears sorely driven, the impounding of the animal
seeming to have triggered all, and he was eventually noted as *pauper*
(1316). It is not difficult to see how basic economic hardship fuelled
such an outcry.

Another two slanders occurred within households, William
Hobbe (A) defaming John Hobbe as a thief in 1306, and Nicholas, son
of Richard of Broughton (A), false claiming against a brother, Ralph,
in 1316. The remaining arraignments saw five main family members
beset either an isolated resident or an outsider; an equal number of the
latter returned the injury.[62]

Altogether, the fifty-two enrollments present us with a range of humanity and outpourings, yet two charges clearly dominate. Promiscuity notices are striking for their precision, *infidele et meretrice* constituting vivid obloquy. Yet, theft and debt denunciations were heard most often, predominating in church court records for the later middle ages as well.[63] When substantial villagers, such as, an Attehalle (A), Aspelon (A), and Attegate (C) made wrongful accusations of debt, and likewise an Ad Portam (A) and Hobbe (A) slandered others as thieves, we may suspect either very real difficulties for these core residents, or simply an initial good will having gone sour. Possibly a slight ambiguity regarding the terms of a loan had fanned itself into a deep irritant. Add to these charges the five theft/debt allegations made against women, and the testiness surrounding goods — the slightest license or tampering with them — is obvious.

Firmer clues as to motives are best sought in complete court-roll biographies, especially those for recurrent offenders, e.g., Thomas Mohaut (1292, 1297), Simon le Bon (1288, 1297), John Beneyt (1292, [2]), and Thomas Gore (1306, 1314, 1316, 1334, 1340), and similarly for families with more than one violator, viz., Cranes (2), Fabers (2), Le Bons (3), Peges (2), Parsons (2), and Coupers (2).

In 1288, Walter Crane (A) rebuked opprobriously John Beneyt (D) during the harvest works, John, son of Simon Crane, two years later attacking John Gore (A) in his courtyard with filthy words and stones. Both seemed markedly tempestuous, yet their records are relatively clean thereafter. Walter received outsiders (1297, 1306, 1316) and owed debts (1311, 1322), yet also pledged on five occasions; John was arraigned for a work default (1306). Their initial indictments strongly suggest adolescent pique and vexatiousness, a sorry scourge at the time, but obviously remediable. The pattern holds for Thomas Mohaut (A) as well. In 1292, he defamed a neighbour and in 1297 slandered the threesome of Henry, son of Richard (Out), John Randolf (A), and Elias Carpenter (Trade); yet, by 1297, he had also become a taster, subsequently a juror (1299), the reeve (1306–07, 1311–12), a taster again (1316), and pledged ten times as well (1297–1334).

More interesting were the eventual transgressions of their victims. John Beneyt (D) defamed Katherine Bele (Inter) as a thief, also false claiming against her for debt in 1294; in fact, he owed her 6d. He was charged with another two debts, theft, assault, and break and entry in the same year. He seems to have been notably hounding the woman, urging that the theft was against her sister. Katherine Bele was a simple gleaner (1290, 1291), virtually a vagrant, and unfortunately charged with adultery in 1294. There were obviously ties, circumstantial and otherwise between the defendant and the woman, and both disappeared from the village in 1294.

Thomas Gore inflicted the greatest amount of this damage on the village between 1270–1350, wrongly prosecuting on five occasions. Again, it is not difficult to discover an incitement. In the case of John of Broughton (A), a debt was owed by a Gore to a Broughton in 1297 and contrariwise in 1306,[64] enough straw indeed for the camel's back. Similarly, Agnes Smith (Trade) was already on the roll for 1314 for having broken an agreement with Thomas Gore concerning a piece of meadow which she was renting from him. Robert Lenot was an outsider and falsely charged with trespass (1316) while Catherine Hobbe (A) was once more a resident and the accusation, debt (1334). William Hanecok (D) was also well known to Thomas Gore, having been presented prior to the false claim in 1340 for unjustly detaining 2s. 7d. plus one bushel of peas from him. Once more, we are pointedly reminded of the place of property in the psyche of villagers. Any threat whatever to material resources was a powerful incentive for action. Being a tradesmen, a butcher, Thomas Gore may have felt the burden of delayed debts more keenly than most. His credit activities were certainly as central to his concerns as his butchery, and increasingly he emerges as a frenzied character who was finally presented for igniting his house in 1339, damages at 10s.

Smiths (Trade), Hobbes (A), and Broughtons (A) virtually gave as much trouble as they received. Agnes Smith false claimed in 1307, as did her son in 1291, and they certainly add to the notion that tradesmen were more defiant and hot-tempered than most. Stephen Smith was fresh on the rolls in 1291, i.e., a youth, and the further meaning of his action is possibly best discovered in his victim. John Ballard (B) was as reputable a villager as one might expect to find, five times a juror, fourteen times a pledge, and also a capital pledge over the years (1288–1316). But it may have been exactly these accolades that triggered the youth's scorn.

John Hobbes (A) was assuredly slandered — twice as a thief in 1306. In 1297, he and his brother, William, had been censured as vagabonds who broke in the doors and windows of neighbors to the terror of the village, John being again presented for this. In 1306, he forestalled, waylaid a cart, and with his wife stole fowl, six pledges being enlisted to ensure that they would behave and respect their neighbors.

Disappearing for a time, he resurfaced from 1334 to 1340, six hues being raised over him in as many years. Although the slanders of 1306 were personal initiatives — the respected John ad Portam (A) being one of the defendants — they may certainly have epitomized wider sentiments. As Gluckman notes, gossip expresses group values and is not simply delimited personal activity; it helps to identify and firm up a common code, thus ensuring unity.[65]

William Hobbes who was the other party to denounce his brother in 1306 is certainly a more interesting case study. Until 1306, he remained an assailant, housebreaker, and fornicator, and was also wrongly prosecuted.[66] He then changed dramatically, becoming several times a juror, a taster, and nineteen times a pledge. He was once more falsely sued, for debt in 1320, and was certainly owing the defendant, Stephen of Burton (Out), 5s. 5d. His debts remained a problem. In 1320, he was also owing Robert Crane (A) (5s. 5d. plus two lbs. of wool) and Thomas Clerk (B) (one ring of peas and one quarter of wheat). Moreover, although slandering his brother as a thief in 1306, it was he who owed the victim 15d.

The Broughton household experienced a defamation within its walls as well, but they were most often innocent victims. John of Broughton (A), falsely prosecuted by Thomas Gore (1306) was again slandered in 1316. His varied and constant involvement in village life renders him remarkably similar to John Ballard. He acquired and defended land (1306[2], 1311), extended credit (1297), received villagers (1314 [2]), pledged on twenty-four occasions, was a juror (1292), a taster (1299, 1301) and also trespassed thirteen times. But his detractor in 1316, John the Couper (Trade), had no less impressive credentials — five times a juror, eleven times a pledge, defended land, trespassed, and sought concords (1306–1339). The situation clearly bolsters Paine's notion that *mauvaise langue* is most often the weapon of equals to forward self-interest.[67] A man climbs by disparaging and humbling others: throw dirt enough and possibly some will stick. There are other examples of equals truly reviling each other, yet with the fortunes of neither party seemingly greatly harmed. William Couper insulted Andrew Outy (A) in 1291 yet continued to function as a juror and pledge, as did his victim. Ralph Everard (B) who defamed the wife of John le Bon (A) similarly remained a creditable pledge and juror.[68] The situation seems to parallel present-day Sarakatsani society where there is really no shame in delivering insults.[69]

With the Le Bons (A), Peges (Inter) and another two intermediate villagers, we confront an especially ill-willed lot. Three Le Bons were presented for their tongues, Simon defaming a brewer (1288), Petronilla decrying her neighbors (1292), and Simon and his wife attacking the bailiff (1297). Although a major village family, John was the only steady member in a generation, the others flitting hopelessly on and off the records. Ultimately, their indiscipline was more baneful for self than others, Simon being enrolled as *pauper* in 1288.

William Pege, and Agnes, wife of John Pege, were three times guilty of slander, the former finally being placed in stocks for his abusive theft allegation. Agnes Pege's battle with Christina Couper (Trade) whom she defamed as a whore (1314) was especially heated. The latter had assaulted Pege, leading to the slander, then trounced her again, Agnes replying with a hamsocn. Nine years later, Agnes Pege was again under suspicion, the object of a hue and cry.

Margaret Knyt (Inter) who slandered a villager as a "receiver of thieves" in 1291 was in 1297 arraigned with her husband for being a malefactor in autumn; they were required to surrender their bodies as pledge to the bailiff. John le Stake (Inter) who defamed a neighbor in 1292, stole a tunic in 1294, and by 1297 was to be arrested if he came onto the fee because he was inquituous.

Conclusions: Slanderous cries of theft and promiscuity are indeed shocking. Several entries clearly reflect a routine anxiety having converted itself into a major obsession; others simply confirm a commonplace, viz., that familiarity unquestionably does breed contempt. The ordinary tensions of rural life had "already soured relationships between the parties in a cause" says J. A. Sharpe.[70] When Thomas ad Pontem (A) wrongly sued John ad Portam (A) in 1340, 16d. were owing the defendant. In the case of Parson (1311), Attehille (1325), Webester (Jan. 1322) and Randolf (1306) the stakes were increasingly higher — 2s. 2d., one quarter of beans, 27s., and 31s. 4d.[71] Occasionally, an entry candidly reveals the petty ways of villagers:

> Convictus est per juratos quod Johannes filius Ricardus de Hyrst falso imposuit Henricem ad Portam quod idem Henricem per minas suas coegit ipsum Johannem dare 1 busellum braseum pretium septem denarias cuidam de herhyth(?) pro denaris suis habendi de brasei prius eidem vendito. Ideo dictus Johannes in misericordia, 3d. Plg. Thomae Bedellus.[72]

Besides spitefulness, fear would seem a major factor in several suits involving goods. Debt is an anxious burden in any age, and entirely relative: the ten pence binding one man can be as vexing as the twenty-seven shillings holding another. John Martyn who false claimed against John Erhith in 1316, for example, owed the latter only 12d. Creditors had few devices at their disposal.[73] They could resort to a court-ordered distraint of a pot, billhook, or bundle of cloths, but this served only to compel the debtor to appear in court.[74] Moreover, judgement would not be given against a defendant until he had appeared, three summonses being permitted.[75] So, loans clearly warned of difficulties.

As for eventual solutions to these conflicts, more than a dozen offenders, such as Thomas Aspelon (A), William Aleyn (B) John, son of William ad Portam (A) simply dropped from the rolls.[76] Some doubtless left the vill, but the suggestion is largely that fines and pledging, the usual court guarantees, worked, main families, in particular, having a good deal to lose by their recalcitrance. Says Sharpe also: villagers knew that it was not "the beste meanes" to sue one another and that they should try to "make frendes." The law could be a weapon to further a feud, but its principal goal is to bring quarrelling people to an amicable settlement. They were also aware that defamation was a breach of Christian charity and violation of neighborly ethics, and they were broadly trying to conduct themselves in accord with these.[77] Obviously, the censured were by no means miraculously cured, remaining a fragile mixture of amiability and spitefulness, pledging neighbors but trespassing and receiving against their interests as well. As Susan D. Amussen expresses it, humanity like great social processes operates in more than one direction and often in quite contradictory ones.[78]

It was isolated intermediate villagers, such as the Peges, Knyts, and John le Stake who remained truly problematic. They compounded their *mauvaise langue* with increasingly serious felonies, and the court ultimately invoked multiple pledges, the stocks, and increasingly higher fines to deal with them.

And what of their victims, defied so publicly and impulsively? Most, e.g., Henry, son of John (B), John Outy (A), William Abbot (A) among several others were little damaged, maintaining their juror, pledging and ale-tasting responsibilities.[79] So, it would seem that those who are ill-named are not half-hanged, calumny being a rather unpromising weapon in the Hobbesian contests of villagers.

We shall turn now to three themes conspicuous in the data for the five villages.

Women and Defamation

"Women are like wasps in their anger." "A woman's sword is her tongue and she does not let it rust." Such sayings are not difficult to multiply. But are they artifice only, the contrivances of playwrights-cum-poets and intended simply to amuse?

Out of thirteen slanders at Warboys between 1290–1353, seven were committed by women, five of their victims were men, the most abusive remarks issued from their tongues, and they sustained their challenge the longest, mustering additional resources — husbands *et al.* — as need be. In 1292, for instance, Elena Scut (A) insulted with *turpibus verbis* Simon Gerold (A) and Thomas of Broughton (D). In January 1316, Anabile Lenot slandered Philippa Shepherd (Trade), the incident fanning itself into a false claim and counter false claim, Robert Lenot vs. Philippa Shepherd and Roger Shepherd vs. Robert Lenot. Women were responsible for two of forty-three false claims,[80] and four females were wrongly sued by men.[81]

Wistow women committed only five of thirteen slanders, yet the incidents were remarkable for their spectacle. In 1294, Alice Bole (Inter) defamed in a single stroke twenty-six workers regarding a cash agreement, thereby bringing the autumn works of the lord to a halt.[82] In 1307–08, her sister Agnes attacked with foul words Thomas Lanerok (A), Robert Attebrok (A), Michael le Palmer (A), and Robert Baroun (A).[83] The two were like Valkyries, fearless in flight and assiduously scouring the landscape. We meet as well a common gossip, Amitia, wife of Simon, son of Richard (A) who greatly subverted the dignity of her neighbors, burdening the substantial fine of one-half mark for her trouble (Nov. 1353). Ten of fifty false claims originated with women,[84] and ten women were falsely prosecuted by men.[85]

In the two upland villages cases were fewer and seemingly less stormy, yet women were still central figures. They executed three of six defamations and four of seventeen wrongful prosecutions at Abbots Ripton. Two of the slanders (1308, 1313) alleged theft of goods worth only 3d. and we might readily deduce the extreme poverty of both defendants.[86] However, with Agnes Attelane breaching the ale assize six times over succeeding years, 1309–1343, she obviously had a fairly decent living. Juliana Wake was even more a force to be reckoned with. She answered an assault by Roger Derlyng (B) in 1274 with a false claim, was presented for various assize infractions (4), trespass and default, undertaking a return assault on Derlyng accompanied by an unjust hue in 1308-09 in addition to the slander (1313). She was a sturdy stem indeed, and the widow of John Vernoun (A) who false claimed versus her son for carrying off fen worth 3d. (1274) was every bit to be heeded. Yet, the fact of certain need cannot entirely be erased from our picture. Margaret Balle (A) who wrongly sued Andrew Martyn (A) in 1301 was inscribed by the court as *pauper.*

One female only defamed at Upwood and one false claimed. It is the aid lent by spouses and the trade background of three of the litigants — Pykelers, Miller, Webester — that are the most interesting details.[87] Finally, four men false claimed against women.[88] The entire Upwood situation, namely, three defamations only over seventy-five years (1278–1353) yet thirty-three false claims, an action involving greater social distance, and less raucous than slander, but with exactly the same intent, suggest a village conditioned somewhat differently than its neighbors.

In fine, why the frequency and marked intensity of women as defamers?[89] Slander is a potent assault weapon, its effects often more devastating than an outright physical thrashing. It allowed the weaker sex to strike first, contend face-to-face with a quarry, frequently with a blow so numbing as to facilitate escape from immediate counterattack. It suited the physique of women, and perhaps a psychological moment, and beyond this we might best look to the various entries. The wife of William of London (D) assailed with *turpibus verbis* the forester and the reeve of Warboys (1290) because they had caught her son stealing wood at night. The Warboys woodward was again a victim (Jan. 1294), and also the reeve and a taster at Wistow (1307–08).[90] In other words, overseers of some key village resources and industries were major targets for attack, doubtless because of their efficiency in curtailing initiative.

Suspicions of the "loose woman" and of the Lothario also excited a frenzy. They were a worry to both esteem and security, Matilda Bugge (D) slandering the butcher, John the Pondere, as a false seducer and hurling other enormities at him (Warboys, 1301) and Matilda Folyot heatedly denouncing Juliana Parys (D) as a whore (Wistow, 1301).

Stronger still were their fears regarding property: two Abbots Ripton women and one each from Wistow, Warboys, and Broughton slanderously charged theft.[91] And they false claimed for debt almost as frequently as men. Yet, we can surely sympathize with the widow of Geoffrey Prepositus of Caldecote (Out) who was owed 21d., 8d. for woodland, a half ring of grout and three sheaves of feed-wheat by her victim,[92] the court in fact condoning her claim (Warboys, 1290). Similarly, Johanna Warde (D) was owed 12d. by her victim (Abbots Ripton, 1343).[93] Yet, Sarra Attehalle (D) who wrongly sued (Wistow, 1347) was owing the plaintiff[94] 12s. 5d. Hers was an especially dramatic gesture. She was recently a widow and had trespassed her victim too. One suspects outright desperation. Originally the heir and eventually executors were responsible for a man's debts, and the widow of a villein was indeed his principal heir.[95]

A number of women clearly did have trouble with debt. Dionysia Nunne (D) of Warboys who was wrongly prosecuted by Richard Wilkes (D) (Oct. 1322) was still owing him three years later. Agnes Lacy (B) and her husband owed a false claimant 6d. (Wistow, 1342).[96] Sarra Haukyn (A) (Wistow, 1326) and Matilda, widow of Andrew Sabyn (A) (Wistow, 1347) were also alleged to be debtors.[97] Note the presence of widows three times in these suits; their condition could be a precarious one indeed.

Simple trespass could fuel an anger that eventually exploded in a false prosecution too. When William Leunye (Out) wrongly sued Agnes Webster (Warboys, 1343) he had trespassed her, she had trespassed him, then came the claim. A similar charge by Joan Clairvaux (Wistow, 1353) is recorded amidst three intrusions made by her victim upon the Clairvauxs, an exasperating affair without doubt and clearly telling of villager obduracy.[98] The pattern in suing was not always so predictable. When Margaret Gernoun false claimed vs. John Aylmar (Wistow, 1291) it was she who had disturbed his cart while taking dung into the fields, and also torn the tunic of his son. Upon a return false claim, she appropriated from Aylmar's meadow, and damaged the corn of lord and neighbors by breaching a fence (1291). But her male kinsmen were just as peevish and hostile, two of them defaming.

All told, while women slandered almost as frequently as men and perhaps more flamboyantly, their reasons for doing so were no more erratic. They monopolized only one charge, namely, sexual license. Indeed, it is their social origins, not their sex that cast the most light on them. Ninety percent came either from D households, i.e., families with a minor involvement in public life, or from intermediate isolated ranks.[99] They had little to lose by their boldness, the lives of Agnes and Alice Bole affording graphic testimony. The former went from a presentment for fornication and pregnancy outside of marriage (1278) to receiving and gleaning wrongly, defaming, trespass, assault, finally marrying a freeman without license (1334). Alice was raped in 1278, went on to glean wrongly, trespass, defame, and was finally prohibited the vill in 1307–08. Four female defendants — Agnes Reve (Wistow, 1318), Agnes Wymar (Warboys, 1299), Matilda of Upwood (Wistow, 1326), and Margaret Balle (Abbots Ripton, 1301) — were certified as poor, a stark test indeed for one's self-discipline and goodwill.[100]

Nonetheless, it is interesting that women were extending and securing credit as often as they were. Elaine Clark reckons that they constituted 14% of Writtle's moneylenders over the years 1382–1490.[101] In the case of John Haukyn (A), Upwood, who wrongly prosecuted Alice West (1353), he owed her the considerable sum of 6s. The entries highlight the hazards of such operations, especially for the *femme sole*, but women seemed duly capable of defending themselves. When Mariota Andrew (B) of Wistow was false claimed by Thomas, son of Thomas Arnold (D), she promptly raised the hue and cry not only on him, but his sister (1291).

At bottom, the most striking detail to emerge from this study of women and defamation pertains not immediately to them at all. It was men who slandered most often. Women have usually been reckoned the major detractors in society because of their insufficient interests. Yet, precisely because men were so involved in business, economics, and public service, they seemed prey to a notable envy/mistrust and thence slander. Medieval women are certainly known to have participated in their communities, especially the economy, more extensively than their sixteenth- and seventeenth-century counterparts; they shared in the baser stratagems connected with this involvement as well.[102]

Property and Defamation

In the 1970s, Michael M. Postan suggested the presence of a fairly extensive credit system in medieval villages,[103] and by 1981 Elaine Clark had fleshed in a number of its details, including the identification of tradesmen as 31% of creditors, substantial cultivators, 18%, village officials, 14%, and women 14%.[104] For information about the collateral and sureties of a potential debtor, creditors largely relied on their own devices.[105] They would often allow customers to remain in their debt for a number of years (61% of 265 cases), yet clearly debts were due "when requested" (20.6% of suits).[106] All told, it is not difficult to envisage a party giving way to either impatience or anxiety and lashing out. George Foster has also pointed to economic disputes as the most frequent cause of poor interpersonal relations in peasant societies.[107]

Warboys saw nine wrongful prosecutions involving debt over the 1270–1350s, Wistow, the same number, and Abbots Ripton and Upwood, three cases respectively. Mindful that the courts did not usually indicate the charge, the notices are significant. Even a detinue of 1d.[108] was sufficient to move a creditor to wrongly sue. Other goods noted were:

Table 2

Goods and Money Associated with Wrongful Prosecutions[109]

Village	Sum
Warboys	a mixed debt involving cash, grout, wood and wheat (1290); two baskets (Oct. 1301); 12d. (1305); 2s.10d. (Jan. 1316); one-third of a patrimony (Jan. 1320); 6s.3d. (1343)
Wistow	10s. (1320); 12d. (1325); 23d. (1329); 12s.5d. (1347); one measuring vessel (1350); 3s.6d. (1350)
Abbots Ripton	4s. (1318); 12d. (1343)
Upwood	18s. (1318); 5d. ob. (1328-29); one barrel worth 6d. (1332)

Expectably, the patrimony in contention at Warboys involved two brothers from a substantial (i.e., A) household.[110] The 10s noted for Wistow were being sought by an outsider, while the 18s. at Upwood were being claimed against an outsider, both suits revealing just how substantially credit and its complications traversed local boundaries.[111] The 3s. 6d. noted at Wistow were an unhappy yet acknowledged outcome of a trespass.[112] The offenders in these prosecutions had previously been generous with their goods and sentiments, substantially so, yet an underlying mistrust vitiated these arrangements.

Given the sums owed by debtors who falsely sued, dread seems a likely motive. Nicholas Robbe (A) owed 4s. to John Rose, custodian of the light at Abbots Ripton (1318); Simon Brid (D) was in arrears 6s. 3d. to John Pilche (Trade), Warboys (1343); John Higgeneye (A) owed 2s. 10d. to William Fine (D), Warboys (Jan. 1316). His relative, William

Higgeneye, shows graphically the pace of borrowing and lending for some villagers. In 1339 he was three times a lender and twice a debtor, his wife once lending and twice borrowing as well; the next roll (1343) saw him a debtor and falsely prosecuting; 1347 saw him false claim again and he was returned the insult; and in 1350 he was once more a debtor. Creditors, however, remain of greatest interest, wrongly suing as they did even for 5d. ob. (Upwood, 1328), 12d. (Abbots Ripton, 1343; Warboys, 1305) and two baskets (Warboys, 1301).

Five of nine Warboys lenders were from D households. Elsewhere, they included A families, but notably D residents again, followed by intermediate villagers, tradesmen at Abbots Ripton, and outsiders at Upwood. The modest means of these individuals, the consequence of market fluctuations for some, doubtless nudged them towards this initiative. Elaine Clark puts the situation more bluntly: villagers needed to reciprocate credit in order to continue receiving it;[113] even the smallest amount of property set in tow obligations. What is most critical however, is that the limitations on their resources often made their gesture a decidedly contradictory one, a gift of poison.

Professor Clark also notes that village credit arrangements cut across class distinctions, effecting a redistribution of goods and chattels that evened out villager disparities; in other words, it was not simply one villager regularly providing produce, land, livestock, etc. to another who had to pay for them with cash.[114] However, illegal suits, especially by lesser D creditors, countered the positiveness of this situation somewhat.

A number of wrongful suits alleging trespass involved debts too. When John Haukyn (A) of Upwood thus arraigned John Pikeler (Trade), he owed him the price of a tree — 18d. (1350). When he similarly arraigned Alice West, he owed her 6s. (1353). All told, such allegations total seven for Warboys, seventeen for Wistow, thirteen for Upwood and two for Abbots Ripton. And, last but by no means least were the defamations charging theft — six at Broughton, two at Abbots Ripton, Warboys, and Wistow respectively, and one at Upwood — sheaves of reeds and woolen cloths being noted.[115] They are perhaps a fitting capstone to the property issue: the ownership, lack thereof, and circulation of goods alike engendered notable tensions and aggression.

Officials, Tradesmen, and Families and Defamation

Officials: All five villages show their officials as routinely slandered, some of the severest condemnations being thrown at them. Nor has the situation changed notably. The gossip of twentieth-century Makah Indians as well as Italian and Welsh villagers involves constant criticism of those trying to run affairs; residents wish to punish anyone who appears to get too much prestige as a leader.[116] But were medieval bailiffs, woodwards and the like decried simply because they were leaders? Did the denunciations carry any hint of truth, moot a possible officiousness, prejudice, or dishonesty? Did villagers resort to slander in an effort to change regulations? John Beard Haviland notes that gossip is a powerful instrument for manipulating cultural rules, helping to redefine the conditions of their application, hence keeping them up to date.[117]

A number of incidents indeed reveal a patent contempt for authority simply because of its too ready defence of established precept. Woodwards were attacked on at least five occasions, John Gernoun (A) for example, calling the woodward of Wistow a thief, together with other enormities (1307–08).[118] The behaviour of the offenders was in general afflictive with Gernoun being arraigned for several trespasses, assault, break and entry, and forestalling as a hayward (1294–1342).[119] But the presentments also seem to express a demand by villagers for greater access to the woodlands. In other words, one suspects an element of protest in some of the confrontations, a desire as Haviland notes to revamp the regulations.

Other outbursts that seemed clearly a criticism of administrative correctness were Richard of Hyrst's (Inter) defamation of the bailiff of Broughton (1297); William Horseman's (Inter) false prosecution of the bailiff of Wistow (1342); and Adam Brun's (A) wrongful prosecution of Richard Revison, Wistow, 1349.[120] Still, the difficult and unpromising existence of the defendants seems equally an issue. They came almost entirely from intermediate villager ranks, Horseman and Hyrst, having attained to virtually no public recognition in a lifetime. Such frustration doubtless abetted slander more than once.

Respect for duty by no means impaled either a hayward of Abbots Ripton in 1313, the forester of Warboys in 1290, and possibly a clerk of Warboys in 1299. As officials, they, themselves slandered, assaulted, and otherwise intimidated residents, their offenses culminating in public censure and dismissal. The hayward attacked and wounded William le Bond (A), being fined 5s., then defamed Agnes le Bond, who had doubtless come to the defense of her kinsmen (damages at 20d.), finally false claiming against John le Bond, his wife, and son, the bedel serving as his pledge. He also assaulted the daughter of the Reeve in 1313, damages amounting to 10s. His deeds link him with the most injurious of villagers and he was dropped from all offices by year's end.

Although the forester of Warboys had impeccably foiled the London family theft, he was also charged with non-presentment (i.e., contempt) and fined 40d. in 1290. Perhaps neglect only and not preferential treatment explains the default; nonetheless, he had jeopardized himself, opened the way for criticism. Financial deception may have been suspected of clerks, Agnes Wymar (Out) defaming a clerk of Warboys as a thief in 1299. William Clerke of the same village wrongly prosecuted Richard Berenger (A) for breach of covenant (1334), and given his notarial competence, the act seems more distasteful than usual.

Also violating a public trust were a custodian of the marsh of Upwood (1308), a cowherd of Wistow (1347), the reeve of Upwood (1311) and William Marshall of Wistow (1279), all of them illegally suing. The latter two might be charged with incitement as well since their victims counter-sued, Marshall, in fact being opprobriously defamed.[121]

The reeve of Upwood in the above instance had moved against a tradesman, a cook, but the situation was usually the reverse, and money the incitement. John the Webester wrongly prosecuted Ralph, the reeve of Broughton (Jan. 1322), the latter owing him 27s. William the Smith of Warboys also false claimed against the reeve (1343).

Completely disreputable in their condemning of officials were John le Pondere (Warboys), John Crane (Wistow), and the Le Bons (Broughton). Their actions tell of little else than their exceptional disdain. In 1299, le Pondere (pound-keeper and butcher) defamed then false claimed vs. the birdwarren, poaching very likely being the issue. In 1305, he pronounced the bedel useless in the service of the lord, alleging other enormities, and went on to wrongly sue him. He was notably self-aggrandizing with five land acquisitions in four years (1290–1294), owing debts, illegally receiving outsiders, and raising the hue wrongly. Only Matilda Bugge boldly, if wrongly, challenged him (1301). It is difficult not to envisage a burly, aproned John le Pondere, perhaps lusty too (*vide* M. Bugge), a man who knew little restraint of any sort. The Le Bons misuse of the bailiff of Broughton (1297) likewise focuses attention primarily on their own erraticism, the myriad trespasses, and the damage caused by the household over the years. John Crane (A) beset the swineherd and bedel-to-be of Wistow, denouncing his food and potables, then illegally suing him (1297).[122] The defendant was already known for abandoning property (1278) and as a vagabond who skulks under the walls of his neighbours. He later assaulted, damaged property, and was to be arrested.

In the face of these taunts, local courts gave strong and unequivocal support to their officials, as they could. Geoffrey, the bedel of Upwood, was condoned when accused of wrongly prosecuting Richard Heryng (Trade) (1297), and Robert the Dyker's false claim against a foursome at Wistow in 1322 was similarly pardoned.[123]

The numbers of women who participated in attacks again attracts attention. David E. Underdown in a portrait of the village scold notes that women who were poor and otherwise at the margins of society (i.e., D and intermediate villagers in the present context) were very likely to vent their frustration on village notables.[124] Meanwhile, Susan Amussen reminds us that insult was a claim to equality,[125] and we might certainly expect this assertion on the part of A offenders, such as, the Gernouns, le Bonds, and Bruns, as well as more substantial tradesmen, John le Pondere (Warboys), William the Smith (Warboys), and John the Webester (Broughton). With officials achieving their offices and prestige largely through personal energy,[126] the jealousy and *mauvaise langue* of their peers is not surprising. Finally, the affronts levelled at them — thief, treacherous, seducers, etc., — are an interesting comment on the virtues expected of officials.[127]

Tradesmen: "Honour is not in his hand who is honoured, but in the hearts and opinions of other men."[128] A sobering adage, and merchant-tradesmen through the centuries have doubtless experienced its weight more decisively than most. Thirteenth-fourteenth century society saw them as prone to regrating and to violating price statutes: they were prepared to batten on a community. Their routine involvement in the marketplace also gave them ready tongues and an imperturbableness in the face of criticism, i.e., the wherewithal to intimidate clients.[129] Ernest Pulbrook says that cobblers have always been ready to scent a grievance and tailors are renowned for their peevishness.[130]

At Upwood, four villagers, A, D, and intermediate individuals, false claimed against a Cook (1311), Cowman (1307), Pykeler (1350), and Hering (1295, condoned). Almost twice as many tradesmen, namely a Haringmonger (1328–29), two Millers (1307, 1308), a Smith (1350), Swon (1339–40), Pilche (skinner) (1333), and Ponder (1339, 1350) did the same. In only one instance was their victim a tradesman, namely, a miller *et ux* impleading a weaver (webester) in 1308. They did not resort to the more dramatic technique of slander, seemingly managing effectively otherwise. Thomas Aspelon (A), however, was certainly riled enough to defame both a herringer and swanherd (Swon) in 1326. On balance, Upwood traders certainly menaced their clientele more successfully than *vice versa*.

At neighboring Warboys the experience was very different. Tradesmen were victims in four slanders and seven wrongful prosecutions, but executed only three of each themselves. January, 1316 saw William the Smith not only slandered but twice falsely sued by A residents.[131] Also among the wrongly indicted were a shepherd (Jan. 1313, 1316), two webesters (Nov. 1320, 1343), a miller (1305), a pilche (1343), and a tradeswoman, Matilda Harying (1301),[132] with D residents largely undertaking the subjection.[133] Nonetheless, the hot-headed threatening tradesman emerges here too, Richard and Geoffrey Gardiner attacking Roger Carpenter as a thief in 1299 and shouting other shameful things at him; the egregious John le Pondere also hailed from this vill.[134]

Abbots Ripton saw two defamations and eight illegal prosecutions involving tradesmen, but they basically summed up two classic disputes, viz., John Carpenter vs. Roger Derlyng (B) and Thomas Ternour vs. Robert Brewester. In 1302, Roger Derlyng hamsoked John Carpenter and struck his wife; Carpenter responded with a false claim, then attacked and beat Roger twice, the latter eventually countering with another break and entry. The second was an even more furious affair, Ternour likely a supplier of pottles and casks, hence dealings between the two being virtually obligatory. In 1353, he owed a debt to Robert Brewester, following which he trespassed him (damages at 5d); Robert then wrongly prosecuted, and Thomas promptly defamed him, twice. The Brewester again false claimed and Ternour countered with his own illegal suit; Robert went on to trespass and Ternour wrongly sued twice again; Robert trespassed again and Thomas responded with yet another false claim. There were two defamations and six illegal prosecutions associated with this one dispute alone, as genuine a donnybrook as court rolls are likely to offer.[135]

Wistow tradesmen nine times wrongly prosecuted and were once a victim; they were three times slandered and once authored such abuse. Three trade types dominate the entries — smiths, millers, and shepherds. Smiths were four times transgressors, millers twice so and once a victim, and herdsmen three times offenders and four times victims. The degree of their insolence was indeed impressive. Simon the

Shepherd had four times trespassed and also assaulted his victim,[136] then false claimed against him for trespass (1353). Similarly, William Miller had assaulted his victim in 1313[137] before wrongly prosecuting him, and also false claimed against Ivo Walter (D) (1320) who just as readily defamed him. And, Roger Shepherd who falsely sued for trespass (1344)[138] was himself the intruder. Herds were returned some of this menace, Richard Shepherd (father of Simon) being defamed twice, and wrongly sued.[139] Ivo Shepherd was wrongly prosecuted by a shoemaker, Agnes Sutor, the plea possibly involving materials furnished to her workbench.(1318).

All told, millers were litigants in four villages, and similarly smiths and herdsmen; shoemakers and webesters surface in three communities and ponders and pilches in at least two.[140] Credit was again a thorny issue: the miller of Warboys owed a debt of 12d. to Alan Haugate (D), the latter illegally suing (1305); Simon Brid (D), defendant, Warboys, owed 6s. 3d. to John Pilche (1343); the smith of Wistow false claimed vs. Thomas and Sarra Haukyn (A) for a debt (1326).[141] As previously noted, Elaine Clark found tradesmen to be 31% of Writtle's money lenders.[142] In sum, the trade set had punishing tongues, but they were often notably harassed as well.

Main Families: We shall note overall patterns only. Of forty-three false claimants at Warboys, twenty-six were from main families, one-third of these deriving from substantial A households. The nine uniformly impleaded a lesser, i.e., a D villager, a situation that could point to an overly wary and even repressive A contingent, or a genuinely thorny undergroup. That seven D individuals thus beset members of their own ranks confirms a definite bumptiousness, fuller court-roll biographies revealing that these individuals were housebreakers, assailants and property-damagers as well. Richard Bryd was five times the object of a hue and cry (1316, 1325 [2], 1332, 1339), drew blood,(1325), "hamsoc'ed" (1325), trespassed (1331, 1339) and falsely claimed (Nov. 1320). Robert Lenot three times damaged property (1313, 1316, Oct. 1322) and three times trespassed (Jan. 1322, Oct. 1322, 1326) in addition to twice wrongly prosecuting (1316, 1325).[143] In part, A claimants may have been trying to shore up community standards against an exceedingly contrary D group (*vide* Gluckman)[144] while their D counterparts seem to have been quite self-interestedly challenging equal and superior alike (*vide* Paine). The pattern varies notably from nearby Broughton where more marginal households were far less implicated.

At Wistow, A residents initiated sixteen of fifty wrongful prosecutions, half of these being against equals and only three against D residents. Trespass was the chief grievance.[145] D villagers were again notable offenders, spiting three of their own and three A residents, a debt being alleged four times.[146] Interestingly, four budding C householders threw themselves at a well-entrenched A resident.

With four and three of its seventeen mispleadings originating with A and D residents, Abbots Ripton is consistent with the above. The distinctive feature is the fewer incidents overall.

At Upwood, the genuine curiosity is the eight intermediate defendants; surrounding communities saw only three or four such offenders. They may well hint of a village life less centred on main tenants and their influence, including their disciplinary control. These essentially isolated residents also raise the question of a more solitary pattern of village existence generally. Notwithstanding, eleven of thirty-three false claims originated with main villagers.

Geography and Defamation

Tenth-century foundation charters reveal an Upwood prized for its hunting and hawking, its copse and chase.[147] In 1086, woodland for pannage measured one and one-half leagues in length and one in breadth,[148] with Henry III granting free warren in the manor providing its lands were not within the bounds of the royal forest (1251 A.D.).[149] David E. Underdown urges that unlike arable parishes with their nucleated centers and concentrated institutions for social control, including strong habits of neighborhood and cooperative labor systems, wood-pasture communities are characterized by scattered modes of economy and settlement that were likely to spell weaker restraint and mediation devices.[150] A generous fen allotment and consistent attention to it probably strengthened the separate character of Upwood life.[151]

Interestingly, the village saw only four defamations but thirty-three false claims over 1278–1350, suggesting indeed less direct relations yet a marked litigiousness. Moreover, an unusual thirteen prosecutions asserted trespass. The charge involves high feelings: as Pollock and Maitland note, it amounts to an intrusion on property, committed with force and violence *cvi et armis)*, even if only the breaking of a blade of grass.[152] Nonetheless, it is the individual at a remove — no more — who is aggrieved; the impersonal nature of the action holds. By contrast, there were only four charges of debt, credit arrangements inevitably involving close communication of needs, of gages, of friends willing to serve as pledges, etc. It is also noteworthy that major villagers, such as, Andrew Gernoun (A) (1318) and William atte Snape (A) (1328), sought their loans from outsiders. Only three villagers[153] wrongly prosecuted more than once, and only one household[154] had more than one offender. Finally, in only two instances was there anything resembling a sequence of events, a charge and counter-charge.[155] The vill remains a curious blend of remoteness yet intensity of feeling.

At Abbots Ripton where significant stands of ash, elm, oak, and birch, some of the best in the county, still survive,[156] the effects were even more conspicuous. The vill was twice the size of Broughton, 4,100 acres,[157] yet as already noted, it numbered only 690 persons as opposed to its neighbor's 834 over 1274–1350. It saw only seventeen false claims. Nonetheless, its offenders were some of the most die-hard of the region. There were six highly-charged defamations, two alleging theft, and an unusual three wrongful prosecutions were linked with assault. We recall the spate of denunciations that flew between both Roger Derlyng and John Carpenter (1350) and Thomas Ternour and Robert Brewester (1350). The malevolent hayward, William, who so thoroughly menaced the Le Bonds and mangled Joan Reeve (damages at 10s.) was a resident. And so was Juliana Wake who nursed a grudge against Roger Derlyng for thirty-five years. Nor did these uplanders seem to change over time. The sixteenth century saw numerous collisions between the inhabitants and the bailiff. They were reacting to the new lordship of Sir John St. John, his increased rents and crack-down on forest privileges.[158] They surely had a taste for the fray and a notable spirit in adversity.

Conclusion

One of the most deeply-rooted assumptions about villagers is their relish for gossip — prying, tattling, newsmongering, and criticizing. We recall the many occasions for female exchange at Montaillou — the mill, fetching water, trade, in bed (with three to a bed, two peasant women and a noblewoman) the village square, spinning, lending, and simply chatting.[159] The present study has considered the legal extreme of this talk, viz., defamation and aggravated defamation in five English villages.

The offenders represented every walk of life, from major tenants, officials, women, youth, and tradesmen[160] to the marginal isolated resident. Their motives were just as varied. Several A residents, main tenants, who denounced an equal or an inferior were in part asserting an individual superiority while also shoring up the *status quo*. G. H. Mead and Erving Goffman long ago recognized the self-interested nature of gossip,[161] while P. Spacks and Max Gluckman acknowledge its influence as "building on shared values of intimates,"[162] "consolidating social power,"[163] thus "keeping cliques and aspiring individuals" in their place.[164]

Yet these tidy assumptions are often intruded upon by much plainer truths, in particular, the trespass and debt actions already linking litigants. Lending and borrowing went on constantly in village life, engaging and connecting every class. Anxiety, confusion and thence a delict seemed to overtake debtors, while impatience consumed a number of creditors. Several wrongful prosecutions by and against tradesmen were credit-driven. The system was by no means *free* in nature, the lenders purely self-determining in their initiatives; nor was it simply an economic institution.

The theme of social disparity raised its head on several occasions. A number of the offenses savour of frustration, i.e., disappointment turned to contempt. As P. Spacks notes, gossip is a resource of the subordinated, the underclasses, a means of disrespecting, ridiculing, and satirizing a world that impinges on them.[165] D and intermediate residents frequently attacked A villagers and officials, as did women.

Other incidents bespeak pure unabashed aggression rather than hopelessness. Samuel Heilman speaks of gossip as "surreptitious aggression which enables one to wrest power, manipulate, and strike out at another without the other's being able to strike back."[166] Medieval villagers, especially the marginal, were risking open attack and seemed quite unafraid to do so.

A striking boldness characterized the offenses of women and youth in particular. For the former, slander was a dramatic yet safe action, and perhaps called attention, if only intermittently, to the special difficulties of women. Nicholas Bugge's (D) first court-roll infraction (Warboys, 1290) was a slanderous cry of theft and Robert Segeley's (A), a wrongful prosecution in 1316. They went on to become jurors and pledges,[167] but the outcome was not always so satisfactory. In 1307–08, four Wistow youths[168] maliciously insulted, beat, and drew the blood of John, servant of Andrew Outy, and attacked and bloodied John Crane. They were definitely a clique, their viciousness striking, and ten and twenty-five years later one of them, Roger Attebroke, was still engaging in assault.

Two of the most fundamental underpinnings of social life are the impulses of cooperation and competition, defamation seemingly representing the latter distorted to an extreme enmity. Lorraine Blaxter refines the point effectively: small intensely intimate communities demand that the individual find a successful balance between avoidance and sociability, malice and slander resulting as much from an excess of one as of the other. Excessive avoidance suggests too much individual pride, greed, cunning and self-protection, as well as an incivility, an inability to deal with others.[169] Too much neighborliness and *bonne volonté* makes a man's help too obvious and may arouse fear (especially if he refuses reciprocity).[170] As F. G. Bailey concludes, successful relationship (community) is achieved by dealing with whole persons and rejecting impersonal interactions; however, it is safeguarded by doing just the opposite — a thoroughgoing paradox indeed.[171]

Villagers were seldom ostracized for their offenses, fines and pledges being used as correctives. They then carried on as a typical blend of helpfulness and harmfulness, friendship and mistrust. John Aylmar (A) (Wistow), for example, false claimed in 1291, 1294, and 1297, yet fully retained his respectability as a juror and pledge over the years.[172] Thomas Arnold (A) of Wistow, Richard Segeley (A), John Higgeneye (A), and Henry Pakeral (A) of Warboys are other examples.[173] It was lesser D and intermediate villagers, Robert Kyng (Inter), John Lyon (Inter), and Ivo Walter (D) of Wistow, and Simon Brid (D) of Warboys who handled sanctions and themselves least effectively. The first of these was presented for listening under the walls of his neighbors at night (1294) and by 1309 he had slipped fully into a pattern of defamation, debt, assault, receiving, contempt, and false claiming, being again presented in 1333 as a harmful vagabond who listens under the walls of his neighbors.[174] But a taste for mayhem seems as much personal as circumstantial. John Crane, from a major tenant family (Wistow), became a vagabond in 1297 and lived the rest of his days as a defamer, waster, and assailant.

Slander and wrongful prosecution are genuinely harmful acts. Yet, villagers seemed to weather a good deal of this caterwauling and cantankerousness and carry on. More than forty years ago George C. Homans wrote:

Of course in any particular village, neighbourhood might break down into mutual distrust. Perhaps it was always in danger of breaking down, and perhaps when it did so the bitterness was all the greater because of the closeness of the contacts between men. But if we can judge by farming communities in modern times, the traditions of cooperation were probably so well established that they could survive a great deal of petty bickering. Neighbours groused at one another, but worked together just the same.[175]

He seemed to sense the situation very effectively.

NOTES

1. Professor Natalie Davis, "The Reasons of Misrule" in *Society and Culture in Early Modern France* (Stanford, 1975), pp. 97–123, (esp. pp. 104–10) was one of the first to call attention to these rituals. A much more elaborate investigation now exists, Jacques Le Goff et Jeans-Claude Schmitt, eds., *Le Charivari* (Paris, 1981).

2. Carlo M. Cipolla, *Faith, Reason and the Plague in Seventeenth Century Tuscany* (Ithaca, N.Y., 1979); Carlo Ginsberg, *The Cheese and the Worms* (Baltimore, 1980); Phillippe Ariès, *L'Homme devant La Mort* (Paris, 1977); Emmanuel LeRoy Ladurie, *Montaillou, Village occitan de 1294 à 1324* (Paris, 1975); Jacques Le Goff, *Your Money or Your Life*, trans Patricia Ranum (Cambridge, Mass., 1988) are just a few examples.

3. John Kennedy Campbell, *Honour, Family and Patronage* (Oxford, 1976); J. G. Peristiany, ed., *Honour and Shame, The Values of Mediterranean Society* (Chicago, 1966); Julian Pitt-Rivers, Mana (Welwyn Garden City, Herts., 1973); *The Fate of Scechem or the Politics of Sex* (Cambridge, 1977); Paul Stirling, *Turkish Village* (London, 1965), pp. 27–28, 68, 192, 230–33 et passim; Juliet Du Boulay, *Portrait of a Greek Mountain Village* (Oxford, 1974), pp. 16, 22, 38, 102, 104–12, 142–43, 194 et passim. This initial literature has been steadily added to, more recent scholars engaging in increasingly precise linguistic analysis to refine notions of honor; or, probing more carefully the links between honor and different social statuses; or, tracing the actual processes of recognizing honor, i.e., the interactional context and its impact, rather than simply informing further on the substantive meaning of honor. V, e.g., J. Davis, *People of the Mediterranean, An Essay in Comparative Social Anthropology* (London, 1977), pp. 89–101; Michael Herzfeld, "Honour and Shame: Problems in the Comparative Analysis of Moral Systems", Man, n.s. 15 (1980), 339–51; Unni Wikan, "Shame and Honour: A Contestable Pair" *Man*, n.s. 19 (1984), 635–52.

4. "Gossip and Scandal", *Current Anthropology*, 4 (1963), 307–16; "Psychological, Sociological and Anthropological Explanations of Witchcraft and Gossip: A Clarification," Man, n.s. 3 (1968), 20–34, esp. 28–34. v also Du Boulay, *Portrait of a Greek Mountain Village*, pp. 201-13; and Elizabeth Colson *The Makah Indians* (Manchester, 1953), pp. 201–36, among others.

5. "What is Gossip About? An Alternative Hypothesis", *Man*, n.s. 2 (1967), 278–85 esp. pp. 280–81; "Gossip and Transaction", *Man*, n.s. 3 (1968), 305–08.

6. "Filcher of Good Names: An Enquiry into Anthropology and Gossip", *Man*, n.s., 9 (1974), 93–102. Other significant works on gossip are F. G. Bailey, ed., *Gifts and*

Poison (Toronto, 1971); Patricia Myer Spacks, *Gossip* (Chicago, 1985); George M. Foster, "Interpersonal Relations in Peasant Society", *Human Organization*, 19 (1960), 174–78; John Beard Haviland, *Gossip, Reputation, and Knowledge in Zinacantan* (Chicago, 1977); Edward C. Banfield, *The Moral Basis of a Backward Society* (Chicago, 1958).

7. *Defamation and Sexual Slander in Early Modern England: The Church Courts at York*, Borthwick Papers, No. 58 (York, 1981).

8. Ibid., p. 5. The author notes Star Chamber, King's Bench, the Court of Chivalry, the quarter sessions and assizes, borough and manorial courts, church courts, as well as the common law courts at Westminster.

9. Pitt-Rivers in Peristiany, ed., *Honour and Shame*, pp. 21–22; id., *Mana* p. 8; Davis, *People of the Mediterranean*, p. 77. However, Wikan, "Honour and Shame" 635–52 shows just how complex judging honour is, and similarly the question of value in one's own and in others' eyes.

10. Arthur W. H. Adkins, *Merit and Responsibility, A Study in Greek Values* (Oxford, 1960), pp. 181–89, 295, and especially pp. 316, and 337ff. The Middle Ages emphasized actions and intentions directed toward a common Good greater than that envisioned by Aristotle and which thus transcended the confines of the city-state and civic acclaim. *V* Jacques Maritain, *Moral Philosophy* (New York, 1964), pp. 45–51 and 71–91. *v* also id., *The Person and the Common Good* (New York, 1947), pp. 75–76.

11. *V Leviathan*, ch. 10; *Elements of Law*, ch. 8, sec. 5: honor is "those signs for which one man acknowledgeth power or excess above his concurrent in another". In other words competition and the achievement of precedence are the defining elements of honor. For a useful analysis of Hobbes's thinking, *v* Leo Strauss, *The Political Philosophy of Hobbes, Its Basis and Its Genesis* (Chicago, 1952), esp. pp. 50ff.

12. Campbell, *Honour*, pp. 39, 193, 268–306 *et passim*. For several societies of the Mediterranean Basin — Andalusians, Cypriots, Kabyles, Bedouin — these are noted as central criteria of honour. *V* Peristiany, *Honour and Shame*, pp. 45–61, 178–89, 199, 202, 211, 214–29, 249–56 et passim. Davis, *People of the Mediterranean*, pp. 90, 91, 95–97 et passim.

13. Bailey, ed., *Gifts*, pp. 41–68 and esp. 49. A man's moral character is achieved, is in his control, and this makes it the truest measure of his worth. Wealth, numbers and quality of kinsmen, etc., depend on various demographic, economic and physical contingencies.

14. Ibid., pp. 4–6, 22, 100 et passim.

15. Davis, *People of the Mediterranean*, pp. 92–101. Efforts of inferiors to dishonour superiors and *vice versa* involve very different effects. So too, the penalties attaching to the efforts of these parties vary. *V* also, Bailey, ed., *Gifts*, pp. 14–16, 182–211, esp. 187–89, Pitt-Rivers, *Mana*, p. 8; Peristiany, *Honour and Shame*, pp. 35–36, 61ff.

16. Analytical jurisprudence is also known as legal positivism and sees law as nothing more than its concrete manifestations (statutes, cases, etc.), discarding any notions of innate ideas, eternal truths and the like, and it is essentially a command of the sovereign power (state). In other words, positivism implies that law is the product of somebody's very palpable decision — what Max Weber called "formal rationality" or "logical formalism" — and it is definitely changeable by some further decision. John Austin is the father of English analytical jurisprudence. *V* his *Province of Jurisprudence Determined* (London, 1954), pp. 30ff., 163ff.; *Lectures on Jurisprudence*, 2 (London, 1863), pp. 222ff. By contrast, the historical school regards law as the prod-

uct of the "common consciousness" or "spirit of a people"; it grows out of the history and traditions of a nation. Friedrich Carl von Savigny *(System des heutigen Römischen Rechts,* Berlin, 1840, pp. 171–75 et passim*)* is regarded as the founder of this school. *V,* more recently, Lawrence M. Friedman, *Law and Society (*Englewood Cliffs, N.J., 1977).

17. *Law and Revolution, The Formation of the Western Legal Tradition* (Cambridge, Mass., 1983), pp. vi–vii, 44. As he otherwise states, "law has to be believed in or it will not work" (p. vii). V also H. L. Hanbury, *English Courts of Law* (Oxford, 1945), p. 15 on the reconciliability of the analytical and historical schools of jurisprudence.

18. As Friedman, *Law and Society,* p. 37 notes, this shift (expedient) does imply changes in the way laws are applied and enforced, and also changes in the authority system.

19. *The Laws of the Earliest English Kings,* ed. and tr. by F. L. Attenborough (Cambridge, 1922), pp. 21 (Hlothere and Eadric, c. 11), 77 (Alfred, c. 32); *The Laws of the Kings of England from Edmund to Henry I,* ed. and tr. by A. J. Robertson (Cambridge, 1925), p. 127 (Aethelred, c. 33). Late Roman law had evolved the terms *infamia* and *turpitudo* to refer to actions resulting in a loss of honor, and as Rudolf Huebner, *A History of Germanic Private Law,* trans. Francis S. Philbrick (New York, 1968), pp. 47, 102–08 notes, early Germanic cultures borrowed and extensively developed these. Sir F. Pollock and F. W. Maitland, *The History of English Law,* 2nd ed. (Cambridge, 1911), I, 536–38 and Theodore F. T. Plucknett, *A Concise History of English Law,* 5th ed. (London, 1956), pp. 483–88 note the Middle Ages as adding the terms *diffamatio* and *scandalum,* with the year 1275 A.D. marking the appearance of the statute *scandalum magnatum.* According to Sharpe, *Defamation and Sexual Slander,* p. 10, defamatory accusations in England by the sixteenth century included "whore, witch, scold, disturber of neighbours, perjurer, liar, cheat, drunkard, knave, slave, thief, cuckold, illicitly begets child, adulterer, fornicator".

20. R. H. Helmholz, ed., *Select Cases on Defamation to 1600,* Selden Society, Vol. 101 (London, 1985), pp. v–xlvii for an excellent analysis of the development of church law on defamation. Ibid., p. xlviii–lxv on the nature of defamation in local courts. *V* also "Canonical Defamation in Medieval England," *American Journal of Legal History,* 15 (1971), pp. 255–68.

21. Helmholz, *Select Cases,* pp. lxvi–cxi on the appearance and early growth of Common Law jurisdiction. F. W. Maitland, *Forms of Action at Common Law* (Cambridge, 1981), p. 54 notes the writ (titles) under which this action initially and eventually fell.

22. Sir William Holdsworth, *A History of English Law,* II, 4th ed. rpt. (London, 1966), p. 383.

23. Bailey, ed., *Gifts,,* pp. 1–2, 104, 122–24, 153–56, 287; Haviland, *Gossip, Reputation,* p. 28; Spacks, *Gossip,* pp. 4–5 et passim.

24. Bailey, ed., *Gifts,* p. 171.

25. *Portrait of a Greek Mountain Village,* pp. 203–04. It allows the speaker to sow the seeds of doubt while not actually implicating himself or herself in the act of slander. In local reckoning, it is a fault rather than a sin.

26. Bailey, ed., *Gifts,* pp. 154–55; Paine, *Man,* n.s. 2 (1967), p. 283; Spacks, *Gossip,* pp. 12–15, 47.

27. Bailey, ed., *Gifts,* pp. 156–58, 236; Laurence Wylie, *Village in the Vaucluse* (Cambridge, Mass., 1957), pp. 194, 196–98, 202, 271–74; Haviland, *Gossip, Reputation,* pp. 74–75 and 204–13 give an extensive list of gossip topics.

28. Pollock and Maitland, *History of English Law,* II, pp. 539–40.

29. Bailey, ed., *Gifts*, pp. 4–6.
30. Ibid., pp. 7, 16–18, 187–92, 292.
31. Ibid., pp. 282, 292.
32. Plucknett, *A Concise History*, p. 483.
33. Pollock and Maitland, *History of English Law*, II, pp. 538.
34. The Public Record Office court roll collection is identified as S.C.2, Portfolio Nos. 178/1ff. and 179/1ff. The British Library Collection consists of Additional Rolls, identified by five digits, e.g., 39754, 34774, etc. *Broughton Rolls:* 1288 (179/5) 1290 (39754) 1291 (39849) 1292 (34335) 1294 (34894) Jan. 1294 (39597) 1297 (179/9) 1299 (179/10) 1301 (39913) 1301 (34913) 1306 (39459) 1306 (179/12) 1307 (34916) 1308 (34304) 1309 (34342) 1311 (34305) 1313 (34768) 1314 (39463) 1316 (39464) 1316 (39465) 1318 (34803) 1320 (39758) 1320 (39759) 1321–22 (179/20) 1322 (39467)1325 (179/22) 1329 (39468) 1331 (39469) 1332–33 (34363) 1333 (39470) 1334 (39762) 1334–35 (179/28) 1337 (34899) 1339 (34808) 1339–40 (179/30). *Warboys Rolls:* 1290 (39754) 1292 (34335) 1294 (39755) 1294 (39597) 1294 (34894) 1299 (179/10) 1301 (39850) 1301 (179/11) 1305 (34774) 1306 (34895) 1306 (39756) 1309 (34342) 1313 (34910) 1313 (34324) Jan. 1316 (34896) 1316 (34897) 1318 (39757) 1320 (34918) 1320 (39758) 1320 (39759) 1322 (34777) 1322 (179/20) 1325 (34898) 1325 (39851) 1326 (39760) 1331 (39761) 1332-33 (34363) 1333 (34919) 1333 (39470) 1334 (39762) 1337 (34899) 1339 (39853) 1343 (179/31) 1347 (39856) 1347–48 (34900) 1349 (39763) 1350 (179/34) 1353 (179/35). *Wistow Rolls:* 1278 (179/4) 1279 (34911) 1291 (39849) 1292 (34335) 1294 (39597) 1297 (39562) 1299 (179/10) 1301 (34913) 1301 (39850) 1306 (39755) 1307 (34799) 1307–08 (34915) 1308 (34916) 1308 (34801) 1309 (34342) 1313 (34917) 1316 (34896) 1316 (39465) 1318 (39757) 1320 (34804) 1320 (34918) 1322 (34805) 1325 (34806) 1325 (39851) 1326 (39760) 1329 (39852) 1333 (34919) 1333 (34810) 1334 (34809) 1339 (39853) 1342 (39854) 1347 (39856) 1349 (39763) 1350 (179/34) 1353 (39855).
35. There are twenty-eight court rolls for Upwood and twenty-one for Abbots Ripton. *Upwood:* 1278 (179/4) 1279 (34911) 1294 (34769) 1295 (179/9) 1297 (34798) 1299 (179/10) 1302 (179/12) 1307 (34799) 1307 (179/15) 1308 (34801) 1311 (34802) 1313 (34917) 1318 (34803) 1320 (34804) 1322 (34805) 1325 (34806) 1325 (39851) 1326 (34807) 1328–29 (39852) 1331 (34321) 1332 (39582) 1333 (34810) 1334 (34809) 1339 (34808) 1339–40 (34811) 1344 (39854) 1347 (34849) 1349 (34850) 1350 (179/34) 1353 (39855). *Abbots Ripton:* 1274 (39586) 1292 (34337) 1294 (39597) 1295 (179/9) 1296 (179/9) 1299 (179/10) 1301 (179/11) 1306 (34895) 1306 (179/12) 1307 (179/15) 1308–09 (39739) 1313 (179/17) 1318 (179/18) 1321 (179/20) 1326 (34807) 1332 (179/26) 1334 (179/28)1339–40 (179/30 Ed. III (39738) 1343 (179/31) 1350 (179/34).
36. J. A. Raftis, *The Estates of Ramsey Abbey, A Study in Economic Growth and Organization* (Toronto, 1957), pp. 7–8, 19.
37. *The Victoria County History of Huntingdonshire*, ed. William Page and Granville Proby (London, 1932) I, pp. 342–44 (= *VCH: ...etc., Hunts.*).
38. *VCH:Hunts.*, II, pp. 202, 238.
39. Ibid., pp. 242–43.
40. J. A. Raftis, "Social Structures in Five East Midland Villages", *Economic History Review*, ser. 2, 18 (1965), p. 100: Wistow, 1,064; Warboys, 1,235; Broughton, 834; Upwood, 993.

41. *VCH:Hunts.*, II, pp. 158.
42. J.A. Raftis, "Commutation in a Fourteenth-Century Village" in *Essays in Medieval History Presented to Bertie Wilkinson*, eds. T. A. Sanquist and M. R. Powicke (Toronto, 1969), pp. 291–93, 296–97 for tallies of customary labor. Raftis, *Estates*, pp. 199–208 indicates wages for both regular (famuli) and hired labor.
43. *V* Edward Britton, *The Community of the Vill* (Toronto, 1977), pp. 16–19, 94–130, 166–78 et passim.
44. Dates for the defamations were: 1288 (2); 1290 (1); 1291 (3); 1292 (4); 1294 (2); 1297 (3); 1306 (2); 1307 (2); 1311 (1); 1314 (1); 1316 (1). Those for the false claims were: 1291 (1); Jan. 1294 (1); 1294 (1); 1297 (1); 1299 (1); 1301 (1); 1306 (3); 1307 (3); 1311 (3); 1314 (2); 1316 (3); 1320 (1); 1321 (1); 1325 (1); 1334 (2); 1337 (3); 1340 (2).
45. Pollock and Maitland, *History of English Law*, II, p. 539.
46. 1297 — debt; 1316 — trespass; 1325 — debt; 1334 — debt (2); 1337 — debt (2); breach of covenant.
47. Ian Kershaw, "The Great Famine and Agrarian Crisis in England, 1315–1322", *Past and Present*, 59 (1973) 3–50; M. M. Postan, "Medieval Agrarian Society in Its Prime: England", in *The Cambridge Economic History of Europe*, I, (Cambridge, 1966), pp. 548–70, J. Z. Titow, "Some Evidence of the Thirteenth-Century Population Increase", *Economic History Review*, ser. 2., 14 (1961) 218–24; M.M. Postan and J. Titow, "Heriots and Prices on the Winchester Manors", *Economic History Review*, ser. 2, 11 (1959), 392–410. Cf. H. E. Hallam, *Rural England 1066–1348* (Glasgow, 1981), pp. 10–16. There is a wide literature on the Malthusian issue.
48. Raftis, *Economic History Review*, ser. 2., 18 (1965); "The Concentration of Responsibility in Five Villages", *Mediaeval Studies*, 28 (1966). pp. 92–118.
49. Campbell, *Honour*, p. 267; Davis, *People of the Mediterranean*, pp. 94, 95, 101; Pitt-Rivers in Peristiany, *Honour and Shame*, pp. 24, 60. Village main families fall clearly within this middle stratum.
50. Insecurity fuelling envy is a classic well-spring of gossip and scandal. *V* Bailey, ed., *Gifts*, p. 171; Foster, *Human Organization*, 19 (1960), pp. 174, 175; Banfield, *Moral Basis*, pp. 116, 121–22, 126; Stanley L. Olinick, "The Gossiping Psychoanalyst", *International Review of Psycho-Analysis*, 7 (1980), 442–43; Spacks, *Gossip*, p. 48.
51. Gluckman, *Current Anthropology*, 4 (1963), p. 309; Paine, Man n.s. 2 (1967), p. 282.
52. Also, John of London (Inter) vs. Agnes, wife of John Pege (Inter) (1307); Richard Parson (D) vs. Agnes Cateline (D) (1311, debt owed?); Thomas Gore (A) vs. Agnes Faber (Trade) (1314, breach of covenant); Thomas Gore (A) vs. Caterine Hobbe (A) (1334, debt); Thomas Aspelon (A) vs. Agnes Pellage (A) (1337).
53. Spacks, *Gossip*, p. 32.
54. Bailey, ed., *Gifts*, p.259.
55. Ibid., p. 170.
56. Petronilla Le Bon (A) vs. a *vicinus* (1292); Matilda, wife of Simon of Caldecote (Out) vs. William Maresechall (Off) (1297, debt); Agnes Smith (Trade) vs. (? illegible) (1307); Johanna, dau. of John Parson (D) vs. Thomas le Fenere (Out) (1311).
57. *V* also Sharpe, *Defamation and Sexual Slander*, pp. 9, 11, 16, 20.
58. Spacks, *Gossip*, pp. 38–42, 152, 155–56, 262. V also Bailey, ed., *Gifts*, pp. 1, 170, 259; Du Boulay, *Portrait of a Greek Mountain Village*, pp. 102, 134, 204–05.
59. *V* S. F. C. Milson, *Historical Foundations of the Common Law* (London, 1969), pp. 332–33 regarding slander of goods. Essentially, personal dignity transfers itself to

whatever one becomes easily identified with; hence, to slander goods was to impute professional incompetence.

60. 1291: William Couper (Trade) foully insulted Andrew Outy (A); Simon, son of Thomas Smith (Trade) slandered John Ballard (B). 1316: John Couper (Trade) defamed John of Broughton (A).

61. Also, John le Webester (Inter) false claimed vs. Ralph le Reve (Jan. 1332), a debt of 27s. owed?; Matilda of Caldecote (Out) vs. William Maresechall (Off) (1297), a debt of 25d. owed.

62. *Main Families:* Thomas Mohaut (A) defamed a *vicinus* (1292); William and Mariota Russell (A) vs. Henry Pochyn (Inter) (1307); Ralph Elecok (B) vs. Thomas, son of William (Out) (1314); Ralph Attehill (A) vs. John Webester (Inter) (1325). *Intermediates and Outsiders:* John, son of Richard of Hyrst (Inter) vs. Henry Ad Portam (A) (1291); John le Stake (Inter) defamed a *vicinus* (1292); John And [?] defamed a *vicinus* (1292); William, son of Elye' (Out) vs. Ralph Elecok (B) (1299); John Martyn (Out) vs. John de Erhith (Out) (1316, debt owing?).

63. Sharpe, *Defamation and Sexual Slander,* p. 14 citing K. F. Burns, "The Administrative System of the Ecclesiastical Courts in the Dioceses and Province of York: Part I, the Medieval Courts" (unpublished typescript deposited at the Borthwick Institute, 1962), p. 186.

64. John Gore owed 2 1/2 bu. of wheat plus 2s. 8d. in silver to John of Broughton (1297); Richard of Broughton owed 1 bu. of wheat to Thomas Gore (1306).

65. Gluckman, *Current Anthropology* 4 (1963) pp. 307–16; id., *Man,* n.s. 3 (1968) pp. 28–34.

66. John Kyng (B) vs. William Hobbe (A).

67. Paine, *Man,* n.s. 2 (1967), pp. 278–85; *"Man,* n.s. 3 (1968), pp. 305–08. Wilson, *"Man,* n.s. 9 (1974), pp. 96, 98 claims that simply maintaining equality requires such denigration. While Broughtons and Coupers had different economic foundations, they were clearly social equals.

68. *William Couper:* 1288 — juror, trespass; 1290 — juror; 1291 — juror, concord, defamer; 1294 — juror, pledge (5); 1294? — pledge; 1297 — pledge (2), work default; 1299 — work default; 1301 — juror. *Andrew Outy:* 1288 — juror, defended land; 1290 — juror; 1291 — special juror, concord; 1294? — pledge, work default (2); 1297 — pledge; 1299 — juror, work default. *Ralph Everard:* 1288 — capital pledge, trespass; 1290 — capital pledge, work default; 1291 — capital pledge, juror, pledge; Jan. 1294 — juror, defamer; 1294 — pledge; 1297 — pledge.

69. Campbell, *Honour,* p. 286.

70. Sharpe, *Defamation and Sexual Slander,* p. 22.

71. Note also: Gore (1340) 2s. 7d. and 1 bu. of peas; Burton (Nov., 1320) 5s. 5d. The 31s. 4d. owed by John Kyng to John Randolf included 7 bu. of wheat worth 3s. 6d., and one qu. of barley worth 40d., one robe worth one mark, one-half mark in silver, one large tub worth 30d. and one pitcher worth 2s.

72. B. L. Add. Roll 39849 (1291).

73. Self-help had been virtually prohibited from Anglo-Saxon times. Pollock and Maitland *History of English Law,* II, p. 574; Holdsworth, *History of English Law,* II, p. 100. Bracton, *Notebook,* no. 900 (1224) eventually argued that debt and damages ought to be levied from a defaulter's personal property, but as Pollock and Maitland II, p. 595 note, it took six hundred years for this view to prevail. V also Plucknett, *A Concise History,* p. 386.

74. Holdsworth, *History of English Law,* II, pp. 101, 104; Pollock and Maitland *History of*

English Law II, p. 575; Elaine Clark, "Debt Litigation in a Late Medieval English Vill" in *Pathways to Medieval Peasants*, ed. J. A. Raftis (Toronto, 1981), p. 264.

75. Pollock and Maitland op.cit., II, pp. 594–95; Plucknett, *A Concise History*, pp. 384, 386.

76. Also: Petronilla le Bon (A), Nicholas of Broughton (A), John Beneyt (D), Simon le Bon (A) and his wife, Henry Hanecok (D), William Attegate (C), Simon Smith (Trade).

77. J. A. Sharpe, "'Such Disagreement betwyx Neighbours': Litigation and Human Relations in Early Modern England" in *Disputes and Settlements, Law and Human Relations in the West*, ed. John Bossy (Cambridge, 1983), pp. 176–82; Helmholz, "Canonical Defamation," p. 267.

78. See S. D. Amussen, "Gender, Family and the Social Order, 1560–1725" in *Order and Disorder in Early Modern England*, eds. Anthony Fletcher and John Stevenson (Cambridge, 1985), pp. 207, 209. V also D. E. Underdown, "The Taming of the Scold: the Enforcement of Patriarchal Authority in Early Modern England", ibid., p. 122.

79. Also: John of Broughton (A), Andrew Outy (A), John Ballard (B), Richard Fysshere (A) and William Hobbe (A). To note the complete files of three: *Henry, son of John:* 1288 — pledge (2), trespass; 1291 — work default, land (two cottages); Jan. 1294 — juror, taster, pledge, debt owing, false claimed; 1294 — taster; 1297 — juror, trespass, work default (2); 1306 — juror; 1307 — juror; 1308 — work defaults (5); 1311 — nonappearance; 1314 — juror. *John Outy:* 1308 — pledge; 1311 — juror, pledge (2); 1314 — pledge (4), work default; 1316 — juror (2), taster, pledge (5), taster (default); 1320 — juror, pledge (2); 1322 — juror, pledge (4); 1325 — trespass; 1331 — juror, pledge, exchanged land; 1322 — pledge, concord, received gleaners; 1333 — juror, pledge; 1334 — false claimed; 1337 — pledge (defaulted and then came); 1339 — juror; 1340 — juror, trespass. *William Abbot:* 1288 — pledge; 1290 — juror; 1294 — juror; 1294? — trespass; 1307 — juror; 1308 — defaulted; 1311 — juror, work default; 1314 — pledge, assault; 1316 — false claimed; Nov. 1320 — pledge; Jan. 1322 — juror, exchanged land; 1325 — juror, pledge (2); 1331 — juror, trespass, exchanged land; 1332 — juror, pledge; 1333 — juror; 1334 — juror, pledge; 1340 — juror.

80. Mabil, widow of Geoffrey Prepositus of Caldecote (Off) vs. Lawrence Pakerel (A) (1290 debt, condoned); Cecilia Drake (Inter) vs. Juliana Wilkes (D) (Jan. 1320).

81. Robert Lenot (D) vs. Philippa Shepherd (Trade) (Jan. 1316), Richard Wilkes (D) vs. Dionysia Nunne (D) (Oct. 1322), William Leunye (Out) vs. Agnes, daughter of Alexander Webester (Trade) (1343), William Hyggeneye (A) vs. Agnes Attewode (D) (1347).

82. The next entry notes Alice as having wrongly mowed herbage in le Milneweye; her body is her pledge.

83. Mariota Holy (Inter) appears no less defiant, having both insulted and defamed Alice Cotes (C) (1316).

84. Margaret, widow of Walter Gernoun (A) vs. John Aylmar (A) (1291); Agnes, daughter of the Smith (Trade) vs. Richard Shepherd (Trade) (1297); Margaret Kyng (Inter) vs. Agnes Manger (D) (1313); Agnes Sutor (Trade) vs. Ivo Shepherd (Trade) (1318); Agnes le Reve (Off) vs. Ivo Walter and his wife, Margaret (1318); Matilda of Upwood (Out) vs. Ivo Walter (D) (1326 trespass, condoned); Agnes Pires (Parys) (D) vs. Ivo Walter (D) (1329 debt); Margaret Jowel (A) vs. [?] (1333); Sarra, widow

of Thomas Attehalle (D) vs. John Jowel (A) (1347); Joan Clairvaux (A) vs. John Wrighte (D) (1353).

85. Thomas Arnold (D) vs. Mariota Andrew (B) (1291); John Aylmar (A) vs. Margaret, widow of Walter Gernoun (A) (1291); Robert Richard (A) vs. Alice, wife of Roger (A) (1313); John le Bonde (Inter) vs. Alice Lauwe (B) (1320); Robert de Bykere (Dyker) (Off) vs. Christina Rede (A), Thomas Lanerok (A), Michael Palmer (A) and Galfridus le Rede (A) (1322, condoned); Robert Smith (Trade) vs. Sarra Haukyn and her husband Thomas (A) (1326 debt); Robert Palmer (A) vs. the wife of Thomas Arnold and her husband (D) (1326 trespass, condoned); Stephen Crane (A) vs. Agnes Lacey and her husband (B) (1342 debt); Henry Couhirde (Off) vs. Matilda, widow of Andrew Sabyn (A) (1347 debt); John Drinere (C) vs. Joan Clairvaux (A) (1353 trespass).

86. Agnes, wife of Andrew Attelane (D) defamed Agnes Attegrave (Inter) as having stolen her scissors (1308); Juliana Wake (D) defamed Sarra Haulond (A) as having stolen herring worth 3d. (1313). The remaining entry saw Agnes Horseman (D) slander Margaret Austyn (Inter) (1334).

87. The wife of Ralph Miller together with her husband (Trade) false claimed vs. John the Webester (Trade) (1308). Matilda Baroun (D) slandered the wife of William Pykeler (Trade) (1326), both the husband and wife having previously trespassed her; William then counter-slandered and was condoned.

88. Four men false claimed against women: John de Morden (Inter) vs. Emma Blunt (Inter) and Agnes Baseley (Out) (1325); Geoffrey Haringmonger (D) vs. Alice Wenington (A) (1328, trespass); William Payn (Out) vs. Agnes atte Barre (Inter) (1333), a previous entry noting that he had trespassed her; John Haukyn (A) vs. Alice West (D) (1353, trespass).

89. In total, sixteen of thirty-five defamations in these four villages were committed by women, 46%.

90. The reeve, Thomas Lanerok, and a taster, Robert Attebrok, were among the foursome slandered by Agnes Bole as untrustworthy, Wistow (1307–08). A woodward was defamed by Juliana le Bond (A) Warboys (Jan. 1294).

91. Supra, n. 86 for the Abbots Ripton entries. Agnes Wymar (Out), Warboys, denounced Robert Clerk (A) as a thief (1299). Juliana Parys (D), Wistow, denounced Ivo Walter as a thief (1320). Her husband, John Parys, false claimed against him for trespass in 1320 as well.

92. Lawrence Pakeral (A).

93. John atte Dam (A) was the debtor and her victim. Note also, Agnes Pires (D) of Wistow who was owed by Ivo Walter when she falsely sued him (1329).

94. John Jowel (A).

95. V A. W. B. Simpson, *A History of the Common Law of Contract* (Oxford, 1974), pp. 82-84 on the transmission of these liabilities on death. Holdsworth, *History of English Law* II, pp. 96–97, III, pp. 572–83 and Pollock and Maitland, op. cit., II, pp.334–37, 340–48 give fuller details. Ibid., II, pp. 427, 428 on the status of villein widows as heirs.

96. Stephen Crane (A).

97. Robert Smith (Trade); Henry Couhirde (Trade) and Robert [?] were the claimants respectively.

98. Her victim was John Wrighte (Out). Joan Clairvaux had herself trespassed John Drinere and was wrongly prosecuted by him in 1353.

99. Only Wistow false claimers represented a wider sweep of society, namely, two A households and two Trade households. Warboys and Abbots Ripton offenders were largely from D ranks while four of five Wistow defamers were intermediate villagers.

100. In addition, two plaintiffs in false claims are noted as poor, viz., Agnes, daughter of Ralph, the butcher (Broughton, 1291) and Emma Blunt (Upwood, 1325). Underdown, in Fletcher and Stevenson (eds.), *Order and Disorder* p. 120 also notes that women who were poor, social outcasts, widows or otherwise lacking in the protection of a family, or newcomers to their communities, were most commonly the village scolds.

101. Clark, in Raftis (ed.) *Pathways to Medieval Peasants*, p. 263.

102. Barbara, A. Hanawalt, ed., *Women and Work in Preindustrial Europe* (Bloomington, Ind., 1986), pp. xiv–xv, 10–13, 20–27 for medieval village women in particular; Judith M. Bennett, *Women in the Medieval English Countryside* (New York, 1987), pp. 5, 115–18, 120–26, 190–95. V also Rodney H. Hilton, "Women in the Village" in *The English Peasantry in the Later Middle Ages* (Oxford, 1975), pp. 95–110, esp. 105–06; Britton, Community of the Vill, pp. 16–37.

103. *The Medieval Economy and Society* (London, 1972), p. 137.

104. Clark, *(v* n. 101), p. 263

105. Ibid., p. 264.

106. Ibid., pp. 270–71. As an example, the author noted the case of John Borrell, a well-to-do cultivator, owed a debt of £4 5s. by Walter atte Tye. He sued for 36s. In September 1408; for 12s. 1d. plus 5s. 4d. as rent due for pasture and 6s. 1d. for services rendered by his son to Tye in June 1411; for 26s. 4d. in January 1414; for 3 bushels of peas also in January 1414 Ibid., pp. 278–79).

107. Foster, "*v* n. 6", p. 176.

108. Owed by Roger Shepherd (Trade) to Richard Attewode (D) (Warboys, Jan. 1313).

109. Clark, *(v* n. 101), pp. 253–54 also notes credit as ranging from land, animals, grains, and wood to various manufactured items.

110. It was owed to Simon Noble by Geoffrey Noble, Simon wrongly suing.

111. John Brandon (Out) vs. Thomas Akerman (D); Andrew Gernoun (A) vs. John, son of Stephen (Out).

112. John Aubyn (Inter) trespassed Thomas Rede (A), the latter wrongly suing.

113. Clark, *(v* n. 101), p. 270.

114. Ibid.

115. Nicholas Bugge (D) accused Geoffrey Heron (Inter) of taking 40 sheaves of reeds from his work in the marsh (Warboys, 1290). John Crane (A) slandered an unidentifiable villager as having taken his woollen cloth worth 12d. (Upwood, 1307).

116. Colson, *The Makah Indians*, pp. 201–36, esp. 219–20; Ronald Frankenberg, *Village on the Border* (London, 1957), pp. 65–66 et passim; Banfield, *Moral Basis*, pp. 28–29, 34–35.

117. Haviland, *Gossip, Reputation*, p. 170.

118. *V* also, Warboys (1290); Broughton (1311) (2); and Warboys (Jan. 1294).

119. Similarly, Juliana le Bond who maligned the Warboys woodward (1290) was to be relaxed her fine if she would behave better.

120. Supra, n. 56 and p. 23 for similarly motivated attacks by women.

121. The custodian of the Upwood marsh vs. Martin West (D) and Thomas Cholle (Inter); Henry Couhirde vs. Matilda Sabyn (A); the reeve of Upwood vs. Robert Cook (Trade); William, son of Geoffrey Marshall vs. Thomas Aylmar (A) and John [?].

122. Thomas Lanerok, bedel in 1299, 1304, and 1316.
123. Thomas Lanerok, Michael Palmer, Geoffrey Rede and Christina Rede.
124. *Vn.* 78, p. 120.
125. *Vn.* 78., p. 211–12.
126. Edwin B. DeWindt, *Land and People in Holywell-cum-Needingworth* (Toronto, 1972), p. 220: "...sheer competence was therefore a more highly valued element than merely economic position. ...The premium was on competence...." A. J. Fletcher, "Honour, Reputation and Local Officeholding in Elizabethan and Stuart England" in *Order and Disorder,* eds. Fletcher and Stevenson, p. 93 notes the same situation for the 16th and 17th centuries.
127. Ibid., p. 111.
128. John Cleland, *Institution of a Young Nobleman* (1607) as cited by Fletcher, op. cit. (n.126), p. 93.
129. Sylvia L. Thrupp, *The Merchant Class of Medieval London 1300–1500* (Ann Arbor, 1962), pp. 92–97 gives several examples of the fraudulent practices of merchants and efforts to police them. There were constant complaints that brewers and caterers sold above the official price (p. 94). W. Cunningham, *The Growth of English Industry and Commerce,* 5th ed. (Cambridge, 1922), I, 214 notes the following tradesmen and offenses as routinely falling within the jurisdiction of Leet courts over the years 1066-1272 A.D.: "...forestallers, regraters and engrossers, butchers who sold diseased meat, shoemakers, tanners and glovers who sold bad goods or dear, bakers and brewers who broke the assize, as well as those who used false weights and measures...." With the three Edwards (1272–1377 A.D.) there were even greater efforts to regulate abuses. (Ibid., I, 263). Indications of regrating and of breaches of the assize are also very familiar in university records. *V* Hastings Rashdall, *The Universities of Europe in the Middle Ages,* eds. F.M. Powicke and A.B. Emden (Oxford, 1936), III, pp. 85, 94, 100, 102–03, 110, 280, 287. *V* further, Thrupp, *Merchant Class,* p. 75 who notes that the mass of London citizens of the 1360s were suspicious that the great merchants were battening on them. In 1364, the vintners, fishmongers and drapers of London secured monopolies. Cunningham, *Growth,* I, 250 notes that "common folk had a strong suspicion that the man who was able to secure a monopoly by engrossing or by buying up the available supply of any article, would retail on terms that were to his own profit but not to the advantage of the community".
130. *English Country Life and Work* (Wakefield, West Yorkshire, 1976), pp. 89, 90. *v,* also, George Ewart Evans, *The Farm and the Village* (London, 1974), pp. 128–33.
131. Richard and Robert Segeley.
132. She was defamed by Matilda Bugge (D).
133. Lenots, Brids, Bugge, Haugate.
134. Also noteworthy is Alexander Sutor (cobbler) who simultaneously sued two villagers.
135. The remaining entry saw John Sutor having falsely sued John Martyn (A).
136. An A resident, Henry Bissop.
137. Robert le Lord (Inter).
138. Vs. Robert Kyng (Inter).
139. Agnes Smith (1297) and Ivo Walter (1313) (2) vs. Richard Shepherd.
140. *Millers:* Upwood, Warboys, Wistow, Broughton; *Herdsmen:* Warboys, Upwood, Wistow, Broughton; *Smiths:* Upwood, Wistow, Warboys, Broughton; *Shoemakers:* Abbots Ripton, Warboys, Wistow; *Webesters:* Upwood, Warboys, Broughton; *Ponders:* Upwood, Warboys; *Pilches:* Upwood, Warboys.

141. A Pikeler (Warboys, 1350) and Couhirde (Wistow, 1347) were also owed debts when they false claimed.

142. Clark, *(v* n. 101), p. 263.

143. To note three others: (1) Simon Bryd was presented on a morals charge (1320), for contempt (Jan. 1322), assault (1325), drew blood three times (1325 [2], 1333), damaged reeds (1331), hamsoc'ed (1333), trespassed (1337, 1339), false claimed (1343), and was declared a fugitive in 1344–45. (2) Richard Wilkes false claimed (Oct. 1322), trespassed eight times (1331, 1333 [2], 1334 [4], 1337), received (Oct. 1322), and was twice a debtor (Oct. 1322, 1325). (3) John Lenot trespassed eight times (1333, 1334, 1347, 1350 [3], 1353 [2]), false claimed (1349), six times defaulted on opera (1353), and the hue was raised over him in 1339.

144. *V* also Spacks, *Gossip*, p. 34 on gossip and social control.

145. It was alleged twice against an A party (1299, 1353) and twice against a D victim (1325, 1349).

146. *V* court rolls for 1329, 1347, 1349 and 1350.

147. *VCH:Hunts.*, II, p. 238.

148. Ibid., I, p. 343; also Carts., II, p. 342.

149. Ibid., II, pp. 65, 66.

150. Underdown, *v* n. 78, pp. 125–26.

151. J. A. Raftis, *Tenure and Mobility, Studies in the Social History of the Medieval English Village* (Toronto, 1964), pp. 122–25, 261–63 notes extensive by-laws at Upwood pertaining to turving and the harvesting of reeds and also notable violations of them.

152. Pollock and Maitland, *op. cit.*, II, 511ff.; Plucknett, *Concise History*, pp. 366–72.

153. John Haukyn (A), Reginald le Pondere (Trade), and John de Morden (Inter).

154. The Haukyns (A).

155. Robert Cook (Trade) was false claimed by William, son of the Reeve (Off) (1311) and returned the insult. John Kymbolton (D) trespassed and false claimed vs. John Love (C) (1353) who false claimed in turn, alleging trespass.

156. D. W. Fryer, Huntingdonshire, in *The Land of Britain*. The Report of the Land Utilization Survey of Britain, ed. L. Dudley Stamp, Part 75 (London, 1941), pp. 426–27. *VCH:Hunts.*, II, p. 202 contains various references to the medieval timber, noting that its value remained high until well into the sixteenth century.

157. *VCH:Hunts.*, II, pp. 158, 202.

158. Ibid., II, p. 202.

159. Emmanuel LeRoy Ladurie, Montaillou, *The Promised Land of Error* (London, 1978), pp. 253–54. V also, Du Boulay, *Portrait of a Greek Mountain Village*, pp. 204, 208–09,

160. In addition to the Broughtons and Hobbes of Broughton, the Nobles of Warboys, Gernouns of Wistow, and Vernouns of Abbots Ripton experienced a wrongful prosecution within family ranks. They were all A households.

161. G. H. Mead, *Mind, Self and Society* (Chicago, 1959), pp. 204-09; E. Goffman, *The Presentation of Self in Everyday Life* (New York, 1959), p. 85. *v* also, Paine, *Man*, n.s. 2 (1967), p. 283; Bailey, ed. Gifts, p. 123: "everyone is out for themselves".

162. Spacks, *Gossip*, p. 15.

163. Ibid., p. 22.

164. Bailey, ed. *Gifts*, p. 103 citing Gluckman, "Gossip and Scandal". *V* further Spacks, *Gossip*, pp. 20, 34, 48.

165. Spacks, *Gossip*, pp. 5, 15–16, 30 et passim.

166. *Synagogue Life: A Study in Symbolic Interaction* (Chicago, 1976), p. 156.

167. *Roger Segeley:* Jan. 1316 — false claimed, trespassed the lord's grain (beasts); Jan. 1320 — juror; Jan. 1320 — juror; Jan. 1322 — pledge; 1326 — juror. *Nicholas Bugge:* 1290 - defamed; 1299 — trespassed the lord's woods (2), pledge (4), special juror; 1306 — juror; Jan. 1313 — trespassed the lord's grain (oxen); 1313 — pledge; 1316 — pledge.

168. John, son of Robert Smith (Trade), Simon, son of Richard Shepherd (Trade), Roger, son of Robert Attebrok (B) and John Lyon (Inter).

169. Bailey, ed. *Gifts,* pp. 120–23.

170. Ibid., p. 125.

171. Ibid., p. 292.

172. *John Aylmar:* 1279 — pledge; 1291 — juror, false claimed; 1292 — pledge (2); 1294 — false claimed, juror, pledge; 1297 — false claimed; 1299 — juror; 1310 — juror.

173. *Thomas Arnold* false claimed in 1291, pledged in 1278, 1292 and 1318, and false claimed again in 1320. *Richard Segeley* defamed and false claimed in 1316, yet pledged in that year and several times over the 1320s–1330s, also serving as a taster in 1322 and 1325. *John Higgeneye* twice false claimed (Jan. 1294, 1316) as well as trespassed his neighbours. He was also a bird warren, taster, twice a capital pledge, twice a juror and several times a pledge over 1292–1316. *Henry Pakerel* false claimed in 1306 and pledged twice in 1316 and again 1339.

174. *Ivo Walter* (1294–1334) defamed twice, false claimed once, trespassed several times, received, damaged property, worked poorly, sold reeds illegally and more. (He was also wrongly prosecuted five times and defamed once by fellow residents.) *Simon Brid* (1320–1345) executed three assaults, damaged reeds, hamsoc'ed, trespassed, false claimed and was, as we have seen, declared a fugitive in 1345. *John Lyon* trespassed in 1301 and defamed and twice assaulted in 1307–08.

175. *English Villagers of the Thirteenth Century* (Cambridge, Mass., 1941), p. 106.

On Claude Dupuy
(1545–1594)

William McCuaig

*Queen's University,
Kingston, Canada*

On Claude Dupuy (1545–1594)

Claude Dupuy, a *conseiller* or magistrate of the Parlement de Paris and a notable figure in the history of culture in the European sixteenth century, died on 1 December 1594 in the French capital. His whole life had been centered on the city of Paris — more specifically on the left bank, the Faubourg St.–Germain, and the Ile de la Cité, on which the Palais de Justice stood. Four episodes of absence from Paris are significant: his years of university study at Toulouse and Bourges; his voyage to Venice, Padua, Bologna, Florence and Rome in 1570–1571; his sojourn in Guyenne in 1582–1584 as a member of the Chambre de Justice sent to the region to reestablish impartial justice; and his departure from the capital (when it was in the grip of the Catholic League) to join the royalist parlement at Tours in 1591. Claude Dupuy returned to Paris with Henri IV in March of 1594, and thus was able to live out the final months of his life in the city that had always been his home. It was a life commemorated (under the Latin form of his name, Claudius Puteanus) in a memorial brochure published in 1607, *Claudii Puteani Tumulus*.[1] The *Tumulus* contains for the most part obsequies in verse of the usual stylized and uninformative kind, but it gives his age at death — 49 years completed — and therefore establishes that his birth must have occurred in the year between 1 December 1544 and 1 December 1545.

Claude Dupuy was a man of great learning, and might have been a distinguished professional scholar had he not chosen the career of a parlementaire. As it was he was able to work desultorily on the texts of a number of classical authors, and to aim at the preparation of an edition of the Latin Panegyrics, which was not however completed. His patrimony of erudition and humanity were therefore transmitted to France and to posterity in three forms: the first is the holdings of the Bibliothèque Nationale of Paris, including the manuscripts of the

Collection Dupuy,[2] the manuscripts once possessed by him which passed to the main series of Greek, Latin, and French MSS, and the many editions bearing his *ex libris* to be found among the *imprimés*. The second is the lives and careers of his devoted wife and children, among whom were Pierre and Jacques Dupuy, both eminent in the seventeenth century. The third legacy left by Claude Dupuy is his surviving letters to Gian Vincenzo Pinelli of Padua, the only extensive body of correspondence (in fact the only extensive body of text of any kind, I believe) from his hand to survive.

The purpose of the present contribution is, first, to give a brief account of the facts of his life, some salient and a few trivial, as they have been recorded in the historical literature, a task which has not before been undertaken. But the main intention is to portray the man as he appears in the third of the three "legacies" mentioned above, his correspondence with Gian Vincenzo Pinelli. The letters from Dupuy, written in Latin and French, are to be found in the Biblioteca Ambrosiana of Milan,[3] while those from Pinelli, written in Italian, are in a manuscript of the Collection Dupuy at Paris.[4] These are letters of marvellous richness, and have been consulted by a number of scholars over the years — those from Dupuy with great ease, those from Pinelli with a little more initial difficulty, until one gets accustomed to his scrawling hand. But it is a hand with which it is possible to become acquainted not only in the Bibliothèque Nationale but also in the British Library, the Biblioteca Apostolica Vaticana, the Ambrosiana, and any number of other repositories, for Pinelli, unlike Dupuy, was not distracted from his self-imposed burden of assiduous correspondence with learned acquaintances by the duties of a magistrate or the cares of a family. He resembles Dupuy, however, in that neither man allowed himself to be distracted from scholarship by a professorship: Pinelli was a *libero studioso*, an independent intellectual.

The correspondence has normally been drawn upon by scholars who have had a particular interest in one or another of the illustrious contemporaries with whom Pinelli and Dupuy were on familiar terms; the one whose intellectual power was most startling and about whom they therefore have the most to say was Joseph Scaliger. The personality of Joseph Scaliger exercised a peculiar fascination upon all who knew him and many others who wished to know something, even at second hand, of his character and methods. Dupuy figures in the published correspondence of Scaliger, and he was the dedicatee of Scaliger's edition of Catullus, Tibullus, and Propertius of 1577. Grafton's *Joseph Scaliger* is the best guide to the intellectual world of

Scaliger, and indeed of Claude Dupuy.[5] I myself began to read the letters in 1983 with a search for information about Pinelli's friend (and
Dupuy's honored acquaintance), Carlo Sigonio, a search which was
fruitful and which made it possible to quote extracts from the letters
having to do with the publication of Sigonio's books in Italy, France,
and Germany.[6]

In what follows, after a brief biographical sketch, Claude
Dupuy will be allowed for the first time to speak for himself about his
friends and family; about his world of books and learning and the
grotesque reflection of it in the world of censorship; and about France
in the 1570s (for which decade his letters are much fuller and more frequent than they are for the 1580s), as she struggled unsuccessfully to
strangle the demons of civil and religious war.

* * * *

Suzanne Solente was able, using MS Dupuy 638 and other resources of
the Collection Dupuy, to give the best available (albeit brief) sketch of
the background of Clément Dupuy (1506–11 August 1554), the father
of Claude Dupuy.[7] The family was from the region of the Monts du
Forez, near Lyon: the town of St.–Galmier is named as their place of
origin; Claude Dupuy was born in Montbrison;[8] Clément Dupuy purchased the seigneury of St.–Germain-Laval in 1550. All three towns are
in the *département* of the Loire, in the region of Rhone-Alpes, with Lyon
as their metropolis. Clément Dupuy migrated to the capital and
became an *avocat* in the Parlement de Paris, marrying Philippe Poncet,
the daughter of a Parisian family, on 23 June 1539.[9] She survived until
1586, and bore two siblings to Claude Dupuy, Clément Dupuy S.J. (d.
16 April 1598) and Judith Dupuy, who married Claude Séguier, Sieur
de Verrière, a member of an eminent family of "the robe" — that is, of
judicial and administrative professionals with legal training. Likewise
eminent, likewise *robin*, were the families with whom Claude Dupuy
eventually contracted his own marriage alliance: his wife was Claude
Sanguin, daughter of Jacques Sanguin and Barbe De Thou. The latter
was the sister of Christophe De Thou, *premier président* of the Parlement
and father of Jacques-Auguste De Thou. There was a marriage alliance
in the generation of Jacques-Auguste between one of his sisters and
Achille de Harlay, who was to succeed Christophe De Thou as *premier
président* — and with that enough has been said to connote the milieu
into which the ascending curve of his family fortunes, and his own character and intellect, were to carry Claude Dupuy. The circumstances in

which he left his own numerous offspring, on the other hand, were insufficient in light of the inflation of the price of offices in the kingdom of France to sustain his son Pierre at the level of a *conseiller* of the Parlement de Paris. Nicolas Rigault states explicitly that this was an avenue which was in effect closed to Pierre Dupuy,[10] even had he wished to follow it. But Pierre and Jacques Dupuy, best known of the offspring of Claude Dupuy, were to leave their mark not in Parlement but on the literary civilization of France in the seventeenth century.

Claude Dupuy must have shown early aptitude for languages and literature, and was able to study under Jean Strazel, Jean Dorat, Adrien Turnèbe (Turnebus), and Denis Lambin in Paris.[11] His legal studies were done at Toulouse,[12] and under Jacques Cujas at Bourges.[13]

In 1571, when he was about twenty-six years old and had just returned from his Italian voyage, Claude Dupuy was residing with his widowed mother at her house in the parish of St.–André-des-Arts[14] on the left bank — which was not however called "la rive gauche" at that time, but rather "l'Université." It will be safe to assume that this was the same house in which she had lived with her husband from the time her married life began, and in which her son had been raised. Claude Dupuy, in other words, was a child of St.–André-des-Arts, the quarter of magistrates and intellectuals. The De Thou were among the leading families (were perhaps the leading family) of this parish. In 1576, at the age of 31, Claude Dupuy married and obtained the office of *conseiller* of the Parlement de Paris, and perhaps soon after he moved himself and his family to the fashionable and growing suburb of the Faubourg St.–Germain. This removal did not in any case carry him far from St.–André-des-Arts and his other native haunts on the *rive gauche*.

As an adult Claude Dupuy stated that his oldest and closest friend, with whom he had been intimate since youth, was Jacques Houllier, the homonymous son of the great Parisian professor of medicine, and practitioner, Jacques Houllier (Jacobus Hollerius, d. 1562). The younger Houllier chose a different profession to that of his father, taking legal training at Toulouse with Dupuy and choosing, like Dupuy, a magisterial career. But unlike Dupuy, Jacques Houllier the younger did not serve in the Parlement de Paris.[15] In a letter to Gian Vincenzo Pinelli, Claude Dupuy presents Jacques Houllier in terms which make it clear that he was a *conseiller d'état,* a member of the *grand conseil.* The letter contains interesting references to Joseph Scaliger ("de la Scala") and Jacques-Auguste De Thou, as well as to Houllier, and is short enough to quote in its entirety:

Monsieur vous recevréz la presente par Monsieur Houlier Conseillier
du Roi en ceste cour, l'un de mes plus anciens et intimes amis. Nous
avons esté nourris ieunes ensemble, et depuis avec l'age nostre amitié a pris telle accroissance, ut nihil ad eam possit accedere. Quand il
n'y auroit que cela, encores ie m'asseurerois qu'il seroit bien receu et
favorisé de vous. mais il y a bien plus. car ie vous puis bien dire, et en
cela ie ne me laisse point transporter de l'amitié que ie lui porte, que
c'est un des premiers hommes de nostre robe et qui a peu de sec-
onds qui le suivent de pres, fort eloquent, grand iurisconsulte, fort
docte en toutes les parties de philosophie, et de Mathematiques, bien
versé en toute histoire, en la geographie, et langue Grecque, Et quod
familiam ducit, homme de grand esprit, de grand iugement, et de
singuliere integrité. la doctrine et la vertu lui sont comme heredi-
taires. car il est fils de feu Iacobus Holerius Medecin tres-renommé et
lequel a tenu un des premiers lieux entre ceux de sa profession tant
en la practique que theorique. ledit Sieur Houlier meu d'une
honneste curiosité, et comme naturellement toute personne bien
née est desireuse de voir et voiager, va faire une course en Italie, et
fait dessein d'aller premièrement à Venise et Padoue, et de là à
Romme, Naples, et Gennes. Ie vous supplie Monsieur de lui faire
tous les plaisirs, faveurs, et courtoisies, qu'un tel personnage peut
desirer d'un Gentilhomme docte, courtois et vertueux tel que vous
estes: singulierement de lui donner des adresses en toutes lesdites
villes et autres lieux ou son chemin s'adonnera selon l'humeur et
naturel que connoistréz en lui. n'estiméz point que ceste recomman-
dation soit vulgaire; ie ne vous sçaurois escrire plus affectueusement
pour mon propre pere, que ie fais pour Monsieur Houlier, lequel est
un des plus intimes et feaux amis que i'aie en ce monde, Et l'amitié
plus que fraternelle qui est entre lui et moi, est connue à tous ceux
de pardeça. Ie vous envoierai pour la foire prochaine les livres que
me demandéz. i'ai tout prests pour vous envoier deux briefs traitéz
de Monsieur de la Scala, l'un de Critica et criticis, et l'autre contre le
Papyrus de nostre ami,[16] lesquels ie vous ferai tenir par le premier, et
i'estime que vous les auréz receus avant que la presente vous soit ren-
due. Ie ne sçai qu'est devenu un pacquet de lettres que ie vous ai
envoié il y a quelques mois par la voie de l'Ambassadeur de Ferrare,
dedans lequel il y en avoit une de Monsieur de Thou, par laquelle il
vous remercioit du plaisir, que lui aviéz fait. ie desirerois que vous lui
escrivissiéz: car ie vous iure que i'ai veu et leu ladite lettre pleine
d'honnestes offres, et vous puis encores mieux tesmoigner la bonne

affection qu'il a de vous servir. Ie ferai fin en cest endroit par mes
treshumbles recommandations à vos bonnes graces, et prierai nostre
Seigneur vous
donner
Monsieur longue et heureuse vie. de Paris ce XVme iour d'Aoust
M.D. LXXIX.
Monsieur de la Scala se recommande humblement à vos bonnes
graces, et vous observe infiniement
Vostre treshumble serviteur Claude Dupuy.[17]

        Though Dupuy himself travelled to Italy only once and
remained there for merely a matter of months, this voyage was to be
one of the important periods of his life. His correspondence with
Pinelli begins not long after they had parted in Padua, with a letter
from Bologna of 28 September 1570.[18] It is probable that Dupuy arrived
in Italy in late August or early September; he was with Pinelli in
September 1570. It was to be the only time in their lives that they met
face to face. Dupuy was in Rome by November, engaging there in philological work, and in discussion with Marc-Antoine Muret, Fulvio Orsini,
and other humanists. He left Rome in mid-February 1571 and his voyage from Rome to Lyon took twenty-three days.[19] Claude Dupuy was
anxious to commence his legal and magisterial career, and anxious for
his country as it became mired in religious and civil war.
        From 1571 until 1576, Claude Dupuy must have served his
legal apprenticeship in the Palais de Justice. There is no published
information on his professional activities at this period of his life, and
in writing to Pinelli, Dupuy preferred to discuss politics and literature
rather than to report to his Italian correspondent on such practical
matters. Claude Dupuy will have served in one of the five subordinate
sections of the Parlement de Paris which were known as the Enquêtes.[20]
He was never, as it seems, an avocat.
        But if the middle 1570s represent a prelude in the profession-
al life of Claude Dupuy, they were years of the greatest importance for
the cultural life of France in the sixteenth and seventeenth centuries
for, in the recollection of Jacques-Auguste De Thou, it was ca. 1574–75
that his group of scholarly friends began the series of informal but regular meetings that were in essence the origin of the intellectual salon
which, after civil peace had returned to France, had its focus in his residence in the vicinity of St.–André-des-Arts, and which was continued
after his death by Pierre and Jacques Dupuy. It is worth comparing two

accounts of the origins of this cénacle, the first given by De Thou himself in his memoirs, the second appearing in his recorded table talk. In the memoirs, De Thou speaks of his return, towards the end of 1574, from an Italian voyage, and of how he dedicated the subsquent four years to study and intellectual intercourse with Pierre and François Pithou, Antoine Loisel, Jacques Houllier, Claude Dupuy, and Nicolas Le Fèvre:

> Ex Italia reversus Thuanus domo se tenuit, literis vacaturus; et librorum lectioni totum quadriennium impendit: sed nec tam privato studio, quam amicorum literatorum colloquiis ac consuetudine, profecit; in quibus primas ferebant Petrus et Franciscus Pithoei fratres, Antonius Oisellus, Jacobus Hollerius, magni illius Hollerii dignissimus filius, et Claudius Puteanus, qui, sub id in senatum cooptatus, Claudiam Sanguineam proxima secum cognatione conjunctam in uxorem duxit; eoque vinculo, qui iam doctrinae et virtutis opinione coaluerant, arctius deinceps uniti sunt. Sed omnium maxime cum Nicolao Fabro conjunctissime ac diutissime vixit....[21]

In the *Thuana* (a text whose complete reliability cannot be taken for granted[22]) it is recorded that this company met in the evening on holidays chez De Thou — but also that the day had often included an earlier rendez-vous at the Cordeliers, the great Franciscan convent situated between the Porte St.–Michel and the Porte St.–Germain. The church itself was destroyed by fire in 1580, and subsequently rebuilt, but it was in the cloister that the men of letters gathered. It may be noted that (as this reminiscence seems to state) they were often joined by Joseph Scaliger at their evening gathering in a private residence, but that he did not come with them to the cloister of the Cordeliers. Those whom De Thou recalled as having met there were: himself, Dupuy, Houllier, Le Fèvre, Pithou (Pierre, apparently), Louis Servin on occasions, and a member, not clearly identified, of the Hotman family. It was the personality of Jacques Houllier — immensely learned, yet a mocker of bibliophiles, cosmopolitan, versatile, persifleur and raconteur — that left the strongest impression from the meetings at the Cordeliers on the memory of the young De Thou:

> M. Houlier estoit un tres-sçavant homme, fils du Medecin, tres-habile homme. Il sçavoit beaucoup de choses. Il estoit fort eloquent, sçavoit bien l'Histoire. Ils avoient estudié aux loix à Toulouse M<essieurs>

du Puy, le Fevre et lui. Il estoit grand railleur et faisoit un conte fort proprement et eloquemment. Il avoit fort voyagé; se mocquoit de ceux qui estoient si curieux en livres.

Ils'assembloient tous les dimanches et festes aux Cordeliers, dans le cloistre, depuis huict heures jusques à onze, Mess<ieurs> Pithou, du Puy, le Fevre, de Thou, Houlier, Hotman,[23] quelquesfois Servin, qui servoit pour faire rire. M. Houlier se mocquoit de luy et luy faisoit accroire de grandes absurditez. Là ils communiquoient des Lettres, et falloit estre bien fondé pour estre de leur compagnie: et pour moy, je ne faisois qu'escouter. Cette compagnie se trouvoit chez moy les festes après disner, où M. Scaliger estoit souvent. J'ay appris tout ce que je sçay en leur compagnie.[24]

When composing the necrology of Jacques Houllier the elder for the *Histories,* De Thou also included a memorial notice of Jacques Houllier the younger, which may be compared with the two portraits of him given above in Dupuy's letter to Pinelli and in the *Thuana.* This notice records, once again, his impressive intellect and learning, and also emphasizes that the career as a royal office-holder of Jacques Houllier was not passed in the relatively sedentary fashion of a par-lementaire such as Dupuy, but that "peregrationibus longinquis... bonam aevi brevis ipsi a Deo concessi partem contrivit."[25]

Claude Dupuy aspired to become a *conseiller,* a member of the Grand'Chambre, one of the premier magistrates of the city of Paris and in fact of the kingdom of France. This aspiration was made possible by his own superior intelligence and legal training, and — one has to pre-sume — by an accumulation of capital in his family which gave him the means to contemplate such a purchase. Dupuy's career fell during the period of modern French history at which the venality of offices, while universally practiced, was not officially admitted. He would have been required to purchase his office, and then at the moment of investiture to swear an oath to the effect that no price had been paid for his advancement[26] — a distasteful ordeal.

He was received as a lay councillor of the Parlement de Paris on 6 February 1576. The place he took had previously been held by the late Jean Morelet du Muiseau.[27] On 28 October 1587, Dupuy, and another councillor, Jacques (II) Allegrin, received ratification of lettres patentes permitting each to resign his place when, and to whom, he pleased, in accordance with the edict of July 1586.[28] (Within two decades, in the France of Henri IV, this right to dispose of one's office as a fully private economic asset would be formalized and guaranteed by the payment of an annual fee — the Paulette.)

Dupuy's marriage to Claude Sanguin took place very shortly after he became a *conseiller*. Solente states that the contract for the marriage was passed on 29 April 1576.[29] Gian Vincenzo Pinelli wrote to congratulate Dupuy on this marital union on 21 June 1576.[30] In a letter to Pinelli of 14 September 1576, Claude Dupuy evaluated his marriage to Claude Sanguin (and also, in passing, the perceived constraints of the social world in which he lived his life) in these terms:

> Monsieur ie vous remercie humblement de la congratulation que vous me faites à raison de mon mariage. certainement i'ai tres-grande occasion de m'en louer, graces à Dieu, aiant espousé une femme uxoria forma, bien apparentée et alliée en ceste Ville et des mieux, riche moiennement, et davantage, ce que ie devois dire premier, bien nourrie et de bonnes meurs. Ie suis receu en mon estat de Conseillier de ce Parlement dés le mois de Fevrier, apres avoir souffert beaucoup de peine et de travaux. Ces offices sont honorables entre ceux de nostre robe, au-reste penibles, suiets, et peu propres à mon humeur et naturel. Mais en France on ne peut honnestement demeurer privé, ores que lon le desirast, sic vivitur apud nos. O que vous estes heureux en Italie, qui pouvéz passer vos ans in otio simul et in honore. Ces deux empeschemens, qui sont tres-grans, comme vous pouvéz iuger, ont causé que ie ne vous ai point escrit long-temps-a....[31]

Claude Sanguin survived her husband by many years, living until 1631. Claude Dupuy and Claude Sanguin had numerous progeny: eight children survived infancy.[32] Pierre and Jacques are well known to the literature of France in the seventeenth century; letters of Christophe Dupuy, (who became a Carthusian) to Jacques-Auguste De Thou have recently been published.[33]

With Claude Dupuy's marriage in 1576, or probably not long after, there came a move beyond the city wall of Paris to the Faubourg St.–Germain. But the first document which states clearly that he lived in the faubourg is from 1587: a letter in which Dupuy gives Pinelli precise instructions about the address to be used in writing to him at Paris: "A Monsieur Dupuy Conseiller du Roi en sa Cour de Parlement, demeurant au Fauxbourg de St.–Germain des Prez."[34] It is, as it happens, possible to know with some precision where the residence of Claude Dupuy was in the faubourg, for the name of the street and that of the parish were recorded on a posthumous inventory of his goods that has been preserved. Chez Dupuy was "Rue des Deux Portes, parroisse Saint Benoist."[35] Many parishes in the sixteenth century had a rue des Deux Portes, for it was not unusual for residential streets to be closed off by a barrier at either end, and all of the old streets of Paris (except for one insignificant impasse) that once were designated in this way have received a more modern appellation. But consultation of the *Dictionnaire historique des rues de Paris* makes it fairly certain that the one in which Dupuy resided was the modern rue de Nevers in the sixth arrondissement.[36] It opened, and opens, onto the quai opposite the eastern end of the Ile de la Cité, very near the bridgehead on the left bank of the Pont Neuf. When the Pont Neuf was sufficiently complete to be usable (early 1580s?), Claude Dupuy will have traversed it before dawn most mornings on his way to the Palais de Justice. Before that he would of course have used the Pont St.–Michel. The whole quarter was made raw and raucous by the enormous amount of new construction taking place there in the sixteenth century, including that of the new bridge itself, begun in 1578, and that of the many new residential developments such as the rue des Deux Portes: Dupuy will likely have been the first occupier of the house he lived in there, and his move was in every sense comparable to the decision of any young, affluent, urban professional with a new family to move to a recent but upscale semi-suburban development in any twentieth century city. His street was too recent to appear on any of the published sixteenth-century plans of Paris, all of which were based on a single master plan developed before 1550 and which fail to reflect urban growth in the second half.[37]

The Faubourg St.–Germain bore, for contemporaries, a series of connotations, all of which are relevant for the nuances they give us concerning the social and cultural orientation of Claude Dupuy. It was the quarter favored by the Italians in Paris, as well as by the Huguenots, and since the Middle Ages by the licentious students of the university. The Foire St.–Germain, which was as much of a Saturnalia as official Christianity would tolerate in the capital city of the kingdom, took place there every year before Lent. The life of the faubourg was associated with an openness to cultural influences arriving in Paris from all parts of Europe, and as such was an object of particular suspicion on the part of the ligueurs of the city.[38] And of course Dupuy remained within easy reach of St.–André-des-Arts, of the booksellers in the rue St.–Jacques, and of the Cordeliers.

The Sanguin, unlike the Dupuy, were a Parisian family of long standing, just as Dupuy told Pinelli. Their origins are traced by Barbara Diefendorf: "The Luilliers and the Sanguins were famous as money changers in the late fourteenth and early fifteenth centuries..."[39] and by the sixteenth century had risen to prominence among city office-holding families. The father of Claude Sanguin, Claude Dupuy's bride, was Jacques Sanguin, sieur de Livry, a city councillor,[40] an échevin in 1567,[41] a *lieutenant de justice* of the prévôt des marchands in 1569,[42] and *lieutenant-général aux Eaux et Forêts*. His father had been a *conseiller* at the Parlement.[43] The mother of Claude Sanguin was Barbe De Thou, daughter of président Augustin de Thou, sister of *premier président* Christophe De Thou, aunt of président Jacques-Auguste De Thou, the historian.

One of Claude Sanguin's brothers returned the family to full parlementaire standing shortly after Claude Dupuy became a *conseiller:* he was Jacques Sanguin the younger, who entered upon the office of *conseiller* on 1 July 1580 after having frequented the Palais de Justice as an *avocat*. At this time he bore the title of sieur de Livry, so we can conclude that his homonymous father Jacques Sanguin was by then deceased. *Conseiller* Jacques Sanguin would survive his brother-in-law Claude Dupuy to become *prévôt des marchands* in 1606–1612. His wife was Marie du Mesnil, daughter of an *avocat*.[44]

Mademoiselle Claude Sanguin and *conseiller* Jacques Sanguin had at least one other brother who was to play a role in the history of Paris at the end of the sixteenth century, and for biographical references to him we must turn to the literature on the Ligue rather than that on the Parlement. He was Christophe Sanguin, canon of Notre-Dame and ligueur. The entry on Christophe Sanguin in Robert Descimon's *Qui étaient les Seize?* notes that he had been a *conseiller de ville* as well as a member of the *conseil secret des Seize*.[45] Further details are provided in Elie Barnavi's *Le Parti de Dieu:* Christophe Sanguin belonged to the earlier, socially superior generation of leaders of the Parisian Ligue. Not only was he a canon and *chambrier* at Notre-Dame, he held the priory of Aton as well. Barnavi records the career of his brother Jacques Sanguin, and the marriages of two of his sisters, Madeleine and Jeanne, but has failed to record the marriage, or even the existence, of a third sister, Claude Sanguin, wife of Claude Dupuy.[46]

When they composed the epitaph for the *Tumulus* of their father, the sons of Claude Dupuy thought it worthwhile to draw attention to two aspects of unusual importance in his public life. The first was a period of two and a half years, January 1582 to June 1584, during which his service as a *conseiller* of the Parlement de Paris took on a relief which it did not normally have when he was merely a part, albeit an eminent one, of the vast machinery of the Palais de Justice on the Ile de la Cité. His qualities of erudition, memory, judgment, and diligence brought him this distinction: "inter delectos ex amplissimo ordine recuperatores qui res Aquitanicas componerent a Christianissimo rege adsumptus... "[47] Dupuy, in other words, was a member of the Chambre de Justice sent from Paris to the province of Guyenne in 1582, where it sat as a court of appeal for the purpose of hearing cases in which Huguenots were involved — cases which the incendiary atmosphere of those years in that province (a province which fell within the sphere of influence of Henri de Navarre) had made it impossible for the Parlement de Bordeaux to deal with. Contemporary documents concerning the mission of the Chambre de Justice include the memoirs of J.-A. De Thou,[48] who was initially a part of it, and the speeches of Antoine Loisel, published in his *Guyenne*. Loisel participated in the court as *avocat général du roi*. Surviving archival documents relevant to this mission were discovered and studied in the nineteenth century by E. Brives-Cazes, and the brief account which follows depends on his two monographs of 1866 and 1874.[49] The significance of the work done by the Chambre de Justice is evaluated in the monograph of Roman Schnur: all of its members were Catholics, but its mission to judge, on a purely legal basis and without reference to religion, cases which were quintessentially offshoots of the religious struggle, made it a perfect *politique* organism. Loisel's speeches on the theme of amnesty mark a stage in the growth of the idea of the modern state, a state that is in which religious allegiance is not paramount but subordinate to membership in the national community.[50]

In the 1570s a special section of the Parlement de Bordeaux, composed at first of equal representation from Catholics and Huguenots, then of representation two thirds Catholic and one third Huguenot (*chambre mi-partie, chambre tri-partie*) had been established to deal with cases in which a difference of religion was involved. They had proved unable to function, and the emergency had to be dealt with at the national level. The idea of sending a special section from the Parlement de Paris to Guyenne was broached in 1580 and took concrete form in an edict of November 1581, which appointed the members. Their number was intended to be nineteen in total, but there occurred the usual amount of last-minute substitution and re-shuffling of the membership, and the late arrival of at least one member. The group which set out from Paris and arrived in Bordeaux in January of 1582 comprised *président* Pierre (II) Séguier and thirteen *conseillers*, while Antoine Loisel as *avocat général du roi* and Pierre Pithou as *procureur général du roi* represented the state. Pierre Pithou was of course one of the greatest men of letters of sixteenth-century France, as were J.-A. De Thou and Antoine Loisel.[51] One's subjective (and perhaps unduly partial) feeling about Claude Dupuy is that he was their equal in every respect except that of literary distinction in the eyes of posterity, to which, had he felt the spur of ambition, he might have left a legacy as substantial as that of Pithou, if not that of De Thou.

At Bordeaux the Chambre de Justice was quartered in the Jacobin convent of the city. Its first sessions were held there at the end of January 1582. Bordeaux had a new mayor at this time: Michel de Montaigne had just returned from his voyage to Italy in order to occupy this position. He was to have frequent social and professional contact with the *conseillers* of the Chambre de Justice, both in Bordeaux and while they were in session elsewhere, and his surviving correspondence includes one letter from him to Claude Dupuy. It is dated 23 April, the year is 1584, and the Chambre is in session at Saintes. A protégé of Montaigne, the Sieur de Verres, was accused before it of a crime of violence, and Montaigne wrote to defend his character and the necessity of whatever it was he had done in the context of the military emergency prevailing in France; and to claim that the charge brought against him was malicious.[52] Though Montaigne does not enter into the details of the charge, we can see clearly that the case of the Sieur de Verres was typical of the sort of cases handled by the Chambre de Justice: he is perhaps as likely to have been a Huguenot as he is to have been a Catholic, and he had been involved in an armed conflict of some sort with members of the opposite confession, a conflict in which his actions, whatever they were, could be excused on the grounds of self-defence, or at any rate on the grounds that the normal standards by which armed actions were to be judged had effectively been suspended in France. According to Brives-Cazes, the sort of deeds that were felt to fall into this state of legal limbo were acts of pillage: religious turmoil, the consequent military emergency, and the protection that could be obtained from local magnates, had combined to put them beyond the bounds of jurisdiction.[53] The same author in his monograph publishes many letters (similar to the one from Montaigne to Dupuy) written by Henri de Navarre to the Chambre de Justice in favor of his protégés who had acted in a similar fashion. An interesting historical parallel: it is well known that the city of Rome and her surrounding territory were afflicted with a species of outlawry not dissimilar in its effects, though different in origin, to that which afflicted south-west France at exactly the same time. In both cases jurisdiction had lost its capacity to repress criminality. At Rome this was because Pope Gregory XIII lacked the political will to confront Roman banditism; but his successor Sixtus V was to prove more forceful, just as he was to prove more forceful in his attempts to interfere in the national affairs of the kingdom of France.

French justice had not been rendered entirely impotent, and it was still possible to try and to punish crimes of a more drastic nature. The most notable judgment pronounced by the Chambre de Justice in Bordeaux was the death sentence imposed, and executed, on Jean de Rostaing, a Huguenot and a terrorist. That such a sentence could be imposed and carried out in France, even during the emergency, was exceptional for a different reason: Rostaing was a gentilhomme. De Thou himself mentions this notorious case.[54] Other death sentences were pronounced and carried out in a more routine way. Judicial torture was not seldom used, under the so-called extraordinary procedure which was adopted in order to deal with many criminal cases, just as it was in Paris and elsewhere in Europe. Claude Dupuy will often have had to supervise, or be present at, the tormenting of prisoners.

The Chambre de Justice met in Agen from October 1582 to May 1583, at Périgueux from July 1583 to January 1584, and at Saintes from February 1584 to June 1584. The opening and the closing of these sessions were regularly the occasion for the delivery of the famous speeches of Antoine Loisel, and once of Pierre Pithou, in favor of amnesty and civil peace — and for the formal recitation of the latest royal edict of pacification. The removal of the court from one city to another was not a simple matter, for the number of persons included in its function was very much larger than the small number of magistrates who sat at its summit: sergeants, *greffiers* (clerks), *huissiers* (literally "ushers," but in fact policemen), *procureurs* and others were all necessary for the administration of justice.

Occasional glimpses of the working life of the magistrates are offered in the documents used by Brives-Cazes. The Chambre normally held audiences on Monday, Wednesday, and Friday beginning at 7 A.M., and the magistrates probably met in council on every working day, given their caseload. Each will have functioned in turn as *rapporteur* for a portion of the cases before them, that is, as the magistrate charged with sifting and summarizing the written evidence for his colleagues. It was the *rapporteur* who could expect to receive "épices" — an honorarium offered to the magistrate by the parties to the cause and accepted quite openly. If torture was to be used under the extraordinary procedure, the *rapporteur* would supervise it.

The birth record of the offspring produced by Claude Dupuy and Claude Sanguin in the course of a fecund marriage illuminates for a moment the private life of the magistrate during these years, revealing that Claude Sanguin accompanied her husband during his sojourn in south-west France, for their son Pierre was born at Agen in November 1582, and their son Clément was born in Saintes in May 1584.[55] The decision to have his wife, and presumably his children, accompany him on a difficult and dangerous mission, far from Paris, testifies to the affection that characterized this ménage.

All of the members of the Chambre de Justice were gladdened when they could finally return to the capital. But within a short time, at the mid-point of the decade, the Ligue was re-founded in Paris, and France began to slide towards open civil war: it is not by chance that Jacques-Auguste De Thou felt the need to imitate T. Livius and to write a new preface to the subsequent portion of his *Histories* when he reached the year 1585.[56] Before describing the vicissitudes of Claude Dupuy during the years of the Ligue, mention may fittingly be made of the garden which gave him interludes of peaceful recreation in the 1580s, as the situation in France worsened. The testimony concerning the garden, which was part of a country property he had acquired at Balizy, on the outskirts of Paris, is to be found in Dupuy's correspondence with Pinelli, and has been well synthesized in a recent article.[57] The flowers and vegetables he cultivated there brought great solace to the spirit of Claude Dupuy.

He was to step into the spotlight of history once more, on the day in January 1589 when he and the other *conseillers* of the Parlement de Paris, choosing to follow their *premier président* Achille de Harlay, were led to the Bastille and imprisoned there by Bussy Leclerc. For the rest, his role as historical actor is, quite simply, typical and characteristic of the Politiques. When he had to make the difficult decision, a crux for so many, about whether or not to remain in Paris and collaborate with the Parlement there, he chose to depart and join the king. These are the salient facts; but what would we not give to know if he escaped from Paris in the same dangerous and dramatic way that Jacques-Auguste De Thou did, and if and how his numerous family escaped to join him! The *Journaux* of Pierre de l'Estoile for the reigns of Henri III and Henri IV tell us summarily of his arrest in 1589 and of his death in 1594.[58] It is a pity, for there are, or were, legitimate motives to hope that Pierre de l'Estoile might have had more to say concerning Claude Dupuy, whom he will have known well. They were practically coevals (l'Estoile was born in 1546) and both were residents of the Université quarter, and in fact of the same parish, St.–André-des-Arts. Their fathers would have been colleagues in the Parlement de Paris, where Louis de l'Estoile had been a *président* in the *Enquêtes*. Both were office-holders themselves (Pierre de l'Estoile as *grand audiencier* at the Chancellerie) and Politiques of an identical stripe, as far as one can judge. Both were famous for their collections of all the ephemeral literature connected with the turbulence of their times; they had the same archival instinct.[59]

The events of 16 January 1589 were the second of the two occasions in the public life of Claude Dupuy that were thought worthy of explicit commemoration in his *Tumulus*: "a coniuratis perniciosissimae factionis ministris cum reliquis ordinis sui quos ob vitae probitatem constantiamque in fide permansuros scirent, in carcerem coniectus est." Paris had been barricaded, and the king had surrendered his capital to the Duc de Guise, in May 1588. The assassination of the Duc de Guise and his brother at Blois in December 1588 had revealed that even Henri de Valois was capable of violently dispatching his enemies in defence of his sovereignty and his kingdom. Within a few days of the murders, one *président* and a handful of the *conseillers* of the Grand'Chambre of Parlement had already left Paris to join the king.[60] From this time all of the *conseillers* were to be faced with a crisis of moral choice. Achille de Harlay, *premier président*, knowing that the use of force against his person was now imminent and inevitable, continued to preside. On 16 January 1589, he and two colleagues, Potier and Augustin De Thou, opened a session of the Grand'Chambre.[61] Claude Dupuy was present. The Seize, the leaders of the Ligue in Paris, feared that the Parlement might publish *lettres patentes* from the king in which he justified the executions at Blois and ordered the submission of the city; the preventive arrest of the leaders of the Parlement was therefore determined upon, and carried out by the new ligueur governor of the Bastille, Bussy Leclerc. But, in a famous example of constancy, all of the *conseillers* present declared that they also would suffer the fate of their chief, and Bussy Leclerc conducted them to the Bastille with difficulty. A number of them were to remain there as prisoners, and it is certain that Claude Dupuy was among them. The author of the *Dialogue d'entre le maheustre et le manant* declares that these magistrates repented of their firmness when they found how hostile the Parisian crowd were to them as they were led through the streets, and we can believe at any rate that a trial was made of their courage, for such an unexpected arrest would have left them with no time to provide for the safety of their families.

In a letter of Pietro Del Bene to Joseph Scaliger, written from Tours on 8 March 1589, there is testimony to the apparent effect that Claude Dupuy, rather than attending the session of the Grand 'Chambre of 16 January and volunteering there to be arrested in company with Harlay, was sought out and arrested at his home by the ligueurs.[62] The veracity of this statement is doubtful. In the same letter Pietro Del Bene declares that he has lived through the recent vicissitudes of France in an unsettled and itinerant manner. As far as one can tell from Colliard's monograph, he was not in Paris at the time of the arrests and not in a position to know at first hand what had occurred. Del Bene describes Claude Dupuy as having been snatched from the midst of his wife and children, and from the bosom of the Muses (a reference to his private library and studies). This is a topos: it reports accurately the significance of the arrest, not the factual details of it. Claude Dupuy's constitution was not robust and his friends feared for the effect on his health of the months of privation he suffered while in prison (this concern is evident in the letter of Del Bene to Scaliger).

There was dissension between the Duc de Mayenne, representing the Ligue as Lieutenant général of the kingdom, and the ligueurs of Paris, as to what should be done with the imprisoned parlementaires. Some remained in the Bastille for up to a year. Mayenne wished to have the parlementaires released, but this policy was opposed by Bussy and the Seize, who were unable to prevent the release, but able to extort a ransom from their prisoners.[63] Claude Dupuy must have paid this ransom. He left the Bastille on 18 March 1589, according to l'Estoile.[64] Achille de Harlay remained captive until later in the year, and may have had to come to some kind of compromise with his enemies in order to obtain release.[65] Those released in March were confined to their homes until they should have sworn allegiance to the Ligue; and the Parlement resumed its function under the influence of the Seize and the presidency of Barnabé Brisson.

From the surviving records of the Parlement, studied by Maugis, it can be stated with confidence that Claude Dupuy took no such oath, nor made any other act of accommodation to the wishes of the ligueurs. He did not return to the Palais de Justice once he had left the Bastille, but will have aimed to escape from Paris and rejoin the royalist Parlement at Tours. He was not able to accomplish this until 1591, and it can be assumed that he eventually did so in a clandestine fashion, and at risk to himself and his family. In the interval he must have lived privately in ligueur Paris for possibly up to two years, perhaps in a reduced state of health because of the rigors of the Bastille and the subsequent rigors of life in the besieged capital. Perhaps he and his family were for much of the time confined to their house and their neighborhood. Their preoccupation will simply have been that of obtaining sufficient nourishment to stay alive, for the horror of famine in Paris in these years is notorious. The survival of most or all of Dupuy's papers and books in the Collection Dupuy argues that his house was not put to the sack during the years of peril, not even after he had left the city.

The next firm date to which the chronology of Claude Dupuy's life can be anchored is 24 July 1591, on which date he was reintegrated into the Parlement at Tours.[66] To achieve such reintegration was not easy, for reasons that are very well explained by Maugis.[67]: the institutional life of this Parlement was largely occupied in protecting the position and the revenues of those who had rallied to Henri III in the first hour against those who, for whatever reason, attempted to rally to Henri IV at a later date. The claims of each "rallié" to have been loyal in adversity were scrutinized and the procedure was dragged out as long as possible in each case. It is this fact which makes it impossible to assume that Claude Dupuy had left Paris only a short time before July 1591; perhaps he had been at Tours for six months or more before officially regaining his status.

Dupuy had fewer difficulties than many colleagues in attaining reinstatement. Maugis includes him in the list of those "réintegrés sans enquête ni delai... sur simple présentation de lettres du roi."[68] These letters had been obtained from Henri IV by Dupuy on 29 May 1591, in return for Dupuy's oath that he had "neither subscribed nor participated" while still in Paris, i.e. he had not taken the oath of adhesion to the Ligue, nor even gone to the Palais de Justice.[69] The case of a colleague, Jean Amelot, may be compared: Amelot had been locked up in the Bastille at the same time as Dupuy, and released like Dupuy in March 1589 via the payment of a ransom of 10,000 livres. Amelot had been able to avoid taking the oath, but had to admit that he had repaired to the Palais de Justice (i.e. had collaborated to some extent with the ligueur Parlement in Paris) after the death of Henri III on 1 August 1589. He confessed to this at Tours on 18 September 1591, and reintegration in his case was a more difficult business that it was for Claude

Dupuy. But by the end of September or early October 1591 he was a functioning member of the branch of the royalist Parlement set up at Châlons.[70] (It appears that Claude Dupuy himself was deputed at some point to serve at Châlons, but that he did not actually do so.)[71]

What of Dupuy's brother-in-law Jacques Sanguin? We find that he took the oath of the Ligue on 26 January 1589, in company with Brisson and many others.[72] Jacques Sanguin was pliable therefore, like Brisson, and did not have to pay the price of moral courage that was demanded of his brother-in-law. Or was he truly closer in sentiment to the Ligue, of which his brother Christophe was an important member? At any rate he chose the royalist option before long, or found it preferable to the hardship of life in Paris, for his name is found in the records of the Parlement at Châlons from late in 1590.[73] Unlike many others recorded in the pages of Maugis, who had to undergo *épuration* of some kind (even though they may have been the prisoners of Bussy Leclerc, like Claude Dupuy) before finding acceptance among the royalists, Jacques Sanguin slides easily and silently in those same pages from the ranks of the ligueur Parlement to those of the royalist one.[74] He was one of the smooth men who always seem to emerge serenely out of civil broils in which more principled folk suffer harm.

His brother at least remained faithful to the Ligue until Paris finally fell. Christophe Sanguin too has his moment in the limelight of history, in connection with an episode even more notorious in the Parisian annals of the time than the incarceration of the magistrates in January 1589. The canon of Notre-Dame was one of the ringleaders of the conspiracy of November 1591 to hang Président Brisson, and Larcher and Tardif — a deed whose principal instigator was, again, Bussy Leclerc, the man who had imprisoned Harlay, Dupuy, and the others.[75] Christophe Sanguin was to suffer brief banishment from Paris after the royal restoration, but was able to return in May 1595 and resume his benefices thanks to the protection of Geoffroy Camus de Pontcarré. An inquest was held on the death of Brisson, and judgments of guilt were pronounced, including one which fell on the head of Morin, author of the *Dialogue d'entre le maheustre et le manant*. Many of these guilty men, in contrast to Christophe Sanguin, lived in misery and died in exile in the Spanish Netherlands.[76] In sum, Christophe Sanguin escaped paying a penalty that many others had to pay for having been an active Seize. Like his brother Jacques, he was one of those who float to salvation in times of trouble.

The fortunes of Henri IV rose as he abjured the Huguenot

faith in July 1593; his coronation followed in February 1594. In that month Claude Dupuy, with less than a year now to live, but with a few moments of happiness still reserved for him, took part in a deputation of Parlement to the king.[77] One of these occasions for rejoicing arrived when Henri IV entered Paris on 22 March: on that day or soon after Claude Dupuy must have been able to return with his wife and children to their own home, their own belongings, in the Faubourg St.–Germain. Nicolas, his last child, was born in Paris on 14 July 1594.

On 1 December Claude Dupuy died from the effects of a gross kidney stone — the characteristic affliction of the man of letters, in the common opinion of the time. His death was preceded by a period of painful suffering, so much so that Nicolas Rigault, who was in a position to know intimate facts of this kind from those closest to Claude Dupuy, states that it was only Christian fortitude that kept him from resorting to self-annihilation. He was buried not far from his home, in St.–Sulpice, the funeral laudation pronounced by Achille de Harlay.[78]

The inventory of Claude Dupuy's estate began on 20 January 1595, in the presence of a notary.[79] The estimate of the value of his library, which was completed on 31 January 1595, was carried out by Denis Duval, a bookseller and publisher whom Dupuy had known and dealt with for many years. Duval listed a total of approximately 1000 printed and MS books. He placed a value on them of 334 écus and 4 sous.[80]

The major published monument of Claude Dupuy's life was of course the *Tumulus* which appeared in 1607. In 1608 his textual notes on Velleius Paterculus were published in a combined edition of the works of that author and Tacitus.[81] The ancient text upon which Claude Dupuy had lavished the greatest amount of philological attention during his life was that of the Latin Panegyrics. An edition of the panegyric delivered to Theodosius in 389 CE by Pacatus Drepanius, published in Amsterdam in 1753, contained Dupuy's collations of some MSS of the text, and also his notes, most of which adduce parallel passages in other authors of the Silver and Late Latin periods.[82]

As a preliminary to any full account of Dupuy's contribution to the texts of Velleius Paterculus and the Panegyrics, it would be necessary to make a complete census of the relevant MS material in the Collection Dupuy and elsewhere. The colleague with whom he discussed his work on these authors most fully was not Gian Vincenzo Pinelli but Pietro Del Bene. Letters written from Italy in 1571–1572 by Del Bene to Dupuy, now in MS Dupuy 490, would be of importance in this respect. At the Biblioteca Ambrosiana, MS G 77 inf. contains transcriptions, made for Pinelli, of five letters written by Dupuy in Paris to Del Bene in Italy between November 1571 and November 1572.[83] They are rich in philological discussion, especially of the Panegyrics. The same is true of other fragments of the correspondence of Dupuy and Del Bene.[84]

Of the distinguished men of letters and scholars with whom Claude Dupuy was on familiar terms, De Thou, Pithou, and others have been mentioned above. The letters of Marc–Antoine Muret to Dupuy from Rome have been published.[85] The figure of Gian Vincenzo Pinelli requires less introduction than that of his correspondent Claude Dupuy. He was one of Europe's leading writers of letters in a century in which private correspondence was a principal means of communication — yet only when the complete edition of his epistolary exchange with Dupuy appears in print will any considerable portion of his letters be available in other than manuscript form. A biography of him by an acolyte, Paolo Gualdo, appeared in 1607, and unlike Dupuy's *Tumulus,* which was published in the same year, it is filled with valuable information and with human insight into the life of its subject and his circle.[86] Modern studies of Pinelli are focused primarily on the contents and formation of the Biblioteca Ambrosiana, which incorporated the surviving portion of his manuscripts. The guide to the Pinelli MSS by Adolfo Rivolta is a very incomplete instrument, but useful as an introduction to Pinelli and as a rapid guide to the contents of the codices studied.[87] A major article by Marcella Grendler sets a new standard in studies on Pinelli and the Ambrosiana.[88] A.M. Raugei has published a transcription of Pinelli's notes on French grammar, in addition to her paper on Dupuy's love of gardening.[89]

* * * *

The subject discussed most frequently, and most animatedly, in the letters of Claude Dupuy and Gian Vincenzo Pinelli was not life, but books, and everything to do with books, including authors, publishers, printers, vendors, prices, bindings, and libraries. Pinelli's own collection was of European importance, and the posthumous biography of him by Paulo Gualdo contains a detailed description of its organization and system of shelfmarks. Dupuy could not afford to house his collection in such a grand manner, but he was able to send Pinelli a carefully drafted description of a library in France (more precisely, a combination of library and museum) which did rival Pinelli's in fame — that of the French statesman, Henri de Mesmes, sieur de Roissy.[90] It is published here *in extenso,* since it is surely one of the more complete and evocative descriptions of an important sixteenth-century library:

Quant est de l'estude de Monsieur de Roissi, ie ne vous en puis escrire qu'en general, a scavoir qu'elle est composée de tous bons livres impriméz en toutes langues et sciences, entre lesquels il y en a beaucoup marquéz de la main de grans personnages comme Budee, Ranconet, etc., et plusieurs tant Grecs que Latins conferéz sur vieus exemplaires par gens qu'il a entretenu pour cela. d'un grand nombre d'escrits a la main Grecs, Latins, et Francois. de plusieurs livres de Geographie et de portraits des plus excellens sculpteurs de nostre temps impriméz; et d'autres a la main de descriptions de pais, villes, Chasteaus et belles maisons, paisages, histoires, portraits d'hommes au vif, de poissons, d'oiseaus, animaus, simples etc. le tout fait par bons maistres. Il a infinies copies de choses appartenantes aus affaires d'estat, comme de traitéz de paix entre Princes, tresves, ligues, mariages, harengues, lettres, assemblées, solennitéz, ordonnances, histoires et choses semblables tant ancienes que modernes: plusieurs memoires des plus excellens et renomméz Ambassadeurs, qui ont negotié de nostre temps pour le Roi hors le Roiaume, lesquelles il a recouvré a grans cousts et peines de leurs secretaires ou heritiers. Sa bibliotheque est asséz grande, de laquelle les murailles depuis le haut iusques au bas sont tendues de toile verde gommée, et la gomme qu'on y a mis empesche que les vers ne s'y mettent, a quoi les tapisseries de laine sont fort subietes. tout a l'entour d'icelle sont poulpitres couvers aussi de la mesme toile de la hauteur d'environ huit pieds, aians chacun sept ou huit ais plats, sur lesquels les livres sont colloquéz droits, comme nous avons coustume en France de les mettre; et sont disposéz selon les professions, verbi gratia, les livres en droit in folio tous ensemble, puis en un autre poulpitre ceux de la mesme science in 4°. puis ceux in 8° ensemble, et ainsi des autres. Les livres sont reliéz fort magnifiquement, la plus grand'part en marroquin de Levant de toutes couleurs avec compartimens et fueillages d'or dessus, les uns en velin tout doré, aucuns en marroquin ou veau à pieces entées et rapportées de diverses couleurs, plusieurs couvers de velours. En chacun poupitre est un rideau aussi de toile verde, lequel on peut tirer. Au dessus des poupitres tout entour sont tableaus et portraits au vif de Princes et Princesses, Seigneurs de

renom et gens illustres tant de France que d'autres nations tam nos-
trae quàm superioris aetatis. aupres la grand'librairie il a deux cabi-
nets, en l'un desquels sont les livres escrits a la main, desquels il a
grand' quantité en toutes langues, et les tient dans les armoires. En
l'autre sont les medailles, desquelles il a aussi un grand nombre,
grecques et Romaines, de la Republique, de l'Empire, des derniers
temps, d'or, d'argent, de bronze, et diverses pieces anciennes et nou-
velles de France et autres nations battues ou pour avoir cours ou
pour memoire, lesquelles sont disposées par laiettes selon les temps:
en ce mesme cabinet sont infinies singularitéz d'or et d'argent, de
crystal, diverses pierres rares, habillemens, et armes des Indes et
autres pais estranges, instrumens de mathematique, et autres choses
exquises que ie ne puis reciter. Monsieur de Roissi tient auiourd'hui
un des premiers lieus a la Court, et est depuis quelque temps
Superintendant des Finances, qui est une charge de grand mani-
ment.[91]

Especially in the early years of their correspondence, both
Dupuy and Pinelli were capable of making enormous demands on each
other's time and patience in connection with the building of their
respective collections. The erudition of each was universal in tendency,
and both ranged over the ancient, medieval, and modern periods with
the assurance of men of learning for whom the entire range of
European history formed a single gamut. In the same month in which
he sent Dupuy his description of the library of De Mesmes, Dupuy
requested a complete current bibliography of the recent history of
Italy, and gave explicit instructions that whatever ecclesiastical censorship was in effect was to be disregarded:

et pour ce que je suis ia en train de vous bailler des affaires, ie vous
prierai encores de m'envoier a vostre commodité un indice de tous
les Historiens, au moins de ceux qui sont venus a vostre congnoissance, qui ont escrit les choses des derniers temps d'Italie, en Italien,
ou Latin, en general ou particulier, prohibéz ou permis. et cotter a
un chacun quae tempora historia complexus sit, et le lieu, l'année, et
la marge de la meilleure impression, et aussi distinguer par quelque
marque les bons et plus estiméz des autres.[92]

Dupuy's interest in the current polemical and historical literature generated by the crisis through which his country was living is

apparent from the first. In a letter written to Pinelli in the month preceding the St. Bartholomew Massacre he reviewed in detail the principal publications available, using the tone of deliberate and judicious
neutrality that was second nature to him, emphasizing the bibliographical aspect rather than the ideological content.

> Cinq volumes de *Recueil,* qui sont ramas et farragines de plusieurs
> livrets, discours, edits, mandemens, lettres, actes iudiciaires, protesta-
> tions, remonstrances, complaintes, requestes, placars, et choses sem-
> blables, disposéz selon l'ordre des temps. les trois premiers se suivent
> depuis la mort du Roi Henri iusques a l'an 1565. in 8°. Le IIIIme con-
> tient les choses appartenantes aus secons troubles 1567 in 8°. Le Ve
> est de la derniere guerre in 8°.[93]

As for the massacre which took place in Paris on St.
Bartholomew's day, 24 August 1572, Dupuy's letters to Pinelli are a
good example of a phenomenon which apparently was widespread
among the parlementaires and among wider sections of the population
which shared their attitudes — horrified taciturnity, the feeling that
the enormity committed in the capital city was impossible to speak of.
Another Parisian correspondent of Pinelli (and a notable figure in the
literary history of Italy), Jacopo Corbinelli, was not restrained by the
compromising bonds of national complicity and professional discretion, and wrote for Pinelli an account of the massacre that has attained
classic status.[94] No such account appears in the letters of Dupuy. His
only reaction was a bibliographic one: early in 1573 he wrote to Pinelli
in hopes of obtaining a copy of the notorious pamphlet of Camillo
Capilupi, *Lo Stratogema di Carlo nono re di Francia contro gli Ugonotti rebelli
di Dio et suoi,* a production inspired by the cardinal de Guise which
praised the French monarchy for the patient craft and subtlety it had
shown in preparing the dispatch of Coligny and the Huguenot leaders
— at a time when the official line from Paris was that the massacre had
been an emergency measure taken on the spot to deal with an insurrec-
tion. Agents of the throne were attempting to suppress this embarrass-
ing pamphlet, which as it seems had a wide circulation in manuscript
between its composition in 1572 and its publication in 1574, and Dupuy
(and some eminent unnamed patrons of his) urgently desired to obtain
one.[95] But the *Stratogema,* which was an embarrassment to the Roman
Curia as well, had become unobtainable. The same letter from Dupuy
contains impassive testimony to the similar chilling effect the massacre

had had on the publication and sale of polemical literature, which had been so ebullient in the first phase of the wars of religion. Following Dupuy's detailed description of them, Pinelli had requested to be sent the volumes of the Recueil, but it was too late:

Le livre de Saintes intitulé, *Examen doctrinae Calvinianae et Bezanae de Coena Domini,* ne se trouve plus longtemps a. Les volumes du *Recueil* que vous me demandéz et livres semblables ne sont plus de saison depuis la St. Barthelemi.[96]

Many pages of the letters written by Dupuy to Pinelli through the 1570s and 1580s contain long and detailed resumés of the most important recent books published in France, Germany, and Belgium. An example of the grave and exact style with which this bookish information was relayed may be given, from a letter of 1575, in which Dupuy discusses du Haillan and La Popelinière, contemporary historians who have been the object of recent historiographical studies:

Girard, dit autrement du Haillan, fait imprimer un' histoire de France depuis Pharamond, quem vulgò monarchiae Francicae conditorem statuunt, iusques à Louis XII, auquel celle de Langeai commence.[97] à quoi ie ne pense point qu'il ait eu autres memoires, que des chroniqueurs et historiens communs: car il n'a esté curieux par le passé de rechercher les librairies et chartres anciennes, par lesquelles nostre histoire, qui autrement est fause et defectueuse en plusieurs endroits, se doit verifier et restituer; comme celui qui depuis peu de temps a entrepris ceste charge. toutesfois elle ne sera à contemner, consideré mesmement que lon aura ensemble en un corps ce qui est espars ça et là, et pour la plus part en mauvais stile et en langue grossier. combien que ie crains fort, qu' en ce qu'il tirera des auteurs Latins, il ne bronche souvent par ignorance d'icelle langue; comm'il lui est advenu en quelques traductions.

L'histoire des guerres civiles innominati auctoris a esté imprimée deux fois: celle que ie vous envoiai, est de la derniere edition; au-moins ie n'ai point oui dire qu'on l'ait rimprimée depuis, et ie ne le pense point. L'auteur d'icelle se nomme Lancelot du Voësin, dit de la Popelliniere, Poitevin d'asséz bon lieu et de gentil esprit, et bien conneu en ce Palais, lequel il a hanté par quelques années: mais durant les troubles derniers (i'entens les troisiemes) il s'est trouvé parmi les trouppes de ceux de la religion nouvelle avec reputation de bon soldat, et a esté present à une bonne partie des choses, qu'il a mis par escrit. Quòd iudicium meum exquiris; equidem video plerosque omnes magnam cùm fidei tum diligentiae laudem ipsi tribuere: meritò an secus, ie m'en rapporte à eux. certainement quant à la plume, *isorropian*[98] in primis professus est, neque quemquam omnium asperè ac contumeliosè appellat. les gens de guerre principalement en font estime, pour-autant qu'il s'est fort amusé à representer et depeindre les lieux, villes et places, les sieges et campemens d'armées devant icelles, bateries, escarmouches, batailles et choses semblables; desquelles ils disent qu'il parle per-tinemment et en termes propres. car au reste son stile est fort affecté, et comme tout deguisé de façons de parler et dictions estrangeres, et principalement Italiennes, desquelles le plus du temps il se pourroit bien passer.[99]

Some of the more disreputable and presumptuous grub-streeters of the time, such as André Thevet, were however capable of driving Dupuy to exasperation and vehemence as he denounced their *sottise et ignorance*.[100] Dupuy was exceptionally sensitive to style. He thought that of Cujas underwent an odd alteration when the great jurist turned from legal science to write about current affairs: "Il a maintenant un estrange stile."[101] François Hotman, another distin-guished jurist and a Huguenot, had on the contrary a natural talent for controversy, and Dupuy often remarks on the biting effectiveness of his polemic style.[102]

Dupuy reports and comments upon the publication of two of the most renowned treatises of the Huguenot "monarchomachs," Hotman's *Francogallia* and Beza's *Du droit des Magistrats*. Perhaps the first observation to make is that his comments are summary and objec-tive: there was a lack of passion or scandal in Dupuy's reaction to the *religion prétendue reformée*. In part this attitude is dictated by the context in which he wrote, for his letters to Pinelli are bulletins to a foreign friend who had never visited France, and the common ground between them was their profound knowledge of history and literature, and their cosmopolitan admiration for learned men of whatever religion. If it were possible for us to recover in some magical way the private, face-to-face conversations of Claude Dupuy with his wife or with his compatri-ots and colleagues about the crisis of France, we might conceivably find that he detested with emotional vigor the apostasy of the Protestants; but I think it unlikely. In the testimony Claude Dupuy has left us in the letters to Pinelli, the attitude is analytical and the emotional tone sub-dued. His analysis touches the likely political result of the writings of Beza and Hotman; he deplored the passion and polarization which they would arouse — and that is what it means to be a *politique*.

The literature of the ancient world contained accounts of, and first-hand testimony from, periods of civil war; it will be enough to mention the works of Cicero. Dupuy's attitude is that of a Roman senator caught up in the civil war between the Caesarian and Pompeian factions, but a senator attentive only to the pragmatic aspects of the situation. From a modern historical perspective, the civil war through which France was passing was a conflict both like and unlike that of the late Roman republic, for in both cases action and conviction on a very large scale had important ideological bases of a social and political nature, but the civil war in France was also a religious war of a kind unknown to antiquity. If Dupuy had self-consciously drawn a parallel with the age of Cicero, or used a recognizable classical citation from that period to convey the thought, it might, paradoxically, be easier to detect an awareness on his part that the historical situations were not identical, a perception of the historical specificity of religious war in the modern world. But the senatorial approach is entirely spontaneous, as spontaneous as his effortless switching between French and Latin, and, as I think, he does not reflect on it himself. He does use a citation from ancient literature, but it is from the age of the panegyrists, that is, of the later Roman empire, when ideological conviction and action were virtually unknown, or at any rate played little part in the periodic turbulence provoked by contests among dynasts and power groups nakedly bent on occupying the Palace. There is a difference, which Dupuy ignores, between turbulence of this kind, whatever the scale of the military operations involved, and civil war with an ideological and religious dimension. For him, the absence of royal authority in France has allowed factions to rise up and to contend for power: Huguenots, and Guisards even more, belong to the same pragmatic category.

This too is what it means to be a *politique*. Thus he is not perceptive (does not attempt to be perceptive) about the historical specificity and independent importance as intellectual products of the books of Hotman and Beza:

Francisci Hotomani....Francogallia 8° Gene\<va\>; en ce livre il a voulu illustrer nostre antiquité Françoise, de laquelle il traite plusieurs points notables; quibus asdpersit nonnulla, qui ne plaisent pas fort a

nos Courtisans, combien qu'il ne parle point nommement du gou-
vernement present, et i'entens qu'ils lui font respondre par Regius:
et veu l'estat auquel les choses se retrouvent au iourd'hui en ce
Roiaume, liber iste videtur aliquod seditionis, ut Panegyristae nostri
verbum usurpem, incentivum habere.[103]

Traité du droit des Magistrats 8°. ce livre a un beau et specieux titre;
mais au dedans il est tres pernicieux, veu l'estat present et l'humeur
qui regne pour le iour-d'hui en France, n'estans les esprits que trop
enclins à mutinerie et rebellion, sans qu'il soit besoing huiusmodi
flabellis seditionis, car l'auteur d'icelui (c'est De-Beze) entre autres
choses s'efforce de prouver, Que les suiets peuvent par droit divin et
en bonne conscience s'opposer et resister, mesme par la voie des
armes, à leur prince autrement legitime, devenu tyran manifeste: qui
est une question fort demenée de ce temps; pleust à Dieu que ce fust
de parolles seulement.[104]

   Other observations by this intelligent and subtle writer might
have political (and *politique*) resonance as well. A facetious but very
pregnant remark, made when the famous commentary of Justus Lipsius
on Tacitus was imminent, not only reveals the strong feeling of sixteenth-century readers that the works of Tacitus were directly relevant
to their world, but alludes to the contemporary principate that in
Dupuy's mind most resembled that of the Julio-Claudian emperors:
"(Lipsius) promet de nous donner en brief son commentaire sur
Tacitus: mais i'y vois un grand inconvenient; c'est qu'il n'est pas gentilhomme Florentin, qualité essentielle requise pour entendre cest
auteur."[105] It was the Florentine grand-ducal court of the Medici whose
statecraft recalled the duplicitous and sanguinary actions perpetrated
(on the showing of Tacitus) by members of the Julio-Claudian line.
Dupuy's learned and elliptical way of implying this is to suggest that a
Netherlandish scholar would not be capable of getting to the heart of
Tacitus since he lacked the experience of life at a court such as that of
the Medici (*scilicet:* where life was lived as it had been lived under
Tiberius or Nero). The further pregnancy of the observation derives
from the fact that the Florentine grand-ducal house, in the person of
Catherine de Médicis, had joined its bloodline to that of the monarchy
of France, and that Catherine herself had taken a dominant role in
directing the policies of France for many years. Her influence on those
policies, and on the strategies adopted by the throne, including the

strategy adopted in August of 1572, was deplored by Dupuy and those who thought like him. And of this he allows Pinelli, and us, to catch the faint echo.

* * * *

The letters of Dupuy and Pinelli are, among other things, a good introduction to the problems of inflation and the conversion of currencies in the sixteenth century (there is also a good deal of information on current prices of books). Dupuy and Pinelli periodically in the 1570s attempted to draw up accounts for the value of the books they had sent and received, to determine which of the two was the creditor and which the debtor. Dupuy in particular carried out this exercise laboriously. To obtain a common standard by which to measure the outlays made in Paris and Padua, he had to convert the monies spent in each case to *écus pistolets*, which as he explained to Pinelli was the generic term for gold coins of the scutum type (called in Italian *scudi* or *scuti*) minted outside France. They circulated in France in competition with the native *écu soleil* (called simply *écu sol*). The *écu pistolet* was at this time constantly worth two *sous tournois* less than the *écu soleil*, but the rate at which either type of *écu* was convertible to *sous* could vary, and in fact had risen throughout the century as the *sou* lost value. Some portions of the accounts drawn up by Dupuy for money spent by him in France are drawn up in terms of *livres* (=*francs*), *sous*, and *deniers*. Here of course the *livres* are a unit of account, equalling 20 *sous*.

Between 1572 and 1575 Dupuy remarked that the *écu pistolet* underwent inflation from a price of 56 sous to 58 *sous*. In 1576 its value had risen to the level of 63 sous, but in 1579 it had fallen again to 58 *sous*.[106] This was the result of monetary reforms imposed by Henry III in 1577 which made the *écu soleil* convertible at a rate of exactly 60 *sous*, and therefore fixed the value of the *écu pistolet* at 58 *sous*. To reduce the sums spent in Venetian coin by Pinelli to the same standard, Dupuy calculated the *écu pistolet* as equivalent to 7 Venetian *lire*.

The costliest book mentioned in the correspondence, though it was not among the books sent by Dupuy to his friend, was the Plantin polyglot Bible, which cost 36 *écus soleil* in Paris in 1574, and 50 ducats in Venice. Most of the books which Dupuy sent to Pinelli and whose price he recorded cost less than 1 *franc* (20 sous). The Manilius of Scaliger was slightly dearer at 1 *livre*, 12 *sous*. The *Annales de France* of Belleforest were very dear at 16 *livres*.

One of the most interesting aspects of the correspondence, and one discussed endlessly by the two men, was the best and most secure way to send books to each other. The available channels were, first, the public carriers operating the postal service between France and Italy, and second, the couriers used by international business firms and merchants to conduct their business. A complicating factor was the threat of having books confiscated by ecclesiastical censors, even though Pinelli and Dupuy had no interest in heretical literature as such, and not many of the books sent by them were at all likely to appear suspect, except to the excessively zealous local inquisitors of the time. The 1570s were the decade of maximum censorial pressure at the frontiers of Italy. Pinelli acknowledged more than once that in any given package of books sent by him to France, or vice versa, there were bound to be a few that had "un poco del curioso."[107] In the early months of 1573 a package of books sent by Dupuy was inspected by the Inquisitor ("il Padre Inquisitore") at Genoa, the port of entry into Italy, and a number of volumes that evidently fell into this category were confiscated.[108] Dupuy of course was dismayed and irritated by this, for he had taken care to insert those books that might be suspect among the gatherings of other, more innocuous ones. This mild form of concealment was practicable because the books sent by Pinelli and Dupuy were normally purchased new and were shipped unbound. In any case it failed to deceive the Inquisitor's men in Genoa. Dupuy resolved to find a better way in future to outwit "these harpies":

> I'ai entendu que l'Inquisiteur vous retint quelques livres de ceux que ie vous envoiai l'année passée par Gennes, de quoi i'ai esté moult esbahi: hic valde Lynceus fuerit necesse est; car en les faisant empacqueter, i'avois mis ceux qui estoient suiets a censure dedans d'autres, quò istas harpyias fallerent. mais puis qu'elles ont si bon néz, un' autre fois ie m'adviserai de quelque meilleure ruse.[109]

By mid- 1574, Dupuy and Pinelli had settled upon a method of sending books to each other which they considered to be the most efficient, cheapest, and least exposed to the risk of confiscation, one they were to employ from that time forward. They prevailed upon various Parisian and Venetian printers and publishers, with whom they were well acquainted, to carry these books to the semi-annual book fair at Frankfurt along with the merchandise the bookmen were sending there to be sold, and pass them on in the German city for forwarding to the ultimate destination. The advantage in Pinelli's case was that the port of entry into Italy for the shipments of the Italian printers and publishers returning from Frankfurt was Venice, and in Venice he could exert personal influence to obtain the release of books that might otherwise have been confiscated.

In the autumn of 1573 Pinelli sounded out the Venetian bookseller Pietro Longo — or perhaps "prevailed upon" would be the appropriate verb in this case, since one's impression is that for fifteen years Pinelli and Dupuy abused the time and patience of the hapless booksellers, especially the unfortunate Longo, by forcing them to play the role of shippers and forwarders of small parcels. There was little or no profit in it for the bookmen, since they charged Pinelli and Dupuy only the cost of the freight for these. Pinelli asked Longo to name a Parisian publisher with whom he (Longo) could expect to be in contact at Frankfurt. Longo named Jacques Du Puys (no relation to Claude Dupuy), one of the leading publishers in France and one of the most important figures in the history of the culture of the book in sixteenth-century Europe. Pinelli wrote to Claude Dupuy suggesting that books intended for him (Pinelli) should be given to Jacques Du Puys in Paris to be carried by Du Puys to Frankfurt and given there to Pietro Longo. Longo would bring them back to Venice where Pinelli would receive them.

V.S. mi dica, chi libraro suo amico si parta di Parigi, per la fiera di Francfort, al quale ella potesse dare alcuni libri per me, per consegnarli in Fiera ad un altro libraro di qua. che questa mi pare la miglior strada di servirsi, et io farei il medesimo di quanto V.S. desiderasse da queste parti. il libraro di qua, che si chiama Pietro Longo, mi nota un Dupuy, come suo conoscente. V.S. di gratia l'intenda et poi me ne scriva.[110]

Claude Dupuy followed this plan to the letter. He was well acquainted with Jacques Du Puys, and in a position to prevail upon him in the same way that Pinelli was able to prevail upon Longo. When Jacques Du Puys left for the Easter fair in 1574, he brought with him a packet of books to give to Longo. Dupuy informed Pinelli of this on 28 March 1574.

Ie congnois tous les libraires de ceste Université qui trafiquent a Francfort, et n'y a pas un d'entre eux, qui ne me face volontiers

plaisir en ce que vous m'escrivéz. i'en ai parlé entr' autres au susdit
du-Puys, qui est celui que Pietro Longo vous a nommé, et lui ai baillé
un petit pacquet de livres pour vous; lequel i'ai adressé a Francfort
audit Longo. ceste voie me semble fort bonne et seure au temps des
Foires: et en autre temps i'ai commodité de vous faire tenir tout et
seurement par celle de Gennes ce que vous voudréz, par le moien
d'un marchant Genevois, qui commigravit huic viciniae....[111]

At the moment of writing this, Dupuy received a letter from
Pinelli containing a further list of desiderata. Dupuy went directly to
the quarter of the rue St.-Jacques in the University, where the booksellers were, and managed to obtain most of them. They were given to
Denis Duval, the factor in Paris for Andreas Wechel, himself formerly
of Paris and now active as a publisher in Frankfurt, so that they could
follow the others to the city on the Main and be handed over likewise
to Pietro Longo.

Monsieur comme ie fermois mon autre lettre, i'ai receu la vostre du
16me de Fevrier avec un memoire de livres, desquels ie vous ai recou-
vré la plus grand' part, et les ai bailléz a un libraire de ceste
Université nommé Denis du-Val facteur de Wechel (car lacques du-
Puys estoit ia parti) pour les faire tenir a Francfort es mains de Pietro
Longo, comme les autres.[112]

By 26 May Pinelli had received notice from Frankfurt that
both packets had duly been handed over to Longo by Du Puys and
Duval. This was good news in itself and it augured well for the future.[113]
In addition Pinelli had another reason to view with confidence his
future prospects of actually taking delivery of books from France and
Germany: the important position of Inquisitor for Venice had recently
been assigned to a Dominican of Verona who soon showed himself ami-
able, a friend of men of letters.

Though he is never named by Pinelli, the new Inquisitor was
in fact Marco Medici of Verona, OP. He was to fill the role of Padre
Inquisitore in Venice until December 1578, when he became bishop of
Chioggia.[114] Marco Medici died in August 1583. He enters the ken of
historians of the sixteenth century at around this time for another reason connected with his inquisitorial role: it was Marco Medici who carried out a further expurgation of the works of Gasparo Contarini,
works whose texts had already been posthumously emended for publi-

cation in Paris. After further alterations had been imposed upon them by Marco Medici, they were to be reprinted in Venice by Aldo Manuzio Jr. in 1578.[115]

The letters of Pinelli and Dupuy allow us to add one or two further elements to our knowledge of the career of this Inquisitor. Marco Medici was a friend of an Italian *letterato* living in Paris, Guido Lolgi. The two had met in Paris in the past, at the time when "Monsignore di Ceneda" had been papal nunzio there, and Marco Medici had been a member of his entourage. The nunzio referred to was Michele della Torre, bishop of Ceneda in the region of Aquileia. He had served an early term as nunzio in France in 1547, and a later one in 1566–68. It was certainly on the latter occasion that Marco Medici accompanied him, and became a friend of Guido Lolgi. Though Pinelli and Marco Medici might have been acquainted before Medici became Inquisitor in Venice, Pinelli took care to cultivate him soon after he was appointed:

> saluto caramente... [il] Signor Guidi Lolgi, non solo a nome mio, ma et <iam> dio d'un Padre di Predicatori, il quale si fa tutto suo, et mi dice, ch'ai tempi che Monsignor di Ceneda era nuntio costà si trovavano insieme spesse volte. esso padre hora è stato fatto inquisitore per conto di libri etc. in Vinetia.[116]

We can deduce that when the packets of books for Pinelli were brought back to Venice after the spring fair in 1574, Marco Medici showed himself to be an accommodating Inquisitor by releasing them to Pinelli without too much difficulty. In future, Pinelli wrote to Dupuy, shipment via Frankfurt should be the norm in all cases in which there was any scent of suspicion attached to the books to be sent — for Marco Medici, unlike other Inquisitors, would let him have anything that was not utterly depraved and pernicious:

> della strada di mandarmi questi libri, ch'ella troverà, à me è riuscita assai buona, questa di Francfort. et desidero, che sia seguita sempre che non siamo troppo lontani dal tempo della Fiera, altrimente mi rimetto alla cortese diligenza di V.S., alla quale son certo che non mancheranno altre strade, come è quella che lei mi nomina del mercante Genovese suo vicino, et amico. l'avertisco bene di questo, che riservi tutte quelle cose, ch'haranno un po del curioso alla via di Francfort, accioche non mi siano tolte per strada, come fu di quelle

di Genova. perche qui in Vinetia ho il padre inquisitore, ch'è mio amico. et mi renderà subito ogni cosa, quando non sii veramente perniciosa in tota substantia, che non m'avverrebbe con altri Inquisitori.[117]

As an appendix to this notice of Marco Medici, it may be worth adding that there exists another item of testimony showing his benignity to men of letters. Carlo Sigonio's great historical work *De Regno Italiae* had its first edition in Venice from the presses of Giordano Ziletti in 1574. To obtain an imprimatur for *De Regno Italiae* proved not to be an easy matter during the months in which it was in the press: in fact there was more resistance from the authorities of the Venetian state than there was from ecclesiastical authority, but in the end both obstacles were overcome with some minor alterations to the text. In 1576 Sigonio published an *Index* to *De Regno Italiae* which included thanks to men of learning and humanity in Italy who had aided him in research and publication. They included "Fr. Marcus Medices Veronensis, Inquisitor Venetiis." This sincere testimony is proof that Marco Medici had done as much as his office allowed to ease the passage of *De Regno Italiae* into print at a difficult time.[118] It constitutes a title of honor for this Dominican, and goes some way to offset the less creditable role for which he is known in the expurgation of the works of Gasparo Contarini.

Throughout the 1570s and 1580s, until his death in January 1588, it was Pietro Longo upon whom Pinelli relied for the portage of books to and from Frankfurt. The life and activities of this merchant and transporter of books have been investigated by Paul F. Grendler in his monograph on the effects of censorship in Venice.[119] Longo's background is unknown; he and his brother were carriers of books, but they quarreled in 1570. Longo apparently made the voyage from Venice to Frankfurt throughout the 1570s and 1580s for other bookmen and on behalf of private clients. He carried manuscripts for Girolamo Mercuriale, professor of medicine at Padua, and Antonio Riccoboni, professor of humanity at Padua, to Basel for publication by Pietro Perna. And he obtained a copy of Konrad Gesner's *Bibliotheca Universalis* (a banned book) for Mercuriale. Longo seems not to have kept a shop or published books. His name appears on only one imprint, together with that of the Venetian printer Gaspare Bindoni.

Longo was imprisoned by the Inquisition in late August 1587; and the Inquisition was gathering information in the course of other interrogations. Gaspare Bindoni testified that Longo had had connections with Pietro Perna in Basel and through Perna in Strasbourg as well, where he was accepted as a Protestant. The normal practice of the Venetian booksellers who were returning up the Rhine to Italy was to make a halt at Basel in order to acquire and pack additional books for shipment back to Venice. On these occasions "Longo always packed his barrels apart from the others, so that his companions could not determine what titles he carried."[120]

There is not a complete record of Longo's trial. An official of the Inquisition talked with him on the night of 27 January 1588. He seems to have confessed to no more than obtaining a couple of scandalous books for Venetian patricians. The Holy Office put him to death a few days later. A letter in Basel, found by Antonio Rotondò, reports his death on or about 31 January 1588. The writer compares this death to that of Girolamo Donzellini a year earlier, and a Venetian chronicle records that the cause of Longo's death was the importation of books from distant lands. The true reasons for this judicial murder would appear to have been a combination of smuggling — and clearly proved Protestant beliefs.

Grendler's thesis is that there was a definite network of book smugglers with Longo at its center, which was a continuation of a network run by Pietro Perna in the 1550s. The hazardous role of carrier was assigned to Longo himself. We gather that Longo "simply packed his contraband together with his legal merchandise in Basel and proceeded south. He had no need of secret routes or clandestine methods until he reached the Holy Office inspection at the Venetian customs house. Perhaps he evaded the inspection entirely by taking the books across the lagoon to the city in a small boat by night.[121] Also, it appears that there was so much tedious confusion in the customs shed that many illegal books must have gone through. If the suspect books were packed in the bottom of a barrel, an inspector might easily be tricked. The large number of prohibited volumes available in Venice, on Grendler's reconstruction, suggests to him that Longo was not alone and that the clandestine trade had many members — virtually the entire fraternity of Venetian bookmen.

The letters of Pinelli can perhaps add one or two details to our knowledge of Pietro Longo. By September 1585 Pinelli was impatient with Longo, who for his part had had enough of carrying small packets of books for Pinelli, and took to eluding Pinelli's importunities in a fairly transparent fashion.[122] Theirs had been a business relationship, not one based on *amicizia*. The social distance between them, by the standards of the time, was too great for that. Nevertheless, and despite all one's own sympathy for Pinelli, one has to ask whether Pinelli was not in some way callous, or careless of past services rendered him by Pietro Longo (including the transport of suspect books at the risk, as the event showed, of his own life), when he reported to Dupuy in the following words the death of Longo, about three weeks after the body of the bookman had been cast into the Venetian lagoon in the dead of night:

> Emmi anco piaciuto l'aviso delli libri mandatili la Pascha passata per via di Francfort che fussero in salvo, et più mi piacerà quando intenderò che già siano in man sua, che me ne faceva alquanto dubitare il mal esito di quel poveraccio di Pietro Lungo capitato male per suoi peccati vecchi et nuovi et questo suo caso è stato di più cagione ch'io non habbia mandati a V.S. alcuni libri che di già haveva apparecchiati per lei, che di già erano in poter suo a questo fine; ma di tutto appresso.[123]

The evidence which Grendler found of Longo's ties to Strasbourg receives confirmation too in the letters of Pinelli, which reveal that a close collaborator of Longo was Lazarus Zetzner, who began publishing in Strasbourg in 1582.[124] In the previous decade, before becoming an independent entrepreneur, he had acted as the agent — in Strasbourg apparently, perhaps also at Frankfurt — of Pietro Longo. Zetzner was a fixture at the Frankfurt book fair.

> et poi che stiamo in questo, raggioniamo di libri ancora dietro, et le dico, che mi maraviglio, come sin qui non le sia capito quel mazzetto piccolo, che l'inviai tanto fà, che se bene non potette accompagnarsi con le balle che si mandorno in fiera alla Pasqua dell'anno passato del 1577, fu nondimeno avviato, poco appresso, et raccomandato a Messer Lazaro Zetzner tedesco, altre volte agente di Pietro Lungo, et hora libraro in Argentina, il quale si trova sempre in fiera a suoi tempi. Ma il Lungo, che serà in fiera tra poco, et s'abboccarà con esso Lazaro, intenderà come sia passata la cosa, et vi darà quel rimedio, che bisognerà, et se per sorte troverà, che detto pacchetto non sia per ancora mosso verso V.S., glielo manderà insieme con l'altro fagottino, che gl'ho consegnato un mese fà.[125]

As this quotation reveals, there was a contretemps for Pinelli and Dupuy in the spring of 1578 (and not for the first or last time) with

regard to the sending of their books through Frankfurt. The easy and
secure method they had discovered four years earlier had proved not to
be flawless. One of Pinelli's codices containing letters from Dupuy also
contains a transcript of a letter in Italian from Dupuy to Longo, concerning the same missing books. To my knowledge, no other text in
Italian by Claude Dupuy has been preserved, and this would be a document of great linguistic interest — if not for the fact that it was almost
certainly drafted by one of Dupuy's many Italian friends and signed by
him. At the very least one of them will have gone over and corrected an
original draft in Italian by Dupuy. The letter shows too much facility to
be an entirely authentic product of Dupuy's pen, for although he had a
good reading knowledge of Italian, he would have had little opportunity in the course of his life to exercise himself in writing or speaking it.
The text is as follows:

Magnifico Messer Pietro. Per questa Fiera io non mando niente al
Signor Pinelli, per che le lettere ch'ei m'ha scritte son giunte troppo
tardi, et i vetturali erono di gia partiti. Aspetterò un'altra occasione
per mandargli quello che mi chiedeva. E' mi ha scritto per piu sue
circa un pacchetto di libri che dice havervi consegnato un'anno fa,
per farmelo tenere per via del Signor Andrea Wechel di Francfort: et
per l'ultima sua mi fa a sapere che voi lo lasciaste a Strasbourg, et per
che da quel tempo in qua io non ho havuto altre nuove, io vi prego
farmi intendere quel che n'è seguito, il nome dell'huomo, a chi voi
lo lasciasti à Strasburg; a fin che io mi sforzi di rinvenirlo, se non s'è
perso. Io mandai al detto Signor Pinelli per l'ultima fiera di
Settembre un grosso pacchetto di libri, il quale io detti qua a Sire
Denis du Val corrispondente di detto Wechel per farlo consegnare
nelle Vostre mani in Francfort. ma il detto Signor Pinelli non l'ha
ricevuto: et scrive d'haver ricevuto solamente per ordine mia, un
libro, intitolato Chopinus *de sacra politia forensi*.[126] il quale io non gli
ho gia mandato io: Io non so se qualcun'altro de suoi amici
gliel'havessi mandato, o se si fusse preso un pacchetto per un altro; o
se per sorte fusse rimasto per inavvertenza a detto Wechel: al quale io
vi prego di parlarne, a fine che si sappia quel che n'è stato. Et con
questo farò fine, raccomandandomi affetionatamente à vostra buona
gratia. Pregando il Signor Dio che vi conservi. Di Parigi il primo di
Marzo 1578. Vostro miglior amico per farvi servitio Claude Dupuy.[127]

The great publisher Andreas Wechel of Paris and Frankfurt

has been mentioned in passing in these pages above, as has Denis Duval, who began as his factor and eventually took over the Parisian branch of Wechel's firm. Claude Dupuy's contacts with Duval and through him with Wechel were frequent, and Dupuy as a young man clearly had known Wechel himself in Paris in the years before 1572, when Wechel moved to Frankfurt in the wake of the St. Bartholomew.[128] Dupuy normally sent books for Pinelli to Frankfurt by means of Duval and Wechel, who handed them over at the fair to Pietro Longo. The only work of Carlo Sigonio to be published by Wechel's firm while Wechel himself was alive (his heirs were to publish many others) was a reprint of De Regno Italiae (1575), and the contact between author and publisher in this case was through Pinelli and the circle of Dupuy. Pinelli and Dupuy also negotiated with both Jacques Du Puys and Andreas Wechel on Sigonio's behalf in preparation for the authorised reprint of Sigonio's De antiquo iure populi Romani, which was eventually published by Jacques Du Puys in 1576.[129] Claude Dupuy often used the services of Jacques Du Puys to have books for Pinelli carried to Frankfurt, as an alternative to the services of Denis Duval. The book-men charged Dupuy the cost of the transport they provided — 3 sous for each book, coming usually to around 2 francs for a parcel of 12 to 15 books — and perhaps they counted on earning his good will as an aid in their relations with the Parlement and the city. Even so they found the business of transporting these packages as irksome as Longo did, and sometimes evaded the importunate requests for their services advanced by Dupuy.

Jacques Du Puys, as the publisher of Bodin and Sigonio, authors of European importance, and as an assiduous frequenter of the Frankfurt fair, has a role in the cultural history of the period not per-haps inferior by much to that of Andreas Wechel.[130] But we learn from Claude Dupuy that his approach to his business was more entrepreneurial, farther removed from the tradition of the great schol-ar-printers of the past, than that of Wechel. The context of the follow-ing quotation is the negotiations being carried on by Pinelli (represent-ing the interests of Carlo Sigonio) and Dupuy (mediating between the interests of Sigonio on one hand and the interests of Jacques Du Puys on the other) for the republication of Sigonio's works on Roman antiq-uities. Pinelli had expressed the view that a recent edition by Du Puys of a work by Jacques Charpentier had been defective, and that therefore Du Puys was not a suitable choice to publish Sigonio. Claude Dupuy replied as follows:

Iacques du-Puys m'a dit, que pour cest' heure il ne pouvoit entendre à l'impression des livres du Seigneur Sigonio. et ce que vous dites qu'il s'est mal porté en l'Alcinous de Charpentier, n'est pas considerable (pace tua dixerim) audit du-Puys, qui n'est pas imprimeur, mais libraire seulement; faisant imprimer par autres et en divers lieux, tantost bien, tantost mal, selon que les auteurs des copies en sont plus ou moins curieux, et comm'ils y tiennent la main. et quand il m'en fit porter parole, il me promit nomméement de les faire imprimer par Robert Estienne l'un des meilleurs et plus diligens imprimeurs de ceste Ville; et non content de sa simple promesse, la copie estant envoiée par-deça ie l'eusse fait obliger par escrit, vous asseurant que ie ne me voudrois point mesler d'une chose, laquelle ie penserois devoir reussir autrement, qu'au contentement de ceux, à qui elle touche.[131]

Perhaps it is as well to add that when Sigonio's *De antiquo iure populi Romani* was reprinted for Jacques Du Puys a year later, the work was executed not by Robert Estienne but by the firm of De Tournes of Lyon, and that the result was satisfactory.[132]

Some further information on the Paris publishers and the role of the Frankfurt book fair: Dupuy states that in selecting the merchandise to be packed and shipped to the fair, they were inclined to give preference to works published in the larger folio format. The margin of profit on these would have been greater for each unit of weight than that for works published in octavo or quarto. Dupuy could assume that Pinelli would have less difficulty in obtaining works such as these in the regular manner through the Venice bookshops, and therefore made an effort to send him specialized works in the smaller formats, which might not otherwise have appeared for sale in Venice.[133] The same was true from Pinelli's end: in a letter of 1578 he states that he has not sent a copy of Pier Vettori's recent edition and translation of Aristotle's *Politics* to Dupuy because it would have been supererogatory to do so: merchandise of such value would certainly have been imported directly for commercial sale in France. The value and importance of this particular edition derive as much or more from Vettori's part in it as from the permanent relevance of Aristotle to the political and cultural world of the time.[134]

* * * *

The letters of Dupuy and Pinelli contain a first-hand record of one of the notable cases of ecclesiastical censorship of the sixteenth century. The object of the attempted suppression was the Greek historian Zosimus, who, writing ca. 500 CE, made the accusation, which had already been made in the past by Eunapius of Sardis among others, that the Christian emperors had brought about the decline of the Roman Empire. A translation of this work by a German humanist, Johannes Löwenklau or Leunclavius was to appear in 1576, but before that year there were at least two interested scholars who desired strongly to be able to read the work of Zosimus. They were Dupuy and Muret, with De Thou also becoming interested in the matter. Dupuy had a particular interest because of his project to publish the Latin Panegyrics with a commentary. His systematic review of the complete range of sources for the history of late antiquity would be incomplete, he felt, if Zosimus were to escape him. The Greek manuscript used by Leunclavius remained in private hands; exactly whose will be revealed. The Biblioteca Vaticana, a library with which Dupuy had managed to make himself rapidly familiar in the course of his brief visit to Rome in 1570–71, contained a manuscript of Zosimus. The head of the library was cardinal Guglielmo Sirleto of Calabria, a scholar of great attainments and piety, and a figure around whom the history of Catholic Counter-Reformation scholarship and censorship in the sixteenth century could almost be said to pivot. Sirleto was the most active and authoritative member of the group of cardinals charged with administering the Index Librorum Prohibitorum.[135]

Dupuy's active attempt to be granted the use of the Vatican Zosimus commenced in 1574. He recalled to Pinelli that citations from Zosimus had been published by Politian and Onofrio Panvinio ("Onufre") and that three years earlier in Rome he had been able to see the first part of a transcript of it that was being made by a friend of his. This unnamed friend is in fact Muret. Dupuy also makes it clear why Muret's labor of transcription had not been completed: Pope Pius V (Michele Ghislieri) had ordered it to be withdrawn from consultation — but Gregory XIII (Ugo Boncompagni) might prove to be more liberal in this matter, and there was also, as it seemed, a manuscript in Florence:

Mais sur toute chose ie desire de recouvrer les histoires de Zosime Sophiste Grec, desquelles il y a un exemplaire en la Vaticane. estant a Romme i'en vis le premier livre et le commencement du second par le moien d'un mien ami qui les faisoit copier: mais il advint que le Pape Pie V à la suggestion de quelques uns, qui lui soufflerent aus oreilles qu'en cest auteur y avoit plusieurs choses contre la religion Chrestienne, le fit serrer in intimam bibliothecam, damnandum tenebris et carcere saeptum. ce peu que i'en ai leu, (car il y a six livres) outre les autoritéz que Politian et Onufre en recitent, m'a laissé une fort grand' envie de voir le reste, pour avoir quelque congnoissance de l'histoire civile depuis le regne de Diocletian et Maximian iusques a la dissipation de l'Empire, laquelle nous est presqu' incongneue. car outre qu' elle est de soi grandement recommandable, voire necessaire; encores sans cela ie ne puis sortir a mon honneur de mes Panegyristes, desquels l'intelligence en infinis lieus depend de l'histoire. i'ai pensé que vous m'y pouviéz plus aider que nul autre que ie congnoisse par-delà; au moins scai-ie bien que ie ne me puis adresser a homme, qui s'y emploie plus volontiers que vous: qui me fait vous prier d'essaier par quelcun de vos amis d'en avoir une copie pour moi. car ie croi que sous ce Pape, lequel i'entens estre homme raisonnable et amateur des lettres, on n'y tiendra ceste rigueur. le plus grand mal qui soit en Zosime est, qu' en quelques endroits il detracte de Constantin et de Theodose, qui sont princes a la verité optimè meriti de Christianismo: mais de la religion verbum nullum; comm' aussi il n'en pouvoit pas avoir grand' congnoissance, aiant esté tousiours nourri au Paganisme. Et vous supplie qu'aiant eu response de Romme vous me mandiéz comme la chose pourra passer; car ie suis deliberé nullum non movere lapidem pour en venir a bout, et deusse-ie emploier la faveur de quelques grans de ceste Court: toutesfois ie ne voudrois venir là sans avoir preallablement tenté toute autre voie. ce qu'il coustera à copier, curabo statim Romae rescribi à celui que vous me nommeréz. i'ai oui dire qu'il y avoit un autre exemplaire de cest'histoire en la librairie du feu Cardinal Salviati, laquelle est de present a Florence: et il n'est pas qu'il n'y en ait quelques copies à Romme. i'ai sceu davantage que feu Onufre l'avoit fait traduire en Latin: et peut-estre qu'au defaut de l'original on pourroit recouvrer ceste traduction ou de ceux es mains desquels la librairie dudit Onufre est tombée, ou bien du translateur mesme.[136]

In the same year, 1574, Jacques-Auguste De Thou was in Italy as a member of the entourage of the diplomat Paul de Foix (Latinè Foxius) and Muret now hoped to use the influence of Foix with the

Grand Duke of Tuscany, Francesco I, to obtain the use of the manuscript of Zosimus in Florence. But Foix's influence was not enough to overcome the fears of the Grand Duke. At a time of religious suspicion and hostility in Europe, the idea of making available the unpublished writings of an ancient opponent of the Christian emperors seemed to have impressed the pious minds of the popes and princes of Italy with superstitious dread. This aroused the sarcasm of the French men of letters. The experience of actually living through crisis had given the French a hardier attitude, whereas Catholic Italy, straining to keep herself free of all the ills of heresy and war that had erupted in the transalpine world, had become morbidly fearful and cautious. At any rate, here is the report from De Thou's memoirs for 1574:

> Ibi [Florence] Thuanus, memor Muretum Zozimi, qui historiam Eunapianam contraxit, videndi desiderio tantopere flagrare, et quia exemplar, quod in Vaticana bibliotheca asservabatur, habere non potuerat, Florentinum ut habere posset Foxii interventu sperasse, Foxio aurem vellit, ut illius ad aliquot menseis usum a Francisco impetraret. Quod initio concessum; sed postea compertum ut Romae, sic Florentiae, Pii V temporibus interdictam huius libri lectionem fuisse. Adeo ingens illud odium, quo Zozimus, pollente fanaticorum Gentilium superstitione, ob infestum in Christianos animum, et quaedam in Constantinum et Theodosium libere dicta, flagrabat, in animo pii senis post tot saecula adhuc recens erat, ut idem metus, qui Evagrii tempore Christianos nondum bene confirmatos invaserat, abolitis penitus gentium erroribus, et Christiano nomine ubique constituto, ipsum nunc etiam incesseret.[137]

Pinelli for his part had no more success on Dupuy's behalf than De Thou was having on Muret's behalf. He used two methods of approach: the first was to write to Fulvio Orsini in Rome, the second to write to Carlo Sigonio in Bologna. Carlo Sigonio had the ear of cardinal Gabriele Paleotti, bishop of Bologna, who as a member of the commission for the Index was in theory the peer of Sirleto. In practice, as those who have studied the history of the Index know, Sirleto was not a peer but a princeps in matters of censorship. In any case, as cardinal librarian, he could command the fate of the manuscript of Zosimus independently of his other official role, and that is what he did, uttering a passionate *nego* which was reported by Orsini to Pinelli, and by Pinelli to Dupuy, in the following terms:

Scrissi a V.S. co'l corriero passato, come io era in qualche speranze di poter havere il Zosimo, per le parole che me ne scrisse di Bologna il Signor Sigonio, il quale pensava di potermi servire co'l mezzo del Cardinale Paleotto. ho poi havute due lettere del Signor Fulvio Orsino che me n'hanno escluso affatto, dicendomi in esse d'haverne parlato col Cardinale Sirleto, perche me ne compiacesse et che non c'e stata via d'indurlo a contentarsene, con dire, che'l libro è scandalossimo e degno d'essere brusciato.[138]

In the sequel there appears to have been some talk of releasing a bowdlerized text of Zosimus for the use of Catholic scholars. Dupuy took an appropriately brusque attitude to this suggestion, and in a splendid passage, finely comprising mordant regret, colloquial pungency, and lancing indignation he informed Pinelli that it had been a mistake to approach Sirleto straight off rather than go through an underling, and declared further that Sirleto, though his great learning had raised him above his humble origins, had shown himself unfaithful, in an ignoble fashion, to the very world of learning on whose summit he now stood.

Mais le plus grand aide que ie pouvois esperer, c'estoit de Zosime, lequel a traité diligemment celle partie de l'histoire, dont i'ai affaire; vous remerciant humblement de la peine, qu'en avéz pris et donné à vos amis pour l'amour de moi mais puis qu'il n'y a nul moien de l'avoir, patience pour cest'heure. certainement dés-lors que ie sceus que vous vous adressiéz aus Cardinaux, i'entrai en desfiance que la chose ne reussiroit point à nostre gré: et qu'il faloit y proceder sourdement, et, comme lon dit en France, par comperes et commeres, envers ceux qui ont charge de la librairie sous eux; lesquels sont ordinairement personnes plus traitables, et qui se laissent aisément aller, quand ils sont maniéz dextrement et par moien. ceste superstition, ou, pour dire mieux, cafardise me semble par trop affectée, et totalement indigne de gens faisans profession des lettres, et qui tiennent tout leur avancement d'icelles. qu'ils n'aient pas peur, que de ce costé là respublica Christiana detrimentum accipiat: le mal qui est plus à craindre, vient des nostres mesmes. Ceterùm Zosimo facilius caruerim que de l'avoir tronqué et chastré à l'appetit de ces Messieurs: ausquels Zosime pourroit dire, ce que Martial disoit à un quidam, qui se plaignoit de l'obscenité de ses vers; "Ne castrare velis meos libellos, etc." ce seroit un tres-mauvais exemple et preiudice pour supprimer, ou à tout le moins pour gaster et interpoler les livres de Tacite, Suetone, Lucian, Galien, Julian, Eunape, Cyrille, Numatian et autres, contenans quelques iniures et gosseries contre nostre religion. sed est fortissima omnium veritas; nedum futilia convicia, et sepultas Ethnicae superstitionis reliquias reformidet. Celui de Florence que ie disois, est entre les mains du Signor Jacopo Salviati, l'un des plus riches et apparens gentilshommes de la Ville, qui a herité de la librairie du feu Cardinal Salviati: de laquelle, à ce que lon m'a dit, il est merveilleusement chiche et ialoux, iaçoit qu'il n'y entend rien; et le bon homme Vittorio s'en est plaint à quelques uns, que ie scai. Aureste ie ne puis penser, veu l'importance et elegance de cest' auteur, et le long temps qu'il a esté en veue, qu'il n'y en ait quelques copies à Romme par les estudes privées; ce que ie vous prierois de descouvrir par le moien de quelque ami, si ie ne craignois de vous estre trop importun pour ce regard. il est certain qu'Onuphre l'avoit fait tourner, autrement il ne s'en eust sceu aider; et Monsieur Muret m'a nommé autrefois le traducteur: mais il ne m'en souvient plus.[139]

By 1575 Dupuy was relieved to learn that the translation of Zosimus by Leunclavius was imminent. But to complicate matters, the brothers Pierre and François Pithou (the latter was living in Italy at that time under the name Monsieur de Luyeres, and seeing Pinelli often), both of whom were famous for their canine nose for manuscripts and canine jealousy of those they possessed, were indulging in the kind of mystification they liked to practice on their friends, each of them claiming that his brother was in possession of an exemplar of Zosimus, while playing the *ingénu* himself. Dupuy, who badly wanted to see a manuscript of Zosimus, declared that neither one of them would have shared it even if he did have it, and reproved both of them for their illiberality:

Monsieur de Luieres se mocque des gens, de dire, que Monsieur Pithou a Zosime; d'autre costé Pithou afferme que Luieres l'a: utri fidem habebimus? ego certe neque hunc neque illum, in hac quidem parte, verum esse arbitror. toutesfois pour certain Luieres l'a veu en Alemaigne ou en Suisse de ce dernier voiage, et (qui plus est) il l'a leu diligemment: et de ce font foi quelques siennes notes, que i'ai veu entre les mains de sondit frere, sur les constitutions Grecques du Code, lesquelles il a recueilli de divers auteurs. mais ie vous peux bien asseurer que Monsieur Pithou ne le veit iamais. Et ores que l'un ou l'autre d'eux l'eust, ie ne laisserois pourtant de faire toutes diligences à moi possibles pour le recouvrer d'ailleurs: car ils sont merveilleusement chiches de leurs livres, et sans discretion de personnes, chose peu civile ac illiberalis, et mal convenable à leur profession.[140]

Many years later Jacques-Auguste De Thou claimed the credit for bringing the story of the vicissitudes of the Greek text of Zosimus to a triumphant turn by procuring its first edition and defeating those who desired its suppression, thus keeping faith with the late Marc-Antoine Muret. The veritable *ingénu* had been Pierre Pithou, the false one François. De Thou relates that François Pithou had indeed obtained from Leunclavius at Basel, while on his voyage to Italy in 1574, the Greek exemplar of Zosimus used by Leunclavius for his translation, and that a promise had been given to Leunclavius that no edition would be printed without his prior consent. (This was very likely mendacity, a mere pretext used by François Pithou to justify his keeping the MS unpublished.) De Thou was able, however, to get the manuscript on loan from François Pithou, and in what amounted to a ruse, had it copied, after which he took it upon himself to have the copy transmitted to Frankfurt, where Fridericus Sylburgius, a learned collaborator of the Wechel heirs, used it as the copy text for the first complete edition of Zosimus in the original Greek in 1590.[141] In sum, it is fairly clear from the outlines of this story that François Pithou had done a disservice to scholarship by sequestering a manuscript of Zosimus rather than seeing to its publication. He brought about the same result as the one aimed at by Sirleto, and for much less honorable motives, viz. that he enjoyed having and being able to read a text that was unavailable to other people who wanted to do so, like Claude Dupuy. Though both the translation and then the Greek editio princeps of Zosimus did eventually appear while Claude Dupuy was still alive, and notionally able to take advantage of them, they came too late to give him the incentive he needed to conclude his work on the Panegyrics: it was a philological project that fell victim to Dupuy's professional and family life, and the onset of civil war in France.

* * * *

Dupuy's letters reveal his poor opinion of the capacities of two individuals who achieved notoriety as intellectual innovators in the sixteenth century (and whose fame is kept alive by modern Renaissance studies), but who were thought of by men of Dupuy's calibre simply as bad scholars and extravagant reasoners. The first was Petrus Ramus, who had had a fierce dispute with Dupuy's old teacher, Turnebus, on a front on which Turnebus was strongest and Ramus weakest, *humanitas* — the study of classical history and literature. Ramus had published a commentary on the speeches of Cicero against the agrarian law proposed by P. Servilius Rullus in 63 BC, and Turnebus had turned his fire on it. Dupuy, in a letter written to Pinelli just a few months before the St. Bartholomew's Night massacre in which Ramus was to lose his life, listed the polemics that had been published on both sides, and for the most part was neutral, but did add his own qualifying judgment to his notice of Turnebus's attack on Ramus's Cicero commentary. The fact that he did so is an indication of his own orientation to the type of historical erudition at which Ramus was a failure: *"Animadversiones in Rullianos Petri Rami commentarios;* ou il [Turnebus] monstre la grand' bestise et ignorance dudit Ramus en les commentaires sur les Agraries de Ciceron."[142]

Jean Bodin was a more considerable figure than Ramus, and his *Six livres de la République,* which appeared first in 1576 and developed his theory of political sovereignty with a wealth of comparative historical, political, and geographical information, was a timely and important work which had immediate impact on the intellectual world (and retained its force for a century at least). No scholar who reads the works of Bodin, or consults the secondary literature on him, should have any doubt about the carelessness with which Bodin cited not only historical but also juristic sources, nor about the fact that many of his comparisons are far-fetched. But neither should there be any doubt about the importance and influence of his political theorizing. Dupuy showed the limitations of his own erudite humanist and magisterial circle when he commented upon the lack of sound judgment shown by Bodin, while failing to appreciate the importance of his work, which to the savants of the city seemed, he said, to be a mere "farrago and rhapsody":

> Quant à ce que vous desiréz sçavoir quel iugement lon fait ici du livre de Bodin *de la Republique:* si vous demandéz du commun, il est asséz estimé et bien recueilli, et il s'en est desia vendu deux impressions sans celle de Lausanne en petite marge, laquelle a esté faite sur la

premiere de ceste Ville; en la seconde il n'a pas changé ni adiousté grand' chose, qui est presque ce qu'il a tiré de *la Republique des Suisses* de Simlere, laquelle il recouvra peu apres la premiere edition. si vous entendéz des savans, ils en font cas comme d'une farrage et rapsodie contenant beaucoup de choses superflues et qui sont hors son suiet; plusieurs rares et bonnes, et de laquelle un homme de meilleur iugement que lui pourra bien faire son proufit, aiant tout, bon et mauvais ramassé ensemble: au demeurant en beaucoup d'endroits iudicium illius requirunt.[143]

There is a similarity to be found in Dupuy's response to the most important work of political theory to be published in France in the sixteenth century, and in his responses to the more overtly publicistic, but also very influential, works of Hotman and Beza. Claude Dupuy, as a royal magistrate and an heir by personal inclination to the values of the Renaissance humanist tradition, was hindered in his ability to come to grips with *Francogallia, Du droit des Magistrats,* and *Six livres de la République.* To the royal magistrate and orthodox Catholic, the doctrine of resistance enunciated by the Huguenot monarchomach writers had to seem, at bottom, a piece of sedition. To the Renaissance humanist and eminent parlementaire the new doctrine of absolute sovereignty must have seemed not much less pernicious. Of the doctrine of resistance, itself a political ideology of fairly ad hoc character, he was capable of formulating a critique in terms, likewise limited, of its probable effect. But in the case of Bodin's more ambitious work, Dupuy's critique fell correspondingly short of its target, just because his scholarship made him so acutely sensitive to the work's palpable defects, and because as a *parlementaire* he had passed his career close to the vertex of the body, the Parlement de Paris, which, more than any other, represented an idiosyncratically French form of constitutionalism which opposed absolutism.

There is little or no direct testimony in the letters of Dupuy to Pinelli, concerning his public life as an office-holder. Yet they show us the mind of a magistrate whose professional conduct during the wars of religion conformed perfectly to all the most positive connotations of the term *politique* (even though the revelation of his thought and character in this correspondence is conditioned by the character of its addressee, a man of exquisitely non-political nature). It was both as a *politique* and as an exponent of humanistic culture that Dupuy expressed his disdain for the ineptitude of the ecclesiastical censors.

How strongly one hopes that the short space of time between
its appearance and his demise, and the precarious state of his health,
enabled him to read the *Satyre Menippée*. Culture and politics, books
and the Palais de Justice (but also his family and his garden) were
linked in the life of Claude Dupuy. It was the formidable culture of the
man that made him the magistrate he was.

Notes

1. *Claudii Puteani Tumulus* (1607). Copy seen: Paris, BN, cote 4° Ln. 27, 6853.
2. The published catalogue of the Collection Dupuy by Léon Dorez and Suzanne
    Solente (1899–1928) is of course an indispensable guide, and a reprint of it by the
    Bibliothèque Nationale is a desideratum.
3. BAM, MS G 77 inf., fols. 1–91; and MS T 167 sup., fols. 204–258. The last surviving
    letter from Dupuy (MS T 167 sup., fols. 257–58) is dated 25 January 1588.
    Quotations in the present article from these codices will be lightly modernized in
    respect of punctuation, but in matters of spelling and the use of accents will repro-
    duce as faithfully as possible the original texts, since Dupuy was fairly consistent in
    his usage.
4. BNP, MS Dupuy 704, fols. 2–112. The last letter from Pinelli (fol. 112) is dated 2
    June 1593, the penultimate one (fol. 111) 22 August 1589. To my knowledge, the
    most extensive publication to date of the letters of Pinelli from this codex was in
    Rita Calderini De Marchi, *Jacopo Corbinelli et les érudits Français* (1914), app. D, com-
    prising ten letters. MS Dupuy 663 contains a further letter from Pinelli to Claude
    Dupuy (fol. 110). It was published, in an imperfect transcription, by Castellani,
    "Lettera inedita di Gianvincenzo Pinelli a Pietro Dupuy" [sic].
5. The important references to Dupuy in Grafton, *Scaliger* 1 are at pp. 98–99 and nn.
    154–162 to those pages. His article "Rhetoric, Philology, and Egyptomania in the
    1570s: J.J. Scaliger's invective against M. Guilandinus's *Papyrus*" (1979) traces in
    detail an episode of scholarly commerce involving Scaliger, Melchior Guilandinus,
    Pinelli and Dupuy, and adduces a number of letters from the correspondence of
    Pinelli and Dupuy at nn. 20, 23. For the wider context, Donald R. Kelley's
    *Foundations of Modern Historical Scholarship. Language, Law, and History in the French
    Renaissance* (1970) is indispensable. Another aid to general orientation in the world
    of the French and Italian scholars of the sixteenth century is Pierre De Nolhac, *La
    bibliothèque de Fulvio Orsini* (1887).
6. Citations from the letters of Pinelli and Dupuy appeared in my article "Carlo
    Sigonio storico e la censura" and in *Carlo Sigonio* (*v* bibliography)
7. Solente, "Les manuscrits des Dupuy," pp. 177–78.
8. Or at any rate this is stated in Grente, *Dictionnaire des lettres françaises — Le seizième siè-
    cle* s.v. Claude Dupuy. The *Tumulus* describes Clément Dupuy as follows: "Clementis
    disertissimi oratoris ac iurisconsulti ex nobili apud Segusianos familia orti" (f. 2r).
    "Apud Segusianos" (rectè Segusiavos) is a classicizing way of designating the modern
    département of the Loire.
9. She is identified as Philippe Poncet de Venart in the *Dictionnaire de Biographie
    Française* t. 12, s.v. Claude Dupuy.
10. Rigault, *Petri Puteani Vita*, in De Thou, *Historiarum libri* (1733), t. 7, part II, p. 44.
11. The *Tumulus* itself contains no independent information on Dupuy's career of stud-

ies, but it excerpts the obituary notice of Claude Dupuy from De Thou's *Historiarum libri*, a notice which appears in book 109 under the year 1594 (vol. 5, pp. 381–82 in the London edition of 1733). It is De Thou who names Strazel, Dorat, Turnèbe, and Lambin as Claude Dupuy's early teachers in Paris. The last three are sufficiently well known to the general literature on the cultural history of France in the sixteenth century. As for Jean Strazel, cf. A.C. Dionisotti, "Polybius and the Royal Professor" (*v* Bibliography).

12. From the recollections of J. -A. De Thou: "Ils avoient estudié aux loix à Toulouse, M<essieurs> du Puy, le Fevre et lui [Houllier]." *Thuana*, in De Thou, *Historiarum libri*, t. 7, pp. 187–88, a passage cited further at n. 24 below.

13. De Thou in his formal necrology (as in n. 11) records the fact that Dupuy studied law under Cujas. Dupuy never gives any specific information about his education in his letters to Pinelli; such information would have been relayed *viva voce* when they met.

14. Pinelli to Dupuy, 7 April 1571, the first letter from Pinelli to be addressed to Dupuy in Paris; MS Dupuy 704, fol. 7; the address on fol. 7v is as follows: "A Monsieur Claude Dupuy au Logis de Madamoiselle Dupuy pres de St. Andre des artz a Paris."

15. His name is not recorded anywhere in the volumes of Maugis, *Histoire du Parlement de Paris*.

16. Melchior Guilandinus. Cf. Grafton, "Rhetoric, Philology, and Egyptomania in the 1570s: J.J. Scaliger's invective against M. Guilandinus's *Papyrus.*"

17. Dupuy to Pinelli, 15 August 1579; MS T 167 sup., fol. 208r-v. Houllier did vist Pinelli at Pauda and did proceed to Rome. He was back in Paris by January 1580.

18. Dupuy to Pinelli, Bologna, a.d. III Kal Oct. = 28 Sept, 1570; MS G 77 inf., fol. 1.

19. Dupuy to Pinelli, Lyon, s.d. (March 1571); MS G 77 inf., fol. 7.

20. The functioning of the Parlement de Paris and the Palais de Justice is described in R. Doucet, *Les Institutions de la France au XVIe siècle*, 1, pp. 167–88; and J.H. Shennan, *The Parlement of Paris* (1968).

21. De Thou, *Commentariorum de vita sui libri*, book 1, anno 1574, p. 25.

22. Cf. the account of the editions and MSS of the *Thuana* in Kinser, *The Works of Jacques-August De Thou* (1966).

23. It is not clear to me whether the great jurist and publicist François Hotman is meant, nor at what period he would have attended these reunions in Paris, if it were he. The modern account of his life is Donald R. Kelley, *François Hotman* (1973). I am grateful to Professor Kelley for private epistolary discussion of this passage. It may be that Jean Hotman, the son of François Hotman, was the person in question. But the slender line of transmission from De Thou's remembered table talk (which in itself harked back to a remembered past) to the text printed as *Thuana* seems to me to make it a question not worth pursuing.

24. *Thuana* in London ed. (1733) t. 7 (separate pagination), pp. 187–88. Letters from Dupuy to Pinelli sent in January and February 1580 include express salutations from De Thou, Houllier, and Pierre Pithou (MST 167 sup., fols. 214r, 217v). The conjunction of these names indicates, I think, that the meetings of this learned circle were a fixture at that time, although they would have been interrupted within a year by the absence of Dupuy, Pithou, and De Thou, all of whom left Paris together on the same mission to Guyenne.

25. De Thou, *Historiarum libri*, II, book 34, anno 1562, p. 325.

26. The custom of exacting this oath fell into disuse before the end of the century. Salmon, *Society in Crisis*, pp. 77, and 322: "In 1598 the crown abandoned the

hypocrisy of requiring the judges to swear an oath that they had not bought their office."

27. Maugis, *Histoire du Parlement de Paris*, III, p. 258. Dupuy is not described in this entry as having served previously as an avocat, which was the case with many others who became conseillers. It is this which allows the conjecture that his previous service had been as a judge in the Enquêtes. On the date, NB that Solente, "Les manuscrits des Dupuy," p. 179, states that "Dupuy avait été pourvu de l'office de conseiller au Parlement de Paris (23 September 1575)." She does not clearly identify the source of this information and I think that it must be wrong. Maugis is the more reliable guide to this aspect of Dupuy's life.

28. Maugis, III, pp. 253, 258.

29. Solente, p. 179, citing BNP, Dossiers bleus 548, dossier 14393, fol. 2 ff.

30. Pinelli to Dupuy, 21 June 1576, MS Dupuy 704, fol. 50r.

31. Dupuy to Pinelli, 14 September 1576, MS G 77 inf., fol. 78r.

32. Solente, pp. 180–82 and n. 5. MS Dupuy 638, f. 92r–v contains the basic list of the dates and places of birth of the children of Claude Dupuy and Claude Sanguin, information which Solente has supplemented from other sources. I have been unable to consult a note by M.P. Flament from *Bibliothèque de l'Ecole des Chartes* 62 (1901), pp. 720–22, publishing autograph notes by Claude Dupuy on the birth of his children, from a family Bible now in the BNP. The children were:
Anne (1 February 1578–1647),
Christophe (25 May 1580–28 June 1654),
Augustin (11 June 1581–May 1641),
Pierre (15 November 1582–14 December 1651),
Clément (15 May 1584–1635),
Marie (28 February 1587 — ?),
Jacques (28 September 1591–17 November 1656),
Nicolas (14 July 1594–1 July 1625).

33. Cf. Alfred Soman, *De Thou and the Index. Letters from Christophe Dupuy (1603–1607).*, (1972).

34. Dupuy to Pinelli, 12 April 1587; MS T 167 sup, fol. 252r.

35. "Inventaire des manuscrits de Claude Dupuy (1595)," published in *Bibliothèque de l'école des Chartes* (1915), p. 4.

36. Hillairet, *Dictionnaire historique des rues de Paris*(Paris, 1963), I, (for the list of superseded street names) and II (s.v. rue de Nevers).

37. Cf. J.-P. Babelon, *Paris au XVIe siècle*. The end-papers of this volume contain a reproduction of the plan of Paris by Truschet and Hoyau. On p. 249 there is an enlarged reproduction of the view of the quarters of St.–André-des-Arts and the bourg St.–Germain from the same plan. It shows as open terrain the area just outside the city wall, between the Porte de Buci and the Tour de Nesle, where the rue des Deux Portes (rue de Nevers) was to be built. Nor does it show the new bridge, on which see Babelon pp. 138–39 and 285. On the plans of Paris: Babelon, pp. 37–42.

38. Babelon, p. 133 (Italians), p. 170 (Huguenots), pp. 247–253 (general character of the faubourg) and passim for related subjects.

39. Diefendorf, *Paris City Councillors* p. 90. On p. 38 she notes that the family first began to hold civic offices in the period 1400–1450, and on p. 36 that many members of the Sanguin served as prévôts des marchands, échevins, and city councillors in the sixteenth century.

40. Diefendorf, *Paris City Councillors*, p. 349, an index reference.
41. Babelon, p. 543. At this time he also had the status of conseiller aux Eaux et Forêts.
42. Babelon, p. 548. The entry here appears to indicate that he also had this position in 1576.
43. Cf. Barnavi, *Le Parti de Dieu,* p. 87. He does not identify the father of Jacques Sanguin, city councillor. It must have been André Sanguin de Livry, made conseiller clerc in 1536, who died in 1539. Cf Maugis, t. 3, p. 175.
44. Maugis, *Histoire du Parlement de Paris,* III, pp. 261–62. All further references to Jacques Sanguin will be to the parlementaire son, not the city councillor father.
45. Descimon, *Qui étaient les Seize?,* no. 207. Christophe had another brother-in-law of distinction in addition to Claude Dupuy; he was Geoffrey Camus de Pontcarré, *conseiller d'Etat.* Christophe Sanguin's date of death was 1599.
46. Barnavi, *Le Parti de Dieu,* pp. 82, 87.
47. *Claudii Puteani Tumulus* f. 2r.
48. De Thou, *Commentariorum de vita sua libri VI,* 2, pp. 37–46. It is regrettable, from the point of view of institutional history, that De Thou refers only in passing to the work of the Chambre de Justice. The pages cited are filled, for the most part, with lyrical accounts of the author's recreational excursions amid the natural beauties of Acquitaine. De Thou was one of two clerical *conseillers* of the Chambre. The other was Lazare Coquilley. They were able to sit in judgement on civil cases, but not criminal ones. De Thou withdrew from the Chambre in August 1582 in order to return to Paris, where his father lay ill. As for Dupuy, he apparently did not write to Pinelli at all during the period of the deputation in Guyenne.
49. Emile Brives-Cazes, *Le Parlement de Bordeaux et la Chambre de Justice de Guyenne en 1582* (1866); *La Chambre de Justice de Guyenne en 1583–84* (1874).
50. Roman Schnur, *Die französischen Juristen im konfessionellen Bürgerkrieg des 16. Jahrhunderts. Ein Beitrag zur Entstehungsgeschichte des modernen Staates* (1962), pp. 36 ff.
51. Loisel and Pithou receive special attention in Donald R. Kelley, *Foundations of Modern Historical Scholarship* (1970), chapter 9.
52. Montaigne, *Oeuvres complètes* (1962), pp. 1380–81, letter no. 14
53. Brives-Cazes (1866), pp. 185–86.
54. Brives-Cazes (1866), pp. 99 ff., De Thou, *Commentariorum de vita sua libri,* p. 44.
55. BNP, MS Dupuy 638, fol. 92v; and Solente, "Les manuscrits des Dupuy," pp. 180–82; Nicolas Rigault, "Petri Puteani Vita," in De Thou, *Historiarum libri* (London ed., VII), pp. 42–43. Pierre Dupuy was sometimes called, informally and affectionately, "le Gascon," because of his birth under meridional skies.
56. De Thou *Historiarum libri* bk. 81 (vol. 4 in the London edition).
57. Anna Maria Raugei, "'Je me délecte à présent du jardinage…': Natura e artificio nel giardino di Claude Dupuy" (1987).
58. Pierre de l'Estoile, *Journal Henri III, Journal Henri IV* (1943, 1948), ad indicem. For what follows I refer especially to the editorial introduction by Louis-Raymond Lefèvre to the first volume.
59. *Scaligeriana* (1668), p. 259: "*Pasquils.* Monsieur du Puis a amassé tout ce qui se faisoit de Pasquils durant la Ligue bon et mauvais. Le Roy fait chercher les Auteurs, il veut bien faire et ne veut pas qu'on en parle." Claude Dupuy's attentive collecting of this literature is reflected in the letters to Pinelli.
60. Maugis vol. 2, p. 58.
61. The embastillement of 16 January 1589 is recounted by Maugis, vol. 2, pp. 59–60. In

Morin's *Dialogue d'entre le maheustre et le manant* (published in December 1593) the events are told from the point of view of the Seize, who planned and executed the manoeuvre. In Ascoli's edition of the *Dialogue* (1977) the true significance of what occurred is analyzed coolly: cf. text pp. 109–10 and n. 147.

62. Pietro del Bene to Joseph Scaliger, 8 March [1589], published in *Epistres françaises des personnages illustres et doctes à Mons. Joseph Juste de la Scala* (1624, pp. 380–85), cited here from Colliard, *Pierre d'Elbène*, pp. 318–20.

63. Morin, *Dialogue d'entre le maheustre et le manant*, ed. Ascoli, pp. 112, 124, 127–28, with the editor's notes.

64. L'Estoile, *Journal Henri III*, p. 620. I note that Dorez records the following document in MS Dupuy 87 (not seen by me), fol. 288: "Elargissment de Claude Dupuy, par ordre du Conseil de l'Union, 28 mars 1589, copie authentique."

65. Maugis, II, p. 71 ff.

66. Maugis, III, p. 288. Solente, "Les manuscrits des Dupuy," p. 180 and n. 3, gives the date 12 July 1592 for this reintegration. But the date given by Maugis will be the right one.

67. Maugis, II, pp. 136 ff, "Le Parlement de Tours."

68. Maugis, III, p. 287.

69. Maugis, III, p. 288.

70. Maugis, II, pp. 141–43, p. 183 n. 5, and vol. 3, p. 276.

71. Maugis, II, p. 183, and vol. III, p. 297

72. Maugis, III, pp. 275 ff. and 280.

73. Maugis, III p. 296.

74. But it must be admitted that the records of this turbulent period, as Maugis himself makes clear, were incomplete.

75. Maugis, II, pp. 83 ff; Barnavi, *Le parti de Dieu*, pp. 206 ff; the most detailed account of the conspiracy and its aftermath in Barnavi and Descimon, *La Sainte Ligue, le Juge, et la Potence* (1985).

76. Barnavi, *Le parti de Dieu*, pp. 243–47; Descimon, *Qui étaient les Seize?*. no. 207.

77. Solente, "Les manuscrits des Dupuy," p. 180.

78. De Thou, necrology of Dupuy (as in n. 11 above); Rigault, *Petri Puteani vita* (in De Thou, VII, separate pagination), pp. 42–43.

79. "Inventaire des manuscrits de Claude Dupuy (1595)." This article, published without attribution in the *Bibliothèque de l'École des Chartes* 76 (1915), reports the discovery of the Dupuy inventory in the minutier of a Parisian notarial practice (Étude Fardeau, aujourd'hui M. Faroux, liasse 443, art. 1). The author of the article devotes particular attention to the MS portion of Dupuy's library, and identifies many MSS by their modern BNP shelfmark.

80. For a rapid and suggestive comparison of the numbers of books to be found in the very large collection of Barnabé Brisson and several other contemporaries, and their value, cf. Barnavi and Descimon, *La Sainte Ligue* pp. 88–89. Brisson, a man of learning who was rich and greedy, possessed more than two-and-half times as many books as Claude Dupuy. But Dupuy's library contained far more books than the number normally to be found in the library of an average, or even an exceptional, parlementaire.

81. *C. Cornelii Taciti et C. Vellei Paterculi scripta quae exstant* (Paris: P. Chevalier, 1608). Texts of the two historians and notes are paginated separately. The fly-title for Velleius makes it clear that this is the first edition of Dupuy's textual notes. The edi-

torial note, evidently inspired by Dupuy's sons, is well informed about the contretemps dating back to the 1570s between Aldo Manuzio Jr and Dupuy over the
attribution and priority of notes on Velleius.

82. *Latini Pacati Drepanii Panegyricus cum notis integris Claudii Puteani et al.,* ed. Joannes
Arntzenius (Amsterdam: heirs of S. Schouten, 1753). This panegyric is number 2 in
the traditional ordering of the panegyrics.

83. Milan, BAM, MS G 77 inf.; the dates of the letters, with the relevant foliation in the
MS in brackets, are as follows: 10 November 1571 (fols. 35–40); 29 November 1571
(fols. 13–14); 25 March 1572 (fols. 17–22); 19 July 1572 (fol. 28); 9 November 1572
(fols. 31–33).

84. V Grafton, *Scaliger* 1 (1983), p. 273, nn. 162–64, citing MSS Dupuy 16 and 808.

85. Pierre De Nolhac, "Lettres inédites de Muret," publishing letters from MS Dupuy
490.

86.. Paulus Gualdus, *Vita Ioannis Vincenti Pinelli* (1607).

87 Rivolta, *Catalogo dei codici pinelliani dell'Ambrosiana* (1933).

88. Marcella Grendler, "A Greek Collection in Padua: the library of Gian Vincenzo
Pinelli (1535–1601)" and cf. the briefer resumé in her "Book Collecting in Counter-
Reformation Italy: the library of Gian Vincenzo Pinelli (1535–1601)."

89. Anna Maria Raugei, *Un abbozzo di grammatica francese del '500. Le note di Gian Vincenzo
Pinelli;* "'Je me délecte à présent du jardinage...': Natura e artificio nel giardino di
Claude Dupuy" (1987).

90. See the recent volume, edited by Claude Jolly, *Histoire des Bibliothèques Françaises: Les
Bibliothèques sous l'Ancien Régime, 1530–1789.* ad indicem for references to the library
of de Mesmes and many others. There are a handful of rather generic references to
Claude Dupuy as well.

91. Dupuy to Pinelli, 10 November 1571; MS G 77 inf., fols. 9v–10r. In reply to a request
from Pinelli to explain more fully the nature of the protective wall hangings in
Roissy's library, Dupuy replied on 19 July 1572: "Toile gommée en l'estude de
Monsieur de Roissi signifie toile trempée ou adspersa leviter d'eau, en laquelle on a
infusé de la gomme Arabique ou de Tragagant." (MS G 77 inf., fol. 27r.)

92. Dupuy to Pinelli, 29 November 1571; MS G 77 inf., fol. 12r.

93. Dupuy to Pinelli, 19 July 1572; MS G 77 inf., fol. 26v. The bibliographical problems
posed by the proliferation during the wars of religion of the ephemeral literature
which Dupuy here characterizes so clearly are well known. Tome 1 of the *Catalogue
de l'histoire de France* contains a repertoire of such pieces and collections of pieces:
Recueil appears as the title or designation of a number of them (Lb.33, numbers 51,
219, 220, 235), some of which are probably to be identified with the items Dupuy
describes here.

94. Jacopo Corbinelli's letter to Pinelli about the massacre was published in Pio Rajna,
"Jacopo Corbinelli e la strage di S. Bartolomeo." Rajna was not entirely at home in
Corbinelli's milieu and there are inexactitudes, including a misidentification of
Claude Dupuy. For an expert monograph on Corbinelli (and Pinelli, Dupuy, and
others) Rita Calderini De Marchi, *Jacopo Corbinelli et les érudits Français* (1914). The
original of Corbinelli's letter on the massacre is in MS T 167 sup. The entry on
Corbinelli in *Dizionario biografico degli italiani* (vol. 28, 1983, pp. 750–60) is by G.
Benzoni.

95. Dupuy to Pinelli, 2 February 1573; MS G 77 inf., fol. 42r. Pinelli replied from Rome
on 20 March 1573 (MS 704, fol. 22r): Capilupi's piece was being suppressed. The

entry on Capilupi in *Dizionario biografico degli italiani* 18 1975, pp. 531–35) is by G. De
Caro. It reports the printing of the *Stratogema* in Rome in 1574 without giving bibliographical details. It is unclear to me how many copies survived and can be consulted; I have never seen one.

96. Dupuy to Pinelli, 2 February 1573; MS G 77 inf., fol. 41v.
97. Bernard de Girard, sieur du Haillan. The work here described by Dupuy as in the
press was evidently the *Histoire générale des rois de France*, which appeared with the
imprint 1576. Du Haillan is discussed in De Caprariis, *Propaganda e pensiero politico*,
pp. 305–17, and in Kelley, *Foundations of Modern Historical Scholarship*, pp. 233–38.
98. This word, which means equilibrium, hence impartiality, is written in Greek characters in the MS and transliterated here.
99. Dupuy to Pinelli, 17 January 1575; MS G 77 inf., fols. 71v–72r. The judgement given
here of La Popelinière may be compared with that given in, for instance, Huppert,
The Idea of Perfect History, pp. 135–50, and in Kelley, *Foundations of Modern Historical
Scholarship*, pp. 139–41 (with further bibliography).
100. E.g., Dupuy to Pinelli, 25 March 1575; MS G 77 inf., 67v, denouncing Thevet. A letter of 12 December 1579 is even harder on the impostor Thevet, and also blasts
Goropius Becanus, the savant of Antwerpen, as a "fol, impudent, et outrecuidé." MS
T 167 sup., fol. 209r.
101. Dupuy to Pinelli, 25 March 1575; MS G 77 inf., fol. 69v.
102. The monograph which deals especially with this aspect of the life of Hotman is
Donald R. Kelley, *François Hotman. A revolutionary's ordeal* (1973).
103. Dupuy to Pinelli, 28 March 1574; MS G 77 inf., fol. 52v. Dupuy is not only on solid
ground philologically (the word *incentivum* is quite non-classical and belongs to later
Latin), but has chosen a historical reference packed with meaning. He alludes to
the panegyric numbered twelfth in the traditional order, and specifically to a passage (12.1.4) in which the writer, in a topos of modesty, compares his own halting
praises to the thin note of the reed-pipe on the battlefield: feeble in comparison to
the trumpet or the curved war-horn, yet not utterly ineffective in giving *incentivum*
(stimulus, arousal) to combative spirits — which is what Dupuy accuses Hotman of
doing. Not only that: this panegyric is a composition of 313 CE in which the pane-
gyrist felicitates Constantine for his victory over the usurper Maxentius at Rome in
312 — that is, for success in a dynastic power struggle, success which culminates
when Constantine enters the Palace, followed by the longing eyes of the grateful
populace (12.19.3–4). Dupuy and Pinelli operated at such a high level of erudition
that Dupuy was able to convey, in a glancing allusion to the source of his lexical
choice, an entire point of view on the troubles of France.
104. Dupuy to Pinelli, 25 March 1575; MS G 77 inf., fol. 69r. On the historical specificity
of ideological consciousness in early modern France during Dupuy's lifetime, readers are referred to Donald R. Kelley, *The Beginning of Ideology. Consciousness and
Society in the French Reformation* (1981).
105. Dupuy to Pinelli, 12 December 1579; MS T 167 sup., fol. 212r.
106. "Quant a vos comptes, ie ne sache point de meilleur moien de les arrester, qu'en
reduisant (comme vous faites) les livres et francs à escus pistolets; ainsi appellons
nous tous escus de coing estranger, lesquels valent deux sols moins que ceux de
France, dits vulgairement escus sol ou au souleil. mais pource que le pris des escus
et autres especes est fort incertain et desreglé en France, comme toute autre chose,
et croist de iour à autre par l'avarice et monopole des marchans, lesquels donnent

ordinairement loi aus monnoies: en la reduction des trois premieres sommes par moi fournies, i'avaluerai les escus au plus haut cours de l'an 1572. qui estoit de 56 sols piece; et pour le regard des deux dernieres, à 58 sols, lequel pris a cours pour le iour-d'hui. ie dresserai ci-dessous tout le compte, comme ie l'entens; le soumettant toutesfois à vostre advis, et à meilleur calcul." Dupuy to Pinelli, 25 March 1575; MS G 77 inf., fol. 67v. The same letter contains an extensive reckoning. Cf. Dupuy's letter of 14 September 1576, same MS, fol. 79r: "I'ai arresté nos comptes ici bas, reduisant les livres (dico libellas) tant Françoises que Venitiennes à ΔΔ [écus] pistolets, lesquels pour le regard de la derniere mise par moi faite, i'ai avalué à 63 sols tourn <ois> piece, comme ils ont cours au-iourd'hui." An extensive reckoning follows. And finally, cf. Dupuy's letter of 12 December 1579, MS T 167 sup., fols. 209–212.

107. Pinelli to Dupuy, 9 July 1574; MS Dupuy 704, fol. 30r.

108. This confiscation is first mentioned in Pinelli's letter to Dupuy of 29 May 1573; MS Dupuy 704, fol. 24r: "...et se bene il Padre Inquisitore se n'ha tenuti alquanti, spero nondimeno di potergli ricuperare." This hope was not to be gratified. (A further reference to the incident is in his letter of 5 August 1574; same MS, fol. 28r–v.)

109. Dupuy to Pinelli, 28 March 1574; MS G 77 inf., fol. 51v.

110. Pinelli to Dupuy, 13 November 1573; MS Dupuy 704, fol. 26r.

111. Dupuy to Pinelli, 28 March 1574; MS G 77 inf., fol. 54r. Dupuy refers to Du Puys as "susdit" because the publisher had already been mentioned frequently in this letter in connection with a plan to have the works of Carlo Sigonio reprinted in Paris. Details about this, with citations from the same letter, can be found in McCuaig, *Carlo Sigonio*, as can other references to Jacques Du Puys, ad indicem. The Genoan merchant living in Paris with whom Dupuy was acquainted was named Dorino Iouardo.

112. Dupuy to Pinelli, 30 March 1574; MS G 77 inf., fol. 57r.

113. Pinelli to Dupuy, 26 May 1574; MS Dupuy 704, fol. 26c verso: "mi piace che piaccia anche a V.S. la via della fiera di Francfort, et la seguiremo ne nostri bisogni. già ho nuova delli due pacquetti consegnati a Messer Pietro Longo in fiera, et secondo mi dicono, seranno qui fra 13 giorni al più tardi."

114. Paul F. Grendler, *The Roman Inquisition and the Venetian Press 1540–1605.* (1977), p. 49 (with further references given there to Eubel, *Hierarchia Catholica*).

115. Gigliola Fragnito, *Memoria individuale e costruzione biografica* (1978), pp. 26–27; and eadem, "Aspetti della censura ecclesiastica nell'Europa della Controriforma. L'edizione parigina delle opere di Gasparo Contarini," p. 45.

116. Pinelli to Dupuy, 26 May 1574; MS Dupuy 704, fol. 26c verso.

117. Pinelli to Dupuy, 5 August 1574; MS Dupuy 704, fol. 28r. The last lines of this passage are cited in Paul F. Grendler's contribution ("Printing and Censorship") to *The Cambridge History of Renaissance Philosophy* (1988), pp. 52–53, with the erroneous reading *sia* for *sii* (the fault is mine, not his). Grendler there makes the argument for the ineffectiveness of censorship which he made first in his monograph of 1977, *The Roman Inquisition and the Venetian Press, 1540–1605.*

118. McCuaig, *Carlo Sigonio*, chapters 1 and 4.

119. Paul F. Grendler, *The Roman Inquisition,* cf. pp. 186–89; 266; 193–95, 200, 255. Grendler's pages incorporate the results of research by Antonio Rotondò and Leandro Perini as well as himself.

120. Grendler, pp. 187–88.

121. Grendler, p. 194.
122. Pinelli to Dupuy, 8 September 1585; MS Dupuy 704, fol. 87r; and 24 August 1586, fol. 94r.
123. Pinelli to Dupuy, 22 February 1588; MS Dupuy 704, fol. 108r.
124. Miriam Usher Chrisman, *Lay Culture, Learned Culture* (New Haven 1982), p. 4 and other references to Zetzner ad indicem. He was active until 1616.
125. Pinelli to Dupuy, 22 February 1578; MS Dupuy 704, fol. 53r–v.
126. The work of this title to which Dupuy refers was published in 1577 by René Choppin, a jurist, a Gallican in his approach to church-state relations, and something of a ligueur.
127. Claude Dupuy to Pietro Longo, 1 March 1578, non-autograph; MS G 77 inf., fol. 85–v. The address is on a separate sheet, a plico, fol. 87v. It reads: "Au Seigneur Pietro Longo Marchant Italien estant de present a Francfort [and in the hand of Pinelli:] primo di Marzo 1578 Parigi C. Dupuy al Lungo de libris."
128. Cf. R.J.W. Evans, *The Wechel Presses: Humanism and Calvinism in Central Europe 1572–1627* (1975). The most recent and fullest researches on Wechel are to be found in Ian Maclean, "André Wechel at Frankfurt, 1572–1581" (*v* Bibliography).
129. On all of the above, cf. McCuaig, *Carlo Sigonio*, chapter 1.
130. On Jacques Du Puys, *v* Philippe Renouard, *Documents sur les imprimeurs* (1901), pp. 84–86; and idem, *Répertoire des imprimeurs Parisiens*, (1965), pp. 135–36.
131. Dupuy to Pinelli, 17 January 1575; MS G 77 inf., fol. 71r. The text of "Alcinous," translated with commentary by Jacques Charpentier, to which Pinelli and Dupuy refer, is in fact the work of the Platonic philosopher Albinus. This edition had appeared under the title *Platonis cum Aristotele in universa philosophia comparatio* (Paris: Du Puys, 1573).
132. Dupuy to Pinelli, 14 September 1576: "L'oeuvre du Seigneur Sigonio *de antiquo iure populi Romani* a esté imprimé par De-tournes de Lion à la diligence de Iacques Dupuys, fort bien et correctement, i'ose dire mieux qu'à Boulongne: sinon qu'ils y ont mis un grand et sot titre à l'Allemande, lequel à mon opinion desplaira à l'auteur." MS G 77 inf., fol. 78v. This edition appeared under two slightly different titles, *De antiquo iure populi Romani and De antiquo iure civium Romanorum*. Cf. H. M. Adams, *Catalogue of Books 1501–1600 in Cambridge Libraries* (Cambridge: UP, 1967) items S 1099 and 1100 for full particulars.
133. Dupuy to Pinelli, 15 September 1584: "le vous ai envoié a ceste foire tout ce que i'ai trouvé de nouveau pardeça, hors mis les gros volumes, dont les libraires se chargent ordinairement, comme Tertulianus Pamelii; Brissonius *de formulis antiquis*, Scaliger *de emendatione temporum; Ambrosii Paraei opera* in Latinam linguam conversa." MS T 167 sup., fol. 225r.
134. Pinelli to Dupuy, 2 January 1578: "non le mando la politica del Vittorio, perche m'imagino ch'ella l'habbia havuta per via di Lione, non essendo quel libro zoppo ad arrivare a qualsivoglia loco." (MS Dupuy 704, fol. 51r), The edition referred to by Pinelli is *Petri Victorii Commentarii in VIII libros Aristotelis de optimo statu civitatis* (Florentiae apud Iuntas, 1576; folio). N.B. that this edition contained the complete Greek text and translation, as well as Vettori's commentary.
135. I refer to my own *Carlo Sigonio* chapter four, and further bibliography mentioned there. On the Biblioteca Vaticana, cf. Jeanne Bignami Odier, *La Bibliothèque Vaticane de Sixte IV à Pie XI* (1973, ad indicem for Sirleto). On the Congregation for the Index, F.H. Reusch, *Der Index der verbotenen Bücher* (1883), vol. 1, pp. 429–34.

136. Dupuy to Pinelli, 15 July 1574; MS G 77 inf., fol. 63r–v. N.B. that the folios of this letter have been deranged in the binding of the codex, and are to be read in the order 61–63–64–62. Dupuy was au courant because he had received letters from Muret himself, giving information which he now gives to Pinelli about the MSS of Zosimus and their availability. Cf. De Nolhac, "Lettres inédites de Muret," p. 390 (Muret to Dupuy, 2 November 1572). By December 1573 Dupuy had received from Muret copies of the notes Muret had been able to make before the MS was withdrawn, and had realized that he needed to consult the complete text of Zosimus; cf. ibid., p. 394 (Muret to Dupuy, 27 December 1573).

137. De Thou, *Commentariorum de vita sua libri*, book 1, anno 1574, p. 24. I have modernized the punctuation.

138. Pinelli to Dupuy, 15 October 1574; MS Dupuy 704, fol. 34r.

139. Dupuy to Pinelli, 17 January 1575; MS G 77 inf., fol. 72v.

140. Dupuy to Pinelli, 25 March 1575; MS G 77 inf., fol. 68r–v. Cf. Dupuy to Pinelli, 4 September 1575: "De Zosimo eò nunc laboro minus, quòd is propediem edetur in Germania. ie vous ai desia dit et vous le dis encores, que Monsieur Pithou ne l'a eu ni veu onques, et vous le pouvéz maintenir de ma part à Monsieur de Luieres; lequel l'a veu sans doute: s'il l'a ou non, ie n'en sçaurois que dire; ledit Pithou afferme que si." (MS G 77 inf., fol. 76v.) (And cf. Pinelli to Dupuy, 4 Feb. 1575; MS Dupuy 704, fol. 34a recto.)

141. De Thou, *Commentariorum de vita sua libri*, book 3, anno 1588, pp. 91–92. It will be evident that I have eschewed philological and codicological detail in recounting this story. Readers are referred to Mendelssohn's preface to his edition of Zosimus for notices concerning the Vatican codex of the Greek historian, the publication of material from Zosimus by Politian and Onofrio Panvinio, and related matters. Mendelssohn took account in this preface of two sources I cite: the Muret letters to Dupuy and the memoirs of De Thou. NB that De Thou claims that the MS owned by Leunclavius and then François Pithou had been brought to Europe directly from Constantinople by Leunclavius, a claim denied by Mendelssohn.

142. Dupuy to Pinelli, 26 March 1572; MS G 77 inf., fol. 23r. Dupuy goes on to point out that this and an earlier work by Turnebus had been published under the name of Léger Duchesne, of whom Dupuy's opinion, in contrast to his opinion of Turnebus, was very low: "mais les deux derniers sont mis en lumiere au nom de Leodegarius à Quercu, lequel y a tant seulement presté son nom, et par la lecture de moins d'une demi-page il est aisé de descouvrir que quelque autre y a mis la main que ledit Leodegarius, id est, homo ineptissimus et infantissimus. "The commentary of Ramus on the agrarian speeches had been published in 1552; the *Animadversiones* of Duchesne/Turnebus which Dupuy cites here had appeared in 1553.

143. Dupuy to Pinelli, 23 September 1577; MS G 77 inf., fol. 83v. A few years later Dupuy corrected in part the information he had earlier given to Pinelli about Bodin's book, but proved to be badly informed in another respect by declaring to Pinelli that Bodin would not translate the *République* into Latin: "Ne croiéz pas que Bodin s'amuse à traduire sa *Republique* en Latin. ie vous ai autresfois mandé que l'impression de Geneve in 8° avoit esté faite sur la premiere de Paris; mais ie m'abusois, car ils l'ont chastrée en plusieurs endroits, malo more; et l'auteur s'en est plaint en la derniere edition de ce livre. la Table de droit, de laquelle vous dites qu'il fait mention en sa *Methode de l'histoire*, est sortie en lumiere depuis un an en-ça; c'est fort peu de chose à mon iugement. il fait imprimer un gros livre des Sorciers, id est, de sorti-

legis et veneficis." Dupuy to Pinelli, 12 December 1579; MS T 167 sup., fol. 210 r.

BIBLIOGRAPHY

Manuscripts
Milan, Biblioteca Ambrosiana (=BAM):
　　MS G 77 inf.
　　MS T 167 sup.
Paris, Bibliothèque Nationale (=BNP):
　　MS Dupuy 704
(All three MSS are miscellanies of sixteenth-century letters.)
Printed works
Babelon, Jean-Pierre. *Paris au XVIe siècle (Nouvelle histoire de Paris)*. Paris: Association pour la publication d'une Histoire de Paris/Hachette, 1986.
Barnavi, Elie. *Le Parti de Dieu. Étude sociale et politique des chefs de la Ligue parisienne 1585–1594*. (Publications de la Sorbonne, n.s. Recherches 34). Louvain: Nauwelaerts. 1980.
Barnavi, Elie — Robert Descimon. *La Sainte Ligue, le juge, et la potence: L'assassinat du président Brisson (15 novembre 1591)*. Paris: Hachette, 1985.
Bignami Odier, Jeanne. *La Bibliothèque Vaticane de Sixte IV à Pie XI*. Città del Vaticano: Biblioteca Apostolica Vaticana, 1973.
Brives-Cazes, Emile. *Le Parlement de Bordeaux et la Chambre de Justice de Guyenne en 1582*. Bordeaux: Gounouilhou, 1866.
——— *La Chambre de Justice de Guyenne en 1583–84*. Bordeaux: Gounouilhou, 1874.
Calderini De Marchi, Rita. *Jacopo Corbinelli et les érudits Français d'après la correspondance inédite Corbinelli-Pinelli (1566–1587)*. Milan: Hoepli, 1914.
Castellani, C. "Lettera inedita di Gianvincenzo Pinelli a Pietro Dupuy," *Nuovo archivio veneto* anno 3, t. 5 (1983), pp. 487–93.
Catalogue de l'histoire de France t. 1. Paris: Bibliothèque Nationale, 1968 (ed. pr. 1855).
Chrisman, Miriam Usher. *Lay Culture, Learned Culture: Books and social change in Strasbourg, 1480–1599*. New Haven and London: Yale University Press, 1982.
Colliard, Lauro A. *Un dottore dell'Ateneo patavino alla Corte di Francia: Pierre d'Elbène (1550–1590)*. Verona: Libreria editrice universitaria, 1972.
De Caprariis, Vittorio. *Propaganda e pensiero politico in Francia durante le guerre di religione (1559–1572)*. Naples: Edizioni scientifiche italiane, 1959.
De Nolhac, Pierre. "Lettres inédites de Muret," in *Mélanges [Charles] Graux*. Paris: Thorin, 1884, pp. 381–403.
——— *La bibliothèque de Fulvio Orsini*. Paris: Boullon et Vieweg. 1887.
Descimon, Robert. *Qui étaient les Seize? Mythes et réalités de la Ligue parisienne (1585–1594)*. (Fédération des sociétés historiques et archéologiques de Paris et de l'Ile de France. Mémoires t. 34.) Paris: Klincksieck, 1983.
De Thou, Jacques-Auguste. *Historiarum sui temporis libri CXXXVIII* (7 vols.). London: Samuel Buckley, 1733.
Commentariorum de vita sua libri VI. (Cited from volume 7 of *Historiarum sui temporis libri*, ed. cit., with separate pagination.)
——— *Thuana*. (Cited from volume 7 of *Historiarum sui temporis libri*, ed. cit., with sepa-

rate pagination.)

Diefendorf, Barbara. *Paris City Councillors in the Sixteenth Century: The Politics of Patrimony*. Princeton: Princeton University Press, 1983.

Dionisotti, A.C. "Polybius and the Royal Professor," in *Tria Corda: Scritti in onore di Arnaldo Momigliano*, ed. E. Gabba, Como: Edizioni New Press, 1983, pp. 179–199.

Dorez, Léon — Suzanne Solente. *Catalogue de la Collection Dupuy* (4 vols.). Paris: Bibliothèque Nationale, 1899 (vols. 1–2, by L. Dorez); 1928 (vols. 3–4 = Table alphabetique, by S. Solente).

Doucet, R. *Les institutions de la France au XVIe siècle* (2 vols.). Paris: Picard 1948.

l'Estoile, Pierre de. *Journal de l'Estoile pour le règne de Henri III (1574–1589)*, ed. L.-R. Lefèvre. Paris: Gallimard, 1943.

——— *Journal de l'Estoile pour le règne de Henri IV (1589–1600)*. ed. L.-R. Lefèvre. Paris: Gallimard, 1948.

Evans, R.J.W. *The Wechel Presses: Humanism and Calvinism in Central Europe, 1572–1627*. Oxford: Past and Present Society, 1975.

Fragnito, Gigliola. *Memoria individuale e costruzione biografica*. Urbino: Argalìa Editore, 1978.

——— "Aspetti della censura ecclesiastica nell'Europa della Controriforma. L'edizione parigina delle opere di Gasparo Contarini," *Rivista di storia e letteratura religiosa* 21 (1985), pp. 3–48.

Grafton, Anthony. "Rhetoric, Philology, and Egyptomania in the 1570s: J.J. Scaliger's invective against M. Guilandinus's *Papyrus*," *Journal of the Warburg and Courtauld Institutes* 42 (1979), pp. 167–94.

——— *Joseph Scaliger. A study in the history of classical scholarship. Vol. 1: Textual criticism and exegesis*. Oxford: Clarendon Press, 1983.

Grendler, Marcella. "A Greek Collection in Padua: the library of Gian Vincenzo Pinelli (1535–1601)," *Renaissance Quarterly* 33 (1980), pp. 386–416.

——— "Book Collecting in Counter-Reformation Italy: the library of Gian Vincenzo Pinelli (1535–1601)," *Journal of Library History* 16 (1981), pp. 143–51.

Grendler, Paul. F. *The Roman Inquisition and the Venetian Press, 1540–1605*. Princeton: Princeton University Press, 1977.

——— "Printing and Censorship," in Charles B. Schmitt, et al., edd., *The Cambridge History of Renaissance Philosophy*. Cambridge: Cambridge University Press, 1988, pp. 25–53.

Grente, Georges, et al. *Dictionnaire des Lettres Françaises: Le seizième siècle*. Paris: Fayard, 1951.

Gualdus, Paulus. *Vita Ioannis Vincentii Pinelli patricii Genuensis*. Augsburg: Ad insigne Pinus [=Marcus Welser], 1607.

Hillairet, Jacques. *Dictionnaire historique des rues de Paris* (2 vols.). Paris: Éditions de Minuit, 1963.

Huppert, George. *The Idea of Perfect History*. Urbana: University of Illinois Press, 1970.

"Inventaire des manuscrits de Claude Dupuy (1595)," extrait de *Bibliothèque de l'École des Chartes* 76 (1915), pp. 1–8.

Jolly, Claude, ed. *Histoire des Bibliothèques Francaises: Les Bibliothèques sous l'Ancien Régime, 1530–1789*. Paris: Promodis: 1989.

Kelley, Donald R. *Foundations of Modern Historical Scholarship: Language, Law, and History in the French Renaissance*. N.Y. and London: Columbia University Press, 1970.

——— *François Hotman. A revolutionary's ordeal*. Princeton: Princeton University Press,

1973.

——— *The Beginning of Ideology. Consciousness and society in the French Reformation.* Cambridge: Cambridge University Press, 1981.

Kinser, Samuel. *The Works of Jacques-Auguste De Thou.* The Hague: Nijhoff, 1966.

Maclean, Ian. "André Wechel at Frankfurt, 1572–1581," *Gutenberg-Jahrbuch* 63 (1988), pp. 146–76.

Maugis, Édouard. *Histoire du Parlement de Paris de l'avènement des rois Valois à la mort d'Henri IV* (3 vols.). Paris: 1914 (vols. 1–2); 1916 (vol. 3). Reprinted New York: Burt Franklin, 1967.

McCuaig, William, "Carlo Sigonio storico e la censura," *Atti e memorie della Deputazione di storia patria per le provincie di Romagna* 35 (1984), pp. 163–93.

——— *Carlo Sigonio. The changing world of the late Renaissance.* Princeton: Princeton University Press, 1989.

Montaigne. *Oeuvres complètes,* ed. A. Thibaudet and M. Rat. Paris: Gallimard (Bibliothèque de la Pléiade), 1962.

Morin, François, sieur de Cromé. *Dialogue d'entre le Maheustre et le Manant.* Ed. Peter M. Ascoli, Droz: Geneva, 1977.

Pacatus Drepanius, Latinus. *Latini Pacati Drepanii Panegyricus cum notis integris Claudii Puteani et al.* Ed. Joannes Arntzenius. Amsterdam: heirs of S. Schouten, 1753.

XII Panegyrici Latini. Ed. R. A. B. Mynors. Oxford: Clarendon Press, 1964.

Rajna, Pio. "Jacopo Corbinelli e la strage di S. Bartolomeo," in *Archivio storico italiano* 21 (1898), pp. 54–103.

Raugei, Anna Maria. *Un abbozzo di grammatica francese del '500. Le note di Gian Vincenzo Pinelli.* Fasano di Puglia/Paris: Schena-Nizet, 1984.

——— "'Je me délecte à présent du jardinage...': Natura e artificio nel giardino di Claude Dupuy," in *La letteratura e i giardini.* Florence: Olschki, 1987, pp. 241–54.

Renouard, Philippe. *Documents sur les imprimeurs, libraires etc, ayant exercé à Paris de 1450 à 1600.* Paris: Champion, 1901.

——— *Répertoire des imprimeurs Parisiens (1470–1600).* Paris: Minard, 1965.

Reusch, Franz Heinrich. *Der Index der verbotenen Bücher.* Aalen: Scientia Verlag, 1967 (ed. pr. 1883).

Rivolta, Adolfo. *Catalogo dei codici pinelliani dell'Ambrosiana.* Milan: Tipografia pontificia arcivescovile S. Giuseppe, 1933.

Salmon, J.H.M. *Society in Crisis. France in the Sixteenth Century.* London: Ernest Benn, 1975.

Scaliger, Joseph. *Scaligeriana, sive excerpta ex ore Josephi Scaligeri per FF PP* (Fratres Puteani). Editio secunda. The Hague: Adrianus Vlacq, 1668.

Shennan, J.H. *The Parlement of Paris.* Ithaca: Cornell University Press, 1968.

Schnur, Roman. *Die französischen Juristen im konfessionellen Bürgerkrieg des 16. Jahrhunderts.* Berlin: Duncker and Humblot, 1962.

Solente, Suzanne. "Les manuscrits des Dupuy à la Bibliothèque Nationale," *Bibliothèque de l'École des Chartes* 88 (1927), pp. 177–250.

Soman, Alfred. *De Thou and the Index. Letters from Christophe Dupuy (1603–1607).* Geneva: Droz, 1972.

Tumulus = Claudii Puteani Tumulus. Paris: 1607.

Velleius Paterculus. *C. Cornelii Taciti et C. Vellei Paterculi scripta quae exstant.* Paris: P. Chevalier, 1608.

Zosimus. *Zosimi comitis et exadvocati fisci Historia nova.* Edidit Ludovicus Mendelssohn. Leipzig: Teubner, 1887 (repr. Hildesheim: Olms, 1963).

THE TOURNAMENT OF POWER: PUBLIC COMBAT AND SOCIAL INFERIORITY IN LATE MEDIEVAL ENGLAND

Victor I. Scherb

Arizona State University
Tempe, Arizona, U.S.A.

The Tournament of Power: Public Combat and Social Inferiority in Late Medieval England[1]

We have been accustomed to look at the jousts, combats, and tournaments of the Late Middle Ages as vestiges of a once vibrant and practical chivalry, a chivalry in which precise horsemanship and the skillful deployment of a sword or spear could truly affect the ways in which wars were fought. Increasingly, however, students of knighthood such as Malcolm Vale, Maurice Keen, and Juliet Barker have shown that it performed some very practical purposes indeed.[2] As late as 1492 Henry VII could call for a tournament at Sheen in order to hone his knights military prowess and precision before his French campaign.[3] Such evidence suggests that Caxton's famous call for yearly "justes of pees to th'ende that every knyght shold have hors and harneys and also the use and craft of a knyght" reflected real beliefs about the efficacy of public combats in perfecting knights in the art of war.[4]

Public combats like tournaments also served purposes beyond martial preparedness, however,[5] and these too have come under increasing scrutiny. Wickham long ago pointed to the theatrical nature of the late medieval tournament, performed by and for an audience of nobles, sometimes scripted, with elaborate costumes, sets, and viewed by throngs of the commons.[6] In light of the new interest in the political and social function of social spectacle it appears that the highly influential view of fifteenth-century chivalry as "in decline" is in some senses inadequate,[7] and, in Howell Chickering's words, that what has been "regarded as empty and elaborate fifteenth-century ceremonies could better be seen as a complicated system of cultural signs manipulated by a social class."[8] We can now perhaps perceive that tournaments stress "the way in which the social structure of a group is strengthened and perpetuated through the ritualistic or mythic symbolization of the underlying social values upon which it rests."[9] In Diane Bornstein's terms, rituals "of chivalry and courtesy served to identify the upper class as a separate group,"[10] and one manner in which they did this was through chivalric games. Cultural signs and practices such as games can simultaneously function both positively, as a banner of inclusion in a privileged class, and negatively, to degrade other members and exclude outsiders. Tournaments were thus among those "stories, ceremonies, insignia, formalities, and appurtenances" which Clifford Geertz has recognized as marking the centers of power and providing those centers with their "aura of being not merely important but in some odd fashion connected with the way the world is built."[11]

An examination of the tournament held in celebration of Prince Henry's creation as Duke of York in 1494, the literary "Tournament of Tottenham" of about 1450, a judicial combat between an approver and a tailor in 1456, and finally the famous tournaments held in honor of a Negress at the court of James IV in 1507 and 1508, reveals the manner in which the late medieval tournament played a pre-eminent and often very theatrical role in strengthening and perpetuating the power of the aristocracy. Attempts by socially inferior members of society to employ tournament symbolism and adopt chivalric practices paradoxically served, or were made to serve, the same purposes of reinforcing the innate skill, power, and glory of the noble classes, even as they created a theatrical space within which the marginal or socially inferior participants could operate. Public combats thus played a complex role in the late medieval symbolics of power; such combats manifested the centers of power, marked their limits, and provided a justification for the control of potentially subversive elements even while allowing these elements a forum.

A host of related social practices — the tournament, the joust, the judicial combat, the mock tournament, and the *pas d'armes* — had had a strongly theatrical character almost from their inception. This is particularly true of the tournament, for as early as the thirteenth century allegory and a sense of theater played an important part in *hastiludes à plaisance*.[12] Costumes were sometimes employed, as when in 1227 Ulrich von Liechtenstein had jousted as Lady Venus.[13] The participants occasionally enhanced the drama of the occasion by the impersonation of another knight or fighting incognito, the better to embellish a knight's reputation if he was victorious.[14] The costuming could some-times be satirically pointed; for example, the 1362 jousts planned for Cheapside were to have included participants in the roles of the seven deadly sins, "which the church had taught were all committed by tour-neying."[15] In later ages, the costuming would become remarkably elabo-rate, as in von Wedel's description of trains of servants capering before Queen Elizabeth, "disguised like savages, or like Irishmen, with the hair hanging down to the girdle like women, [while] others had horses equipped like elephants."[16]

But costuming and impersonation only hint at the theatricali-ty of the tournament. Jousting made necessary elaborate armor, distinct from the armor which a knight might wear to battle, fundamentally set-ting it off from the practice of war.[17] Such *hastiludes à plaisance* differed from the more dangerous and antagonistic *hastiludes à outrance,* which were fought in battle armor with unrebated weapons, with the partici-pants often coming from warring countries.[18] Even in the tournament's ludic form, accidents did occur, as participants settled old grudges or got swept up in the heat of the encounter.[19]

Despite its real dangers and occasional mishaps, the tourna-ment's ritual and pomp placed it outside of ordinary time, in the realm of ceremony and social spectacle; to quote one distinguished scholar of early Tudor pageantry, "with its allegorical cartels, theatrical settings, costumed knights, and imaginative scenarios, the tournament often resembled nothing so much as a disguising that ended in a battle instead of a dance."[20] Scaffolds for the audience surrounded the action, and the field was often further demarcated by being "barryd al abowt" in the manner of *The Castle of Perseverance.*[21] Outside of this walled-off space, ladies and commoners could marvel at the splendor, power, and majesty of the events occurring within, while the lords and knights engaged in the fight could impress upon those outside "the lesson of their inferiority."[22] According to Wickham, the most privileged specta-tors "were invariably given raised positions near the center of the action,"[23] which allowed the noble part of the audience to become themselves a part of the theatrical spectacle of the tournament. While the fighting was real, the violence of such chivalric games was carefully controlled and contained by a complex series of rules which marked them off from the ordinary practice of war, making noble tournaments, if not dramatic, at least a *ludus* which occurred in a theatrical space.[24]

But if the late medieval tourneying field was in some sense a noble theater, it was a theater of power rather than of exchange. By the

mid-fifteenth century the tournament proper had become an exclusively noble performance. Coats of arms, blazons, and devices all proclaimed the aristocratic heritage of the participants. At the 1445 tournament at Nancy held during the wedding celebrations of Queen
Margaret, René of Anjou required coats of arms and crests to be displayed, so that such signs of nobility, " 'forgotten through their ignorance' should be 'recognised and remembered by young and inexperi-
enced noblemen.'... All participants had to be nobles of four quarters
and their arms were proof of this."[25] In addition to the personal prowess
one might demonstrate at an individual joust, the social hierarchy of
the nobility was itself on display in the group combats, called tournoi or
mêlées. Only kings, dukes, counts or barons could bear both a banner
and a pennon; "bannerets bore a banner alone; nobles who were not
barons or bannerets bore only a pennon."[26] These various signs functioned as practical rallying points in disorganized mêlées,[27] but they also
served as visible emblems of the social structure of the aristocracy, even
among apparent chaos and disorder. Crests and coats of arms were
often prominently displayed, identifying the magnates and their private
armies, just as they did in civilian life; such emblems of aristocratic prestige served to stress both the lineage and evident power of the combatants.[28]

Social hierarchy was present in other ways as well.
Tournaments were tightly controlled in England by the King. For
example, the nobles petitioned Henry VII to enact the tournaments
that comprised part of the celebrations surrounding Prince Henry's
elevation to Duke of York in 1494. The nobles requested the tournament in highly formulaic language characteristic of tournament challenges, remembering "theym self [of] that auncyent custume of thys his
noble realme of Englond" where at royal feasts there had always been

> great a[nd] notable actis of armes, for the continuance of the wiche,
> and for the excersice of the same, and lest any oder schuld take that
> enterprinse beffore them, they besought the kyngis grace to licens
> and to permitte them at the said fest to hold and to kepe a justes
> roiall.[29]

A poem written in honor of the 1507 *Justes of the Moneths of
Maye and June* explains that "the chyef thynge / Was to shewe pleasure
to our souerayne the King,"[30] and we can perhaps discern a similar
motive at work in the 1494 tournament. Matters of precedence were

carefully looked to, and decided, first by the heralds and, if all else failed, by the king himself. The tournament in effect became a part of the King's largesse,[31] as did all the ceremonies surrounding Prince Henry's creation as duke. The king's control over them was absolute. The jousts were delayed a full five days because on the intended day "was kept thobitt of the full noble memor [of] the kyngis fader."[32] Prizes could be manipulated, so that although "the proclamacion wer generalle, "referring to 'Who soo ever justethe best,'" the prize — a ruby — was given to the court party.[33] The spectacle itself could be seen as a manifestation of royal power, the challengers having "their hors richely trapped of the kyngis coulours," as they paraded before the king's "house and stage," itself covered "with riche cloth of Aras blew, enramplished with fleurs de lis of gold, and with in fourthe hangid with riche clothe of Arras of oder ystorys, and ij clothes of astate."[34] Even the setting became a symbol of the king's abundant largesse, the tournament field at Westminister being specially prepared and furnished, according to the account, so that "it was the most tryhumphant place that ever I sayw."[35] Such symbolism allowed the tournament to express, in Roy Strong's words, "in festival form the role of the monarch both as liege lord of his knights and as the fount of those two supreme chivalrous qualities, honour and virtue."[36]

Tournaments like this one functioned as a ceremonial display of the legitimacy, wealth, and power of the tournament sponsors and participants. Lengthy lists of names and accompanying titles litter the account, as do descriptions of their costumes, horses, and skill: "There schuld you have syen the good riders; the well doyng horsses, whatt gambadys [leaps], the changelyng of bellis, the glisteryng of spangils and especialle... the lorde Bourgavenny had a small blake hors wiche in montyng soo high a bove grounde did merveilles, and soo oftyn tyme."[37] The jousts display skill, strength, and dexterity rather than mere violence; participants "accomplish" courses, give "good atteyntes," and make "ij speres well brokyn and oon under."[38] Such expert and gentle behavior on the field led naturally to the supper and dances which acted as further manifestations of the cultured wealth of the nobility.[39] To echo Stephen Orgel's words about the court masques of a later age, the social spectacle of tournaments acted as "celebrations of royal power and assertions of aristocratic community."[40]

But while tournaments remained the province of the noble classes, similar knightly sports and activities could cut across social lines, often in ways that served to emphasize rather than efface class distinctions. Running at the quintain and running at the ring were sports practiced by both nobles and commoners in order to increase equestrian skills,[41] while sports done in imitation of the aristocracy, like the water quintain, and tilting at the water butt, seem to have been confined to non-aristocrats.[42] At times commoners performed such sports for the entertainment of the nobility,[43] but in general the primary motives seem to have been their own entertainment, exercise, and the imitation of their social betters. Such sports allowed them to engage in the "symbolic acquisition" of the social practices of the nobility.[44] As Greenblatt argues, the acquisition of such practices comes only at a price, either in public humiliation or in other ways. Commoners performed holiday sports like these on foot or on workhorses, wearing poor clothes, using wooden boards instead of shields, and, course, they remained excluded from the practice of tourneying. Their holiday pastimes, while enjoyable and good exercise, also marked the limitations of their social role, and such was the price they willingly paid in their acquisition of genteel practice.

Support for such a reading of knightly and common practice can be found in literary and historical mock tournaments and judicial combats. There are a few examples of the mock joust or mock tournament in English literature, including Dunbar's early sixteenth-century the "Sowtar and the Tailoris War,"[45] but the mid-fifteenth century "Tournament of Tottenham" and the duel between Fisher and Whithorn in 1456 offer an intriguing comparison. The two documents, the first probably literary and the second certainly historical, are near contemporaries of one another, and both reveal in half-comic, half-frightening ways, the price paid by commoners in their acquisition of chivalric social practices.

Appearing in two mid-fifteenth-century manuscripts,[46] "The Tournament of Tottenham" has sometimes been thought to be an attack on tourneying itself, or against tournaments as portrayed in literature.[47] The poem may bear some relation to an actual dramatic performance, such as the one players offered at Exeter in 1433.[48] The most sensitive reading has been offered by Bonnie Hoffman, who argues that the poem is essentially "mock heroic, and the humor is dependent on the juxtaposition of two poetic and social worlds: the rustic or popular and the chivalric."[49] Mock heroic provokes laughter by treating comparatively low subjects in an elevated manner; in "The Tournament" the author's mock heroic manner also acts as a means of symbolically containing the poem's rustic participants. The poem relates the story of a group of peasant knights who fight for the hand of fair Tyb, the Reeve's daughter, and for the possession "Coppeld," her brood hen and dowry. Perkin, Tyb's father, proposes a tournament as an equitable solution to the assembled "bachelery" (l. 25), all of whom want to marry her. His solution comes, significantly, during "a schurtyng be þe hyway" (l. 11); that is, during a village festival, probably on a holiday. Such is in keeping with George Jones's analysis of German mock tournaments, which were associated with Shrovetide,[50] as well as with other holiday games characterized by an inversion of the social hierarchy.[51] The mock tournament of "Tottenham" thus enjoys much the same status as those other holiday pastimes practiced by Londoners and rural peasants alike, practices acquired from the nobility.

While the portrayal of the two lovers remains largely sympathetic, the "Tottenham" author inverts a good deal of tournament symbolism. The rustics use wicker and wooden boards as shields, bowls as helmets, flails as weapons, hats as crests, and mares and blind work horses as war horses. These accoutrements would of course have been all that was available to peasants, but also serve the more important purpose of blazoning their social class. According to Jones, "by keeping the peasants on workhorses and mares, the nobility could keep their hegemony, which they owed largely to the greater strength and mobility given them by their war horses."[52] The work tools which form the peasants' heraldry ridicules rural and village occupations, and the socially inappropriate imitation of noble practices. The peasants' coats of arms, a sieve and a rake, "Poudred with a brenand drake / And iii cantell of a cake" (ll. 106–07), serve much the same purposes as noble arms do, but these heraldic devices proclaim the lineage and heritage of their bearers as threshers, bakers, and plowmen, people more concerned with where their next "cake" is coming from than with the defense of the realm.

The anonymous Northern author describes the tournament itself in a manner appropriate to its participants. While it is a genuinely funny, even good-spirited poem, when read in relation to tournament accounts like the one described above, "Tottenham" reveals a darker undertone. Gone are the good attaints and skillful horsemanship of noble accounts. In their place are farting, split weapons, clattering shields, and shattered defenses:

þer were flayles al to-slatred
þer were scheldys al to-clatred

Bollys and dysches al to-schatred,
And many hedys brokyn. (ll. 159–62)

Repeatedly the author emphasizes the degrading violence of the tournament. Some "brayn-panes" (l. 165) and "sum... schulder-bonys" (l. 220) are broken, and the men are so weary from the fight that they creep from the field "As þey were croked crepyls" (l. 171). Rather than riding proudly out of the area, the participants have to be carried home by their wives, who come with torches,

To fech hom þer husbandes, þat were þam trouth-plyȝt;
And sum broȝt gret harwes,
Per husbandes hom for to fech;
Sum on dores and sum on hech,*   [gratings]
Sum on hyrdyllys and sum on crech,*   [lattices]
And sum on welebaraws. (ll. 203–07)

Gone are the pennons and banners which distinguish rank in the noble mêlée, replaced instead by maimed men carted home on doors, lattices, grates, and wheelbarrows by their womenfolk. The author portrays the rural tournament as a degrading reversal of actual tournament practice, a reversal which is perfectly in accord with the peasant status of the participants. While some medieval traditions idealize the peasant, even making him a Christ-like figure,[53] side-by-side with this we can find an equally strong tradition, found in such works as the York Psalter, the *Cursor Mundi*, and Caxton's *Game and Playe of Chesse*, which identified peasants with evil, even seeing them as the descendants of Cain, "the first labourere that euer was."[54] Bornstein has drawn our attention to how the author of *Knyghthode and Bataile*, a paraphrase of Vegetius' *De re militari* from the 1450s, "in discussing reasons for rejecting a man, he turns Vegetius' *ignavus* [idle or cowardly] into 'ignoble.'"[55] The rustics' farm implements, here sundered from their intended use and exploited as weapons, might well have recalled the similar sorts of weapons employed by the rebels of 1381 or by the peasant rebels in Jack Cade's 1450 uprising. Such a perception of the peasant class goes some way towards explaining the artistic strategy of the author as he turns the fanfares of actual tournaments into a "fauconfare / At þe rereward" of a peasant's gray mare (ll. 89–90). The immediately following vow of young Harry, another suitor for the hand of Tyb, that he "schal not lefe behende!" (l. 91), hardly seems accidental, but instead serves to lower Harry, and all the rural participants, to the level of the gray mare's fart. Here again, while there's no denying the comedy of the burlesque lowering, the object of ridicule is peasant pretension rather than actual tournament fanfares.

An examination of a judicial combat of 1456 may further help to clarify the direction of the satire. Gregory's *Chronicle* tells the story of Thomas Whithorn, an approver who saved his own life by accusing other men of crimes, and James Fisher, who responded to Whithorn's accusation by challenging him to a judicial combat,[56] saying that "he was fals in hys appelynge, and sayde that [he] wolde preve hyt with hys hondys, and spende hys lyfe and blode a-pone hys fals body."[57] Two lower class combatants thus must ask the nobility for permission to engage in the sort of activity usually limited to their betters. This is, of course, a judicial duel, not a tournament, but the two activities shared the same terminology,[58] and they came to be the exclusive province of the noble classes, often administered by the High Court of Chivalry.[59] Approvers' duels like this one were disreputable, for "the approver had already admitted his guilt and was fighting, not for his own right, but to save himself from being hanged;"[60] Fisher, by contrast, was fighting to prove his innocence.[61] The Whithorn-Fisher combat is particularly instructive, for the judge, "that nobylle man, Mayster Myhelle Skyllyng," who is "a notabylle man, and the moste petefullyste juge of al thys londe in syttyng a-pon lyffe and dethe,"[62] carefully stipulated the terms of the combat, providing us with a detailed account of the judicial spectacle which insists on the principle of symbolic acquisition.

On occasion, the terms of the combat recall those of the contemporary satiric poem. The judge detailed the costume Whithorn and Fisher must wear and the weapons with which they must fight. According to Gregory, the judge required both participants to be "clothyd alle in whyte schepys leter, bothe body, hedde, leggys, fete, face, handys, and alle," an emblem of the ignoble status of the participants. The peasants and tradesman of "Tottenham" thus "sowed þam im schepe-skynnes," in order that they "suld not brest" (l. 64) in the exertion of battle.[63] Fisher and Whithorn's weapons are outlandish and, if not quite flails, at least flail-like, for "they schulde have in hyr hondys ij stavys of grene hasche, the barke beynge a-pon, of iij fote in lenghthe, and at the ende a bat of the same govyn owte as longe as more gevythe any gretenys."[64] Their staves are unpolished, unadorned, and unshorn of bark, impractical in the actual fighting, breaking at the first blow, which suggests that they were more important as visualizations of the humiliated status of the combatants than as actual weapons.[65] Unlike thirteenth-century combats between approvers,[66] neither combatant is allowed a shield as would have been standard practice in noble combats. Furthermore, the stave has a bat attached to it, which suggests that they in some respects resembled those flails with which the heartsick young swains of "Tottenham" fought.

Although, according to Gregory, "hyt ys to schamfulle to reherse alle the condyscyons of thys foule conflycte," it is hard to imagine what he could be withholding. While noble tournaments would be performed at some specially prepared spot, the "foule batayle" between Fisher and Whithorn should be made "a-pone the moste sory and wrecchyd grene that myght be founde a-bowte the towne." And if the field of combat was wretched, it could hardly compare to the physical degradation that Fisher and Whithorn must suffer. They must have

> nothyr mete ne drynke,... bot both moste be fastynge. And yf hyr frowarde wepyn be i-broke they moste fyght with hyr hondys, fystys, naylys, tethe, fete, and leggys... and yf the nede any drynke, they moste take hyr owne pysse.[67]

This judicial combat again recalls "Tottenham" in its degrading insistence on violent physicality, a physicality which recalls some of Bakhtin's exploration of the carnivalesque elements in medieval culture, but without the revivifying, positive associations which he has traced.[68] "Tottenham"'s farting horses, feasting, and violence are refigured here in the degrading insistence on the participants drinking their own urine, as well as the unalleviated (and largely unregulated) violence of the encounter, placed in the appropriate scenic context of "the moste sory and wrecchyd grene that myght be founde a-bowte the towne."

The tournament regulations make clear that the acquisition of noble behavior does not come without a high price. The violence, and the public, largely symbolic proclamation of the participants' inferior status metaphorically circumscribe a limited and painful space within which Fisher and Whithorn are allowed to act. Only by the grace of the king are they allowed even these narrow roles, as this combat was also an opportunity for a display of royal power. If Fisher succeeded in slaying Whithorn, regardless of whether or not Whithorn admitted that he had appealed many men falsely, Fisher himself

> shalle be hangyde by-cause of man sleynge, by soo moche that he

hathe i-slayne the kyngys prover, for by hys meny the kynge hadde mony of such as were appelyd, and that mony þat rosse of hyr stuffe or goodys þat they hadde was put to þe kynge almys, and hys amener dystrybutyd hit unto the pore pepylle.[69]

The stipulations suggest that the "notabylle man" who acted as judge in the case saw the defendant's challenge as an uncharitable act taken in defiance of the king, for it reduced the money the king had available for alms. The account goes on to say that the king might pardon the defendant "by hys grace" if "the defendent be welle namyd and of competent governaunce in the toune or citte there at hys abydyng." Clemency could be hoped for, but not expected. The "vyle and unmanerly fyghtynge" in which Whithorn and Fisher engage puts them beyond the pale: "And by reson [of their fighting] they shulde not ben beryd in noo holy sepulture of Crystyn mannys beryng, but caste owte as a man þat wylfully sleythe hym selfe."[70] In effect, because the fighting is "unmanerly," and the battle is "foule," the judge places the combatants outside civil and even Christian society. Although the combat goes forward, Fisher triumphing over the "fals peler," pardoned by the king, and ending his life as a hermit, the duel can only occur in a symbolic space which makes clear the price the participants must pay in order to simulate the behavior of the socially powerful, a price which potentially entails their complete severance from the social world of fifteenth-century England.

All these cases should make clear that the late medieval tournament, like the royal entry, or the ceremony of knighthood, was a set of social practices and symbols which functioned to re-state, reaffirm, and reinforce the power of the nobility. Most tournaments did this straightforwardly, in their lavish ceremony, costuming, and display of chivalric skill. The prestige which knights could accrue at tournaments was not merely personal, for personal glory quickly became associated with the nobility of their lineage, the power of their social class, and of the honor and magnificence of their court and king. Mock tournaments served similar purposes, but through inverse means. The participants displayed — or were forced to display — skills thought appropriate to the lower classes, demonstrating in the process their worthiness to be ruled and their degraded natures. Where the tournament field becomes a splendid backdrop to the noble lineage, splendid trappings, feats of arms, and precise skill which emanates from the court, the field of "The Tournament of Tottenham," like the "sory and wrecchyd grene" of the judicial combat, serves as a scenic device which com-

plements the poor professions, inappropriate weapons, degrading violence, and chaotic inversions which are portrayed as the natural product of attempts by peasants to acquire and use the symbolic structures
of those in power.

Greenblatt's theoretical model accords less well with my final
example, however, for James IV's famous tournament of the savage
man and the black lady reveals a very different type of cultural negotiation. The tournaments took place in Edinburgh in June 1507, and
again in May 1508. Here, rather than an attempt by the lower class to
imitate courtly forms, we have the court itself employing one of its
socially marginal members in a manner which brings to the fore the
greater glory of the court. Rather than symbolic acquisition, the
Scottish court exploits the symbolic opportunity occasioned by the presence of a number of Negresses.

Called "the justing of the wild knycht for the blak lady," the
tournament was to be held in Edinburgh,[71] where the Wild Knight and
his two companions challenged, "pour l'amour des dames," all comers
to combat for the space of five weeks in the Field of Remembrance.[72] In
the frequent manner of late medieval tournaments, there was a tree of
honor, "in the keeping of the Black Lady, 'accompagnée de Sauvages,
trompettes, et tous instruments.'"[73] The event had European importance, for the 1507 tournament was proclaimed in places as far afield as
Denmark and France at least six months before it actually took place.

As one of Queen Margaret's ladies-in-waiting almost certainly
undertook the role of the tournament "Dame Noir,"[74] "socially
marginal" must be applied with caution. A court Negress would have
been as near the center of power in Scotland as it was possible for a
woman to be. Although the first African slaves did not arrive in
England until the 1550s,[75] court records detail a number of blacks at
the Scottish court acting either as ladies in waiting or (if male) as
clerks.[76] Such preferment, however, did not come without its price.
Negresses, perhaps including the lady of the tournament, tended to be
seen as commodities and were catalogued among the curiosities captured from a Portuguese ship in 1504, along with a musk cat and a
horse with a red tail.[77] According to Dunbar's poem, "Ane Blak Moir,"
the Black Lady of the tournament has "mekle lippis" (l. 5), jaws like an
ape, skin like a toad, a nose like a cat, and is as dark as sap. Unlike the
"laydes quytt" which Dunbar has usually written of, the Black Lady has
the brightness of a tar barrel (l. 12); her nativity was announced by an
eclipse; and the night would feign fight her battles for her. As chief

prize of the tournament, she will be won by he "Quhai for hir saek with speir and scheld" (l. 16), and he will have her love. Whoever,

Preiffis maest mychttelye in the feld
Sall kis and withe hir go in grippis,
And fra thyne furth hir luff sall weld[78]

The apparent reward of her kiss is undercut by the heavy sexual sugges-tion of the knight "going in grips" with her. Those who win only shame, on the other hand, will have the honor of coming "behind and kis[sing] her hippis" (l. 23). We sense an odd sort of ambivalence in the presentation of the mooress; she is exceptional, an oddity whose sojourn in the court enhances its uniqueness and proclaims its far-reaching power; but she is also a satiric butt, a convenient metaphor for ugliness, evil, and shame, associated with dishonor, infamy, and the bes-tial in man. Like Jonson's *Masque of Blackness* of a hundred years later, we have the ideal suggested through a presentation of its antithesis, and the Black Lady need only be seen for the antimasque — or what we might call the anti-tournament — to have taken place.[79]

    The tournament accounts proclaim the glory and lineage of the nobility, qualities which the Black Lady conspicuously lacks. As with most noble tournaments, the display of chivalric power played a large part, the nobility of Scotland taking every opportunity to manifest their prestige, arming themselves "in thair best arrey and in the same armur and waponis that thay thocht thame selffis best to fecht into."[80] James himself participated in the tournament and made lavish displays of hos-pitality to tournament competitors from other countries.[81] James was renowned for his skill at tournaments and received the degree for using "all kynd of turnament maist manlie and knichtlyk of ony that was thair at that tyme."[82] In a manner similar to the author of the tournament account of 1494, Pittscottie carefully enumerates the names and titles of the many nobles who performed notable feats of arms. The rewards were usually weapons, themselves emblematic of knightly accomplish-ment, fashioned in silver, gold, or "doubill ovir gilt," which should be the knights

in memorie for the kingis honour and thair glorie in tymes cuming that thair posteritie micht sie eftir quhat nummer [manner?] thai haue beine and how thay vsit thame sellffis to the kingis graice thair maisteris pleasour and to the adwancment of thair awin honour.[83]

As in Henry's tournament of thirteen or fourteen years before, the prestige of the event becomes a permanent part of the heritage of their noble lineages and more broadly of the nation at large.

The tournament exalts the Black Lady, but only as a curiosity, one who is both singled out and subsumed into the greater glory of the court. Although ostensibly in honor of her, the parodic form of the tournament only permits her to be fought for in the *persona* of the wild knight, which again emphasizes the court perception of her as sub-human, a fitting prize for a savage knight.[84] The tree of honor remains her domain for the duration of the tournament, but its branches demarcate a confining and humiliating space for the tournament lady, even as it also creates as a social space within which a gentle mockery of tournament conventions can take place. Such playfulness with the conventions of the noble tournament, even to the point of having James himself play the part of the wild knight, "quha gave battell to all thame that wald fecht for thair ladyis saik and speciallie of the knichtis and gentilmen of france ingland and denmark,"[85] acts as a further manifesto of the self-assurance, skill, and international prestige of James's court.

The ludic period of festive license and hierarchical inversion permitted by the tournament had a clearly limited scope. Like the *Justes of the Moneths of May and June*, the tournament devisers link the passage of the Queen of the tournament's reign to the passage of time. In the Scottish tournament the end of the festivities was signaled by an unusually grand banquet lasting, according to Pitscottie, from nine in the morning until nine in the evening three days running. Entertainments were provided between every course, the most notable one of which included the Black Lady herself:

> at the hennest [hindmost] bancat pheirs and play vpone the thrid
> day thair come ane clwdd out of the rwffe of the hall as appeirit to
> men and opnit and cleikkit vp the blak lady in presence of thame all
> that scho was no moir seine bot this was done be the art of
> Igramancie for the kingis pleasour.[86]

As in her temporary role as the lady of the tournament, the Black Lady is here allotted a carefully circumscribed space in the entertainment. She does not appear to have been one of those taking part in the banquet, but rather becomes an integral part of the most important of the many "farces" or plays which keep the revellers entertained. Although elevated to the status of the tournament lady, here the entertainment designers elevate her — in her fictional character — right out existence altogether. The account describes a parodic assumption play in which the Black Lady ascends in a cloud by means of a skilfully designed harness.[87] Unlike the participants in modern magic tricks, for her there is no return to earth. While the entertainment works as an extension of the mock element in the tournament, comically elevating a socially marginal figure, it also functions to demarcate the temporal and spatial limits of play: the tournament is over, and even before the revellers leave the banqueting house the lady of tournament will have returned to her previous role.

We can thus see how these Scottish tournaments both elevate and efface a socially marginal figure. The banquet acts as a paradigm for the Black Lady's function in the tournament as a whole. During the time of festive license permitted by the tournament she can briefly become a figure of apparent power and authority — but only within the fiction of the tournament, a fiction which displays the far-reaching wealth and power of the court. Our records do not tell us if the Black Lady, like Princess Mary in the contemporary *Justes of the Moneths of May and June,* held an hourglass with which to measure the amount of time the combatants might fight.[88] If she did so, she also held a provocative emblem of the brevity and fragility of her reign. Although, as lady of the tournament, she can exercise certain chivalric prerogatives — sitting in preferential seating, distributing her favors, overseeing the tree of honor — she remains the butt of coarse court humor, a curiosity, an abbess of misrule whose reign is precisely limited and whose ending coincides with her disappearance.

The foregoing analysis suggests many directions for future exploration. While Tudor and Jacobean pageantry and spectacle have long been fruitful avenues of exploration for scholars like Strong, Bergeron, and Orgel,[89] medieval and early Tudor social spectacle is only beginning to attract the attention it deserves.[90] Not only the productions of the great, but of also the weak, as exemplified in ridings, folk festivals, and holiday entertainments are equally worthy of our serious attention. The role of the audience in social spectacles also deserves further study. The dark undertone of the "Tournament" hardly eclipses the frequent sympathy the author displays for his young hero and heroine, nor is it difficult to imagine a rural audience laughing uproariously at the comic pretensions of their fellows. Even more strikingly, William Gregory's account of the Approver's duel displays some real compassion for the plight of poor Fisher, who seizes the theatrical

moment when he enters the field of combat and kneels down towards
the East and cries "God marcy and alle the world, and prayde every
man of forgevenys, and every man there beyng present prayde for
hym."[91] Gregory plainly sees the judgment of God in the outcome, for
when Whithorn cast Fisher, that "meke innocent,"

> downe to the grownde and bote hym by the membrys,... the sely
> innocent cryde owt. And by happe more thenne strengythe that inno-
> cent recoveryd up on hys kneys and toke that fals peler by the nose
> with hys tethe and put hys thombe in [Whithorn's] yee, that the
> peler cryde owte and prayde hym of marcy, for he was fals unto God
> and unto hym.[92]

Such a swell of public feeling, and such a hearty detestation of the
king's approver, may well have helped to make the combat between
Whithorn and Fisher the last approver's duel for which a detailed
record survives.[93] Thus even within the circumscribed and painful theatrical space allowed to Fisher by social authorities, he is still able to
move the sympathies of his audience. This suggests that while generally
reinforcing the position of the aristocracy, the audience's response to
theatrical social spectacles like these remained complex, uncertain, and
at least potentially subversive.

　　　Both the English and Scottish accounts independently reveal
the manner in which the late medieval aristocracy conceived of the
world of the public combat as an exclusive theater of honor. The field
of combat acted as both playground and stage for the lineages, prowess,
and skill of the nobility. As a *ludic* and theatrical space, the tournament
field was infinitely manipulable; there disguises could be assumed and
socially marginal figures could be briefly and ambivalently elevated to
some of the prerogatives of the nobility. Public combats and mock tournaments can thus be seen to articulate the manner in which the late
medieval nobility's belief structure defined its self-image and sense of
purpose, differentiating it both from its own society and the world at
large. The performance and recording of such social spectacles generally affirmed the aristocracy's perception of itself and its place in the
divine scheme of things even as they allowed the lower classes to exploit
the limited opportunities for self-definition offered to them. The
recorded accounts became, in their own way, the equivalent of heraldic
emblems or tournament prizes, commemorative historical texts of an
individual or a group's skill and honour. Both the visual text of the

event itself and its written account thus came to bear a social meaning which the modern critic needs to encounter, for such encounters explore the connections between culture, literature, and history that can help us in our listening for the text of the past.

Notes

1   My thanks are due to Gordon Kipling and Nancy Gutierrez for their help and criticism and to Jeanie Brink for her patience and encouragement.

2   Maurice Keen, *Chivalry* (New Haven, 1984); Malcolm Vale, *War and Chivalry* (Athens, GA; 1981); Juliet R. V. Barker, *The Tournament in England 1100–1400* (Woodbridge, Suffolk; 1984).

3   Malcolm Vale, *War and Chivalry*, p. 63.

4   "Epilogue" to the *Order of Chivalry, Selections from William Caxton*, ed. N. F. Blake (Oxford, 1973), p. 112.

5   On the function of tournaments in Edward III's court, *v* Juliet Vale, *Edward III and Chivalry: Chivalric Society and Its Context 1270–1350* (Woodbridge, Suffolk; 1982); for a brief account of Richard II's Smithfield tournament of 1390, *v* James L. Gillespie, "Richard II's Knights: Chivalry and Patronage," *Journal of Medieval History* 13 (1987), 143–60, esp. pp. 150–52.

6   On the relations between the tournament and drama, *v* Glynne Wickham, *Early English Stages 1300 to 1600*, 3 vols, (New York, 1959–81), I: 13–50.

7   This view was of course most influentially expressed by Huizinga in his *The Waning of the Middle Ages* (New York, 1954), esp. pp. 84–107; for England, *v* Arthur B. Ferguson, *The Indian Summer of English Chivalry* (Durham, N.C., 1960); a somewhat modified view can be found in *The Chivalric Tradition in Renaissance England* (Washington D.C.; 1986), p. 17. Here, Ferguson finds that the fifteenth century was the last time that the medieval tradition was basically intact. For England and France, *v* Sydney Anglo, "Le Declin du Spectacle Chevaleresque," *Arts Du Spectacle Historie des Idées: Recueil Offert en Hommage à Jean Jacquot* (Tours: Centre d'Etudes Supérieurs de la Renaissance, 1984), 21–37.

8   Howell Chickering, "Introduction" *The Study of Chivalry*, eds. Howell Chickering and Thomas H. Seiler (Kalamazoo; 1988), p. 4.

9   Clifford Geertz, *The Interpretation of Cultures* (New York, 1973), p. 142.

10   Diane Bornstein, *Mirrors of Courtesy* (Hamden, Conn., 1975), p.17.

11   Clifford Geertz, *Local Knowledge* (New York, 1983), p. 124.

12   Barker, *The Tournament*, 84; an older, but still valuable, study of the English tournament, is Francis Henry Cripps-Day, *The History of the Tournament in England and France* (London, 1918; repr. New York: AMS Press), and a good recent introduction to Tudor tournaments can be found in Alan Young, *Tudor and Jacobean Tournaments* (London, 1987).

13   Barker, *The Tournament*, p. 95.

14   Ibid., p. 86.

15   Ibid., p. 95; a good survey of the theatrical nature of noble tournaments can be found in Sydney Anglo, *The Great Tournament Roll of Westminster*, 2 vols (Oxford, 1968), I: 19–40.

16   Roy Strong, *The Cult of Elizabeth* (Berkeley, 1977), pp. 134–45.

17 Anthony Wagner, *Heralds of England: A History of the Office and College of Arms* (London, 1967), p. 2, points out that the introduction of plate armour in the thirteenth century, had the practical effect of making "knights fewer (because they must be richer) and the tournament safer."

18 *V* Richard Barber and Juliet Barker, *Tournaments: Jousts, Chivalry and Pageants in the Middle Ages* (Woodbridge, Suffolk, 1989), pp. 125–32, for description of tournaments held *à outrance* in the fifteenth century.

19 *V* Barber and Barker, *Tournaments*, pp. 139–49.

20 Gordon Kipling, "The Queen of May's Joust at Kennington and the *Justes of the Moneths of May and June.*" Notes and Queries, n.s. 31 (1984), p. 158.

21 *The Castle of Perseverance* in *The Macro Plays*, ed. Mark Eccles, Early English Text Society o.s. 262 (London, 1969), p. 1. On connections between the *Castle* and the late medieval tournament, *v* Steven Pederson, *The Tournament Tradition and the Staging of the Castle of Perseverance*. Theater and Dramatic Studies 38 (Ann Arbor, Michigan: UMI Research Press, 1986).

22 V. G. Kiernan, *The Duel in European History: Honour and the Reign of Aristocracy* (Oxford, 1988), p. 39.

23 *V* Wickham, *Early English Stages* I: 35.

24 On the relations between the tournament and drama *v* Wickham, *Early English Stages*, I: 13–50.

25 Vale, *War and Chivalry*, p. 96; Wagner, *Heralds of England*, p. 36, prints a 1417 letter from Henry V which commands that "no man, of whatever station... should take to himself arms or tunics of arms, unless he should possess the same by ancestral right or by grant of some person having authority sufficient thereunto."

26 Vale, *War and Chivalry*, p. 84.

27 Wagner, *Heralds of England*, p. 25, argues that the primary purpose of armorial bearings came out in war "and in the mimic warfare of the tournament, where their purpose was to render the knights and commanders recognizable to their followers and to one another."

28 Bornstein, *Mirrors of Courtesy*, p. 31.

29 *Letters and Papers Illustrative of the Reigns of Richard III and Henry VII*, ed. J. Gairdner. Rolls Series 24 (London, 1861), I: 388.

30 *The Justes of the Moneths of May and June* in *Remains of Early Popular Poetry of England*, ed. W. C. Hazlitt, 2 vols. (London, 1862), II: 109–30, ll. 236–37.

31 *Letters and Papers*, p. 393.

32 *Letters and Papers*, p. 396.

33 *Letters and Papers*, p. 395.

34 *Letters and Papers*, p. 394.

35 *Letters and Papers*, p. 394.

36 Roy Strong, *Art and Power: Renaissance Festivals 1450–1650* (Woodbridge, Suffolk, 1984), p. 11; for an interesting study of how Tudor monarchs managed to centralize the concept of honor around the figure of the king or queen, *v* Mervyn James, "English Politics and the Concept of Honour, 1485–1642," in *Society, Politics and Culture* (Cambridge, 1986), pp. 308–415.

37 *Letters and Papers*, p. 394.

38 *Letters and Papers*, p. 395.

39 *Letters and Papers*, p. 395.

40 Stephen Orgel, *The Illusion of Power: Political Theater in the English Renaissance* (Berkeley, 1975), p. 7.

41   There were practical reasons for this, as Richard Barber and Juliet Barker (*Tournaments*, p. 6) observe: "The manipulation of a powerful, thoroughbred horse and a heavy lance, complicated by the restricted movement and vision imposed by armour, was a skill acquired only with patient practice at such devices as the quintain and the ring."

42   Joseph Strutt, *The Sports and Pastimes of the People of England,* enlarged and corrected by J. Charles Cox (London: Methuen & Co., 1903), pp. 105–15. "tilting at a water butt" apparently consisted of tilting at a tub full of water, which is struck in such a manner so as not to drench the participants. N.B., p. 109: "the rules of chivalry, at this time, would not admit of any person, under the rank of an esquire, to enter the lists as a combatant at the jousts and tournaments; for which reason the burgesses and yeomen had recourse to the exercise of the quintain, which was not prohibited to any class of the people; but, as the performers were generally young men whose finances would not at all times admit of much expense, the quintain was frequently nothing better than a stake fixed into the ground, with a flat piece of board made fast to the upper part of it, as a substitute for the shield that had been used in times remote; and such as could not procure horses, contented themselves with running at this mark on foot." On popular imitations of noble practices, also *v* Wickham, *Early English Stages,* I: 38–41.

43   Strutt, *Sports,* p. 110, notes the entertainment at Kenilworth for Queen Elizabeth in 1575, where running at the quintain was part of the entertainments.

44   Stephen Greenblatt, *Shakespearean Negotiations* (Berkeley, 1988), p. 10. Symbolic acquisition involves the transference of a mode of social energy by means of a representation for which "no cash payment is made, but the object acquired is not in the realm of things indifferent, and something is implicitly or explicitly given in return for it." The type of symbolic acquisition we are dealing with here would seem to be what Greenblatt terms "acquisition through simulation" in which that "actor simulates what is already understood to be a theatrical representation." The tournament, like the royal pardons which Greenblatt describes, were plainly understood (in some sense) to be theatrical.

45   George Fenwick Jones, "'Christis Kirk,' 'Peblis to the Play,' and the German Peasant Brawl," *PMLA* 68 (1953), 1101–25, points to additional analogues.

46.   MS Cambridge University Library Ff. 5.48 and MS Harley 5396; Bonnie Hoffman, "The 'Turnament of Totenham' and the 'Feest': A Critical Edition." *DAI* 24/08A (1984), p. 2520, also points to two derivative manuscripts, based on the Cambridge text. In the Cambridge MS, it appears with a poem called "Feest," a parody of a medieval marriage feast.

47   George F. Jones, "The Tournaments of Tottenham and Lappenhausen," *PMLA* 66 (1951), 1123–40, speculates on the direction of the satire and provides descriptions of some fascinating German analogues, but draws no definite conclusions. Robert L. Kindrick, "The 'Unknightly Knight': Teaching Satires on Chivalry," in *The Study of Chivalry,* eds. Howell Chickering, and Thomas H. Seiler (Kalamazoo, 1988), 671–72, sees the object of satire as chivalric practice, not the peasants themselves.

48   *V Devon,* ed. John M. Wasson, Records of Early English Drama (Toronto: University of Toronto Press, 1986), pp. 93, 369, 443. Another example of carnivalesque ceremony can be found in the Coventry hock-Tuesday play. *V Coventry,* ed. R. W. Ingram, Records of Early English Drama (Toronto, 1981), pp. 272–75; W. G. Cooke "The Tournament of Tottenham: Provenance, Text, and Lexicography," *English Studies* 69 (1988), pp. 113–16, feels that the poem could have been written by a London scribe

with an East Anglian background, but he doesn't rule out the possibility of a Northern provenance either.

49   Bonnie Hoffman, "The 'Turnament of Totenham' and the 'Feest': A Critical Edition." Unpub. Ph.D. thesis, State University of New York at Stony Brook, 1984, p. 66.

50   Jones, "Tottenham and Lappenhausen," p. 1128.

51   V, e.g., Charles Read Baskerville, "Dramatic Aspects of Medieval Folk Festivals in England," *Studies in Philology* 17 (1920): 19–87; Robert Weimann, *Shakespeare and the Popular Tradition in the Theater*, ed. Robert Schwartz (Baltimore, 1978), pp. 15–48.

52   Jones, "Tottenham and Lappenhausen," p. 1135.

53   The plowman in Chaucer's *General Prologue* and the title figure of Langland's *Piers Plowman* are obvious examples.

54   *The Game and Playe of Chesse* (Caxton, 1476), [26]. V also Henrik Specht, *Poetry and the Iconography of the Peasant*, Anglica et Americana 19 (Copenhagen, 1983), p. 45 on the York psalter, and pp. 46–47 on the *Cursor;* James, "English Politics," p. 310, has drawn our attention to how Caxton's translation of a French version of Raymond Lull's *The Book of the Ordre of Chyvalry*, "actually tightened his author's references to lineage as the essence of knighthood, excluding the latter's occasional brief references to meritocratic criteria as also relevant to chivalric status."

55   Bornstein, *Mirrors of Courtesy*, p. 31.

56   Kiernan, *The Duel*, p. 35, points to another duel in 1453 between an Irishman and an Englishman mentioned in John Benet's *Chronicle*. This was a duel for the accusation of treason, however, fought at Smithfield, and none of the deliberately humiliating measures mentioned by Gregory figure in this duel; a good recent summary of the Fisher/Whithorn duel can be found in John Bellamy, *Crime and Public Order in England in the Later Middle Ages* (Toronto, 1973), p. 132.

57   "Gregory's Chronicle" in *The Historical Collections of A Citizen of London*, ed. James Gairdner, Camden Society n.s. 17 (1876; New York: Johnson Reprint Co., 1965), 199. On approver's duels in general v F. C. Hamil, "The King's Approvers," *Speculum*, 11 (1936), 238–58.

58   Vale, *War and Chivalry*, p. 76.

59   G. D. Squibb, *The High Court of Chivalry* (Oxford, 1959).

60   M. T. Clanchy, "Introduction," to "Highway Robbery and Trial by Battle in the Hamphsire Eyre of 1249," in *Medieval Legal Records*, ed. R. F. Hunnisett and J. B. Post (London, 1978), p. 29.

61   The trial by combat was a type of bilateral ordeal which pitted the opponents against one another. On the status of the ordeal in English legal history, v Paul R. Hymans, "Trial by Ordeal: The Key to Proof in the Early Common Law," in *On the Laws and Customs of England: Essays in Honor of Samuel E. Thorne*, eds. Morris S. Arnold et al, (Chapel Hill, 1984), 90–126.

62   *Gregory's Chronicle*, pp. 200, 199.

63   George Neilson, *Trial by Combat* (Glasgow, 1890), pp. 148–49. This status also seems to be brought out by a crook of horn attached to the staffs of those involved in approvers duels.

64   *Gregory's Chronicle*, p. 200.

65   The crook of horn, described as "i-made lyke unto a rammys horne," may well echo contemporary satiric poetry, such as Lydgate's "Ryght as a Rammes Horne," in *The*

Minor Poems of John Lydgate, Part II, ed. Henry Noble MacCracken, Early English Text Society o.s. 192 (London, 1934 [for 1933]).

66   Clanchy, "Introduction," p. 33.

67   "Gregory's Chronicle," p. 200.

68   Mikhail Bakhtin, *Rabelais and His World,* trans. Hélène Iswolsky (Bloomington, 1984), 1–58.

69   "Gregory's Chronicle," pp. 200–201.

70   "Gregory's Chronicle," p. 201.

71   J. W. Baxter, *William Dunbar: A Biographical Study* (Edinburgh, 1952), p. 165.

72   Baxter, *William Dunbar,* p. 165.

73   Such trees of honour were commonplaces of late medieval tournaments.

74   A. J. G. MacKay, *William Dunbar: 1460–1520* (Edinburgh, 1889), p. cii; and also *v* Baxter, William Dunbar, p. 166.

75   James Walvin, *Black and White: The Negro and English Society: 1555–1945* (London, 1973); also *v* Edward Scobie, Black Britannia: *A History of Blacks in Britain* (Chicago: Johnson Publishing Co., 1972), who briefly mentions James' tournament on p. 8.

76   On blacks in Tudor England, *v* Joseph R. Washington, Jr., *Anti-Blackness in English Religion 1500–1800, Texts and Studies in Religion 19* (New York, 1984), 1–139; Eldred D. Jones, *The Elizabethan Image of Africa* (Washington D.C.: Folger Shakespeare Library, 1971).

77   Patrick Fraser Tytler, *Lives of Scottish Worthies,* 3 vols (London, 1833), III: 331.

78   V "Ane Blak Moir," in *The Poems of William Dunbar,* ed. James Kinsley (Oxford, 1979), p. 106, 11. 16–19.

79   On the *Masque of Blackness, v* Stephen Orgel, *The Jonsonian Masque* (New York, 1965), p. 120.

80   Robert Lindesay of Pitscottie, *The Historie and Cronicles of Scotland,* ed. A. J. G. MacKay, Scottish Text Society 42 (London, 1899), I: 242; for a brief account of knightly activity in late medieval Scotland, *v* Felicity Riddy, "The Revival of Chivalry in Late Medieval Scotland," in *Actes Du 2e Colloque de Langue et de Literature Écossaises* (Moyen Age et Renaissance, ed. Jean-Jacques Blanchot and Claude Graf (Strasbourg, 1978), pp. 55–62.

81   Tytler, *Lives,* 3: 332–33. Francisque-Michel, *Les Écossais en France,* 2 vols, (London, 1862), I: 335–36.

82. Pitscottie, *Historie,* I: 243.

83. Ibid, I: 243.

84   According to Richard Bernheimer, *Wild Men in the Middle Ages* (New York, 1952), p. 20, in the Middle Ages "wildness" implied "everything that eluded Christian norms and the established framework of Christian society, referring to what was uncanny, raw, unpredictable, foreign, uncultured, and uncultivated."

85   Pitscottie, *Historie,* I: 243.

86. Ibid, I: 244.

87   MacKay, p. 167; *v* the *Accounts of the Lord High Treasurer of Scotland,* ed. James Balfour Paul, 6 vols. (Edinburgh, 1902), IV: 129, for the 27 June record of a payment "for bukkilling and grathing of Martin and the blak lady agane the bancat."

88   "Justes," 11. 51–54.

89   Strong, *Art and Power, The Cult of Elizabeth;* David M. Bergeron, *English Civic Pageantry 1558–1642* (Columbia, S.C., 1972; Orgel, *Jonsonian Masque; The Illusion of Power.*

90   v Gordon L. Kipling, *The Triumph of Honor* (Leiden: E.J. Brill, 1977); Sydney Anglo, *Spectacle, Pageantry, and Early Tudor Policy* (Oxford, 1969).

91   "Gregory's Chronicle," p. 202.

92.   Ibid., p. 202.

93   Neilson, *Trial By Combat*, 154; Hamil, "The King's Approvers," p. 257, points to one case in 1470, but it was decided by jury rather than battle.

HUNGER, FLEMISH PARTICIPATION AND THE FLIGHT OF PHILIP VI: CONTEMPORARY ACCOUNTS OF THE SIEGE OF CALAIS, 1346–47

Kelly R. DeVries
Wilfrid Laurier University,
Waterloo, Canada

Hunger, Flemish Participation And The Flight Of Philip VI: Contemporary Accounts of The Siege Of Calais, 1346–47*

Edward III's military strategy in the early stage of the Hundred Years War was simple. He immediately followed a major battlefield victory with the siege of an important French town. In 1340, after defeating the French navy at the battle of Sluys, Edward attempted, although he failed, to take the town of Tournai. And in 1346, following his victory at the battle of Crécy, he repeated this strategy by besieging the port town of Calais. The siege lasted almost a year, but, unlike Tournai, Edward succeeded in gaining this town's surrender. Calais would remain English for nearly two hundred years.

Because Calais remained under English control for so long, enduring sieges and diplomatic treaties, and even outlasting the Hundred Years War itself, modern historians have written much on it. We know of its role in the English and French political, economic, diplomatic, and military history of the fourteenth, fifteenth, and six-teenth centuries. We even know of its defenses, spies, provisioning, and victualling.[1] What is lost among this mass of modern historical commen-

* An earlier version of this article appeared as a chapter of my Ph.D. thesis, *Perceptions of Victory and Defeat in the Southern Low Countries during the Early Fourteenth Century* (University of Toronto, 1987). For assistance in writing this article I wish especially to thank my advisors, Professors Bert S. Hall and Michael R. Powicke. Others who aided me in this endeavor, and to whom I also must pay gratitude, were Professors Joseph Goering, John Munro and John Gilchrist. It should be noted that unless otherwise indicated all translations of texts are the author's.

tary, however, are the reactions of witnesses to the events occuring in and around the city during the English occupation. Principal among these are the reactions of contemporary writers to the initial siege and fall of Calais.

All contemporary or near-contemporary chroniclers and annalists agree that the fall of Calais was a major victory for the English and a major defeat for the French. But this may be the only thing that is universally agreed upon by these early writers. Conflicting stories fill their narratives. Even the details of the siege itself differ as do the reasons given for the outcome. Moreover, most of these differences appear to have a geographical basis. Indeed, a fledgling nationalism can be detected in the writings of these chroniclers. English, French, and southern Low Countries authors each emphasize different details concerning the siege, and each of these emphases serve to support the role played by their countrymen at Calais in 1346–47. For the English this meant attempting to discover who or what they should credit for their victory, for the French, where blame should be placed for the defeat. And, for the authors of the southern Low Countries, there is an attempt to define the role of the Flemings at the siege.

It is the purpose of this article to analyze the contemporary accounts of the siege of Calais in 1346–47. Particular attention will be paid to the chroniclers' discussions of the effects of hunger, Flemish participation and the flight of Philip VI on the siege, as it is through the study of these issues that the nationalistic biases may be most easily seen. By comparing these themes the geographical differences among contemporary commentators become apparent. Also analyzed, for comparative purposes, are modern historical accounts of the siege as well as contemporary "foreign" narratives.

Modern Historical Accounts of the Siege

The Treaty of Espléchin, accepted by Edward III after his retreat from the siege of Tournai, after having been extended several times, expired in March 1345. Edward, who under the terms of the treaty had not attacked the French, immediately planned to lead an assault on their kingdom. In 1346 this assault was made, and Edward chose a route through Normandy to attack the French king.[2] The result was the famous English victory obtained on the battlefield of Crécy on August 26, 1346.[3] Dead on the field were many French nobles including Louis of Nevers, the count of Flanders. Philip VI himself narrowly escaped death in the battle, retreating with the remnants of a large French force to the safety of Paris.

Edward remained only a few days at Crécy celebrating his great victory. Wishing to take advantage of the French retreat, the English king immediately planned to besiege an important French town near the battlefield. His choice after Crécy was the Boulognese seaport, Calais. Strategically, Calais was the perfect target; it was an important seaport and close to his Flemish allies. As well, by conquering this northern port, Edward could effectively eliminate the refuge of Norman and Picard pirates who frequently robbed the English and Flemish merchant vessels which passed through the Channel.[4]

From Crécy, the English army moved quickly to Calais, burning and destroying all the towns between the battlefield and the northern French port.[5] Once the army reached Calais, Edward destroyed the suburbs surrounding the city and then moved to construct his own siegeworks.[6] These works included a rather elaborate city known as Ville-à-Neuve complete with a market place and towers built around the harbor.[7] Calais was completely cut off from any land commerce, and on the sea only the most fearless supply ships dared run the English blockade without being destroyed.[8]

From the beginning of the siege, Edward determined that the only method of subduing Calais was by starvation.[9] Marshlands and sand dunes surrounding the city gave no foundation to the conventional siege engines and early gunpowder artillery that had accompanied other English siege attempts of this period.[10] As well, Edward could sustain a siege of long duration. There was little prospect of a French relieving army arriving after the loss at Crécy, and supplies could easily be obtained from either Flanders or England.[11] Notwithstanding Edward's determination to obtain the town by starvation, his troops were active at Calais; frequent *chevauchées* were made by the English and Flemish armies into Boulogne, Artois, Normandy, and Hainault.[12]

Philip VI was also not inactive in the face of the English besiegers at Calais. Before the end of 1346, the French king tried to gather another army to raise the siege, attempting unsuccessfully to amass his forces at Compiégne on October 1.[13] When this failed he tried, again unsuccessfully, to make peace with the English king.[14] Other French efforts met with the same limited success. Philip was able to get some food into the besieged town, but the amount of victuals was far too small to support the town's population.[15] At the same time, he was able to encourage the Scottish king, David Bruce, to attack England hoping that this would drive Edward III away from the continent. Edward, however, stayed at Calais, entrusting his insular army to the command of military leaders in England, including the queen, and the Scottish incursion met with defeat at the battle of Neville's Cross.[16]

At the end of the winter, early in 1347, Edward was in a strong position outside of the beleaguered French city.[17] The city suffered severe hunger, and the leaders inside had twice tried to lessen some of their suffering by expelling a number of poorer citizens from the town.[18] The Scottish attack on England was not successful. Philip's diplomatic efforts had come to nought. And the papal peacemaking attempts which were ongoing had also failed to gain a peaceful solution to the siege. Edward seemed to have the upper hand in every situation. Only his attempts to marry his daughter, Isabel, to the sixteen-year-old Flemish count, Louis of Male, had been unsuccessful.[19] Even this failure had but limited effect on the English king as the Flemings, embarrassed by their count's actions, afterwards rallied to their ally in larger numbers than before.[20]

In 1347, Philip again tried to raise the siege of Calais. During April and May of that year, the French king successfully gathered the money and the men to confront his English enemy. The French army gathered initially at Amiens and then proceeded north through Arras to Sangatte, arriving within sight of the town walls in July.[21] His army was very large, larger even than the English force, that numbered more than 30,000 men.[22] Despite the size of his force, Philip could see the futility of an assault on the newly strengthened English defences, and his army in many small attacks only gained one insignificant tower.[23] Other attempts at gaining Edward's removal — challenging the English force to battle, offering to duel with Edward alone, and the promise of Guyenne for Calais — failed to move the English.[24] Philip was left with few options. In the first few days of August, the French army retreated to Paris leaving Calais to the English; the town surrendered on August 4, 1347.[25] Edward was merciful to the inhabitants of Calais, accepting surrender without executing anyone. However, all French citizens of the town were exiled, replaced by English merchants and soldiers.[26]

Certainly the taking of Calais was one of the outstanding English victories of the Hundred Years War. Charles de la Roncière likens this siege to the Roman siege of Alesia, claiming that the English tenacity imitated the earlier Roman discipline in order to defeat a very brave French force within the town.[27] And Henri Denifle calls it "the greatest of victories" adding that:

Edward had calculated very well. No other town offered a better point of support for his expeditions against France nor a better depot for his commerce with Flanders. The loss of Calais was for this reason the most sensitive of all those which the French underwent during this period.[28]

But, Denifle is only repeating the feelings of the English during the fourteenth century. Thomas Walsingham, for example, writes that with the victories at Crécy and Calais, "it seemed that a new sun had arisen for the English because of the abundance of peace, the plentitude of goods and the glory of the victory."[29]

Edward's attempts to repopulate the city and to protect it from further French attack show that he wished to hold on to this town for a very long time. That it was held by England for as long as it was is testimony to this king's vision. Calais was to stand as a symbol of English national pride for over two hundred years, holding its own against many sieges and assaults during and after the Hundred Years War. It would finally fall during the reign of Mary Tudor.

Above all, England now had its own "pied-à-terre" on the continent. Not only had the fall of Calais shown the military and governmental inadequacies of the French kingdom, but now Edward held an important naval base on the French coast,[30] a base of continental operations that would be used in nearly every military operation against France during the Hundred Years War.[31]

Edward also conceived of the town as a vibrant economic center for England. Calais and the English merchants who resided there were awarded special economic privileges by the English king.[32] By 1348, Edward had established the staple of tin, lead, and cloth in the town, and in 1363, he succeeded in placing the wool staple there as well, removing it from Bruges.[33] These moves were an attempt by England to make itself militarily and economically independent of its Low Countries allies. As Henry Stephen Lucas writes, "it was obvious that in the future [Edward] would not seek to realize his claims upon the French crown by relying upon his Netherlandish allies."[34]

With the fall of Calais, Edward was also able to rise to a popularity unknown by other English kings in the late Middle Ages. This victory, coupled with that of Crécy, made Edward a conqueror. It also gave him a chivalric image which he had not previously known. Indeed, among the other things which these victories gave an impetus to was the launching of the Order of the Garter which was formally inaugurated in 1348; the symbol of the blue garter for the order was suggested first at a ball held at Calais to celebrate its fall.[35]

However, with all these favorable reports on the results of the victory at Calais, Edward does have some detractors among modern historians. Hans Delbrück criticizes the English king for his inability to make immediate use of his prize,[36] and C.W. Previté-Orten claims that the length of the siege "exhausted" the English army, forcing it to agree to a peace treaty which put off further military activity until 1351.[37] Furthermore, some modern French historians tend to balk at the significance of this victory. In Jean Favier's opinion, the length of the siege at Calais "tarnished the glory of Crécy,"[38] and Edouard Perroy sees the loss of Calais as doing little harm to the French kingdom. He claims that when Edward returned to England, he did so almost "empty-handed:"

> Victor at Crécy, master of Calais, Edward had stretched his forces to the limit. He had shot his bolt and could only go home, full of glory, but almost empty-handed.... The capture of Calais might seem graver, militarily speaking; but it did not touch the royal domain, since it was made at the expense of the Count of Boulogne.[39]

But no one criticizes Edward III as does Colonel Alfred H. Burne who believes that by taking Calais the English king had missed the opportunity to profit from the victory of Crécy. In his opinion, the English army should have marched on Paris.[40]

Contemporary Foreign Accounts

There is much written about the siege of Calais by contemporary writers. Because of its length, the fact that it followed the famous battle of Crécy and the importance of the town to Edward III, the eleven-month siege of Calais attracted many, frequently very detailed, comments from fourteenth- and fifteenth-century chroniclers. Naturally the greatest number of these commentators came from England, France, and the southern Low Countries, but discussion of the siege can also be found in German, Swiss, Dutch, and Italian sources.

While most of the foreign sources mention very little about the activities of Edward's and Philip's armies during the long siege, most are impressed by the French king's inaction when facing the enemy near the walls of the town, and this dominates their comments. A few other details do emerge. For example, the Dutchman, Willem van Berchen, seems greatly impressed by the defenses of the town, a town "strongly fortified with bulwarks and machines of war by the king of France."[41] The Florentine Giovanni Villani and the Swiss Jean de Winterthur describe the strength and large numbers of English soldiers at the siege.[42] And several sources note the low number of losses suffered by this force.[43] Finally, Heinrich von Rebdorf of Germany and the anonymous Italian author of the *Istoria Pistolensi* both mention the Scottish attack on England while Edward III was at Calais, marvelling at the English king's reluctance to abandon his continental fight to protect his homeland.[44]

Although most of these foreign sources relate little about the siege itself, almost all mention Philip VI's gathering of a large army to try to defeat Edward and free the town.[45] Giovanni Villani even notes the number of troops and from what regions of France they came.[46] Also, all mention Philip's flight from Calais. The German Mathias von Nuwenberg even reports that Philip had ordered his army into three lines in simulated battle preparation before fleeing from Edward.[47] Because of this flight, they acknowledge, Calais was forced to surrender to the enemy forces. Villani, for example, concludes:

> Those of Calais, seeing the departure of the king of France and his host, negotiated with the king of England to surrender their land, to save the people from the foreigners. Coming out of the town bare-chested with a noose around their necks, they asked him for mercy.[48]

While these points are agreed upon by the foreign chroniclers of the siege, they cannot agree what led the French king to this flight. Jean de Winterthur claims that Philip merely could "not resist the king of England" therefore he fled from the town.[49] But Giovanni Villani contends that not only was the French king unable to fight against the English without facing "gran pericolo," but that he also was afraid to fight against the Flemish forces who had yet again rebelled against him and were present near Calais on the side of Edward: "The king of France did not wish to accept the decision to go to battle in Flanders against the multitude of Flemings who had rebelled against him."[50] Finally, Willem van Berchem and Heinrich von Rebdorf report that Calais fell simply because *"fortuna* smiled" on Edward after Crécy. Presumably then it was *fortuna* which caused Philip's flight from Calais.[51]

Contemporary English/Southern Low Countries' Accounts

In looking at the writers of the southern Low Countries who discuss the siege of Calais, it becomes immediately apparent that not all of these sources approve of the English king's successes during this time. Although we may question the allegience of sources such as the *Brabantse yeesten* and Edmond de Dynter's *Chronicon ducem Brabantiae* from Brabant, the Liegeois *Chronique* of Jean de Hocsem and the *Chronique Liegeoise de 1402* or Gilles li Muisit's *Chronicon* from Tournai in their commentary on the siege of Calais, none of these sources seem to favor Philip in this engagement despite his political domination of their respective lands at the time.[52] Most seem either to take a "middle-of-the-road" stance, or they concern themselves largely with events taking place in the southern Low Countries themselves commenting only slightly on the occurences about the town to the southwest of them. Other authors of the southern Low Countries, notably Jean le Bel and Jean Froissart, never seem to waver in their feelings towards Edward III at Calais. Indeed, combined with Thomas of Burton's *Chronica monasterii de Melsa* and the works composed by Henry Knighton and Robert of Avesbury, Jean le Bel and Jean Froissart provide the most extensive coverage of the siege and fall of Calais.[53]

One account, that from *La Chronique Liegeoise de 1402*, should be separated from the other English/southern Low Countries sources, as it gives an account of the siege that is completely erroneous.[54] The chief source for the *Chronique Liegeoise's* account is Jean de Hocsem's *Chronique* written earlier in Liège. Jean de Hocsem, after describing at length the English victory at Crécy which he claims was won "on account of archers who with their arrows killed a great number [of French]," writes that afterwards "the king of England proceeded to besiege Calais."[55] His account then digresses to describe several Liègeois matters before returning to the subject of Calais whose fall he credits "pre defectu victualium."[56] However, the author of the later Liègeois work does not take the same historical route in his description of the battle as had his source. In encountering Hocsem's initial, inconclusive description of the siege, and rather than reading on ahead in Hocsem's work where the adventure is resolved, this anonymous author impatiently and erroneously changes the order of the earlier *Chronique's* lines giving the impression that it was English archers defeating an extremely large French force in open battle who had taken the town. He writes:

The king of England, being the victor [at Crécy], withdrew to Calais and besieged it. It was said that the king of France had with him 150,000 armed knights against only 3,000 apart from an infinite number of archers who with their arrows killed a great number.[57]

As for the other, more traditional accounts of this siege written by English and southern Low Countries chroniclers some, as mentioned, give a broad overview of the siege itself. Many report the large amount of destruction made by the English army on its route from Crécy to Calais which later became such a persistent characteristic of the besiegers for the length of the siege.[58] It also became a characteristic of the year itself. The *Récits d'un bourgeois de Valenciennes* describes this destruction:

> During which siege and which time the people [of England] and the French had made many assaults and many battles, where there were many men killed and wounded, on land and on sea, and many noble men of one party or the other were ransomed. And many villages were pillaged, burned and destroyed in Gascony, in Flanders, in Brittany, in Scotland, in England, in France, in Normandy, in Limoges, in Poitou, in and in many other lands, in which there was great damage and pity.[59]

Regarding the siege itself, much commentary is afforded to the English army and its situation around the town of Calais. The *Chronicon anonymi Cantuariensis* notes that Edward had with him a "manus fortis,"[60] and the *Breve chronicon Flandriae* reports that Edward besieged the town with an "artissima obsidione."[61] One of the most impressive features of this "artissima obsidio" was the large siegeworks set up by Edward to house the English army surrounding the besieged town. Known to these writers by the name Ville-à-Neuve, it contained houses, shops, and even a large square in which an open market was held twice a week. Jean Froissart describes this "town":

> When the king of England had come first to the town of Calais, which he desired much to conquer, he besieged it with a great army and in good order, and he constructed and arranged there, between the town and the river and bridge of Niulais, hostels and houses, built from great stone. And they covered these houses which were arranged neatly and easily throughout the streets... And there was in

this new town of the king's all the necessary things pertaining to an army, and more besides. Also located there was a square where a market was held Wednesday and Saturday, and there were merchant's shops, butcher shops, cloth halls, bakeries, and shops for all other necessities, in which anyone could receive anything easily for his money. And there came every day, by sea from England and also from Flanders, those supplies and merchandise by which they were comforted.[62]

Later, after French and Genoese ships successfully ran the English naval blockade and delivered supplies to the starving city, Edward added to his siegeworks by building a large tower on the coast near the Calais port. In this tower, Froissart notes, Edward placed "many espringalles, bombards, mounted crossbows and other instruments," and he outfitted it with men-at-arms and archers.[63]

    The English and southern Low Countries chroniclers further note that Edward did not plan to take the town by assault, due to the large number of men and defensive machines which were inside, nor did he plan to batter the walls down with his own guns and engines because of the sandy and marshy ground which provided them with an unstable foundation. Instead the English king planned to take the town by starving its residents, a plan attested to by both Thomas of Burton and Geoffrey le Baker. Indeed, Baker contests that "the king abstained from assaults and from the shattering of the walls, knowing advisedly that the hunger, which took place within the closed gates, could and ought to tame the pride of the besieged."[64]

    Although it seems from these and other accounts that Edward was unable successfully to attack the town, one source, the Herald of John Chandos's *Life of the Black Prince,* claims that the town was taken only because of the attacks made on it by the English force. The Herald writes:

> And the noble king of England / held there the field. / Many skirmishes and many assaults / were made by both the low and the high / so that the town was taken. / And they [the townspeople] beseeched the king by God's grace / that he would be merciful. / And thus was Calais conquered by force, / by the power and the enterprise / of the noble king and his son / the prince who was so brave.[65]

Little is mentioned by these chroniclers concerning the

French militia and the inhabitants of the besieged town, and any remarks are made principally by the southern Low Countries writers. For example, both Jean le Bel and Jean Froissart record several instances when bands of English troops skirmished with bands of French soldiers.[66] Moreover, they and other Netherlandish authors also note that much fighting took place in the southern Low Countries between Flemish cohorts allied with Edward and their French counterparts; included is extensive coverage of a failed siege on the town of Cassel by the French vanguard of Philip VI's army who came to relieve the siege of Calais.[67]

There seems to be very little concern paid to the inhabitants suffering inside the town. For example, the role of Jean de Vienne, the French leader within Calais, is only mentioned by an English poet, Laurence Minot, and his description of the French leader is negative. Describing Vienne's role in the siege, and telling of its result, Minot writes:

A knight þat was of grete renowne,
   Sir Iohn de Viene was his name,
He was wardaine of þe toune,
   And had done Ingland mekill schame.
   For all þaire boste þai er to blame,
Ful stalworthly þare have þai streuyn;
   A bare es cumen to mak þam tame,
Kayes of þe toun to him er gifen.[68]

Finally, although the Scottish invasion of England is mentioned by all of the English and most of the southern Low Countries' writers, only Jean Froissart and Henry Knighton mention the collusion of Philip VI in the affair, reporting that the French king made a truce with David Bruce, and that he advised him to attack England while Edward and his army lay before Calais.[69] By doing this, Philip vainly hoped that Edward "would depart from his siege of Calais and would return to England."[70]

There is no disagreement concerning the reasons for Calais's surrender to the English. All of the writers commenting on this siege from England and from the southern Low Countries see the hunger of the town as the ultimate cause of its fall.[71] Even the Herald who wrote the *Life of the Black Prince* determined that hunger caused the demoralization of the town, although he ultimately credits Edward and the Black Prince's assaults for the victory, as mentioned above. Indeed, starvation within the town of Calais seems to be a major topic for discussion by these authors.

Nor is this simply discussed at the end of the siege. As reflected in the commentary of the contemporary writers, hunger was a concern for the town from the very outset of the siege. For early in 1347, when the town leaders began to realize the scarcity of their food supplies and the relentless siege of their enemy, they cast out five hundred of the poorer burghers of Calais from the town. The English and southern Low Countries chroniclers, however, differ in their versions of what befell these poor people. Jean le Bel, whose account of the story is later used by Jean Froissart, alleges that this exiled mass was treated well by the English who fed them and allowed them to pass through their lines in safety; he ascribes this treatment to the mercy of Edward III:

> When those people of Calais saw that the king of England had not departed during winter, and that their own supplies were small, they sent five hundred people out [of the town], and they passed among the English army. When the noble king saw the poor people sent outside of the town, he directed them all to come to his great hall and he gave them all an abundance of food and drink. And when they had eaten and drunk much, they were given permission to pass through his army, and to each he gave three shillings of sterling out of the love of God. And they were conducted safely through his army. We should well record such great kindness.[72]

Henry Knighton, on the other hand, claims that there was an unpleasant outcome to this adventure. To these people, Knighton avers, Edward gave no such mercy:

> There were ejected from Calais around five hundred men of the lower class who came to the king of England seeking grace; the king commanded them to return into the town. However, those who were in the town denied entrance to them. And thus they lingered between the army and the town, and suffering much from hunger and the cold, they died day after day.[73]

Another incident concerning the hunger of Calais which is mentioned frequently by these writers is the capture by Edward's forces of a letter written by Jean de Vienne to Philip VI asking for succor as the town was becoming demoralized for lack of food, and Jean feared that it would soon fall to the English:

But, right and dear lord, know that, although the people are all well and of good cheer, yet the town is in much need of corn, wine, and meat. For know that there is nothing herein which has not been eaten, both dogs and cats and horses, so that we can find no more victuals in the town, unless we eat flesh of men.[74]

Edward, realizing the propagandistic purposes of such a letter, immediately sent it to Philip VI. The contents of this letter are of special interest to many of the English and southern Low Countries writers, some of whom include either the whole letter or an excerpt of it in their accounts of the siege.[75]

Eventually the lack of food within the town led to its surrender. Both the English writers and their allies emphasize this point in their works. John of Reading, for example, writes:

Those besieged by the English king, despairing that they did not have any refuge, having consumed their victuals, ate horses, dogs, and rats so that they might not violate their fealty. Finally, it was discovered that no victuals remained among them whom the most miserable hunger would compel either to die evilly or to surrender the town.[76]

Gilles li Muisit describes a similar situation within the town:

During this time, having consumed their victuals, they suffered such penury, hoping to get aid daily, that they ate horses and beasts, and afterwards, they fried the skins of the horses and beasts in oil. Finally, they ate cats, dogs, rats, mice and such other beasts, which they had, on account of which many people died.[77]

Finally, Laurence Minot comments, as if he were one of the besieged:

Oure horses þat war faire and fat
    Er etin vp ilkone bidene;
Have we now er conig ne cat
    þat þai ne er etin and hundes kene.
All er etin vp ful clene,
Es nowther leuid biche ne whelp,
    þat es wele on oure sembland sene,
And þai er fled þat suld vs help.[78]

Thus the town of Calais surrendered to the English army. After its fall, the hunger of the town took still a larger toll, as the people of Calais so engorged themselves with the relief victuals sent in by their oppressors that several more died. Henry Knighton relates the story:

> The king, moved by mercy, took them into his grace, and graciously he handled them. Immediately he sent victuals into the town for the refreshment of the people as they were so famished and affected and annihilated and debilitated by hunger. And they consumed so much of the food and drink that the following night more than three hundred persons died in the town.[79]

Among the accounts of these chroniclers, there is also much description about the negotiations and ceremony of the peace itself. Especially vivid in this regard are the reports of Jean le Bel and Jean Froissart who describe an intricate set of negotiations which went on between Jean de Vienne, who was bargaining for the lives and property of his people, and Walter de Manny, the trusted friend and legate of the English king. Finally, the negotiations having come to a halt, as agreed six of the most wealthy burghers of Calais were led out of the town, without shirts or shoes, wearing nooses around their necks in a symbolic gesture to their captor that he held their lives in his hands.[80]

It is at this point in their discussion of the siege that most of the English and southern Low Countries writers introduce the story of Edward's mercy towards the inhabitants of Calais. However, the English and southern Low Countries authors differ in their versions of the story of Edward's mercy. The English historians are adamant that their king at once showed mercy to the citizens of Calais, putting none of them to death although it is unclear whether he imprisoned any of the nobles; instead, he allowed them to escape with their portable possessions. *The Anonimalle Chronicle* records simply that the townspeople "passed among the English army to the land of the French without evil or molestation, and under the care and command of the king of England."[81] Robert of Avesbury adds: "And the lord king, always merciful and benign, having captured and retained few of the nobles, permitted the community of the town to leave graciously with all their goods."[82] Indeed, the story of Edward's mercy persists into the fifteenth century, as the chronicle known as *The Brut* notes:

And when the King... as a mercyable king and lord, resceyued hym al

to his grace; & a feue of þe grettste persones of stat and of gouer-
naunce of þe toun he sent into Engelond, þer for to abyde hire raun-
some & þe kinges grace; & al þe communialte of þe toun þe king
lete go wher þey wolde in pees, & wiþoute ony harme, & lete ham
bere with ham al hire þing þat þey my te bere & cary away, keping þe
toun and the Castell to hymself.[83]

The southern Low Countries chroniclers, on the other hand,
relate a different account of mercy shown by the English king, for both
Jean le Bel and Jean Froissart mention the active role taken by
Edward's wife, Philippa of Hainault, who, echoing the wishes of his
counsellors, advised the king that he should be merciful to the population of the town. As Froissart describes, Edward did not want to conduct himself mercifully toward the Calaisiens, but he did acquiesce
reluctantly to the queen's wishes, exclaiming:

> Ha! dame, I wish very much that you were elsewhere than here. You
> have asked me so assuredly, that I cannot refuse you. And although I
> do so against my will, you take them. I give them to you, so that you
> may do with them your pleasure.[84]

Queen Philippa then granted the inhabitants of Calais their freedom.
Most of the narratives of the English and southern Low
Countries chroniclers writing on the siege of Calais emphasize the
arrival and almost inexplicable flight of the French army from the siege
without having engaged in battle. While hunger to these writers is the
central cause of the fall of the town, an interesting sidelight for their
analyses are the actions, or more appropriately the inactions, of Philip
VI and his relief force. Several different explanations for this flight are
presented.
Before Philip actually appears on the outskirts of Calais within
striking distance of the English, late in 1347, very little about the
French king and his army is reported. Jean le Bel does tell us that
Philip had been unable to come to relieve the siege of Calais during
the winter of 1346–47, although he does not record the reasons for
such inaction.[85] A century later, however, this neglect had become disdain. For the late fifteenth-century *Kronyk van Vlaenderen* notes that
because he anticipated Philip's approach, an event which did not
occur, Edward III believed that the French did not hold the port-town
in the same esteem as did the English.[86] That an attack from Philip was
anticipated by Edward can be seen in a letter to Margaret, the countess

of Kent, on October 3, 1346.[87] As well, some sources contend that Philip's son, John II, approached the besieged town with his force at the end of 1346, but that he found that he could not attack the English army, and, low on supplies, he was forced to return to France.[88] But other than these remarks, nothing is mentioned by the chroniclers until the French army's arrival at Sangatte Hill.

Once Philip's force had arrived at Calais, some of the writers seem only impressed by the size of the French army using terms such as "grande exercitus,"[89] "grete hoste,"[90] "maxima multitudo armatorum,"[91] "grote ghetale,"[92] and "innumerabilis populus"[93] to describe the mass of the French relief contingent. Others actually try to tally the number of soldiers involved, and these figures range from a very believable 2,000–5,000 knights plus a large number of foot soldiers[94] to a highly unbelievable total of 100,000 soldiers reported in the *Chronique de Pays-Bas*.[95] Still other chroniclers record only the impressive names and number of the nobles who attended the French force.[96]

Only a few contemporary writers relate more details about the French reinforcements. Thomas Walsingham, for example, avers that Philip came to Calais "on account of the promise which he had made to the besieged."[97] Henry Knighton, on the other hand, contends that the purpose for Philip's journey to relieve Calais was less a promise to the town's inhabitants than it was an answer to the beseechings from nobles in nearby Picardy and Artois who feared that if Calais fell, they too might lose their own lands.[98]

Whatever the reason, Philip decided to venture to Calais, arriving nearby and placing his camp within sight of the town and the besieging English army. This certainly encouraged the inhabitants of Calais who hoped that the French presence would lead eventually to their release from the English blockade. However, Jean le Bel reports that when the townspeople realized the weak position of the French relief force in comparison with that of the English besiegers, "they began to despair somewhat."[99] Moreover, the *Chronicon comitum Flandriae* notes that when news of the French approach reached the Flemish army lying nearby at Gravelines, they hastened to join their force with that of their ally, Edward, increasing his numbers at Calais.[100]

Philip's army remained at Sangatte Hill for only a few days. During that time, not only did the French king send out scouts to investigate possible routes by which he might be able to attack the English,[101] but he also became active in peace-making efforts. Legates, probably cardinals, had been sent by Pope Clement VI to negotiate a peace between the two sides, preferably leaving Calais in the hands of the French; Philip, who could only profit from such a treaty, was more than willing to service the needs of these papal mediators.[102] This affinity between Philip and the papal legates brings out a certain enmity in the writings of the English poet Laurence Minot who believed that the papal peace mediators were corrupt and unfairly pro-French in their negotiations. They led the French to tell lies about Edward, and then they tried to beguile the English king into making an accord that would not profit him:

> þe Franche men er fers and fell
>> And mase grete dray when þai er dight;
> of þam men herd slike tales tell
>> With Edward think þai for to fight,
>> Him for to hald out of his right
> And do him treson with þaire tales;
>> þat was paire purpos day and night
> Bi counsail of þe Cardinales
>
> Cardinales with hattes rede
>> War fro Calays wele thre myle;
> þai toke þaire counsail if þat stede
>> How þai might sir Edward bigile.
>> þai lended þare bot litill while
> Till France men to grante þaire grace.[103]

As far as Edward was concerned, however, there would be no peace at Calais; he would not raise the siege until the town was in English hands. This much is certain, at least it is the one point agreed to by the chroniclers who record the peace negotiations. However, the reasons behind Edward's refusal to agree to a peace accord are disputed by these writers. Robert of Avesbury and Henry Knighton claim that Edward simply refused the offered treaty without citing any reasons behind his decision. Knighton writes:

At the same time [as Philip came to Calais], cardinals came to king Edward to negotiate a peace between the kings, and thus a truce was made between the parties for four days for the purpose of negotiating a peace between the kings.... To which Edward responded after a short while that the town and those things which were in it were and ought to be under the will of the king of England, and not as a gift of Philip of Valois.[104]

The Chronicon comitum Flandriae, on the other hand, claims more specifically that Edward refused the peace because he knew that Calais was at the point of surrender due to hunger:

> Cardinals meanwhile negotiated a peace or a truce between the kings, but nothing succeeded because the king of England wanted to have the town of Calais delivered to him entirely before he would proceed with a treaty, because he knew that the Calaisiens besieged by him suffered a fierce hunger and starvation.[105]

Some contemporary writers contend that Edward initially did agree to a peace conference with the cardinals in order to reinforce his numbers and fortifications while making his own defences impregnable against an eventual French attack. Gilles li Muisit, for example, writes:

> Two cardinals, the Lord Hannibal and the lord of Claremont, came and placed themselves between the lines laboring to make peace or to be granted a truce. And they obtained on both sides a respite of only three days during which three days a great abundance of Flemings and English came to the king of England, and his army increased much. And he caused a great ditch to be dug around his army so that the king of France and his force would have no access to the English army nor a way of approaching the town of Calais on account of the sea and the narrowness of passage.[106]

While Edward strengthened his force and his fortifications, Philip was not inactive. During this time, the French king tried to win back the Flemish rebels. He sent messages of fealty and peace to them trying to regain their alliegance. These efforts were unsuccessful, however, for, as Jean Froissart writes, "the king of England for the time being had all of the good men in Flanders...."[107]

When Philip realized that the peace-making efforts of the papal legates had failed, and after undertaking a few small skirmishes which cost him much and resulted in only limited success,[108] the French king tried a tactic which Edward had used against him at the siege of Tournai in 1340: he challenged the English king to combat. Thomas Walsingham writes:

But when he [Philip] saw that he would not be able to satisfy his vows in this affair, on the last day of July, at the hour of Vespers, he offered to the king of England that whenever it pleased him, he might come to battle outside of the besieged place.[109]

Whether Edward accepted this challenge, however, cannot be known based on the contemporary writings of English and southern Low Countries' chroniclers. On the one side, the *Chronique des Pays-Bas* and Jean le Bel claim that Edward refused Philip's challenge to battle. Both report that the English king refused the challenge as he believed that Calais would soon fall and that the French could not aid the town before that would happen.[110] On the other side of the argument, several writers contend that Edward did accept Philip's challenge.[111] Indeed, Edward himself records that he accepted this challenge to do battle with the French. In a letter to Archbishop John Stratford, the king reports:

And then on the Tuesday, towards Vespers, came certain great men and knights from our adversary to the place of conference, and, on behalf of our aforementioned adversary, they offered our people battle so that we would come out of the marsh, and he would give us a fitting place to fight in, at whatsoever hour should please us between that hour and the Friday evening next following; and they would that four knights of ours and four of theirs should choose a place for the one side and the other. Whereupon our people answered that they would show us this offer and would give them an answer on the following Wednesday. Which thing being shown to us, we took counsel and advice with the great men and other wise men of our council and of our army, and, trusting in God and in our right, we gave an answer to them that we accept their offer and take up a battle willingly. And we wrote letters of conduct for four knights of the other side, of whatever estate or condition, to come to our army, in order that we might choose four of their rank, and that the same eight knights might make an oath that they would go view and search out the ground until they were agreed on a suitable place.[112]

Although this acceptance is generally praised by the writers reporting it, the anonymous author of *The Brut* shows some dissatisfaction with Edward's decision:

And [the French] sent to Kyng Edward, and askit hym whedir he durst feight with hym the iijde day, about euensonge tyme, and leve þe seege. And Kyng Edward onon, with-out eny counsaile or avisement, accepted gladly the day; and yette much of his pepill were seke and ded on þe fflux.[113]

Two writers break the normal acceptance/refusal pattern followed by the other chroniclers of the affair. Henry Knighton, for one, claims that Philip initially challenged Edward to combat with only five or six knights per side, and that it was this challenge which the English king refused as he believed that he was "the natural and just heir" of the French crown and thus should not have to prove his right to rule by duelling. After this refusal, Knighton continues, Philip challenged Edward to an open battle "absque impedimento." This challenge Edward accepted heartily:

Edward offered... to fill in all the ditches and to break down all the obstacles around the siege so that the French could have free access and passage with their army to fight a battle without impediment.[114]

The second source which varies on this point is Thomas of Burton's *Chronica monasterii de Melsa* which insists that it was not Philip who challenged Edward to battle, but Edward who challenged Philip to battle:

Legates of the lord Pope, namely the count of Armagnac and two other magnates of France, came for the purpose of negotiating with the magnates of England, assigned by the king for this task in order to make peace.... But when the said lords were unable to agree between them on the establishment of peace, King Edward offered to Philip of Valois that on the battlefield or inside of where the English were encamped, he would fight most freely with him.[115]

Unable to gain Calais by negotiation or by battle, Philip had no recourse but to retreat from the town, leaving it to the English. As Laurence Minot describes the affair:

Sir Philip was funden a file,
He fled and faght noght in at place.
In þat place þe bare was blith,
　For all was funden þat he had soght:

Philip þe Valas fled ful swith
  With þe batail þat he had broght.
  For to haue Calays had he thoght
All at his ledeing loud or still;
  Bot all þaire wiles war for noght,
Edward wan it at his will.[116]

      While most English and southern Low Countries writers report Philip's flight, there is much disagreement among them concerning what caused the retreat. The author of the *Chronique des Pays-Bas,* for example, believes that Philip's retreat was due to his "not being able to aid the town, unless he fought a battle," a battle which Edward refused to give him.[117] *The Brut* blames Philip for the loss of the town claiming that he "treacherously and wiþ fraude" tried to raise the siege.[118] And Jean le Bel, Jean Froissart, the Herald of Chandos, and the *Chronique de Flandre* come to a more active conclusion: Philip retreated because his army was unable to attack advantageously the English.[119] The Herald writes: "But the army was lodged /and the town besieged in such a way / that the king Philip dared not / to raise the siege, but to retreat."[120] Moreover, Jean le Bel, whose account of the siege of Calais is followed closely by Jean Froissart, contends that Philip had sent out "mareschaulx" to investigate possible routes of attack against the English, and it was their report which ultimately dissuaded the French king from further action, for "they did not wish to put their men into a greater defeat than they had at the battle of Crécy."[121]

      Most chroniclers who record this flight, especially the English, perceive its cause to be Philip's fear of Edward and the English army who had defeated the French only the year before. Some of these perceptions are directly related to the English king whose acceptance of Philip's challenge was unexpected and whose bravery on the battlefield was feared. As Thomas Walsingham notes:

On the next day after his approach, he [Philip] fled stealthily at daybreak, leaving the tents behind with victuals stored in abundance, fearing that he might lose doubtlessly because of the bravery of the king who was situated before him.[122]

And Robert of Avesbury adds:

Then Lord Philip, hearing the will of the magnanimous king [that he had accepted Philip's challenge], did not await the result of a battle, but, during the night before the day of Thursday following, having placed his tents on fire, and at that time as if neglecting all his baggage, seeking refuge, he retreated stealthily and subtly vanished from the eyes of the English.[123]

Moreover, Edward III himself also felt that this fear was the reason for the French flight from Calais. Describing the incident to Archbishop John Stratford, Edward writes:

And they of the other side, when now they had heard this answer [that Edward would go to battle against them], began to shift in their offers and to speak of the town all anew, as if putting off the battle; so they would hold nothing certain. And thereupon, on the Thursday before the day, notwithstanding the aforementioned negotiations, our adversary departed with all of his people, as if defeated; and they hurried so much that they burned their tents and a great part of their harness at their departure.[124]

Other chroniclers see the power and numbers of the English army as the deciding factor in the French flight. Geoffrey le Baker writes:

The tyrant of France seeing the capable power of the king, destroying his tents with fire in the morning, having hereby given a sign of powerlessness to the besieged because he dared not aid them, fled foolishly.[125]

And the *Eulogium historiarum* reports:

And it seemed even to the king of France and many others of his army before meeting for battle that there was such a multitude of English that all the world could not resist them, and thus they fled terrified and humbled.[126]

Finally, several southern Low Countries writers record a different reason for Philip's flight. They believe that the French king fled because he had seen the Flemish reinforcements enter the English camp, and he feared to do battle with them. The bourgeois of Valenciennes, for example, reports:

And when the king of France saw that there was summoned more

than one hundred thousand Flemings who had arrived, all having
come to the English side, the said king of France and all his army dis-
lodged themselves and fled without giving any relief to those of
Calais who were in the midst of a great hunger.[127]

     The besieged in Calais witnessed Philip's flight, and they real-
ized that their hopes for aid from the French were lost. Rife with
hunger, they therefore surrendered to Edward.[128]
     While most of the English and southern Low Countries chron-
iclers stress Philip's flight from Calais and the hunger within the town
as the chief cause of English victory, a few other reasons for victory are
also given. Certainly many of the writers from these regions mark the
victory with accounts of Edward's prestige. As mentioned above,
accounts of his, or his queen's, mercy appear frequently in these
sources. But other writers, especially poets who comment on the siege
of Calais, also mention other points concerning Edward's prestige. A
fifteenth-century poet, John Lydgate, the author of *Verses on the Kings of
England,* for example, reports that Edward "gate Calys by his prudent
devyce."[129] The more contemporary Laurence Minot calls the king a
"hound" who successfully hunted the "hare" (Philip VI).[130] And John of
Bridlington uses the image of David to characterize the English ruler.[131]
He also relates a more descriptive "eulogium" on the English king:

I know the *eulogium,* the enemy bulls lost. / For the king robust with
arms, legitimate by everything, / the good and strong king to whom
the evils of death did not harm, / the king never conquered, for
whom the point of sword would not harm; / called Emmanuel, by
whom much was conquered. / In the world, there is not such a fighting general.[132]

     While the presence of God often plays a large role in the
accounts of medieval military narrative, at Calais there is surprisingly
very little mention of the deity on the side of the English. Indeed, many
of the references to God during the 1346–47 conflict occur in situations only marginally connected to the English siege of Calais. For
example, Henry Knighton reports that Henry, duke of Lancaster, was
saved by God when traveling to England from Calais in 1347,[133] and
Robert of Avesbury reports that the Flemings were able to keep the
French from taking Cassel in the same year "with the Lord protecting
them."[134]
     Moreover, the only miracle reported by these sources takes

place at Morin during a *chevauchée* led in 1346 by Henry of Lancaster. The *Chronicon comitum Flandriae* describes the incident:

> And when they [the English] wished to plunder the church cathedral of the glorious Virgin and then to place it on fire, a most beautiful miracle which ought to be committed to memory happened. For an English archer irreverently shot an arrow with his bow into the head of the statue of the blessed Virgin standing within the basilica, wishing to obtain, daring sacrilege, the clothing or the crown with which or with what the venerable head was adorned. But immediately the most strong bow, which the evildoer held in his hands, was broken up into many pieces, which recoiled into this evildoer and even into those standing around him. Through which it occurred most evidently to all that the most beloved son of God did not wish to allow a disgrace made to his most beloved mother. But, as it is said, He vindicated this action immediately. Whence from this indeed all these barbarians were encouraged, prostrate on the ground, humbly to seek the favor of the blessed Virgin. And they offered her very many gifts as if to emend the committed disgraces. On account of this, they spared the said cathedral church and the other churches of the city so that they would not be devastated by fire.[135]

There is, however, a mention of God's role at Calais noted in Thomas of Burton's *Chronica monasterii de Melsa* which is not favorable to the English. Here Thomas of Burton claims that God visited the English troops with dysentery during their stay in front of Calais because of their intimacy with prostitutes. Burton writes:

> Meanwhile, our English remaining at the siege of the town fell to the number of fifteen thousand because of the illness of dysentary. And thus the Lord, as it was believed, whipped them on account of their faults, especially because at that time so many prostitutes came there that their number at most times exceeded the number of soldiers.[136]

Finally, while not much in evidence elsewhere, the English and southern Low Countries chroniclers do differ in their narratives concerning the role of the Flemings at Calais. For, although none of these authors, regardless of their "national" allegiance, denies the presence of Flemish soldiers at Calais, the southern Low Countries writers perceive a much larger role for the Flemish soldiers than do their English counterparts. As mentioned, some Flemish chroniclers believe that Philip VI fled because he had seen the large number of Flemish troops who reinforced the English lines,[137] a charge not found in any English writer's account of the siege, although some English authors do mention the arrival of Flemish troops at this time.[138] Those English sources which do record the Flemish arrival, however, see only a modicum of reinforcements — a total of 3,000 is mentioned by Henry Knighton[139] — while the Flemish chroniclers estimates of troop strength reach as high as 100,000.

Other differences also exist. Two English chronicles, the *Continuatio chronici* of Adam Murimuth and the *Chronica monasterii de Melsa* of Thomas of Burton, mention that the Flemings supplied much of the victuals to the English troops around Calais, a fact surprisingly missing from any southern Low Countries' source.[140] On the other hand, it is only the southern Low Countries writers who claim that, at the outset of the siege, when the Flemish forces tried to join with the English at Calais, they were turned away by Edward; the English king contended that their presence was unnecessary as he had enough of his own soldiers to withstand any French attack. At least this is the impression given in the fifteenth century by the anonymous author of the *Kronyk van Vlaenderen* who writes:

> Around Bamesse, which lasted a week and was very cold, many English soldiers came to help King Edward, and therefore he gave the Flemings leave, and they went home, because King Edward had enough men to withstand the king of France.[141]

Moreover, while both English and southern Low Countries chroniclers comment on Philip's continual attempts to induce the Flemings to desert their English allies — indeed, the most detailed account of these attempts, including an itemized list of French promises made to the Flemings, comes from Robert of Avesbury's *De gestis mirabilibus regis Edwardi III* [142] — only the Low Countries' authors mention similar negotiations and promises made to the Flemings by Edward III.[143] As Jean Froissart insists, Edward very much desired the Flemings as allies in his siege of Calais: "The king of England... wished to hold the love of the Flemings because they had come to his side at Calais and they could prove to be of very great value there."[144] As well, Froissart tells us that in Edward's final preparations to receive a French attack, one which never would come, the Flemings had a very specific role to play in defending the besiegers. It was their responsibility to guard the routes from Gravelines to Calais against possible French conquest. Ultimately, it is this defense which causes Philip to decide not to attack the besiegers. Jean Froissart writes:

> But when they [the French] scouted the pass of Gravelines and the difficult and evil and perilous routes which they would have to use, and that more than sixty thousand Flemings guarded them before Calais, they changed and softened their ideas about this and said: "All our thoughts have come to nought. Calais is lost to us."[145]

Perhaps the most telling difference concerning the Flemish role at Calais, other than a few overtly negative English remarks which will be mentioned later, is the English sources' almost complete disregard for and contradictory remarks on the turmoil surrounding the marriage of the young Flemish count, Louis of Male. The southern Low Countries chroniclers all wrote highly descriptive accounts of the problems of Louis's marriage: Louis wished to marry Margaret, the daughter of Jean III, duke of Brabant, a French ally, while his Flemish subjects, with Edward III's encouragement forced their count into an agreement to marry the English princess, Isabel, even imprisoning him until the day of the marriage. Finally, however, Louis of Male escaped to the French king and married Margaret much to the embarrassment of Edward III and the Flemish people.[146] Despite the role of their king in this affair, however, few English sources concern themselves with it.[147]

Finally, two English writers claim that the Flemings at Calais were not allied with the English, but were inclined to the French and Philip VI instead. One, John of Bridlington, after discussing the refusal of Louis of Male to marry Edward's daughter, writes: "Besides the Flemings were in part French."[148] The second, actually a Welsh chronicle, tells the story of a man from Flanders known only as Jacob who, while visiting the English besiegers at Calais, openly wonders why Edward had not yet taken the town. Edward responded by asking how many men this Flemish leader could supply for his siege. Jacob answered saying that he could very quickly offer only a "dwsing" men to the English. Edward, it is said, was severely disappointed as he reckoned that this meant that Jacob could bring only twelve men to him, but the man from Flanders pacified Edward's fears by explaining that a "dwsing" men in a Flemish guild meant actually 13,452 men (12,000 plus 1,200 plus 240 — twelve twenties — plus 12 men). Here the Welsh account stops to explain that the story of Jacob must be false because not only were the numbers and the speed of gathering unbelievable, but the "forces of Flanders at this time stood on the side of the king of France."[149]

Contemporary French Accounts

In turning to the French narrative accounts on the siege of Calais, it must be noted that not only are there fewer French writers commenting on the siege, but their accounts are also shorter and less detailed than either those of the English chroniclers or those of the southern Low Countries. About the siege itself, prior to the arrival of Philip VI late in 1347, very little information can be gained from these sources, especially about the English forces or their situation around the town. For example, only Cuvelier, the author of the *Chronique de Bertrand de Guesclin,* indicates the "moult puissante" of Edward's force at the siege.[150] As well, only Richard Lescot and the *Grandes chroniques de France* mention the English siege camp including the town Ville-à-Neuve which the *Grandes chroniques* hastens to add was "administered by the money of the Flemings."[151] Jean de Venette does mention the large number of English "machinas et alia genera balistarum" which were present with the besieging force, but he fails to mention anything more about the siegeworks of Edward III.[152]

There is also some commentary on the strong defenses of Calais itself and the fact that they had withstood frequent attacks made on them by the English, a factor in the siege largely neglected by English and southern Low Countries writers.[153] Also included among the French accounts is an assessment of the bravery and prowess of the inhabitants of the town. Jean de Venette writes:

In A.D. 1347, King Edward was before Calais and made many attacks on the town, but the burgesses defended themselves extraordinarily well from within with machines and other sorts of ballista, and they made sorties in which they slew many of the English and triumphed over them.[154]

This town strength led Edward to conclude that he would have to take Calais by siege instead of by assault. *The Grandes chroniques* notes:

And because the king of England was unable to enter the town of Calais as he had wished, he decided to besiege it, and so to deliver the habitations of said town for the hospitality of he and his army.[155]

Still, the French writers insist that Edward desired to capture the town, and he refused to return to England without it as a prize. Richard Lescot writes:

Because the guardian of the town, named Lord Jean de Vienne, refused to surrender, he [Edward] surrounded it with a siege swearing that he would not withdraw from there unless he had first captured the town.[156]

There is also very little commentary on the affairs of Calais immediately after its fall: the surrender of the citizens, the celebration of the English, or the mercy shown the inhabitants of the town by Edward III.[157]

The contemporary French chroniclers also do not vary from their English and southern Low Countries' counterparts in determining that the hunger of Calais ultimately led to its defeat and fall to the English. Although there is no record in these accounts of the exiling of some of the townspeople, the letter captured by the English describing the plight of the town or the deaths of those who engorged themselves after Calais's fall, several of the French writers do use the image of the townspeople consuming cats, dogs, rats, and horses to display their hunger.[158] Moreover, this situation was known to the French, but their king, Philip, was powerless to do anything to ameliorate the woes of the Calaisiens.[159] Still, Jean de Venette reports, Philip had been trying to send food to the town, but on most occasions the English had captured the supplies and had turned them to their own use:

The king of France, Philip, encouraged the Calaisiens by sending victuals to them by land and by sea. Indeed, if there had been enough victuals, they would no doubt have defeated the English. But the provisions which they [the French] sent to them, the English made their own property, as was said, without the king and France and his council knowing it.[160]

The *Grandes chroniques* also reports that the townspeople of Calais became so hungry that they were greatly relieved when Philip arrived to raise the siege. The anonymous author of this work writes:

But the king of England and the duke of Lancaster... and the English who had recently come to their lord, had shut off and enclosed the town of Calais with such a great siege, both by land and by sea, so that supplies in no way were able to be taken to those who were in the said town of Calais, for which they lived in great despair and misery until they knew of the approach of the king, and that he

wished to do battle against their enemy and to deliver the siege surrounding the town.[161]

But Philip's approach did not free the town from its turmoil,
and, finally, Calais was forced to surrender because of the starvation
facing its citizens. The *Grandes chroniques* reports: "And because there
was no food... and they had eaten their horses, dogs, rats and the hides
of beef, they surrendered to the king of England saving their lives."[162]
Also, like the accounts of the siege of Calais written by English and
southern Low Countries chroniclers, the main concern of the French
writers about the siege of the town in 1346–47 is Philip's inability to
meet with the English army in battle or to bring aid to the town.
However, as may be expected, the French judgments of the actions of
their king in this affair are, for the most part, less critical than those of
the authors reporting the siege as a victory.

Although these chroniclers write nothing about Philip's
attempts to raise an army to go against the English at Calais in 1346, a
fact reported by some southern Low Countries' sources, there are several accounts of the French king's success at gathering troops for a 1347
conquest. Jean de Venette notes, for example, that "the king of France,
seeing that the king of England had not relaxed his siege of this place,
came there with a great multitude of armed men since it was said to
him that those of the town did not have any more food."[163] As well, the
Chronique Normande reports that Philip drew his large army mostly from
Arras and other regions near Calais.[164] Finally, Richard Lescot states
that the French king was able to finance his expedition because, with
papal permission, he collected church tithes and borrowed from
Lombard usurers.[165] Moreover, Lescot adds, Philip also took with him
the oriflamme from the church of St. Denis.[166]

The French writers also discuss the unsuccessful peace efforts
made at Calais and the equally unsuccessful challenges to combat made
by the French king. Concerning the former matter, nearly all of the
French writers commenting on the siege claim that Edward initially
agreed to a three-day truce and then deceptively used the time to add
to his already strong defensive fortifications. For example, the
Chronique Normande reports:

There was a truce made for three days by three cardinals who had
been sent by the Holy Father to make peace between the two princes.
And King Philip agreed to the truce for three days, and during that

time the English and the Flemings dug ditches and trenches around their army and across the dunes to the sea in such a way that the French were unable to meet them in battle or to aid the town with supplies or any other thing.[167]

The only difference between this account, agreed to by the authors of the *Grandes chroniques* and the *Chronographia regum Francorum*,[168] and that of Jean de Venette and Richard Lescot is that it mentions the mediation of papal legates. The other two sources for this peace effort all contend that the idea of a truce was solely Edward's who "hearing of his [Philip's] arrival sent ambassadors to him saying guilefully that King Edward would grant him a truce and an armistice of three days." This truce Philip, who was "ill advised," accepted only to be met with the strengthened English siegeworks at its end.[169]

Thus, it is reported, Philip challenged Edward to combat. Here too, as in the accounts of the English and southern Low Countries chroniclers, there is some disagreement among the French commentators. Indeed, several prominent French writers never even discuss Philip's challenges to the English king.[170] Three separate versions of Philip's challenges exist among the French sources. One, from the *Chronographia regum Francorum,* reports that Philip upon arriving at Calais challenged Edward to battle, but before he could recieve an answer to his query the cardinals had induced a truce between the two kings. After the truce and Philip's realization that Edward had strengthened his defenses during it, the French king again challenged Edward to combat. But this time, before Edward could reply, Philip saw that his chances of success were small, and he fled "sad and afraid" into France.[171] A second version of the challenge, recorded in the *Chronique Normande,* differs only in mentioning that Edward refused the second challenge of Philip and thus the French were forced to retreat.[172]

Only Cuvelier reports that Edward accepted the French king's challenge to do battle outside of Calais, and it is this acceptance and Philip's subsequent unwillingness to comply with his own challenge which forms the greater part of his rhyming poetical account of the siege. After mentioning the letters of challenge sent by the French king to Edward, Cuvelier writes:

The chance was there to fight / because he [Philip] required all that day / to put himself in good battle array / against the power of the king [Edward]. / And he said that the army of England / was to come to seek battle / against the king, who had there / done much wrong, as it was said. / The king was not counseled / (about which I marvel greatly) / to fight at this time. / So he [Edward] held the field all day, / and he sought battle often / because he said that was in the right. / But they [the French] did not seek to go there. / Nor were there any who desired / to fight in any place.[173]

Philip then retreated from Calais.

With Philip VI making an "ingloriosum recessum"[174] from the battlefield without engaging the English in battle, the people of Calais were forced to surrender, hoping by this maneuver to save their lives. Jean de Venette describes this incident:

When the men of Calais saw his [Philip's] retreat from afar and perceived that he had withdrawn in confusion without having given them aid or being about to give them any, they were overwhelmed with fear and dismay, because of their lack of reinforcements and of food. Wherefore, not long after, they were forced to surrender themselves and the whole town to the king of England, on condition that their lives should be spared and as many of their goods as they could carry themselves. And thus the king of England took the town of Calais.[175]

All of the French chroniclers blame Philip's flight on his inability to engage the English in battle, either because Edward had (or had not) accepted the challenges to combat, or because the English king had deceptively built defensive siegeworks which could not be penetrated. Only the author of the *Chronique des quatre premiers Valois* varies from this story. He claims that Philip returned to France without raising the siege of Calais not because of any action at the town itself, but because the queen had beckoned him to return to Paris. The anonymous chronicler writes:

King Philip came within one league of Calais, but the letters of the queen had counseled the king to return, which was not good. And thus, when King Philip had left to return to France, the English attacked Calais, and they surrendered to the mercy of King Edward.[176]

Generally, Philip is not blamed for the fall of Calais by these writers. The French authors are sympathetic to his problems at

Sangatte Hill. He is characterized as being "ill advised" by his own councillors and deceived by the enemy who, it seems, should have abided by the truce and not strengthened its position. Or, if we are to believe the *Chronique des quatre premiers Valois,* his wife the queen, dissuaded him from this adventure, an action "qui ne fut bon." Moreover, it is noted, when Philip was finally forced to leave Calais without militarily trying to raise the siege, he does so, as Jean de Venette writes, "so very sorrowful that he could not succor the men of Calais nor attack their enemies."[177]

The defeat of Calais would wound the pride of the French, but, as the *Grandes chroniques* reports, it could not defeat the kingdom's fighting spirit; within a year Philip would be counseled "that he take a great army by land and by sea to England and thus to make an end of this war."[178] England was still the evil aggressor in this conflict, frequently doing "moult grans maux" against the French lands.[179] And God was still with the French despite the loss of Calais.[180]

As for the Flemish role at Calais, the French chroniclers look sternly at the rebels from the towns of the country of Flanders, recording and criticizing many of their actions during the siege. Not only are there generic accusations like that made by the author of the *Chronique des quatre premiers Valois* that the "Flemings were on his [Edward's] side"[181] or that issued in the *Chronographia regum Francorum* that "the Flemings did not wish to obey the king of France,"[182] there is also the assertion that the Flemings "provided victuals" to the English besiegers,[183] and that they supported the English siege town, Ville-à-Neuve, with their money.[184] The French chroniclers also record several instances of French/Flemish conflict, usually skirmishes, which occured duing this time;[185] in particular, they mention the French failure to capture Cassel.[186] Finally, almost all of the French writers describing the siege of Calais also comment on the marriage problems faced by the Flemish count, Louis of Male. These accounts always criticize the role played in the affair by Edward III and the Flemish urban leaders who nearly forced an unwanted marriage onto the young count.[187]

Conclusion

The siege and capture of Calais in 1346–47 was perhaps only one small incident in a late medieval age filled with turmoil and upheaval. The war in which this siege played an early role would last, off and on, for another hundred years, with so much more destruction and loss of life that by its end the siege of Calais was remembered only in the fact that the captured town still remained the possession of England. This, coupled with the presence of the Black Death which within two years would sweep through Europe adding its own far more lethal destructive force to that of the Hundred Years War, would alter warfare for the coming generations. So many people were lost during these crises that it would be nearly 200 years before another town would be besieged by more than 30,000 soldiers as Calais was. As well, despite the fact that sieges became the standard fighting method of the war, the lengths of these sieges would diminish as it became too expensive for an army to besiege a town for almost a year, the time it took to capture Calais. A more competent use of gunpowder weapons than that found at Calais also began to decrease the time needed to take a town.

On the surface, then, the English capture of Calais may have been a last manifestation of feudal warfare. But that is not the impression given by contemporary writers reporting and commenting on the siege. To them this was not a matter of one king, buoyed by the presence of God, triumphantly occupying the town of another. Indeed, God, according to these writers, plays a very small role in the siege, only peripherally attending the affair to perform a miracle in a nearby cathedral or to punish the English soldiers with dysentery for the large number of prostitutes in their camp. Instead, in narrating the events of the siege, all contemporary chroniclers — foreign, English, French or southern Low Countries — agree that it was the hunger of the town which eventually drove it to surrender to Edward III in 1347.

Thus where these writers differ in their narratives, and where they show their fledgling nationalism, is not in the discussion of why the town fell. It is rather in a discussion of other issues leading to the surrender: Philip VI's arrival and subsequent departure from the siege without doing combat with the English army, and the role played (or not played) by the Flemish forces in aiding Edward to bring the town to submission. It is on these two issues that most contemporary writers comment, and over which they differ.

On Philip VI's flight from Calais, ultimately all French writers recognize the powerless position the French king was in when facing the English army and its well-fortified siegeworks, especially after noting that Edward III deceptively added further siegeworks, ditches, and trenches during the three-day truce agreed to by both kings. These writers are thus uncertain about the challenges of combat issued by Philip to Edward III and are sympathetic with his "inglorious" departure from

Calais without further attempting to raise the siege. Some even see this retreat as a charitable maneuver made to save lives within the town. Only the anonymous chronicler of the *Chronique des quatre premiers Valois* differs from this sympathetic view of Philip's retreat; however, it is not Philip whom he blames for the flight from Calais, but the queen who beckoned the king to return to Paris.

The English and southern Low Countries chroniclers, on the other hand, see Philip's flight coming because of his unwillingness or incapability to proceed against the English and Flemish troops entrenched in their fortifications surrounding the town. To these writers, the only possibility Philip had to retain Calais was to negotiate a peace treaty with the English. Therefore, he arranged to have corrupt and unfairly pro-French papal mediators try to "beguile" Edward into accepting a peace treaty which would not profit him, but would instead leave Calais in French hands. However, Edward refused to be beguiled and agreed to a three-day truce during which time he reinforced his numbers and added to his siegeworks.

Philip VI responded by challenging Edward to combat, a point acknowledged by all English and southern Low Countries chroniclers except for Thomas of Burton, but then fled before this combat was to be fought, surrendering the town to its besiegers.

The issue of Philip VI's flight from Calais thus serves as a basis of respective English and French nationalism. The French wish to preserve the reputation of their king, already declining after his defeat at Crécy, while the English wish to show that their forces simply overwhelmed their opponents due to their size or the strength of their fortifications. The southern Low Countries writers generally agree with their English allies on this issue. However, they differ with them and with the French chroniclers on the issue of Flemish involvement at the siege, and in this they too show their nationalism.

On this issue the French writers see the Flemings as a decisive factor in the English victory providing them with victuals, money and soldiers during the siege of Calais. This perception is not, however, held by the English writers. Indeed, contemporary English narrative sources deny the Flemings any significant role at Calais, contending instead that although they did provide most of the victuals to the English during their siege, their military assistance was negligible. English writers record only the presence of a small number of Flemish troops at Calais, and even they were not to be trusted, as the "true" allegiance of these Flemish soldiers is questioned by some English chroniclers. They report that the Flemings were being continually coaxed by Philip VI to desert the English and were in fact a threat to do just that, as they were more "inclined" to the French side than they were to the English. Thus the English authors give the impression that the Flemish presence at Calais was more a nuisance than assistance.

The chroniclers of the southern Low Countries paint an entirely different picture of Flemish involvement at Calais. While there is no mention of Flemish victualling or financial assistance by these chroniclers, a fact not so mysteriously absent as simply taken for granted, their military presence is seen as significant to the outcome. They claim that the Flemings were present in very large numbers, with one estimate reaching as high as 100,000, and more would have been there except that they were turned away by Edward III who felt he had sufficient numbers to withstand the French. More Flemish reinforcements did in fact arrive when they learned of Philip VI's approach, a detail which the bourgeois of Valenciennes and the anonymous author of the *Chronicon comitum Flandriae* insist led directly to Philip's flight from the siege. Furthermore, it is reported by the southern Low Countries writers that Edward III so valued the Flemish participation at the siege that he gave them a specific responsibility, to guard the routes from Gravelines to Calais against a French attack, and that this Flemish defense persuaded Philip VI not to attempt an attack of that otherwise weak position. Finally, if this was not enough proof of the Flemish involvement at Calais, all southern Low Countries chroniclers record at length Louis of Male's marriage problems, including how the Flemings imprisoned him to prohibit his marriage except to the daughter of Edward III. Thus it can be seen that with these favorable comments on the Flemish participation at the siege of Calais, the southern Low Countries chroniclers also exhibit a nationalism despite many of these writers not being from Flanders itself. They seem to want it known that the conflict at Calais was not simply one between France and England but also included the inhabitants of the southern Low Countries, the region most near to Calais and most affected by its English or French occupation.

NOTES

1. *V,* e.g., Georges Daumet, *Calais sous la domination Anglaise* (Arras, 1902); G.A.C. Sandman, *Calais under English Rule* (Oxford, 1908); F. Lennel, *Histoire de Calais,* II: *Calais sous la domination Anglaise* (Calais, 1910); Dorothy Greaves, "Calais under Edward III," in *Finance and Trade under Edward III,* ed. G. Unwin (Manchester, 1918),

pp. 313-50; J.L. Kirby, "The Financing of Calais under Henry V," *Bulletin of the Institute of Historical Research* 23 (1950), 165–77; S.J. Burley, "The Victualling of Calais, 1347–1465," *Bulletin of the Institute of Historical Research* 31 (1958), 49–57; G.L. Harriss, "The Struggle for Calais: An Aspect of the Rivalry between Lancaster and York," *English Historical Review* (EHR) 75 (1960), 30–53; Charles L. Kingsford, "The Earl of Warwick at Calais in 1460," *English Historical Review* 37 (1922), 544–46; S.J. Burley, *The Provisioning of Calais* (M.A. Thesis, Leeds University, 1951); P.T.J. Morgan, *The Government of Calais, 1485–1558* (D.Phil. dissertation, Oxford University, 1966); and John Rainey, Jr., *The Defense of Calais, 1436-1477* (Ph.D. dissertation, Rutgers University, 1987).

2. Edouard Perroy, *The Hundred Years War*, trans. W.B. Wells (London, 1959), pp. 118–19.

3. For modern accounts of the battle of Crécy *V* Perroy, pp. 119–20; Jules Viard, "La campagne de Crécy, juillet-aout 1346," *Le moyen âge* 37 (1926), 1–84; Hans Delbrück, *History of the Art of War within the Framework of Political History, III: The Middle Ages*, trans. Walter J. Renfroe, Jr. (Westport, Conn., 1984), pp. 453–72; Charles Oman, *A History of the Art of War in The Middle Ages*, 2nd ed. (London, 1924), II, pp. 124–47; Ferdinand Lot, *L'art militaire et les armées au moyen âge* (Paris, 1946), I: pp. 340–47; J. Lachauvelaye, *Guerres des Francais et des Anglais du XIe au XVe siècle* (Moulins, 1875), I, pp 212–20; and Alfred H. Burne, *The Crécy War* (London, 1955), pp. 65–203.

4. For the modern historian's analysis of Calais as a strategic choice after the victory at Crécy *V* Lennel, II, pp. 23; Perroy, pp. 119–20; Burne, pp. 204–07; Oman, II, p 148; Lot, I, p 348; Daumet, p. 1; Jules Viard, "Le siege de Calais," *Le moyen âge* 40 (1929), 134; Henry Stephen Lucas, *The Low Countries and the Hundred Years War, 1326–1347* (Ann Arbor, 1929), p. 555; Jean Favier, *La guerre de cent ans* (Paris, 1980), p. 120; and C.F. Richmond, "The War at Sea," in *The Hundred Years War*, ed. Kenneth Fowler (London, 1971), p. 100.

5. *V* Viard, pp. 130–31; Lucas, p. 553; and Henri Denifle, *La guerre de cent ans et la désolation des églises, monasteries et hôpitaux en France,* (Paris, 1899), I, pp 44–45.

6. The English army arrived on 2 September 1346. *v* Viard, p. 133 and Lennel, II:26.

7. *V* Viard, p. 178; Lennel, II, p. 27; and Lachauvelaye, I, p 227.

8. Viard, pp. 134–35 and Lennel, II, p.28

9. *V* Viard, p. 136; Daumet, pp. 2–3; Burne, pp. 208–09; Perroy, p. 120; Lachauvelaye, I, p. 228; and Favier, p. 121.

10.. Viard, p. 137 and Lennel, II, p. 28.

11. Viard, pp. 135, 137. Edward, however, did not need to count on the faithfulness of his Low Countries allies, as he had ensured that he was supplied sufficiently with men and victuals from England. *V* Viard, pp. 141–43; Lennel, II:27–29; H.J. Hewitt, *The Organization of War under Edward III, 1338–62* (Manchester, 1966), p. 57; and Michael R. Powicke, *Military Obligation in Medieval England: A Study in Liberty and Duty* (Oxford, 1962), pp. 185, 197–98.

12. *V* Lucas, p. 554.

13. *V* Viard, pp. 144–45 and John Bell Henneman, *Royal Taxation in Fourteenth Century France: The Development of War Financing, 1322–1356* (Princeton, 1971), pp. 200, 218.

14. *V* Viard, p. 145.

15. Viard, pp. 162–66; Lennel, II:31–32; Daumet, pp. 4–6; and Burne, p. 212.

16. On the Scottish incursion and the battle of Neville's Cross *V* Viard, p. 147; and Burne, p. 212.

17. On Edward's army strength at this time *v* Lot, I:350; J.H. Ramsey, The Strength of English Armies in the Middle Ages," *EHR* 29 (1914), 224; A.E. Prince, "The Strength of English Armies in the Reign of Edward III," *EHR* 46 (1931), 363–64; Michael Prestwich, *The Three Edwards: War and State in England, 1272–1377* (London, 1980), pp. 172–73; and K.B. MacFarlane, "England and the Hundred Years War," *Past and Present* 22 (1962), 4–5. For Edward's naval strength near Calais *V* Charles de la Ronciére, "La marine au siège de Calais," *Bibliothèque de l'école des chartes* 58 (1897), 554–78; Charles de la Roncière, *Histoire de la marine Française* (Paris, 1899), I, pp; 471–97; William Laird Clowes, *The Royal Navy*, (London, 1897), I, pp. 264–67; and Timothy J. Runyan, "Ships and Mariners in Later Medieval England," *Journal of British Studies* 16 (1977), 14. And for Edward's siege defenses and artillery at the beginning of 1347 *V* Hewitt, p. 72; Oman, II, pp. 218, 220; and T.F. Tout, "Firearms in England in the Fourteenth Century," *EHR* 26 (1911), 673.

18. On the hunger of the town and the expulsion of its poorer citizens *v* Lennel, II, pp. 30–31; Daumet, p. 6; Burne, pp. 210, 214; Lachauvelaye, I, pp. 228; Favier, p. 121; and Denifle, p. 47.

19. *V* Lucas, pp. 561–65; Lennel, II, p, 35; Burne, pp. 210–11; Favier, p. 123; and B. Wilkinson, "A Letter to Louis de Male Count of Flanders," *Bulletin of John Rylands Library* 9 (1925), 1–12.

20. Favier, pp. 123–24 and Th. M. Chotzen, "De Vlamingen voor Calais," *Revue Belge de philologie et d'histoire* 7 (1928), 1485–86.

21. *V* Viard, pp. 168–78; Lennel, II, pp. 40–44; Lachauvelaye, I, pp. 230–32; Burne, pp. 212–13; and Oman, II, pp. 153–54. For Philip's monetary woes and solutions *V* Viard, p. 169 and Henneman, pp. 216–18.

22. Henneman, pp. 218–19.

23. Viard, pp. 182–85; Lennel, II, p. 44; Lachauvelaye, I, pp. 232–33; and Burne, p. 215.

24. Viard, pp. 182–85; Lennel, II, pp. 45–47; Lachauvelaye, I, pp. 233– 34; and Daumet, p. 9.

25 Viard, pp. 184–86; Lennel, II, pp. 48–550; Lachauvelaye, I, pp. 234–35; Favier, pp. 124–26; and Lot, I, pp. 349. For a discussion on whether the date of Calais's fall was 3 August or 4 August *V* Roy Martin Haines, *Archbishop John Stratford: Political Revolutionary and Champion of the Liberties of the English Church, ca. 1275/80–1348* (Toronto, 1986), p. 353.

26 *V* Viard, pp. 187-89; Lennel, II, pp. 51–56; Daumet, pp. 10–12; Lachauvelaye, I, pp. 235–42; and Burne, pp. 216–17.

27. Roncière, *Histoire de la marine Française*, p. 565.

28. Denifle, p. 48:

Edouard avait fort bien calculé. Nulle autre ville n'offrait un meilleur point d'appui pour les expéditions contre la France, ni un meilleur entrepot pour le commerce avec la Flandre. La perte de Calais fut pour cette raison la plus sensible de toutes celles que subirent les Francais à cette époque, comme deux siècles après pour les Anglais.

29. Thomas Walsingham, *Historia Anglicana,* ed. H.T. Riley, Rolls Series (London, 1863), I, p. 272: "...videbatur Anglicis quasi novus sol oriri, propter pacis abundantiam, rerum copiam, et victoriarum gloriam."

30. *V* Richmond, p. 100; John Le Patourel, "L'occupation Anglaise de Calais au XIVe

siècle," *Revue de Nord* 33 (1951), 229–30; and May Mckisack, "Edward III and the Historians," *History* 45 (1960), p. 11.

31. *V* Richmond, p. 100; Hewitt, p. 80; and Prestwich, p. 179.

32. *V* Hewitt, pp. 60–62 and Lot, p. 349.

33. *V* Lot, p. 349 and David Nicholas, "Economic Reorientation and Social Change in Fourteenth-Century Flanders," *Past and Present* 70 (1976), 9.

34. Lucas, p. 591. *v* also Prestwich, p. 179.

35. May McKisack, *The Fourteenth Century, 1307–1399*, The Oxford History of England (Oxford, 1959), p. 251.

36. Delbrück, p. 463.

37. C.W. Previté-Orten, *A History of Europe from 1198 to 1378* (London, 1938), p. 282.

38. Favier, p. 125: "...la longueur du siège de Calais ternissait la gloire de Crécy."

39. Perroy, p. 120. *V* also McKisack, "Edward III," p. 8 and John Le Patourel, "Edward III and the Kingdom of France," *History* 43 (1958), p. 188.

40. Burne, pp. 206–07.

41. Willem van Berchen, *Gelderse kroniek*, ed. A.J. de Mooy, Werken uitgegeven door de Vereeniging Gelre, XXIV (Arnhem, 1950), p. 3: "...menibus et apparatu bellicis per regem Francie fortiter munitum..."

42. Giovanni Villani, *Istorie Fiorentine*, in *Scriptores rerum Italiacarum*, XIII. ed. Muratori (Rome, 1728), col. 973. *V* also Heinrich von Rebdorf, *Annales imperatorum et paparum, 1294–1362*, in *Fontes rerum Germanicarum*, vol. 4, ed. J.F. Bohmer (Stuttgart, 1868), p. 530.

43. *V* Villani, col. 974 and Jean de Winterthur, *Chronicon*, ed. F. Baethgen, *Monumenta Germanicae Historicum (MGH) Scriptores* (nova series), iii (Hannover, 1924), p. 273.

44. Heinrich von Rebdorf, p. 530 and *Istorie Pistolensi*, in *Scriptores rerum Italicarum*, XI, ed. Muratori (Rome, 1728), pp. 517–18.

45. *V* Villani, cols, 973–74; Jean de Winterthur, p. 273; and Mathias von Nuwenberg, *Chronica, MGH SS* (nova series), IV (Berlin, 1924), p. 407.

46. Villani, col. 974.

47. Mathias von Nuwenberg, p. 407.

48. Villani, col. 974:

Que' di Calese veggendo partito il Re d'Inghilterra di renderli la terra, salve le persone e'fortestieri, uscendone in camiscia e scalzi col capresto in collo, e'terrazzani alla sua misericordia.

v also Heinrich von Diessenhoven, *Chronicon de Henricus Truchsess von Diessenhoven*, in *Fontes rerum Germanicarum*, IV, ed. J.F. Bohmer (Stuttgart, 1868), p. 57.

49. Jean de Winterthur, p. 273: "Hec eo faciente rex Francie nec civitatem defendere nec regi Anglie resistere presumebat." *v* also Heinrich von Diessenhoven, p. 57.

50. Villani, col. 974: "Lo Re di Francia non volle accettare il partito d'andara a combattere in Fiandra fra la moltitudine de'Fiamminghi suoi ribelli e nimici."

51. Willem van Berchem, p. 3 and Heinrich von Rebdorf, pp. 53–54: "Edwardus rex Anglie, cui fortuna arrisit, post predictum victoriam obsedit civitatem nomine Calicz..."

52. *Brabantse yeesten of rijmkroniek van Braband*, ed. J.F. Willems and J.H. Bormans (Brussels, 1854), II, pp. 575–77; Edmond de Dynter, *Chronicon ducum Brabantiae*, ed. P.F.X. de Ram (Brussels, 1857), II, pp. 644–45; Jean de Hocsem, *La chronique de Jean*

de Hocsem, ed. Godefroid Kurth (Brussels, 1927), pp. 345, 367; *La chronique Liegeoise de 1402*, ed. E. Bacha (Brussels, 1900), p. 339; and Gilles li Muisit, *Chronicon*, in *Corpus chronicorum Flandriae*, II, ed. J.J. de Smet (Brussels, 1841), pp. 263–76.

53. Jean le Bel, *Chronique de Jean le Bel*, ed. J. Viard and E. Deprez (Paris, 1905), II, pp. 111–14, 125–39; 150–73; Jean Froissart, *Chroniques*, in *Oeuvres de Froissart*, ed. Kervyn de Lettenhove (Brussels, 1868), V, pp. 83–88, 118–23, 145–63, 177–222; Thomas of Burton, *Chronica monasterii de Melsa a fundatione usque ad annum 1396*, ed. E.A. Bonds, Rolls Series (London, 1867), II, pp. 60–67; Henry Knighton, *Chronicon*, ed. J.R. Lumby, Rolls Series (London, 1895), II, pp. 39–54; and Robert of Avesbury, *De gestis mirabilibus regis Edwardi III*, ed. E.M. Thompson, Rolls Series (London, 1889), pp. 383–406.

54. *Chronique Liegeoise*, p. 539.

55. Jean de Hocsem, p. 345: "...propter sagittarios infinitos qui telis suis majorem numerum occiderunt. Deinde rex Anglie ad obsidendum Calais se transtulit."

56. Jean de Hocsem, p. 367.

57. *Chronique Liegeois*, p. 339:

Rex vero Anglie victor existens secessit apud Kalas quam obsedit. Dicitur autem rex Francie habuisse secum CL milia equitum armatorum, pars adversa tria milia tantum preter sagittarios infinitos qui telis suis majorem numerum occiderunt.

58. *V* Robert of Avesbury, p. 372; John of Reading, *Chronicon*, in *Chronica Johannis de Reading et anonymi Cantuariensis, 1346–67*, ed. James Tait (Manchester, 1964), p. 101; *The Brut or the Chronicles of England*, ed. F.W.D. Brie, Early English Text Society (London, 1908), II, p. 299; *Breve chronicon Flandriae*, in *Corpus chronicorum Flandriae*, III, ed. J.J. de Smet (Brussels, 1856), p. 12; *Récits d'un bourgeois de Valenciennes*, ed. Kervyn de Lettenhove (Brussels, 1877), pp. 235, 238; *Chronicon comitum Flandriae*, in *Corpus chronicorum Flandriae*, I, ed. J.J. de Smet (Brussels, 1837), p. 219; and *Kronyk van Vlaenderen van 580 tot 1467*, ed. P. Blommaert and C.P. Serriere (Ghent, 1840), I, P. 208.

59. *Récits d'un bourgeois*, p. 258:

Ens ouquel siége et ouquel terme ses gens et les Franchois avoient fait et eu maint assaulx et maintes batailles, dont on avoit maints hommes tués et navrés, par terre et par mer, et maints hommes prins et renchonnés d'une partye et d'aultre, et maintes villes pillyes, brullées et destruites, en Gascongne, en Flandres, en Bretaingne, en Escoce, en Engleterre, en France, en Normendie, en Lymosin, en Poitou, en Angiers et en aultres pluseurs pays, dont che a esté grant domage et pité.

60. *Chronicon anonymi Cantuariensis*, op.cit. p. 292. *V* also Jean le Bel, II, pp. 11–12.

61. *Breve chronicon Flandriae*, p. 12. *V* also Jean Froissart, V, p. 86 and Thomas Walsingham, *Yprodigma Neustria*, ed. H.T. Riley, Rolls Series (London, 1876), p. 291.

62. Jean Froissart, V, pp. 85–86:

Quant li rois d'Engleterre fu venus premièrement devant le ville de Calais, ensi que cils qui moult le désiroit à conquerre, il le asséga par grant manière et de bonne ordenance, et first bastir et ordonner, entre le ville et le riviere et le pont de Niulais, hostels et maisons, et carpenter de gros mairien, et couvrir lesdites maisons, qui estoient assises et ordonnees par rues bien et faiticement... Et avoit en ceste noeve ville de roy toutes coses nécessaires apertenans à une host, et plus encores, et place ordonnée pour tenir marchiet le merkedi et le samedi, et là estoient merceries, bouceries, halles de draps et de pain et de toutes aultres nécessités, et en recouvroit-on tout aisiement pour son argent, et tout ce leur venoit tous les jours, par mer, d'Engleterre, et ossi de Flandres, dont il estoient conforté de vivres et de marchandises.

   v also Henry Knighton, II, p. 39; *Récits d'un bourgeois,* pp. 235–36; Jean le Bel, II, p. 112; and Jean Froissart, V, p. 83.
63. Jean Froissart, V, p. 183: "Et fu pourveus d'espingalles, de bonbardes, d'arcs-à-touret d'aultres instrumens bons et soubtieus." *v* also Jean le Bel, II, pp. 151–52 and Jean Froissart, V, pp. 181, 186–87.
64. Geoffrey le Baker, *Chronicon Galfridi le Baker de Swinbroke,* ed. E.M. Thompson (Oxford, 1899), p. 175:

   Ergo ab insultibus atque murorum conquassatione rex abstinuit, cogitans consulte quod fames, quae foribus clausis ingreditur, posset et deberet obsessorum superbiam domare.

   v also Thomas of Burton, II, pp. 63–64.
65. Herald of John Chandos, *The Life of the Black Prince by the Herald of Sir John Chandos,* ed. M.K. Pope and E.C. Hodge (Oxford, 1910), p. 12:

   Et luy noble Roy dengleterre
   Tient illoeques la piece de terre
   Maint escarmuche et maint assaut
   Y faisoient & bas & haut
   Tant qe la ville se rendy
   Priantz au Roy pur dieu mercy
   Qe a mercy il les vousist prendre
   Et ensement a voir entendre
   ffuist Caleis par force conquise
   P la puissance & p lemprise
   Du noble Roy et de son filtz
   Le Prince qui tant fuist hardiz

66. Jean le Bel, II, p. 132 and Jean Froissart, V, pp. 145–47.
67. *V Kronyk van Vlaenderen,* I, p. 212 and *Chronique des Pays-Bas, de France, d'Angleterre et de Tournai,* in *Corpus chronicorum Flandriae,* III, ed. J.J. de Smet (Brussels, 1856), p. 176.
68. Laurence Minot, *Poems,* ed. J. Hall (Oxford, 1887), p. 30.
69. Jean Froissart, V, pp. 119–22 and Henry Knighton, 41–42.
70. Jean Froissart, V, p. 122: "...il se départiroient dou siege devant Calais et s'en retourneroient en Engleterre."
71. *V* Walsingham, *Historia Anglicana,* I, p. 271; John of Reading, p. 104; Thomas of Burton, II, p. 67; *The Brut,* II, p. 300; Henry Knighton, II, pp; 48, 52; Laurence Minot, p. 29; Jean de Hocsem, p. 345; *Breve chronicon Flandriae,* p. 13; *Chronique de Pays-Bas,* p. 175; *Chronicon comitum Flandriae,* p. 223; Gilles li Muisit, p. 274; Jean le

Bel, II, pp. 151–52, 160–61; Jean Froissart, V, pp. 146–47, 198–99; and *The Anonimalle Chronicle, 1333 to 1381*, ed. V.H. Galbraith (Manchester, 1927), p. 23.

72. Jean le Bel, II, p. 113:

Quant ceulx de Calays virent que le roy Edowart ne se partiroit de cel yver et que leurs pourveances estoient petites, ilz mirent bien Vc personnes dehors et les firent passer parmi l'ost des Angloys. Quant le noble roy vit ainsy ces povres gens mises dehors de leur ville, ilz les fist venir tous devant luy en sa grande sale et leur fist à tous donner à boyre et à manger planteureusement, et quant ilz eurent bien mengié et but, il leur donna congié d'aler hors de son ost, et à chascun fist donner III vielz estrelins pour l'amour de Dieu et les fit conduire bien loing de son ost. On doibt bien cecy recorder pour une grande gentillesse.

The second redaction of Jean Froissart (V, p. 86) places the number of exiled Calaisiens at 1,700 and the third redaction (V, p. 89) numbers the exiles at 2,700 (Kervyn de Lettenhove's order).

73. Henry Knighton, II, p. 48:

Eodem tempore ejecti sunt Calesia de communibus minoribus circiter quingenti viri, qui venerunt ad regem Angliae quaerentes gratiam, quos rex jussit redire in villam; verumtamen qui in villa erant introitum ipsis negaverunt. Et sic moram traxerunt inter exercitum et villam, et fame ac frigore pereuntes spissim de die in diem mortui sunt.

74. This letter may be found in Robert of Avesbury, p. 386:

Mes, tres chier et tres doute seignur, sachetz qe, coment qe lez gentz sont toutz saines et heitez, mais la ville est a graunt defaute des blees, vines, et chares. Car sachietz qe ly naad riens qe ne soit tout maunge, et lez cheens et lez chates et lez chevals, si qe de viver nous ne poions plus trover en la ville, si nous ne mangeons chares dez gentz.

75. *V* Thomas of Burton, II, p. 65; Henry Knighton, II, p. 48; Robert of Avesbury, pp. 385–88; and Jean Froissart, XVIII, pp. 300–301.

76. John of Reading, pp. 104–105.

Desperantes obsessi a dicto rege se aliud refugium non habere, consumptis victualibus suis, equos, canes et mures edebant, ut suam fidelitatem non vilarent. Tandem, compertum est inter eso nichil victui remanere, quos misserima fames aut male mori aut villam reddere coegit, ipsosque domini sui omni succursu atque auxilio viduatos.

77. Gilles li Muisit, p. 274:

Quo tempore consumptis victualibus, tantam sunt passi penuriam, succursum sperantes habere quotidie, quod equos et bestias comederunt, et post, coria equorum et bestiarum frixa in oleo; ad ultimum murilegos, canes, ratos, mures et bestias tales, quas habere poterant, comedebant, propter quod multae personae mortuae sunt.

78. Laurence Minot, p. 29. *v* also *Anonimalle Chronicle*, p. 23 and Jean Froissart, V. pp. 198–99.

79. Henry Knighton, II:52:

Rex vero misericordia motus suscepit eos in gratiam suam, et gratiose eos tractabat; statimque misit victualia in villam ad recreationem populi, sed illi erant adeo famelici et fame affecti et adnihilati ac debilitati, et tantum sumpserunt de victu et potu, nocte proxima sequenti moriebantur in dicta villa plusquam ccc. personae.

80. *V The Brut,* II:300–01; *Récits d'un bourgeois* pp. 258–59; Jean le Bel, II, pp. 160–67; Jean Froissart, V, pp. 198–215; and Thomas Gray, *Scalachronica,* trans. H. Maxwell (Glasgow, 1907), p. 116.

81. *Anonimalle Chronicle,* p. 23: "...passerent parmy lost Dengleterre devers la terre de Fraunce saunz male ou moleste et ceo par conge et commaundement del roi Dengleterre."

82. Robert of Avesbury, p. 396:

Et idem dominus rex semper misericors et begnignus, captis et retentis paucis de majoribus, communitatem dictae villae cum bonis suis omnibus gratiose permisit abire.

83. *The Brut,* II, p. 301. *V* also John of Reading, p. 101; Thomas of Burton, II,p. 67; and Henry Knighton, II, p. 52.

84. Jean Froissart, V, p. 215:

"Ha! dame, je amaisse trop mieuls que vous fuissiés d'aultre part que chi. Vous priés si acertes que je ne vous ose escondire le don que vous me demandés; et comment que je le face envis, tenés, je les vous donne, et en faites vostre plaisir."

v Récits d'un bourgeois pp. 259–61; *Chronique de Pays-Bas,* pp. 176–77; *Kronyk van Vlaenderen,* I:217; Jean le Bel, II, pp. 161–68; and Jean Froissart, V. pp. 198–215.

85. Jean le Bel, II, p. 111.

86. *Kronyk van Vlaenderen,* I, p. 212.

87. This letter can be found in T. Rymer, *Foedera, conventiones,* etc., 3rd ed, (The Hague, 1739), II, p. 205.

88. *V Kronyk van Vlaenderen,* I, p. 212 and Henry Knighton, II, pp. 48–49.

89. John of Reading, p. 104.

90. *Gregory's Chronicle, 1189–1469,* in *Historical Collections of a Citizen in London in the Fifteenth Century,* ed. Jane Gardiner, Camden Society (London, 1876), p. 82.

91. *Breve chronicon Flandriae,* p. 13 and *Chronicon Angliae Petriburgensis,* ed. J.A. Giles (London, 1845), p. 169.

92. *Rijmkroniek van Vlaenderen,* in *Corpus chronicorum Flandriae,* IV, p. 844.

93. Henry Knighton, II, p. 49.

94. Thomas of Burton, p. 66.

95. *Chronique de Pays-Bas,* p. 176.

96. *V* Gilles li Muisit, p. 271.

97. Walsingham, *Historia Anglicana,* I, p. 271:

Cum Rex Angliae strictius obsideret Calesiam, Rex Franciae, juxta promissionem quam obsessis promiserat, collecto exercitu, Calesiam appropinquat, ad dissolvendum obsidionem, si quoquomodo valeret.

98. Henry Knighton, II, pp. 49–50.

99.   Jean le Bel, II, pp. 155–56:

Quant ceulx de Calais le virent sur le mont de Sangate, ilz eurent moult grande joye, car ilz cuidoient bien estre dessiegiez, mais quant ilz virent que on se logoit, ilz se commencerrent ung petit à desesperer.

100.   *Chronicon comitum Flandriae,* p. 223. Other authors who comment on the approach of the French army include: Thomas Walsingham, *Yprodigma Neustria,* p. 291; Thomas Gray, p. 116; Herald of John Chandos, p. 12; Geoffrey le Baker, p. 176; Robert of Avesbury, p. 390; *Récits d'un bourgeois,* p. 257; Jean Froissart, V, pp. 177–85; Ranulph Higden, *Polychronicon,* ed. C. Babington and J.R. Lumby, Rolls Series (London, 1885), VIII: 342–43; and *Vita Edwardi secundi,* in *Chronicles of the Reigns of Edward I and Edward II,* II, ed. William Stubbs, Rolls Series (London, 1882), p. 294.
101.   Jean le Bel, II, p. 157.
102.   *V* Henry Knighton, II, p. 50; Robert of Avesbury, p. 390; *Kronyk van Vlaenderen,* I, p. 217; *Chronicon comitum Flandriae,* p. 223; Gilles li Muisit, p. 271; Jean le Bel, II, pp. 159–60; and Jean Froissart, V, pp. 194–96;.
103.   Laurence Minot, p. 28.
104.   Henry Knighton, II, p. 50:

Et eodem tempore venerunt cardinales ad regem Edwardum tractare de pace inter reges, et sic data est treuga inter partes per iv. dies ad tractandum de pace inter reges.... Ad quod breviter responsum est; quod villa et ea quae in ea erant, erant et esse deberent ad voluntatem regis Angliae, et nihil de dono Philippi de Valoys.

v also Robert of Avesbury, p. 390. (The names of these cardinals are different in many of the chronicles.)
105.   *Chronicon comitum Flandriae,* p. 223:

Cardinales tractabant interim de pace vel treuga inter reges, sed nihil proficiebant, quia rex Angliae omnino volebat habere villam de Calays sibi redditam, priusquam procederet in quocumque tractatu, quia sciebat Casselienses per ipsum obsessos, fame valida et inedia cruciatos.

v also *Kronyk van Vlaenderen,* I, p. 217.
106.   Gilles li Muisit, p. 271:

Venerunt autem duo... cardinales, dominus Hannibal et dominus de Claromonte, et se cum suis inter duas acies posuerunt, laborantes ad pacem reformandam, aut ut treugae donarentur, obtinueruntque ab utraque parte sufferentiam trium dierum solummodo, in quibus tribus diebus venerunt regi Angliae magna copia Flamingorum et Anglicorum, et crevit multum suus exercitus; et fecit fieri fossata magna circa suum exercitum, ita quod rex Franciae et sui ad aciem regis Angliae nullum possent habere accessum nec viam eundi ad villam de Calais propter mare et propter loci parvitatem.

v also Jean le Bel, II, p. 159 and Jean Froissart, V, pp. 194–96.
107.   Jean Froissart, V, p. 178: "Mais li rois d'Engleterre pour ce temps avoit tant de bons amis en Flandres...."

108. *V* Jean le Bel, II, pp. 156–57 and Jean Froissart, V, pp. 188–89.
109. Walsingham, *Ypodigma Neustria,* p. 291:

> Sed cum vidisset se non posse votis suis satisfacere in hac parte, ultimo die dicti mensis Julii, hora Vesperarum, fecit offerri Regi Angliae, quod quandocunque sibi placeret extra locum obsidionis venire ad bellum.

> *v* also Gregory's Chronicle, p. 82 and *Rijmkroniek van Vlaenderen,* p. 845.

110. *Chronique de Pays-Bas,* p. 176 and Jean le Bel, II, pp. 197–98.
111. *V* John of Reading, p. 104; *The Brut,* II, p. 544; Henry Knighton, II, pp. 50–51; and Robert of Avesbury, p. 391.
112. This letter may be found in Robert of Avesbury, pp. 391–95:

> Et puis, la Mardy, vers le vespre, vindrent certeins grauntz et chivalers de part nostre adversarie a la place du tretee, et offrirent a noz gentz la bataille de part nostre adversarie susdit, par ensi qe noz vousissoms venir hors le marreys, et il nous durroit place convenable pur combatre quele heure qe nous plerroit, entre cele heure et Vendredy a soir proschein suant; et vorroient qe iiij. chivalers de noz et aultre iiij. de lour esleirent place covenable pur lune partie et pur lautre. Et sur ceo noz gentz responderent qils nous ferroient monstrer cel offre, et lor durroient respounse le Meskerdy suant. Quele chose monstre a nous, avons eut consail et de nostre host, en affiaunce de Dieux et de nostre droit, nous lour feismes responde qe nous acceptasmes lour offre et prendrissoms le bataille voluntiers; et feismes feare noz lettres de conduyt a iiij. chivalers del autre partye, de quele estat ou condicion qils feussent, de venir a nostre host, a fin qe nous purroions prendre aultre iiij. de lor estat, et qe mesmes les viij. chivalers feissent le serment qe alassent veer et cercher les places tantqe ils fussent en accord.

113. *The Brut,* II, p. 544.
114. Henry Knighton, II, p. 51:

> Rex Edwardus... ad implendum omnes foveas et infringendum omnia obstacula circa obsidionem, ita quod Franci possent habere liberum ingressum et passagium cum suo exercitu ad bellum congrediendum sine impedimento qualicumque.

115. Thomas of Burton, II, p. 66:

> Venerunt legati domini papae, comes videlicet de Ermynak et alii duo magnates Franciae, ad tractandum cum magnantibus Angliae per regem ad hoc assignatis super pace reformanda... Sed cum de pacis reformatione dicti domini inter se nequiverant concordare, obtulit rex Edwardus Philippo de Valesio quod in campi plantie, aut infra ubi hospitabantur Anglici, dimarcaret libentissime cum eodem.

116. Laurence Minot, pp. 28–29.
117. *Chronique de Pays-Bas,* p. 176: "...et bien vit li rois Phelippes que il ne pooit le ville secourir, ne bastaille avoir." *v* also Thomas Walsingham, *Ypodigma Neustria,* p. 29.
118. *The Brut,* II, p. 300.
119. Jean le Bel, II, p. 157; Jean Froissart, V, pp. 189–90, 192, 196–97; Herald of John Chandos, p. 12; and *Chronique de Flandre,* in *Istore et chroniques de Flandres,* II, ed.

Kervyn de Lettenhove (Brussels, 1879), p. 55.
120. Herald of John Chandos, p. 12:

Mais ensi fuist lui hoost logie
Et la ville si assegie
Qe le Roy Philippes noesa
Lever lassege einz retourna.

121. Jean le Bel, II, p. 157:

Ces mareschaulx alerent partout regarder les passages, puis revinrent au roy et luy
dirent à brefves parolles qu'il n'y avoit passage par ou l'ost du roy poeut aprochier l'ost
des Angloys, s'il ne vouloit mettre ses gens à perte mielx qu'ilz ne furent à la bataille de
Cressy.

122. Walsingham, *Historia Anglicana*, I, p. 271:

In crastino vero adventus sui, clam aufugit diluculo, relictis tentoriis, cum victualibus
abunde refertis, metuens nimirum Anglici Regis audaciam, quam expertus fuerat
parum ante, damno suo.

123. Robert of Avesbury, p. 391:

Tunc praefatus dominus Philippus, magnanimi regis Anglorum audiens voluntatem,
eventum belli noluit exspectare, sed de nocte ante diem Jovis proximo tunc
sequentem, tentoriis suis in incendium positis et ibidem quasi omnibus suis sarcinolis
derelictis, quaerens subterfugia, clam recessit et subtiliter evanuit ab oculis
Anglicorum.

124. Found in Robert of Avesbury, p. 393:

Et ceaux de lautre partie maintenaunt, quant ils avoient oye ceste respounse,
comencerent de varier en lour offres et de parler de la ville tut novele, auxi come
entrelessant la bataille; issint ne se voleient tenir a nul certain. Et sur ceo y Jeofdy
devant le jour, nient contre esteantz les parlantz susditz, nostre dit adversarie se depar-
ti, od toutes ses gentz, auxi com disconfit; et hasterent taunt qils arderent lour tentes et
graunt partie de lour herneys a lour departir.

   v also The Brut, II, p. 300, 544; Henry Knighton, II, p. 51; and *Rijmkroniek van
   Vlaenderen*, pp. 845–46.
125. Geoffrey le Baker, p. 177:

Tyrannus Francorum videns potentiam regis auctam, in aurora diei sua tentoria
ignibus depascens, signo proinde funesto obsessis dato quod non auderet ipsis succerrere, vecorditer aufugit.

126. *Eulogium historiarum sive temporis*, ed. F.S. Haydon, Rolls Series (London, 1858), I, p.
   211:

Videbatur regi etiam Franciae et pluribus aliis suorum ante congressionem belli quod tanta fuit multitudo Anglorum quod totus mundus eis non resisteret, et ideo territi fugerunt et contriti.

127. *Récits d'un bourgeois*, p. 257:

Et quant le roy de France vid qu'il avoit mandé bien Cm Flamens qui là virent, tous vestus des paremens d'Engleterre, ledit roy de France et tous ses osts se deslogèrent et s'en ralèrent, sans aultre confort faire à ceulx de Callais, dont ce fut grant honte.

v also *Chronicon comitum Flandriae*, p. 223 and *Kronyk van Vlaenderen*, I, p. 217.
128. *V* Jean le Bel, II, pp. 160–61; Jean Froissart, V, pp. 198–199, 206; *Eulogium historiarum*, I, p. 212; Ranulph Higden, pp. 344–45; *Gregory's Chronicle*, pp. 82–83; Geoffrey le Baker, pp. 176–77; Herald of John Chandos, p. 12; *Vita Edwardi secundi*, p. 294; *Récits d'un bourgeois* pp. 258–59; Thomas Walsingham, *Historia Anglicana*, I, p. 271; John of Reading, pp. 104–05; Thomas of Burton, II, p. 67; *Anonimalle Chronicle*, p. 23; *The Brut*, II, p. 300; Henry Knighton, II, p. 52; Robert of Avesbury, pp. 395-96; and Laurence Minot, pp. 29–30.
129. John Lydgate, "Lydgate's Verses on the Kings of England," in *Historical Collections*, Camden Society, p. 52.
130. Laurence Minot, p. 28.
131. John of Bridlington, *Poem*, in *Political Poems and Songs relating to English History Composed during the Period from the Ascension of Edward III to Richard III*, I, ed. T. Wright, Rolls Series (London, 1859), pp. 158, 166.
132. John of Bridlington, p. 161:

Eulogium didici, tauri perient inimici.
Nam rex robustus armis, per singula justus,
Rex bonus et fortis, cui null nocent mala mortis,
Rex nunquam victus, gladii cui non nocet ictus;
Emanuel dictus, cum quo fit copia victus,
In mundo talis non est pugnans generalis.

134. Robert of Avesbury, p. 384.
135. *Chronicon comitum Flandriae*, p. 220:

Cumque vellent depraedare cathedralem ecclesiam Virginis gloriosae, ac deinde ignem apponere in eadem, accidit ibidem unum miraculum pulcherrimum non immerito memoriae commendandum. Unus enim sagittarius Anglicus irreverenter impegit cum arcu suo in caput imaginis beatae Virginis infra basilicam existentis, volens auferre, ausu sacrilegio, velamen vel coronam, cum quo vel cum qua ejus caput venerabile ornabatur; sed continuo arcus fortissimus, quem tenebat injuriator in manibus, in multa subito confractus est frusta, quae resiliebant illico in ipsum injuriatorem et etiam in cirucmstantes. Per quod cunctis evidentissime patuit, quod benedictus Dei filius dissimulare noluit opprobrium dilectissimae matri suae factum, sed, ut dictum est, illud continuo vindicavit. Unde ex hoc adeo compuncti sunt omnes illi barbari, quod prostrati ad terram veniam humillime a beata Virgine petierunt, et eidem quasi in emendam commissi flagitii munera quam plurima obtulerunt. Ob hoc etiam pepercerunt dictae cathedrali ecclessiae et aliis ecclesiis civitatis, ne per ipsos igne apposito vastarentur.

v also *Kronyk van Vlaenderen*, I, p. 209.
136. Thomas of Burton, II, p. 65:

Interim Anglici nostri in obsidione villae permanentes ex morbo dissenterico usque ad quindecim millia hominum decesserunt. Et sic eos Dominus, ut creditur, propter sua demerita flagellavit, eo praecipue quod tantus fuit ibidem accessus mulierum publicarum quod illarum numerus excessit quandoque numerum armatorum.

137. *V Récits d'un bourgeois*, p. 257; *Chronicon comitum Flandriae*, p. 223; and *Kronyk van Vlaenderen*, I, p. 217.
138. *V* Thomas of Burton, II, p. 66 and Henry Knighton, II, p. 52.
139. Henry Knighton, II, p. 52.
140. Thomas of Burton, II, p. 60 and Adam Murimuth, *Continuatio chronicorum*, ed. E.M. Thompson, Rolls Series (London, 1899), p. 218.
141 Kronyk van Vlaenderen, I:209:

Omtrent Bamesse soe reinet eene weeke lanc ende was zeere cout, doen quamen den coninc Eduwaert veele Inghelssche te hulpen ende daeromme hy gaf den Vlaminghen orlof, ende sy trocken alle t'huuswaert, want de coninc Eduwaert hadde volcx ghenouch om den coninc van Vrankeryke te wederstane.

v also *Chronicon comitum Flandriae*, p. 220.
142. Robert of Avesbury, p. 384.
143. *V* Jean Froissart, V, pp. 178, 181 and *Kronyk van Vlaenderen*, I, p. 214.
144. Jean Froissart, V, p. 161: "Li rois d'Engleterre... voloit tenir à amour les Flamens car à venir à son entente de Calais, il li pooient trop grandement valoir."
145. Jean Froissart, V, p. 197:

Mais quant il regardoient le passage de Gravelines et les destrois et mauvais et périllens passages que il aueroient à passer, et comment bien soissante mille Flamens gisoient de ce lés devant Calais, il rompoient et amolioient lors imaginations et disoient: "Toutes nostres pensées sont vainnes. Il nous faut perdre Calais."

v also Jean Froissart, V, pp. 187–88.
146. *V* Jean le Bel, II, pp. 135–39; Jean Froissart, V, pp. 149–62; Edmond de Dynter, II, pp. 645; *Breve chronicon Flandriae*, pp. 12–13; *Brabantse yeesten*, II, pp. 575–77; *Chronique de Pays-Bas*, pp. 173–74; *Kronyk van Vlaenderen*, I, pp. 210–11; *Chronicon comitum Flandriae*, pp. 221–22; *Rijmkroniek van Vlaenderen*, pp. 841–44, 846; Gilles li Muisit, pp. 264–65, 270–71; and de Budt, *Chronicon Flandriae*, in *Corpus chronicorum Flandriae*, I, pp. 330–31.
147. *V* Thomas Gray, p. 116 and John of Bridlington, p. 159.
148. John of Bridlington, p. 159: "Necnon Flandrenses partim sunt Francigenenses."
149. This story is found in and translated (into Dutch) by Th. M. Chotzen, "De Vlamingen voor Calais," *Revue Belge* 7 (1928), p. 1489:

Wel dyma chwedyl anghyffelib y'w vod ynn wir o herwydd ymrauaelion bethau ar a ellid i roddi a'i ddywedud ynn erbynn y matter hwn ynn gysdal, o herwydd bod pennaethiad Fflandyrs yn dal gida brenin Ffrainck ynn yr amser yma.

150. Cuvelier, *Chronique de Bertrand du Guesclin par Cuvelier, trouvère du XIVe siècle*, ed. E. Charrière (Paris, 1839), I, p. 489.
151. Richard Lescot, *Chronique*, ed. J. Lemoine (Paris, 1896), p. 76 and *Les grandes chroniques de France*, ed. Jules Viard (Paris, 1934), IX, p. 286: "... et li administroient les Flamens vivres par paiant l'argent." *v* also Jean de Venette, *Chronique*, ed. and trans. R.A. Newhall (New York, 1953), p. 46 and *Chronique Normande au xiv siècle*, ed. Auguste and Emil Molinier (Paris, 1882), p. 89.
152. Jean de Venette, p. 45. (Latin in the *Continuatio chronici* of Guillaume de Nangis, ed. H. Geraud (Paris, 1843), II, p. 205.)
153. *Grandes chroniques*, IX, pp. 285–86; Jean de Venette, p. 45; and Eustace Deschamps, *OEuvres completes*, ed. Q. de Sainte Hilaire and G. Raynaud (Paris, 1882), III, pp. 48–49.
154. Jean de Venette, p. 45: (Latin in *Continuatio chronici* of Guillaume de Nangis, II, p. 205.)

Anno domini MCCCXLVII rex Edwardus praedictus, sedens ante Calesium, multos insultus villae facit; sed illi de villa ab infra se egregie defenderunt per machinas et alia genera balistarum: quandocumque etiam exeuntes, quamplures de Anglicis trucidabant, et de ipsis triumphabant.

155. *Grandes chroniques*, IX, pp. 285–86:

Et pour ce que le roy d'Angleterre ne pot pas si tost entrer en la ville de Kalais comme il voult, il la first fermer de siege, et si fist eslever habitacions assez pres de laditte ville pour herbergier li et son ost.

v also Jean de Venette, p. 44.
156. Richard Lescot, p. 75: "Quia custos ville, vocatus dominus Johannes de Vienna, deditionem recusavit, obsidione cinxit, jurans quod inde non recederet, nisi prius capta villa."
157. *V* Jean de Venette, p. 46; Richard Lescot, p. 76; *Chronique Normande*, p. 90; and *Chronographia regum Francorum*, ed. H. Moranville (Paris, 1894), II, pp. 245–46.
158 *V* Jean de Venette, p. 45; Richard Lescot, p. 76; *Chronique Normande*, p. 90; and *Chronographia regum Francorum*, II, pp. 244–45.
159. *V Chronique Normande*, p. 90 and *Chronographia regum Francorum*, II:245.
160. Jean de Venette, p. 45: (Latin in *Continuatio chronici* of Guillaume de Nangis, II, p. 205.)

Rex autem Franciae Philippus confortabat Calesienses, victualia eis per terram ver per mare mittendo. Quae quidem victualia si sufficienter habuissent, nunquam eos de Anglicis dubitare convenisset; sed illi quibus pro eis provisiones committebantur, illas ad propria commoda convertebant, ut dicebatur, rege tamen Francorum et consilio ignorante.

161. *Grandes chroniques*, IX, p. 293:

Mais le roy d'Angleterre et le duc de Lencastre... et les Anglois qui de nouvel estoient venuz a leur seigneur, avoient fermée, et enclose la ville de Kalais de si grant siege, tant par terre comme par mer, que vivres ne pooient en nulle maniere estre portez à ceulz qui estoient en laditte ville de Kalais, pour laquelle chose il vivoient en grant desesperance et en grant misere, jusques atant qu'il sorent la venue du roy et qu'il se vouloit combatre contre son anemi et lever le siège d'entour laditte ville.

162. *Grandes chroniques,* IX, p. 311: "Et pour ce que ilz n'avoient eu point de vitaille... ainçois mengoient leurs chevaux, chaz, chiens, raz et cuirs de buef a tout le poil, se rendirent audit roy d'Angleterre, sauves leurs vies." *v* also *Chronique des quartre premiers Valois,* ed. S. Luce (Paris, 1862), p. 57.

163. Jean de Venette, p. 45: (Latin in *Continuatio chronici* of Guillaume de Nangis, II, p. 205.)

Videns autem rex Franciae, quod rex Angliae ab illo loco obsidionem non dimitteret, cum magna multitudine armatorum ivit illuc, quoniam dictum fuit sibi quod illi de villa victus suos ulterius non habebant, et ita erat.

164. *Chronique Normande,* p. 83.
165. Richard Lescot, p. 75:

Obsidionem audiens rex Philippus, ultra exactiones consuetas et fere importabiles regnicoli alias superaddidit et de consenu pape, decimas ecclesiarum colligens, cum ab usuaraiis Lombardis ingentes pecunias extorsisset.

166. Richard Lescot, p. 75.
167. *Chronique Normande,* pp. 89–90:

Ainçis envoya querre trieves de III jours par III cardinaux, qui y estoient envoiez par le saint pere pour appraisier ces II princes. Et le roy Phelippe accorda les trieves III jours, et en cellui terme les Anglois et les Flamans firent fossez et trenquiez entour leur ost et sur la dune de la mer, par tele maniere que Francois n'y purent assembler à eulz ne secourre la ville de vivres ne d'autres choses.

168. *Grandes chroniques,* IX, p. 311 and *Chronographia regum Francorum,* II, pp. 344–45.
169. Jean de Venette, p. 46 and Richard Lescot, p. 76.
170. *V,* e.g., the accounts found in Jean de Venette (pp. 45–47) and Richard Lescot (pp. 75–77).
171. *Chronographia regum Francorum,* II, p. 245:

Et ergo [rex Francie] mandavit regi Anglie pro bello corporis contra corpus aut centum contra centum, vel mille contra mille, vel exercitus contra exercitum. Sed minime exauditus, videns quod ville succurrere non valeret nec bellum habere cum rege Anglie, tristis et mestus remeavit in Franciam.

172. *Chronique Normande,* p. 90.
173. Cuvelier, I, p. 490:

La chance fut lors bestournée,
Car tousdis requéroit journée

Pour soy combatre en bel arroy
Contre la puissance du roy:
Et disoit que lors d'Angleterre
Estoit venu bataille querre
Contre le roy, qui li avoit
Fait moult de tort, com il disoit
Le roy ne fut pas conseillé
(Dont je fu moult esmerveillé)
De le combatre en celui temps;
Si tenoit-il tousdis les champs
Et bataille souvant requéroit;
Car il disoit que droit avoit.
Mais pour néant l'aloit quérant;
N'estoit celui qui eust talent
De le combatre en nul lieu.

174. V Richard Lescot, p. 76.
175. Jean de Venette, p. 46: (Latin in *Continuatio chronici* of Guillaume de Nangis, II, p. 207.)

Quod percipientes Calesii, a longe recessum videntes, et quod rex sine auxilio eis dato vel dando confusus recedebat, in stuporem et pavorem, tam ex defectu auxilii quam victualium, conversi sunt; unde non post multum temporis se et villam totam regi Angliae, coacti, salvis vitis eorum et salvo quantum super se de bonis suis portare possent, finaliter rediderunt. Et sic rex Angliae villam Calesiensem cepit.

   v also *Chronique Normande,* p. 90.
176. *Chronique des quatre premiers Valois,* p. 18:

Le roy Philippe vint jusques à une lieue pres de Kalais. Mais par les lettres de la roine le roy out conseil de retourner, qui ne fut bon. Et donc quant le roy Philippe se fut mis en chemin de retourner, les Anglois pristrent Calais et se rendirent à la mercy du roy Edouart.

177. Jean de Venette, p. 46: (Latin in *Continuatio chronici* of Guillaume de Nangis, II, pp. 206–07.) "Rex Franciae se deceptum videns, et quod nullo modo posset ad Calesium accedere, dolens nec Calesiensibus succerrere, nec inimicos evadere, reversus est in Franciam indilate."
178. *Grandes chroniques,* IX, p. 312: "...li conseillierent que il feist tost une grant armée par mer pour aler en Angleterre, et aussi par terre; et ainsi pourroit finer sa guerre."
179. V Cuvelier, I, p. 490.
180. Indeed, Eustace Deschamps (III, pp. 47–48) composed a poem concerning the "Perfidie des Anglais" to show that God was still with the French despite their loss at Calais.
181. *Chronique des quatre premiers Valois,* p. 17: "Et furent les Flamens en son [le roy Edouart] aide."
182. *Chronographia regum Francorum,* II, p. 236: "...Flamingi non adhuc volebant obedire regi Francie."

183. Jean de Venette, p. 46.

184. *V Grandes chroniques,* IX, p. 286.

185. *V Chronique Normande,* pp. 82, 83, 88, 89 and *Chronographia regum Francorum,* II, p. 244.

186. *V Chronique Normande,* p. 89 and *Chronographia regum Francorum,* II, p. 244.

187. *V* Jean de Venette, pp. 47–48; Richard Lescot, p. 77; *Chronique des quatre premiers Valois,* p. 18; *Chronique Normande,* pp. 84–85; and *Chronographia regum Francorum,* II, pp. 246–47.

THE FAMILY OF DYNASTIES IN MEDIEVAL EUROPE: DYNASTIES, KINGDOMS AND *TOCHTERSTÄMME*

Armin Wolf

Max-Planck-Institut
für europäische Rechtsgeschichte
Frankfurt-am-Main, Germany
and
Historisches Seminar,
University of Heidelberg, Germany

THE DIRECT LINE OF DESCENT OF QUEEN ELIZABETH II

KING EGBERT = REDBURH

KING ETHELWULF = OSBURH (1st wife)

KING ALFRED = EALHSWITH

Anglo-Saxons   KING EDWARD = EDGIVA (3rd wife)

KING EDMUND I = ELGIVA (1st wife)

KING EDGAR = ELFRIDA (2nd wife)

KING ETHELRED II THE UNREADY = ELFLEDA (1st wife)

KING EDMUND II IRONSIDE = EALDGYTH

EDWARD ATHELING THE EXILE = AGATHA

KING WILLIAM I = MATILDA   ST. MARGARET = KING MALCOLM III
(the Conqueror)   of Scotland

Normans

KING HENRY I = MATILDA (1st wife)

GEOFFREY, Count of Anjou = MATILDA

KING HENRY II = ELEANOR of Aquitaine

Anjou-
Plantagenet   KING JOHN = ISABELLA of Angoulême (2nd wife)

KING HENRY III = ELEANOR of Provence

KING EDWARD I = ELEANOR of Castile (1st wife)

KING EDWARD II = ISABELLA of France

KING EDWARD III = PHILIPPA of Hainault

JOHN of Gaunt = KATHARINE Swynford   EDMUND = ISABEL of Castile
Duke of Lancaster   (3rd wife)   Duke of York   (1st wife)

JOHN, Marquess of Dorset = MARGARET Holland   RICHARD = ANNE Mortimer

JOHN BEAUFORT, Duke of Somerset = MARGARET Beauchamp   RICHARD = CECILY Neville

EDMUND, Earl of Richmond = MARGARET   KING EDWARD IV = ELIZABETH Woodville

KING HENRY VII = ELIZABETH of York

Tudor

KING JAMES IV of Scotland = MARGARET Tudor

KING JAMES V of Scotland = MARY of Lorraine

MARY, Queen of Scots = HENRY STUART, Lord Darnley (2nd husband)

Stuart   KING JAMES I = ANNE of Denmark

FREDERICK, King of Bohemia = ELIZABETH

ERNEST AUGUSTUS, Elector of Hanover = SOPHIA

KING GEORGE I = SOPHIA Dorothea of Celle

Hanover   KING GEORGE II = CAROLINE of Brandenburg-Anspach

FREDERICK LEWIS, Prince of Wales = AUGUSTA of Saxe-Gotha

KING GEORGE III = CHARLOTTE of Mecklenburg-Strelitz

EDWARD, Duke of Kent = VICTORIA of Saxe-Coburg-Saalfeld

QUEEN VICTORIA = PRINCE ALBERT of Saxe-Coburg and Gotha (Prince Consort)

Saxe-Coburg   KING EDWARD VII = PRINCESS ALEXANDRA of Denmark
= Windsor   KING GEORGE V = PRINCESS MARY of Teck

KING GEORGE VI = LADY ELIZABETH BOWES-LYON

HER MAJESTY
QUEEN ELIZABETH II =

H.R.H. THE PRINCE PHILIP,
DUKE OF EDINBURGH

Figure 1.

(Taken from: Patrick W. Montague Smith, The Royal Line of Succession, London 1967)

The Family of Dynasties
In Medieval Europe:

Dynasties, Kingdoms and
Tochterstämme *

Introduction (with figures 1–4)
I. Inheritance and Election: Alfonso the Wise,
   Richard of Cornwall, and the Imperial Electors (with tables A and B)
   1. Alfonso in Castile
   2. Alfonso as Emperor
   3. Richard of Cornwall
   4. Royal Electors and the College of Electors
   5. Summary
II. Principles and System of Inheritance:
   A European Survey
   1. Genealogical and Prosopographical Overview (with tables I–XVII)
   2. Statistical Analysis
   3. Systematic Conclusions

Anyone arriving at Vancouver International airport is first welcomed by a portrait of Her Majesty, Elizabeth II, which documents the fact that Canada is still a monarchy. And when visiting one of the royal castles in England, one can purchase a booklet displaying on the back cover a table of "The direct line of descent of Queen Elizabeth" (fig. 1).This lit-

*Part of this study was presented at the XVII Mediaeval Workshop (November, 1987) at the University of British Columbia. The author wishes to express his thanks to János Bak and Bernhard Heise for preparing the English version and to the Max-Planck-Institut für europäische Rechtsgeschichte, Frankfurt-am-Main for a grant to support publication. The XVII Medieval Workshop was supported by a grant from the Social Sciences and Humanities Research Council of Canada.

185

tle table traces English sovereignty back over thirty-eight generations to King Egbert, who reigned in the year 802. Let us imagine this chain of thirty-eight persons standing in a line, each of whom would be the father or mother of the next; it would take us back to the age of King Egbert and Charlemagne. During one's lifetime, a person can be in touch with five generations: as a child listening to his grandparents, and in his old age talking to his grandchildren. Hence, in our imaginary chain of thirty-eight persons, number one could have heard via number three of number five; number five of number nine, number nine of number thirteen, and so on. Thus, one would need only ten or eleven people as witnesses to span the enormous period of 1100 years back to the birth of Europe.

Although this mental experiment illustrates our proximity to the time of Egbert and Charlemagne, the historical sources do not permit us to reconstitute the complete line of three dozen generations for everybody, but only for dynasties, that is, lines of hereditary rulers. This is one of the reasons why historical research of dynasties has a unique value, even if one is not a monarchist.

Comparative studies of European dynasties can exploit coherent and relatively complete demographic material ranging over more than a thousand years and comprising the whole history of Christian Europe. Their study, therefore, deserves the same attention as the numerous locally restricted investigations of populations of small villages or towns over rather short periods which, in the last few decades, have been hailed as the "new history." The study of dynasties allows us to discover structures of long duration (structures de longue durée), especially the long-lived forms which organized government by laws of descent, the basis of the dynastic system.

As James C. Goldsmith pointed out: "Inheritance systems, broadly conceived, are strategies for the transfer of property from one generation to another."[1] Since pre-modern rulership was connected with certain properties and could even be regarded as a kind of property itself, we can apply Goldsmith's words to our topic and state: dynastic systems, broadly conceived, are strategies for the transfer of power and authority from one generation to another.

The present study is restricted to royal dynasties between 1100 and 1500 in Europe, excluding the Crusader States and Orthodox countries such as the Byzantine Empire and Russia. The area examined consists of eighteen kingdoms: France, England, Scotland, Portugal, Castile-León, Navarre, Aragón, Sicily, Naples, Hungary, Bohemia,

Poland, Sweden, Norway, Denmark, and the Holy Roman Empire, consisting of its three parts, Germany, the kingdom of Burgundy or Arles, and Italy. I did not consider the kingdoms of León, Valencia, Mallorca, Sardinia, or Croatia-Dalmatia because during the period in question they had the same respective rulers as Castile, Aragon, and Hungary.

To begin with, we should survey the dynasties and the nations they ruled. They are presented on three lists. The first one (fig. 2) lists the eighteen kingdoms and their dynasties between AD 1100 and AD 1500. During these four centuries there were in Germany thirteen dynasties; in Sweden, nine; in Hungary, eight; in Bohemia and Norway, seven; in Italy and Denmark, six; in Navarre, Sicily-Naples and Scotland, five; in England and Poland, four; in Aragon, Castile and France, three; in Arles, two; and in Portugal, one. This would make a total of ninety-one royal dynasties, but because several dynasties reigned in more than one kingdom, the actual number of different dynasties is only forty-one.

The second list (fig. 3) is organized the other way around. Here the dynasties are displayed according to the number of kingdoms they ruled or claimed to rule in the four hundred years under review. This list is headed by the Capetian dynasty, reigning in no less than six European kingdoms: permanently in France and, in a cadet line, in Portugal; temporarily in Sicily-Naples, Hungary, Navarre, and Poland. These are followed by the dynasties of Ivrea-Castile, Plantagenet, Wittelsbach and Luxemburg, each of which ruled or claimed to rule five kingdoms. The Hohenstaufen and Habsburg dynasties held four kingdoms each. There are also seven dynasties temporarily ruling up to three kingdoms, nine dynasties with two kingdoms, and finally eighteen dynasties with only one kingdom. Among this last group are not only lesser dynasties like the Schwarzburgs, who claimed the German throne for just five months, but also important dynasties like the Ynglings, Árpáds, Piasts, Duncans, and Stenkils, who were the native dynasties, of Norway, Hungary, Poland, Scotland and Sweden, ruling for many centuries.

The third list (fig. 4) shows the ratio between the number of European kingdoms and the number of different dynasties through the late Middle Ages. Italy and Burgundy were left out, because the thrones of these two kingdoms were vacant most of the time. The first column lists the kingdoms, followed by the names of their respective dynasties in fifty year intervals. This list illustrates that the aforementioned forty-one dynasties never ruled simultaneously. In 1100, most of the existing kingdoms had its own dynasty. Until 1250, the number of dynasties roughly equalled that of kingdoms (thirteen/eleven, fifteen/thirteen, fifteen/fourteen, fifteen/fourteen). But by 1300 (and even more by 1350), the number of dynasties had decreased considerably, due to the fact that several national dynasties had died out while others had accumulated more than one kingdom. By 1300 there were only eleven — in 1350, merely nine — different dynasties ruling the sixteen kingdoms. This process of concentration continued, and in the fifteenth century we find eight dynasties sharing all sixteen kingdoms. A column at the right margin gives the situation in the year 1610, when the condition was extreme: only five dynasties monopolized all sixteen European kingdoms. Afterwards, the number of dynasties increased again.

So far I have distinguished between various dynasties, as is traditional, exclusively by their male line. From now on, however, I intend to treat the interconnections between these dynasties which make them a "family of dynasties." This demands that we look for the females linking these dynasties together. Traditional dynastic history emphasized only the male line. The tables in traditional genealogical handbooks neglect the descendants of daughters. An entirely new book would emerge were we to investigate systematically the descendants of daughters, for which I have introduced the German notion of *Tochterstamm,* meaning literally "daughter's stem." Because this sounds awkward in English, I will retain the German word *Tochterstamm,* in plural, *Tochterstämme.*

Let me illustrate my point with a rather simple and well-known example. On "The direct line of descent of Queen Elizabeth" (fig. 1), I have indicated the various dynasties: the Anglo-Saxons, the Normans, the house of Anjou-Plantagenet (with its lines of Lancaster and York), the dynasties of Tudor, Stuart, Hanover, and finally Saxe-Coburg-Gotha (called the House of Windsor since World War I). These seven English royal dynasties are connected by females — set in blocks on the table. Of the thirty-eight generations listed here, no less than eleven are represented by daughters of an old dynasty who became the mothers of a new one. The present ruling house, starting with Edward VII, is but a *Tochterstamm* of the Hanovers, through Queen Victoria. Beginning with George I, the Hanovers were a *Tochterstamm* of the Stuarts, the Stuarts of the Tudors, the Tudors of the Anjou, who with Henry II were a *Tochterstamm* of both the Norman and Anglo-Saxon dynasties.

This is not very surprising, since England is regarded as a

Figure 2

18 Medieval Kingdoms in Europe and their 91 (41) Dynasties from 1100 to 1500

Germany 13
1 Salians 1024–1125
2 Süpplinburg 1125–37
3 Staufer 1138–1254
4 Guelphs 1198–1218
5 Thuringia 1246–47
6 Holland 1248–56
7 Ivrea–Castile 1257–75
8 Plantagenet 1257–72
9 Habsburg 1273…1740
10 Nassau 1292–98
11 Luxemburg 1308…1437
12 Wittelsbach 1314…1410
13 Schwarzburg 1349

Sweden 9
1 Stenkil c1060–c1129
2 Swen Estridson II 29…1161, ♀ 1412
3 Sverker 1134–1250
4 Folkungs 1250–1363
5 Mecklenburg 1363–89/95
6 Pomerania 1396–1439
7 Wittelsbach 1441–48
8 Bonde 1448…1470
9 Oldenburg 1457–1523

Hungary 8
1 Arpads 1000–1301
2 Capet–Naples 1292–1382/1414
3 Przemyslids 1301–05
4 Wittelsbach 1301–08
5 Luxemburg 1387–1437
6 Habsburg 1438–1457
7 Jagellons 1440…1526
8 Hunyadi 1458–90

Bohemia 7
1 Przemyslids 1086–1306 ♀ 1330
2 Habsburg 1306–07, 1438–57
3 Görz 1307–10
4 Luxemburg 1310–1437
5 Podiebrad 1458–71
6 Hunyadi 1469–90
7 Jagellons 1471–1526

Italy 6
1 Salians 1027…1125
2 Süpplinburg 1133–37
3 Staufer 1155…1250
4 Guelph 1209–1210/18
5 Luxemburg 1311…1378
6 Hapsburg 1452–93

Denmark 6
1 Sven Estridsen 1047–1375 ♀ 1412
2 Mecklenburg 1375, 1387
3 Folkung 1376–87
4 Pomerania 1396–1439
5 Wittelsbach 1440–48
6 Oldenburg 1449–today

Norway 7
1 Ynglings 863–1319
2 Folkungs 1319–1387
3 Sven Estridson 1380 ♀ 14
4 Pomerania 1389–1442
5 Wittelsbach 1442–48
6 Bonde 1449–50
7 Oldenburg 1450…today

Navarra 5
1 Pamplona 905–1234
2 Champagne 1234–1274 ♀ 1305
3 Capet 1305–1425 ♀ 1441
4 Ivrea–Castile 1425–1479 ♀ 1479
5 Foix 1479–87 ♀ 1517

Sicily and Sicily–Naples 5
1 Hauteville 1130–94
2 Staufen 1194–1266/68
3 Capet 1266…1360
4 Barcelona 1282–1410
5 Ivrea–Castile 1412–1516 ♀ 1555

Scotland 5
1 Duncan 1034–1285
2 Baliol 1292–96
3 Plantagenet 1296–1314
4 Bruce 1306–71
5 Stuart 1371–1688 ♀ 1714

England 4
1 Normandy 1066–1135
2 Champagne–Blois 1135–54
3 Plantagenet 1154–1485
4 Tudor 1485–1553 ♀ 1603

Poland 4
1 Piasts 1025…1370/77
2 Przemyslids 1300–06
3 Capet–Hungary 1370–82 ♀ 1399
4 Jagellons 1386–1526

Aragon 3
1 Pamplona 1035–1137 ♀ 1162
2 Barcelona 1162–1410
3 Ivrea–Castile 1412–1516 ♀ 1555

Castile 3
1 Pamplona 1035–1109 ♀ 1126
2 Ivrea 1126–1474 ♀ 1504
3 Plantagenet 1369–87

France 3
1 Capet 987…1848
2 Plantagenet 1340…1485
3 Tudor 1485–1553 ♀ 1603

Arles 2
1 Staufen 1178–90
2 Luxemburg 1365–78

Portugal 1
1 Capet–Burgundy ?1143–1826 ♀ 1853

Figure 3
41 Royal Dynasties in 18 Kingdoms of
Medieval Europe (1100-1500)

Dynasties	Years	Kingdoms	Number of of kingdoms ruled or claimed
Capet	987 ... 1848	France 1	
	?1143 – 1826 ♀1853	Portugal 1	
	1266 ... 1860	Sicily/Naples 3	
	1292 – 1382 / 1414	Hungary 2	
	1305 – 1425 ♀ 1441	Navarra 3	
	1370 – 1382 ♀ 1399	Poland 3	6
Ivrea–Castile	1126 – 1474 ♀ 1504	Castile 2	
	1257 – 1275	Germany 7	
	1412 – 1516 ♀ 1555	Aragon 3	
	1412 – 1516 ♀ 1555	Sicily 5 (Since 1442 also Naples)	
	1425 – 1479 ♀ 1479	Navarra 4	5
Plantagenet	1154 – 1485	England 3	
	1257 – 1272	Germany 8	
	1296 – 1314	Scotland 3	
	1340 ... 1485	France 2	
	1369 – 1387	Castile 3	5
Wittelsbach	1301 – 1308	Hungary 4	
	1314 – 1347		
	1400 – 1410	Germany 12	
	1440 – 1448	Denmark 5	
	1441 – 1448	Sweden 7	
	1442 – 1448	Norway 5	5
Luxemburg	1308 – 1313 ⎱		
	1346 – 1437 ⎰	Germany 11	
	1310 – 1437	Bohemia 4	
	1311 – 1313 ⎱	Italy 5	
	1355 – 1378 ⎰		
	1365 – 1378	Arles 2	
	1387 – 1437	Hungary 5	5
Hohenstaufen	1138 – 1254	Germany 3	
	1155 ... 1250	Italy 3	
	1178 – 1190	Arles 1	
	1194 – 1266	Sicily 2	4
Habsburg	1273 ... 1740	Germany 9	
	1306 – 1307 ⎱		
	1438 – 1457 ⎰	Bohemia 2	
	1438 – 1457	Hungary 6	
	1452 – 1493	Italy 6	4
Pamplona	1000 – 1234	Navarra 1	
	1035 – 1109 ♀ 1126	Castile 1	
	1035 – 1137 ♀ 1162	Aragon 1	3
Przemyslids	1086 – 1306 ♀ 1330	Bohemia 1	
	1300 – 1306	Poland 2	
	1301 – 1305	Hungary 3	3

Dynasty	Dates		Country	
Folkungs	1250 – 1363		Sweden 4	
	1319 – 1387		Norway 2	
	1376 – 1387		Denmark 3	3
Jagellons	1386 – 1526		Poland 4	
	1440 ... 1526		Hungary 7	
	1471 – 1526		Bohemia7	3
Pomerania	1389 – 1442		Norway 4	
	1396 – 1439		Sweden 6	
	1396 – 1439		Denmark 4	3
Oldenburg	1449 – today		Denmark 6	
	1450 ... today		Norway 7	
	1457 ... 1523		Sweden 9	3
Salians	1024 – 1125		Germany 1	
	1046 ... 1125		Italy 1	2
Sven Estridson	1047 – 1375 ♀ 1412		Denmark 1	
	1129 ... 1161 ♀ 1412		Sweden 2	
	1380 – ♀ 1412		Norway 3	3
Süpplinburg	1125 – 1137		Germany 2	
	1133 – 1137		Italy 2	2
Champagne–Blois	1135 – 1154		England 2	
	1234 – 1274 ♀ 1305		Navarra 2	2
Barcelona	1162 – 1410		Aragon 2	
	1282 – 1410		Sicily 4	2
Guelphs	1198 – 1218		Germany 4	
	1209 – 1210 / 18		Italy 4	2
Mecklenburg	1363 – 1395		Sweden 5	
	1375 ... 1388		Denmark 2	2
Bonde	1448 ... 1470		Sweden 8	
	1449 – 1450		Norway 6	2
Hunyadi	1458 – 1490		Hungary 8	
	1469 – 1490		Bohemia 6	2
Tudor	1485 – 1553 ♀ 1603		England 4	
	1485 – 1553 ♀ 1603		France 3	2
Ynglings	863 – 1319		Norway 1	1
Arpads	1000 – 1301		Hungary 1	1
Piasts	1025 – 1370 / 77		Poland 1	1
Duncan	1034 – 1285		Scotland 1	1
Stenkil	c1060 – c1129		Sweden 1	1
Normandy	1066 – 1135		England 1	1
Hauteville	1130 – 1194		Sicily 1	1
Sverkar	1134 – 1250		Sweden 3	1
Thuringia	1246 – 1247		Germany 5	1
Holland	1248 – 1256		Germany 6	1
Nassau	1292 – 1298		Germany 10	1
Baliol	1292 – 1296		Scotland 2	1
Bruce	1306 – 1371		Scotland 4	1
Görz	1307 – 1310		Bohemia 3	1
Schwarzburg	1349 – 1349		Germany 13	1
Stuart	1371 – 1688 ♀ 1714		Scotland 5	1
Podiebrad	1458 – 1471		Bohemia 5	1
Foix	1479 – 1483 ♀ 1517		Navarra 5	1

Figure 4

Ratio between the number of European kingdoms and the number of different dynasties

Year / Kingdom	1100	1150	1200	1250	1300	1350	1400	1450	1500	1610
France	Capet	Capet	Capet	Capet	Capet	Capet-Val	Capet-Val	Capet-Val	Capet-Orl.	Capet Bourbon
England	Normandy	Champ.Blois	Plantagenet	Plantagenet	Plantagenet	Plantagenet	Plantagenet	Plant.Lanc.	Tudor	Stuart
Scotland	Duncan	Duncan	Duncan	Duncan	Plantagenet	Bruce	Stuart	Stuart	Stuart	Stuart
Portugal	—	Capet-Burg.	Capet-Burg.	Capet-Burg.	Capet-Burg.	Capet-Burg.	Capet-Aviz	Capet-Aviz	Capet-Aviz	Habsburg
Castile	Pamplona	Ivrea	Ivrea	Ivrea	Ivrea	Ivrea	Ivrea	Ivrea	Ivrea	Habsburg
Navarra	Pamplona	Pamplona	Pamplona	Champagne	Champagne	Cape t-Evreux	Capet-Evreux	Ivrea	Foix	Capet-Bourbon Habsburg
Aragon	Pamplona	Pamplona	Barcelona	Barcelona	Barcelona	Barcelona	Barcelona	Ivrea	Ivrea	Habsburg
Sicily	—	Hauteville	Staufen	Staufen	Barcelona	Barcelona	Barcelona	Ivrea	Ivrea	Habsburg
Naples	—	—	—	—	Capet Anjou	Capet-Anjou	Capet Duraz.	Ivrea	Iverea	Habsburg
Hungary	Arpad	Arpad	Arpad	Arpad	Arpad	Capet-Naples	Luxemburg	Habsburg	Jagellon	Habsburg
Bohemia	Przemyslid	Przemyslid	Przemyslid	Przemyslid	Przemyslid	Luxemburg	Luxemburg	Habsburg	Jagellon	Habsburg
Poland	Piast	Piast	Piast	Piast	Piast Przemyslid	Piast	Jagellon	Jagellon	Jagellon	Vasa
Sweden	Stenkil	Stenkil	Stenkil	Folkung	Folkung	Folkung	Pomerania	Bonde	Oldenburg	Vasa
Norway	Yngling	Yngling	Yngling	Yngling	Yngling	Folkung	Pomerania	Oldenburg	Oldenburg	Oldenburg
Denmark	Sven Estr.	Sven Estr.	Sven Estr.	Sven Estr.	Sven Estr.	Swen Estr.	Pomerania	Oldenburg	Oldenburg	Oldenburg
Germany	Salian	Staufen Guelph	Staufen Holland	Staufen	Habsburg Wittelsbach	Luxemburg	Luxemburg	Habsburg	Habsburg	Habsburg
Number of Kingdoms	13	15	15	15	16	16	16	16	16	16
Dynasties	11	13	14	14	12	9	9	8	8	5
Ratio %	85	87	93	93	69	56	56	50	50	31

hereditary monarchy which recognizes women's right to succession. But what about those hereditary monarchies which excluded women from succession, like France, or the elective monarchies like Germany or Denmark? It can be shown that such *Tochterstämme* existed not only in England but in other kingdoms as well, and that branches of several dynasties of Europe became *Tochterstämme* of other dynasties. In the following, I wish to demonstrate that the notion of *Tochterstämme* helps to systematize the relationships of numerous dynasties and to clarify the apparent chaos of the comings and goings of dynasties throughout medieval Europe, by revealing some general principles governing the dynastic system. Furthermore, following from these principles there were certain concepts which were significant in determining whether successions were to be accepted or contested, whether there was to be war or peace.

Such systematic and comparative investigations demand extensive studies. Hence, for a start, let us examine a "case study" from the thirteenth-century Holy Roman Empire and a systematic overview of Europe in the late Middle Ages, during the century between 1350 and 1450. The thirteenth-century case, the elections of Alfonso the Wise and of Richard of Cornwall as kings of Germany and Alfonso's inheritance of the Castilian throne, will reveal the all-pervading importance of dynastic principles for both electoral and hereditary kingdoms. It will also show that the principles demonstrated for the later Middle Ages in our broader survey were in operation already before AD 1300.

I
Inheritance and Election: Alfonso the Wise, Richard of Cornwall, and the Imperial Electors[2]

Usually the historical monarchies of Europe are categorized into hereditary and electoral kingdoms. Castile, France, and England count as classic hereditary kingdoms, Germany and Poland as electoral ones. Denmark was originally an electoral kingdom but later became a hereditary one. As far as I know, there is as yet no explanation why one monarchy followed one rule and another the other.

However, upon close scrutiny one can show that there was no essential difference between electoral and hereditary kingdoms, only a partial one. Hereditary kingdoms were a particular form of electoral kingdoms, or, the other way around, electoral systems were a special version of the hereditary principle.

This is an argument that can be supported by the example of Alfonso the Wise. As king of Castile and as king of the Holy Roman Empire, he brought together in his person both the characteristics of a hereditary and an elected ruler. Alfonso was most certainly aware of the fact that there were polities which acquired their rulers by election and others which were ruled by kings who succeeded by the right of succession. In his *Especulo,* the king himself stated:

> *que nos sobre dicho rey don Alfonso avemos poder de facer estas leyes tambien como los otros que fezieron ante de nos...*

> *...por razon, que si los emperadores e los reyes, que los imperios e los regnos ovieron por eleccion, pudieron fazer leys en acquello que tovieron como en comienda, quanto mas nos que avemos el regno por derecho heredamiento.*[3]

Alfonso does not maintain here that there was a fundamental opposition between an elected and a hereditary king, other than possibly the appearance that the one was able to give laws and the other was not. The hereditary monarch was simply an enhanced elected monarch: if the elected king was already able to give laws, to what greater extent could the king who possessed his kingdom by the virtue of the right of succession!

With the death of his father Ferdinand III, Alfonso followed by right of succession as king of Castile, León, etc. on June 1, 1252. And on the basis of a number of elections, in 1256 by the cities of Pisa and Marseilles and later in 1257 by several German princes, he was made king of the Romans and future emperor.

1. Alfonso in Castile

Alfonso X belonged to the younger, Leonian line of the Castilian royal house, which had ruled in León since 1157, and also in Castile after the extinction of the male side of the older line in 1257, and which in 1230 again brought León and Castile together under one king (cf. Table A.)

We have to note here the transmission of the Spanish kingdoms via women. The father of Alfonso X, Ferdinand III, owed his hereditary succession in Castile in the first line to his mother Berenguela, the daughter-heir of the older branch of his house. After the death of her childless brother, she received homage as queen from the Cortes, who had been summoned to Valladolid. Thereupon she

immediately renounced the Castilian throne in favor of her son
Ferdinand (1217). But Ferdinand had to fight for his hereditary succes-
sion in León against his half-sisters, Sancha and Dulcia (1230). Alfonso
IX of León had instituted them as his heiresses in order to protect the
independence of the kingdom and to prevent its reunification with
Castile.

The joint house of Castile-León likewise ruled on the basis of
a female hereditary succession, for Alfonso VII, the first Castilian king
from the house of Ivrea, counts of Burgundy, inherited the realm from
his mother, Queen Urraca, who died in 1126. Urraca was the daughter-
heir of the House of Pamplona. This House of Pamplona, which goes
back to Sancho III (1000–1035), ruled in three lines in Castile until
1109/26, in Aragon until 1137/62, and in Navarre until 1234.

It is also noteworthy that with the extinction of the male
branch of one line, the female branch, not the surviving male branch
of another line, succeeded. Thus the nearer cognates, not the further
agnates, were the heirs. Expressed in a different way: the *Lex Salica* was
not valid here. Succession by cognates was more often successful than a
purely agnate succession. But these successions were by no means
uncontested, as is evident from the failed attempt in 1109 of King
Alfonso I of Aragon to be acknowledged as king in Castile and León as
well.

Not only choices between cognate and agnate hereditary
claims, but also among various cognates were important. Thus in 1253
Alfonso X laid claim to the kingdom of Navarre on the basis that the
House of Castile, like the House of Champagne, stemmed from a
prince of Navarre. In the end, even choices between various agnates
were necessary. The eldest son of Alfonso X Ferdinand de la Cerda,
predeceased his father in 1275. A conflict arose on whether his son
(Alfonso's grandchild) held representation rights, that is, could follow
as an heir to his predeceased father, or whether Alfonso's second son,
Sancho, was to inherit. Thus the principle of the relation closest by
degree (Sancho) opposed the principle of primogeniture (de la
Cerda). King Alfonso convened a council: all those present spoke out
in favor of his grandson, except Manuel, Alfonso's younger brother,
who argued that the law (*ley*) supported the claim of the younger son.
He explained: "Señor, if a main stem of the royal line dies, then the
nearest to the top must step into that place. Three things must remain
solid: the law, the king, and the kingdom; all that which seeks to gain
credence against these things invalid and must not be observed."[4]

This preference of the (younger) son over the grandson (of an older line) was indeed in concert with the stipulations of the *Fuero Juzgo,* based upon the *Lex Visigothorum:*

Lex Visigothorum	Fuero Juzgo
Quod in haereditatis successione filii prima sunt	Que los fiios deven eredar primeramientre en la buena del padre.
In haereditate illius qui moritur si intestatus discesserit, filii primi sunt. Si filii desunt nepotibus debetur haereditas...	En la heredad del padre (si murier sin testamento — ms. toledo) vienen los fiios primeramientre. E si non oviere filios devenlo aver los nietos...[5]

Even the *Especulo* is properly interpreted within the context of this traditional law:

> Onde por todas estas razones que dixiemos el fijo mayor del rey deve heredar el señorio de su padre, o la fija mayor ostrosi fijo no oviere.[6]

The later collection of the *Siete Partidas,* however, pleads for the principle of representation:

> Et aun mandaron, que si el fijo mayor moriese ante que heredase, si dexase fijo o fija, que hobiese de su mujer legitima que aquel aquella lo hobiese et non otro ninguno.[7]

In his first testament (1276), King Alfonso the Wise followed the council of his brother Manuel and declared his younger son, Sancho, as heir:

> Since according to custom and the natural law, to the Fuero and to the law of Spain, the eldest son is to inherit the kingdoms and the power of his father, so should the eldest of the sons of Don Fernando have been the rightful heir, if his father had survived; but since, according to the will of God, the right of the direct line was extinguished by the death of Don Fernando, so we have in accordance with the customary rights and the laws of Spain conferred the succes-

sion upon our now eldest son, Don Sancho, who stands closer to us in a direct line than our grandson, the son of the late Don Fernando.[8]

He later wanted to compensate his grandson — whose mother was the sister of the French king and who was himself supported by France — with at least the kingdom of Jaen (1281). Sancho refused and enlisted the Cortes of Valladolid to overthrow his father and elect himself as king. Thereupon Alfonso disinherited Sancho and declared his own grandson, de la Cerda, as heir of all his kingdoms, or alternatively, the king of France, who was cognatively the great-grandson of Alfonso VIII. When Alfonso the Wise died in 1284, he was followed by Sancho IV; but Alfonso de la Cerda raised his claims on a number of occasions, giving up only in 1331.

Thus even in the hereditary kingdom of Castile, decisions had to be made repeatedly between various claims of inheritance; and thus, in a way, "elections" took place to choose from among different claimants.

2. Alfonso as Emperor

In Germany, that is in the empire, kings and emperors were chosen by election. But even in this electoral system, arguments of lineage and the rights of succession played fundamental roles.

Table B is an excerpt from my systematic genealogical studies of the Roman-German kings and their collateral relations, encompassing three centuries (c.a.1000–1300) and including some 3,000 persons. Here, only the data relevant to the situation of the two elections of Alfonso of Castile and Richard of Cornwall in the years 1256/57 are presented. The table is not an arbitrary collection. The selection of persons is based upon legally relevant and anthropologically fixed criteria.

At the time of Alfonso's and Richard's elections, there existed in Germany a number of factions of royal candidates and electors. On Table B the Spanish faction is framed in continuous, the English faction in broken, and the Hohenstaufen faction in dotted lines. The lines of the two kings' blocks appear in bold, those of their electors in normal lines. The kings appear in bold print and the electors in italics. The ecclesiastical electors, the three Rhenish archbishops from Mainz, Cologne, and Trier, are of course not considered among them, since they were not hereditary princes.

Our table reveals the previously unnoticed fact that the elected kings of 1257 and their secular electors from the various factions were all related *(consanguinei)*. Furthermore, they were not just arbitrarily related, but were in fact representatives of the *Tochterstämme* of the first German royal and imperial house of the Ottonians (or Saxons).

The representative of such a royal *Tochterstamm* was ordinarily the oldest living male in the line of primogeniture. But occasionally the representative was the senior or highest ranking male. According to this definition, the representatives and other members of the same *Tochterstamm* were connected by agnatic (male) relation. In comparison, representatives and members of different *Tochterstämme* were connected by cognatic (female) relation.

Such classification of all descendants of a house into *Tochterstämme* and their presentation through their respective representatives is considerably more than just a genealogical collection of filiations. It makes visible the structure of the consanguine situation according to legally relevant criteria. Basically, such tables can be created for each family which had descendants in the female line.

Table A presents the royal *Tochterstämme* of the House of Pamplona in Spain. Table B comprises a particular selection of *Tochterstämme* of the Ottonian imperial house. By the same method, it is also possible to compile tables of the *Tochterstämme* of the Carolingians or any other European dynasty. Although in part they would comprise the same families, they would offer different perspectives and would make visible the individual structures of the cognatic relationship systems of the given dynasties. Even within the same dynasty, the tables of the *Tochterstämme* vary considerably in different key years.

On Table B the first German king, Henry I, and the three Ottos are listed in the top left. Their house died out in the direct male line in the year 1002, and in the collateral line in 1024. Even though most of the Ottonian princesses entered ecclesiastical positions, four of them — Gerberga and Hedwig (sisters of Otto I), Liudgard (sister of Otto II) and Matilda (sister of Otto III) — married, and, from a total of five different marriages, obtained descendents, thus producing five *primary Tochterstämme*. From the marriages of the daughters of these five *primary* Ottonian *Tochterstämme*, there emerged further *Tochterstämme*, which I designate *secondary Tochterstämme* (thus, for example, the Hohenstaufen are a *primary Tochterstamm* of the Salians and a *secondary Tochterstamm* of the Ottonians). *Tochterstämme* from secondary *Tochterstämme* can be termed tertiary, and so on. These subordinate

Tochterstämme, which are in some way represented by primary *Tochterstämme,* remain out of the picture until, for some specific reason, the primary *Tochterstamm* disappears. Then the secondary ones are promoted to primary *Tochterstämme,* the tertiary to secondary ones, and so on.

Reasons for such moves would be the extinction of the male line of the *primary Tochterstamm,* or the residency of the *primary Tochterstamm* in a foreign country. Since, during the eleventh and the thirteenth century all *initial* primary *Tochterstämme* in Germany had disappeared, all those in the table were in one way or another "promoted" to the primary position.

Using these criteria, Table B displays numerous representatives of the primary and domestic *Tochterstämme* of the Ottonians in their constellation for the key year of 1256/57. For reasons of space and sake of clarity, a number of simplifications were made. Women are framed, and printed in bold face types, in order to emphasize the previously unnoticed lines of descent through females. On the table, kings, queens, and king's daughters are capitalized. Names of non-Germans are underlined.

The two Ottonian *Tochterstämme* most important to the kingdom are in columns 1 and 12. In the first column, the Salian kings and emperors succeed as descendents of the Ottonian daughter, Liudgard. The line then continues through the Salian daughter, Agnes (in column 12), in the imperial house of Hohenstaufen. The table shows that the three main imperial houses of medieval Germany — Ottonian, Salian, and Hohenstaufen — were cognatically joined. The Salians followed as a *Tochterstamm* of the Ottonians, and then the Hohenstaufen as a *Tochterstamm* of the Salians. The successions were, to be sure, decided in elections by the princes of the kingdom. But, as a rule, the king elected belonged to a royal *Tochterstamm* which, with the disappearance of the royal male line, became eligible for inheritance.

When the Hohenstaufen king, Conrad IV, (col. 12) died in Italy in 1254, he left behind a two-year-old son, Conradin. The closest legitimate adult male relatives at this time were the sons of three of King Philip's daughters: the Duke of Brabant, the King of Bohemia, and King Alfonso of Castile (cf. cols. 15, 14, and 13). Similar to the way the Salians had succeeded the Ottonians, and the Hohenstaufen the Salians, so could the Brabantines, Bohemians, and Castilians have followed the Hohenstaufen.

What is also worth mentioning is that not for the first time these three had become representatives of *Tochterstämme* of the Ottonian royal house, through their Hohenstaufen mother, possessing such a position through earlier alliances for many generations. Thus they appear twice on Table B: the Count of Brabant in col. 17; the king of Bohemia in col. 2; and the king of Castile in col. 7. One simply remained largely in the same sphere of *connubium*, with new alliances regenerating old claims again.

In any event, the counts of Brabant (col. 17) were already qualified to become kings before their descent from the Hohenstaufen was established. In the years 1192 and 1208, Count Henry I of Brabant was spoken of as a royal candidate. At the Council of Lyons after the deposition of Emperor Frederick II, Count Henry II of Brabant was offered the Roman-German crown by the papal faction. He nevertheless declined and guided the election of 1247 in favor of his nephew, William of Holland.[9] King William died in January, 1256, leaving behind — just as had his Hohenstaufen counterpart, Conrad IV in 1254 — only a two-year-old son.

Not only in 1254, but also in 1256, King Ottokar of Bohemia was spoken of as a candidate. The archbishop of Cologne tarried over this issue for almost four weeks in July/August 1256 in Prague. A number of princes probably considered electing the by now four-year-old son of King Conrad IV, Conradin (col. 12). Pope Alexander IV, however, in a letter of 28 July 1256, to the three Rhenish archbishops, threatened to excommunicate all electors voting for the young Hohenstaufen.[10] Presently, on August 5, 1256, in Wolmirstedt (near Magdeburg), several princes decided in favor of electing Otto of Brandenburg, *consanguineum nostrum*.[11] He was the younger brother of the Margrave Johann of Brandenburg (col. 5).

Meanwhile, for the first time, two foreign houses belonging to the royal family gathered support from German princes for election to be king of the Romans. In return they offered promises and considerable sums of money. On 13 January 1257, the German supporters of Alfonso of Castile, who had already been declared the king of the Romans by Pisa and Marseilles, assembled in the traditional electoral city of Frankfurt and locked the gates, so that the supporters of Richard of Cornwall could not enter. Thus the brother of the English king was elected in the wrong place, outside the city of Frankfurt. As a result, the election of Alfonso was postponed, and he was not declared king until 1 April 1257.

Such a contest between two kings was nothing new in

Germany. Since the time of Otto IV of Brunswick, from 1198 to 1218, and then after 1246, with the deposition of Emperor Frederick II, Germany almost continuously had two competing rulers at the same time. In the same way that Richard of Cornwall can be considered the successor to William of Holland (died 1256), so can Alfonso of Castile be considered the successor of Conrad IV of Swabia (died 1254) and of the Hohenstaufen emperor. Let us briefly consider the two candidates and their electors.

The significance that descent from the German imperial house had in Castile is indicated by the names which Alfonso's parents, Ferdinand III and Beatrix of Swabia, chose for their children. Of the seven sons of this marriage, excepting Alfonso, only the third and sixth sons (Fernando and Sancho) bore the names of Spanish kings. The remaining four brothers were named Fadrique, Enrique, Felipe, and Manuel, that is, Frederick, Henry, Philip, and Emmanuel. All these were names derived from their maternal ascendent: they were either names of the direct German royal and imperial antecedents back to King Henry I or of emperor Manuel of Constantinople.

Such names were not given arbitrarily. The fact that these names appeared here for the first time in the Castilian royal house is clear testimony to the mentality of King Ferdinand III and his spouse: they were meant as signs of claims and served also to foster an awareness of the mother's relations and the candidacies for inheritance they entailed.

On 4 February 1255, only a few months after the death of King Conrad IV, and while the counter-king, William was still alive we are told that Pope Alexander IV supported the efforts of King Alfonso of Castile to gain the lordship of Swabia. Alfonso expressly called upon his *materna successio.* Thus for Alfonso it was not only *ad acquirendum ducatum Suevie,* but also *quedam alia iura sibi in illis partibus ex materna successione competentia.*[12]

Whether or not, with these other rights, claims were already being laid on the kingdom or empire is not clear. A connection between the claims for Swabia and the empire was, however presented by the Pisan envoys on 18 March 1256 in Soria, at Alfonso's election as king and emperor of the Romans. In the documents drawn up concerning this election, Alfonso is acknowledged as *natum de progenie domus ducatus Suevie, ad quam de privilegio principum et de concessione Romane ecclesie pontificum imperium iuste et digne dignoscitur pertinere et successive ad vos, qui ex ea domo descenditis recta linea....*[13]

At the imperial election of Alfonso by the envoys of the city of
Marseilles on 13 September 1256, in Segovia, it was the *nobilitas* of the
king that was referred to first, and only thereafter his *industria, strenu-
itas, sapienca et prudencia, fides et potencia et clara fama*. The Marseillians
elected Alfonso because he descended *de stirpe imperiali tam Romana et
Constantinopolitana quam Yspana*.[14]

Alfonso's relationship with the Eastern Roman emperors
seems also to have played a role even with the Pisans. Their envoys
exclaimed before Alfonso: "Through you, if you succeed the exalted
Manuel, the late Emperor of Byzance, the unjustly divided Empire
could be joined, united in you with God's grace, as the Empire had
been at the time of Caesar and the most Christian Constantine."[15]

The Marseillians even promised, not only Alfonso, but also his
newly-born son (1256), to serve them as if they were successive heirs of
the empire *(tam sibi quam filio eius heredi in hoc honore succedenti)*.[16] The
office of the emperor was here already clearly being treated as quasi-
hereditary.[17]

The election of an emperor by an Italian and a Burgundian
city was something quite unusual. According to Wilhelm Berges, the
Pisan and Marseillian envoys behaved "as the representatives of the
Italian and Burgundian peoples of the empire." Of course, one may
speculate that the fact that the male line of the House of Castile
stemmed from the kingdom of Burgundy and originally from Ivrea in
Italy played a role in this election. (cf. Table B, col 7). An awareness
that the Castilian royal house originated in Burgundy was obviously present during the lifetime of Alfonso, born in 1221. The contemporary
archbishop of Toledo, the city of the king's birth, Rodrigo Ximenes de
Rada (1210–1247) knew in any case that the Castilian male line
descended from Count William of Burgundy (died 1087). According to
Rodrigo, the betrothal of Berenguela of Castile to Conrad, the son of
Frederick Barbarossa, was broken off on the grounds of close kinship,
which rested on the mutual descent of the pair from the count of
Burgundy.

Roman kings and emperors were customarily elected by the
German princes. In the election year of 1257 Alfonso designated himself *dux Suevie*, he wanted to show that he was a German imperial
prince.[18] Even in his dealings with Pope Gregory X in the summer of
1275 concerning his renunciation of the empire, Alfonso held fast to
his claims to the duchy of Swabia, *ad ipsum pertinens ex successione materna*. This is indicated by the request on the part of the pope to King

Rudolf of Habsburg that Alfonso's claims to Swabia be considered.[19] We have yet to discover whether Alfonso had learned German from his Swabian mother and whether the linguistic argument was significant, as it was with Richard, at his election.

After the death of the Roman-German King William of Holland, Alfonso asked a number of German princes to support his election. In doing so, he appealed primarily to the king of Bohemia and duke of Brabant (cf. cols. 12–15). The fact that Alfonso appealed in particular to the two princes who were his closest relatives in the Empire indicates that Alfonso was certainly aware of this kinship. The fact that this relationship was known at the time is further illustrated by the *Chronicon Hanoniense,* which, by the way, is ascribed to by yet a more distant relative, Balduin of Avesnes, a younger brother of John of Avesnes (col. 18):

> *Des lors que li rois d'Espaigne sot la mort le roi Guilaume, il avoit envoie au roi de Behainne et au duc de Braibant, qui estoient si cousin germain, et a pluseurs autres d'Alemaigne et lor avoit proie qu'il meissent conseil qu'il fus eslus au roiaume. Pour ce se tenoit li rois de Behaingne et plusieurs autres contre le roi Richart.*[20]

Alfonso's election was declared in Frankfurt on 1 April 1257, by the archbishop of Trier, Arnold of Isenburg, in the presence of the bishops of Speyer and Worms, both old Hohenstaufen cities. The description appears in part of the *Gesta Treverorum,* written a few years later (1261/72):

> *Ipse* (the archbishop of Trier), *adductis secum Spirensi et Wormaciensi episcopis ac aliis pluribus nobilibus terre, in manu forti et comitatu decenti die certa Frankinvort assignata processit et ibi virum magnificum dominum Alfonsum regem Hyspanie, illustris regis Boemie et insignis ducis Brabantie nepotem, in Romanorum regem, imperatorem futurum, suo nomine et vice predictorum principum* (duke of Saxony, king of Bohemia, and margrave of Brandenburg) *cum sollempnitate debita elegit, omnium qui aderant accedente applausu letifico et consensu.*[21]

Even from the point of view of Trier, Alfonso was elected because he was the cousin of the king of Bohemia and the duke of Brabant. This close relationship to two of the foremost imperial princes should clearly have identified Alfonso as an indigenous German. For, in view of the vast amount of money that Richard paid his electors, the *Gesta Treverorum* devotes a few lines to relating how the supporters of Alfonso did not wish to vote for a foreigner because of the money *(virum alienigenam pro pecunia nullatenus eligere voluerunt.)*[22]

Here the relationship with the Hohenstaufen was oddly kept secret. Alfonso and his supporters were in a dilemma. On the one hand, Alfonso's claim to the Empire rested upon his Hohenstaufen descent. On the other, it was not opportune vis-à-vis the papacy to emphasize his descent from the banned family of Frederick II.

In the eyes of Alfonso, his right to the empire was obvious *(apud omnes liquidum evidenter)*. And he based this on the fact that in Germany convention and custom dictated that the only kings raised were those whose lineage was known.

> *Nec mirari debet vestre fidelitatis circumspectio, si vos per nostros sacros apices et nuntios non duximus sepius visitandos... cum ius nostrum sit apud omnes liquidum evidenter.... cum de Germanie provintia moris et consuetudinis sit reges assumi ad regnum Romanorum, ex quibus non ignoratis originem nos traxisse...*[23]

This correspondence from Alfonso of October 21, 1258 to the city of Siena is worthy testimony to the consciousness that, even in an *electoral* kingdom, lineage and hereditary claims were considered in royal successions.

3. Richard of Cornwall

Alfonso's argument that in Germany kings were elevated to the throne only if their lineage was known was probably a passing shot at Richard of Cornwall. As opposed to Alfonso, Richard did not descend from a Hohenstaufen emperor. It is true that his sister Isabella was married to Emperor Frederick II, but this union merely procured Richard a relationship by marriage *(affinitas)* and thus no claims of inheritance. In this respect, Alfonso's allusion was justified. But Alfonso did not consider, and maybe was even unaware, that Richard was nevertheless distantly related to the blood-relatives *(consanguinei)* of the German kings (cf. cols. 8 through 10 on Table B). Richard belonged to the Saxon-Brunswick group of Ottonian *Tochterstämme*, as did Emperor Otto IV of Brunswick (died 1218), to whom Richard was even more closely related (to the second canonical degree) than Alfonso was to Conrad IV (to the third canonical degree). Something that is not well known is that together with his older brother, King Henry III of England, Richard of Cornwall was in fact the closest living relative of the late Emperor Otto of Brunswick!

The English court actually attests to a corresponding argument. Matthew Paris, the contemporary English court historiographer, seized upon the following reasons for the election of Richard by the magnates of Germany:

> *Magnates Alemanniae... Elegerut igitur, inito diligenti cum deliberatione consilio, comitem Ricardum, tum propter linguam Anglicanam, quae Alemannicae consonat, et originis communionem et antiquam et novam: antiqua in cronicis poterit reperiri, nova in diebus nostris potest certificari, scilicet de duce de Bruneswic et duce Saxonum, de Ottone imperatore, qui de Anglica scilicet filia Henrici secundi Anglorum regis ortus est.* (written 1257/59)[24]

The brother of the English king was thus elected for two reasons. Both are important in our context, for they characterize the legal conceptions of the time.

I will return later to the first reason. The second reason was that the magnates of Germany elected Richard because of a union of lineages *(propter... originis communionem)*, that is, an old one and a new one *(et antiquam et novam)*. The *new* union of ascent, which could be testified by the duke of Brunswick was based on the fact that Emperor Otto (IV) was born of an English woman (Matilda), a daughter of King Henry II of England. The *old* union of ascent could be found in the chronicles *(antiqua* [originis cummonio] *in cronicis reperiri)*. In a number of English chronicles we are informed that Agatha, a stem-mother of the English royal house (col. 9) was a daughter of a brother of Emperor Henry (III). This emperor's brother must have been Ludolf of Brunswick, son of the Empress Gisela by a previous marriage.[25]

The line of descent of the English kings through both of the Matildas and St. Margaret, the only daughter of Agatha (of Brunswick) and Edward the Exile, is in no way some kind of arbitrary maternal line. It is the very lineage which after the conquest of 1066 procured for the English kings once again the legitimacy of the old Anglo-Saxon kings (fig. 1)! For that reason, they were most certainly aware of it. In this context, this line of maternal descent has a second historical meaning, for it provided the English kings with a lineage giving back to the German king, Henry I.

This, by the way, is not merely a modern genealogical construct, but was also present in the consciousness of the times. This is illustrated by the hereditary transmission of the name Matilda, from the daughter and the wife of Henry I, and the name Henry itself. Richard's grandfather and Richard's brother, kings Henry II and Henry III, bore the names of the first Ottonian kings, as did Richard's oldest son. The latter was knighted by Richard at his coronation in Aachen.[26] He was named *Henricus de Alemannia* and seemed to have entertained hopes of succeeding his father as the Roman-German king. But before his father died, he was murdered as he stopped at the *curia* in Viterbo. According to Guillaume de Nangis, he was supposed to have gone there as *propter regnum, quod pater suus habuerat, si posset facere, obtinendum.*[27] Thus, even in the English faction, we come across conceptions of hereditary rights of succession in an electoral kingdom.

Richard of Cornwall, after all, belonged not only to the Brunswick group of Ottonian *Tochterstämme* but also represented the (secondary) *Tochterstamm* of Poitou-Aquitaine (cf. col. 8). Not only was Richard (just as Emperor Otto IV of Brunswick) a grandson of Eleanor, the heiress of Aquitaine, but he also bore, in the same way as did Emperor Otto IV, the title of a count of Poitou *(comes Pictavie et Cornubie)*. Before he adopted the imperial eagle in its place, Richard's coat of arms combined those of Cornwall and Poitou. Just as in 1198, so also in 1257, a Count of Poitou was elected Roman-German king. This recurrence seems noteworthy, especially since in the royal chronicles of Cologne the line of maternal descent through Agnes of Poitou from the German King Henry I is recorded. It could thus have been well known by the archbishops of Cologne, important supporters of both Otto IV and Richard.[28]

All this speaks for the fact that in the thirteenth century the election of a Roman-German king was not seen as the elector's free and arbitrary choice, but as a legal proceeding in which lineage and thus qualifications concerning rights of succession were of fundamental significance. Accordingly, in a letter about Richard's election, drawn up in the name of his two electors, the archbishop of Cologne and the Count Palatine, reference is expressly made to the nobility of his fine pedigree:

> *dominum Ricardum comitem Cornubie, fratrem domini H(einrici) regis Anglie illustrissimi, tam morum quam generis precipue nobilitate pollentem elegimus in regem Romanorum.*[29]

I now come back to the first reason for the election of Richard which was given by Matthew Paris even before the *originis communio antiqua et nova.*

He wrote that the magnates of Germany had elected Richard because of the English language, which was consonant with German *(propter linguam Anglicanam, quae Alemannicae consonat).*[30]

Maybe this was a passing shot at Alfonso, because with it one could declare Neo-Latin unfit for the German royal dignity. In any event, the following is worth mention: for some time there had already existed foreign, that is non-German, Ottonian *Tochterstämme.* As our table indicates, they included the kings of Poland, Hungary, and France. But until the two elections of Richard and Alfonso, the German princes had never raised an *alienigenus* to the throne. The quality of being German (or belonging to the empire) was clearly part of the tacit legitimation of any imperial candidate. Until the end of the old empire in 1806, despite numerous, particularily French, candidates, the election of an Englishman and a Spaniard in the year 1257 were the only exceptions.

The reference to Richard's Germanic language is much the same as Alfonso's claim to the duchy of Swabia *ex successione materna.* They serve indirectly as evidence for the legal tradition that only a German could become a Roman king.

In a later sentence Matthew Paris set out four further reasons for the election of Richard, not including language or lineage:

> *Elegerunt, inquam, ipsum comitem Ricardum, tum propter ejus fidelitatem, constantiam, et sapientiam, tum propter sui thesauri abundantium.*[31]

There is no doubt that the last reason, the abundance of his wealth, was particularily decisive in the election of Richard; but it must also be maintained that without his kinship with the German kings and princes, the brother of the English king would hardly have figured among the choice of candidates.

4. Royal Electors of 1256/57 and the College of Electors

In order to understand better the relationship between legal elections and hereditary successions in Germany, we must finally investigate who was actually entitled to vote in the German royal elections of 1256/57.

The question is connected with the old, and as of yet unresolved, problem of the origin of the *collegium* of the seven imperial electors.

Originally all German princes were entitled to vote. The *Gesta* of Liège, drawn up just before 1251, still reckoned at the end of the twelfth century with fifty-two voters *(principes quinquaqinta duo, qui imperatorem eligere consueverunt).*[32] If one subtracts from these fifty-two voters the thirty-six bishops certified at least once as electors between 1198 and 1257, the votes of sixteen laymen remain. This corresponds fairly accurately with the number of fifteen secular princes whom we can consider as eligible to vote at the election of 1198/99.[33]

This high initial figure of fifteen or sixteen eligible lay electors receded consideribly in the first half of the thirteenth century, because numerous electoral families died out. And by no means did all those eligible to vote take part in every election. Normally the number of electors was lower than that of those eligible to vote. So we see from one royal election to the next a fluctuating number of participants; in the election of Conrad IV in Vienna (1237), for example, apart from seven bishops, the Count Palatine, the king of Bohemia, the landgrave of Thuringia, and the duke of Carinthia took part.[34] These eleven princes, to whom can also be added Emperor Frederick II, who was duke of Swabia before being elected king, are not identical with the later *college* of seven electors, neither in number nor composition.

How did things appear twenty years later at the elections of Richard and Alfonso? Prevailing opinion teaches: "Ever since the double election of 1257, the seven electors were accepted as exclusive voters: next to the three Rhenish archbishops of Cologne, Mayence and Trier, the four lay-princes: the Count Palatine at the Rhine, the duke of Saxony, the margrave of Brandenburg, and the king of Bohemia..."[35]

However, in my opinion this thesis first put forward by Karl Zeumer in 1905,[36] does not correspond to the constitutional situation of 1256/57. It cannot be shown that these seven electors already held exclusive voting privileges at that time. I maintain that this thesis is a projection of the later college of electors into the past.

It is true that the seven electors are mentioned in the *Cronica de Los Reyes de Castilla* of Jofré de Loaisa:

Mortuo autem imperatore Frederico, quatuor ex septem electoribus, ad quos spectat imperatoris eleccio, prefatum regem Alfonsum, audito de liberalitate et prudencia sua, in imperatorem romani imperii elegerunt. Reliqui vero tres Richartum Cornubie comitem ac regis Anglie fratrem in discordia elegerunt.[37]

According to this, four electors voted for Alfonso, and three for Richard. But the chronicle was not written at the time of the event in 1257. The author, who died in 1307/10, ended his work with the year 1305. Ruling in the year 1305 was Albrecht of Austria, the first Roman king documented to have been elected by the seven electors (Mayence, Cologne, Trier; Bohemia, Palatine, Saxony, Brandenburg).[38] Thus the chronicler's mentioning of the seven electors corresponds exactly with the political reality of his own time.

The testimony of Don Juan (Manuel) (died 1348), a nephew of King Alfonso the Wise, comes even later:

> *que los emperadores primeros que se fazen en Roma, que siempre se fazen por esleycion e son siempre los eslecdores un rey e tres duques e tres arcobispos.*[39]

In contrast to these late testimonies, King Alfonso himself did not give the number of either the eligible voters or his own electors. In 1258 he wrote to the city of Siena that he was *non solum a maiori et saniori parte principum Alemannie, verum etiam ab omnibus illis, qui vocem in electione tantummodo tunc habebant,* elected to the royal title.[40] In the *Siete Partidas,* Alfonso clearly refers to himself as "Emperor who is elected by all or the majority of those who have the power to elect him".[41]

Even in the *Cronica del rey Don Alfonso X,* talk is not about a majority of the seven German electors, but rather of messengers of counts and dukes and other lords from Germany, who would have elected Alfonso as king:

> *...estando el rey en aquella cibdad de Burgos, vinierion y mensajeros de los condes e duques é de las otras gentes de Alemanna que le esleyesen.*[42]

Absent everywhere are the numbers of those eligible to vote and of those who comprised a majority. The absence of the number seven is all the more conspicuous as Alfonso seems to have shown a fascination in the lore of the number seven. His *Setenario* discusses the seven names of God, the seven gifts of the Holy Spirit, the seven virtues of King Ferdinand of Castille, the seven liberal arts, and so on. But nothing is said of seven electors.[43] A review of the German documents contemporary to the elections of Richard and Alfonso reveals that in no way did they refer to "seven" as the number of eligible voters in 1257.[44]

The number "seven" is even absent from the advice attributed to Pope Alexander IV in 1258 when confronted with Alfonso's envoys:

...Elaboret igitur dominus vester rex illustris Hispaniae prudenter et potenter primitus, ut a clero et nobilibus Alemanniae, ad quos jus spectat electionis, in regem Alemanniae rite electus apud Aquisgranum, ut antiqua consuetudo est, consecretur, in regemque solempniter coronetur.[45]

In fact, the number "seven" appears for the first time six years later, in 1263, in a draft of the papal bull, *"Qui celum":*

principes vocem in huiusmodi electione habentes, qui sunt septem numero...[46]

But this does not prove that the German princes at the time held the view that only seven princes had the right to decide royal elections. The passage cited only reiterates the view of the English faction, and is absent from the official version of the bull. Urban IV expressly noted that the validity of the ancient custom alleged by the English envoys was contested by the emissaries of King Alfonso. Adolf Fanta has already pointed out "that the pope does not wish to establish and sanction universally valid principles of constitution, rather he objectively judges what the envoys of both sides bring forward. A misunderstanding of this fact has caused far too much significance to be attributed to this letter in regard to the German constitution."[47]

In Germany the number "seven" is mentioned for the first time in 1275 in a charter of King Rudolf of Habsburg.[48] The first charter jointly drawn up and sealed by the seven electors — without one more or less — dates not earlier than 1298, at the election of Albrecht of Austria, hence 40 years after the elections of Alfonso and Richard![49]

Furthermore, in 1257 there were no assemblies of seven electors voting one for Alfonso and the other for Richard. There were simply two separate assemblies of two factions, each acclaiming its own candidate. Thus, properly speaking, there was no *double election,* but rather two concurrent elections.

Returning once more to Table B in col. 2, we find Ottokar of Bohemia, whose envoy might have voted for Richard,[50] but who certainly voted for Alfonso. In col. 3 there is the Count Palatine and Duke of Bavaria, Ludwig, who spoke for the Wittelsbachs and decided in favor of Richard. According to the Bavarian annals, he voted together with his brother, Henry of Bavaria:

Ubi (before Frankfort) *dum quidam convenissent, Moguntinus et Coloniensis archiepiscopi et Ludwicus comes Palatinus Rheni et frater suus dominus H(einricus) dux Bawarie in Rychardum... convenerunt.*[51]

Ludwicus comes palatinus Reni et Hainricus dux Bawarie frater eius cum episcopis Moguntino et Coloniensi fratrem regis Anglie in regem Romanorum, accepta ab eo magna quantitate pecunie, elegerunt.[52]

In my opinion, the Bavarian vote, which was later to be a source of controversy in the House of Wittelsbach and still is for modern research, can be easily explained if one considers the right of royal election as the royal heritage of a house. In this case, for the time being, the younger brother could therefore claim joint possession of this heritage.

In Table B col. 5, one finds Margrave John of Brandenburg, whose vote was cast for Alfonso. A younger line of the House of Askania, that had received its own vote when it aquired the duchy of Saxony with the fall of Henry the Lion (col. 6), also voted for Alfonso in 1257. Thus, the four secular electors-to-be, from Bohemia, the Palatinate, Brandenburg, and Saxony, all stand together (on the left side of Table B).

However, more princes took part in the elections of 1256/57. Duke Albert of Brunswick-Lüneburg (cols. 4 and 10) decided in August 1256 along with the two Askanians (cols. 5 and 6) for Otto of Brandenburg. In 1257 he took ransom money from Richard of Cornwall and in return freed the archbischop of Mainz whom he had captured, so that the former might be counted among the supporters of his English cousin, Richard.

Duke Henry of Brabant (cols. 15 and 17) did not take part in the elections of January or April, 1257. But he had already been asked by Alfonso in 1256 for support, and in October 1257 he did indeed send an embassy to Burgos to recognize Alfonso as king. In return Alfonso presented the duke with the *cura et universalis custodia* over all *jura ad culmen imperiale spectantes* from Brabant to the Rhine.[53]

In 1259 Duke Frederick of Upper Lorraine (col. 16) proceeded in person to Toledo in order to acknowledge Alfonso's kingship. For this he was named as *summus senescaldus in aula nostra citra Renum* and held the right to carry the first dish to the king on festive days. My impression is that these proceedings in Burgos and Toledo are to be understood as by-elections on the part of individual princes, similar to those which had taken place in earlier German royal elections.

The minor Hohenstaufen, Conradin (col. 12), did not take part in either of the elections of 1257; neither did the House of Wettin (col. 11), loyal to the Hohenstaufen family.

Considering all this, I believe, in opposition to Zeumer and

Giese, that the structure of the later *collegium* of the seven electors had by 1257 not yet been determined. Later proceedings, which saw Alfonso and Richard in mutual opposition approach the curia to be acknowledged as emperor, overwhelm the few contemporary documents and pose difficulties in explaining the two elections of 1257. The historian is thus in danger of projecting later concepts, which may have first arisen from the necessities of the process, back onto the original election.

To be sure, it seems that in fact only those who would later be the seven electors were mentioned in the proceedings at the papal court. If the by-electoral votes of Brabant and Upper Lorraine were not considered, the papal curia could very well have held that the provisions of canonical election and the principle of *unitas actus* were valid. The fact that the vote of the excommunicated Hohenstaufen and their supporters remained unconsidered is obvious. The proceedings of Alfonso and Richard before the curia had great significance for the establishment of the college of electors. One must, however, be careful not to bring this later exclusion of certain parties from the electoral process to bear retroactively upon the question of who was actually eligible to vote and why, according to the understanding of the German princes in 1256/57.

The fact that the number of those *eligible* to vote still exceeded seven in 1256/57, is also attested by contemporary evidence which until now has been unjustly rejected but which, in fact, is of utmost importance. On the election of Richard of Cornwall, Matthew Paris wrote in the *Chronica maiora:* "Those are the greatest in Germany, on whose votes the election of this kingdom depends, that, so to speak, is the earnest *(arra)* of the Empire of the Romans." Thereafter follows an enumeration of the three Rhenish archbishops and fourteen secular princes. All of these princes (if one reads *Lotharingie* instead of *Polonie*) can in fact be shown to have been royal electors at least once between 1198 and 1257. This proves that Matthew's long list is fairly accurate. The text runs:

Primates Alemanniae
Hi sunt maximi in Alemannia, ad quorum nutum pendet electio ipsius regni, quod est quasi arra imperii Romanorum:
    Archiepiscopus Colonie [...]
    Archiepiscopus Maguntinus
    Archiepiscopus Treverensis
    Rex Boemie

Comes palatinus de Reno, [Qui et comes Bavarie]
Dux Austrie
Dux Suavie [...]
Dux Polonie [Lotharingie?]
Marchisius de Miche [Moravia]
Marchisius Brandebord
Dux Saxonie
Dux de Bruneswic
Dux de Carentene [Carinthia]
Dux de Melain [Andechs-Meran]
Dux Braibantie, qui et Lovanie,
Landegravius Duringie
Marchio Mixie [Meissen].[54]

This long list of eligible voters comprises not only the three ecclesiastic and four secular electors who according to received opinion should in 1256/57 have already been the only ones eligible to vote, but also four other dukes and the margrave of Meissen, who at this time seem to have been supporters of Konradin (Swabia, Meissen), of Otto of Brandenburg (Brunswick), or of Alfonso of Castille (Brabant, Lorraine). The list also includes the dukes of Austria and Andechs-Meran, as well as the landgraves of Thuringia. Even though the male lines of these three houses had died out between 1246 and 1248, they, just like the others of this list, had represented *Tochterstämme* of the royal house and had been royal electors. As of 1257, nothing had yet been conclusively decided about their legacy.

Thus the list of Matthew Paris, based on the precedents of previous elections (1247, 1246, 1237 and further back), corresponds fairly accurately to the legal situation of the day, without mentioning any restriction of voting rights. On the contrary, in a later passage, Matthew Paris refers expressly to this list as *nobiles ad quos spectat electio, qui in praecedenti folio tertio annotantur.*[55] Matthew's source was King Henry III of England himself. It must have been in the king's interests to have as accurate a knowledge as possible of the eligible voters in Germany; for he, like Richard of Cornwall himself, was interested in the latter's imperial election to the Roman crown. Matthew even specifies when and where Henry III told him the names of the eligible voters: during a visit of the English king at St. Albans on March 3, 1257. Hence, eight weeks *after* Richard of Cornwall was elected king of the Romans, his brother declared three spiritual and 14 secular princes of the Empire as eligible voters, without any kind of reference to the exclusive rights of the seven electors-to-be!

It was probably Count John of Avesnes who informed the king. The Count was the husband of German King William of Holland's sister, and as such could have been well aquainted with royal affairs in the Empire. Since 1250 he was repeatly in touch with the English court. Apparently, directly after King William's death on January 28, 1256, and in any case on February 5, 1256 "by the council of Count Richard of Cornwall," John obtained the significant sum of £200 as an annual credit from the English Exchequer. On November 26, 1256, in Bacharach along with the Count Palatine, Ludwig, and on December 15, 1256 in Zündorf with the archbishop of Cologne, John concluded decisive agreements concerning the election of Richard.[56] Presumably he also spent time in October and at Christmas of 1256 at the English court, and as the son of the countess of Flanders he was himself related to the royal electors (Table B, col.18).

The identity of the historically documented eligible voters and of the representatives of the *Tochterstämme* of the Ottonian royal house, as I have reconstructed them, indicates that the kings were elected by persons who, by virtue of their particular position within the royal fami-ly, including the female lines, were qualified to vote by right of inheri-tance. Thus we may explain how electors arrived at their *ius eligendi:* they inherited it!

According to the conceptions of the German princes, the king whom they elected could immediately exercise royal power on the basis of the election, hence even before coronation and papal approbation. This concept is attested to by a gloss written in 1212/17 by Johannes Teutonicus to the *Decretum:*

Ex sola enim principum electione dico eum verum imperatorem antequam a papa confirmetur.(ad D. 93c. 24)

The German princes who assembled in 1252 in Brunswick for the by-election of King William spoke out in the same sense:

Rex autem Romanorum, ex quo electus est in concordia eandem potestatem habet quam et imperator, nec dat ei inunctio imperialis nisi nomen.[57]

To be sure, this concept was rejected by the papal curia. Bartholomew of Brescia censured Johannes Teutonicus: *contrarium est verum.*[58] And Hostiensis contradicted the decision of the German princes:

> *Sed, quicquid iudicaverint, non videtur, quod habeat potestatem hanc, quousque per sedem apostolicam fuerit approbatus....*[59]

Alfonso the Wise also agreed with the concepts of the German princes. According to the *Siete Partidas,* the lord or emperor had his power *as soon as* he was elected either unanimously or by a majority of those who had the power to elect a German king (or emperor) at the same place where earlier emperors had been customarily elected, like the election in Frankfurt of Alfonso himself:

Et este poder	
ha el señor	*ha el emperador*
luego que es escogido	*luego que es escogido*
de todos aquellos	*de todos aquellos*
que han poderio	*qui han poder*
de lo escoger	*de lo esleer*
ó de la mayor parte,	*ó de la mayor parte,*
seyendo fecho	*seyendo fecho*
rey en Alemaña	*emperador an aquelle manera*
en aquel lugar	*et en aquel lugar*
do se costumbraron	*do se acostumbraron*
a facer antiquamente	
los que fueron escogidos	
para emperadores.[60]	

Such a concept according to which royal power is based upon election by princes alone, can be well understood if the *ius eligendi* can be considered, in essence, inherited — in the last analysis inherited from kings. In this light, it is true that Germany was an electoral kingdom, but an hereditary electoral kingdom. Hence, in the constitution of the medieval empire, the contradiction between electoral rights and hereditary succession was simply a matter of appearance.

5. Summary

Strictly speaking we observe in Germany principles of succession similar to those of Castile. Royal candidacy depended on one's descent from the first king of the land. Kingship primarily followed the male line, but if the male line died out or was disqualified for some other reason, the relatives via the female line took their turn.

Because most of the German royal houses died out in their male lines after a few generations, their descendency soon consisted of royal *Tochterstämme*, only. And because more and more of these *Tochterstämme* existed elections were necessary to determine the new king. In so far as the new royal houses were still only one of the many *Tochterstämme* of the old royal house, their royal rights had to be confirmed with each new generation by the other *Tochterstämme*, which were themselves in some manner equally eligible. Thus it is clear that German successions based upon elections were actually decisions concerning very complicated matters of inheritance! The apparent changes of dynasties were actually cognate successions decided by means of election. The fact that in these electoral decisions, political means of all kinds could be employed is self-evident, but this does not contradict the thesis that elections were also, strictly speaking, concerned with questions of heredity. While in Castile royal daughters would sometimes themselves become reigning queens, in Germany only their male descendents succeeded.

As in Spain, (see Table A) where the House of Pamplona lived on in its three royal *Tochterstämme*, each of them ruling an individual kingdom — Champagne in Navarre, Ivrea–Burgundy in Castile, and Barcelona in Aragon — so also in Germany (see Table B). The royal *Tochterstämme* of the Ottonian dynasty, however, did not split up the Empire into separate kingdoms, but became royal electors with the possibility of themselves being elected king and future emperor.

We now also understand why Emperor Charles IV in the "Golden Bull" of 1356 did not only codify the hereditary character of the rights of royal election, but also awarded the electors a part in majesty and named them as *pars corporis nostri* and *latera imperii*, that is, part of the emperor's body, and collateral relatives of the empire. He named the *unio* of the electors a *consortium*, that is — in the basic sense of the word — a continuing community of heirs.

But with this we recognize the operation of a *ius commune* in the apparent contradiction between the hereditary kingdom of Castile, and Germany, a kingdom of elected kings and hereditary electors.

II
Principles and Systems of Inheritance:
A European Survey[61]

As a second proof of the foregoing let us undertake a general survey of successions in the European kingdoms between 1350 and 1450, to view these principles of succession from a broader perspective. The results of my investigations will be presented in three sections: first, a survey of genealogical facts; second, a statistical evaluation of these facts; finally, some systematic conclusions.

1. Genealogical and Prosopographical Overview

I have reconstructed the relationships between all of the kings of each of the eighteen countries in the century in question (Cf. tables I–XVII). I have also included the so-called pretenders, a term I find displeasing, for nobody regarded himself a pretender, but rather always as a king.

Let us begin with France. France and her Capetians, who ruled from 987, are the model for a pure male succession over centuries. As indicated on the right side of Table I, between 1350 and 1450 five Capetians followed directly one after the other. Such a continuous line of sons following their fathers occurred quite rarely in European royal dynasties during the century. These five kings belonged to the Valois line of the Capetians that had taken possession of France when the direct line of Capetians died out in the male line with Charles IV in 1328.

Nonetheless, the continuity of Capetian-Valois rule was in danger, for, after the demise of the male line, three daughters still remained, engendering three *Tochterstämme:* Navarre, Burgundy, and England. The names of the three Capetian daughters — Jeanne, Marguerite, and Isabelle — have been printed in bold face. The names of female members of a dynasty are encircled and printed in bold face on all the tables, again to emphasize the importance of women in dynastic history and to make apparent where *Tochterstämme,* so long neglected by historians, led their offspring.

Among the representatives of the three *Tochterstämme* engendered by the daughters of the direct Capetian line, King Edward III of England held the best claim to the French throne since he was the closest kinsman to the deceased King Charles IV of France. Edward was

removed by three degrees of consanguinity, one less than his opponent, King Philip VI of Valois-Anjou, who was removed by four degrees.
(This count is based on the simple Roman method of counting degrees
of consanguinity between two individuals: *Quot generationes, tot gradus,*
that is, the number of generations between two persons determines
their relationship in degrees.) As the closest kinsman of Charles IV,
King Edward III of England did not only have a claim to the French
throne, he in fact claimed it, and used the title "King of France" from
1340 onward. Twenty years later, in the Treaty of Bretigny, Edward
resigned this title, but was given almost half of France as his own
sovereign possession in return. France was practically divided between
the French and English kings. Thus, the Treaty of Bretigny can be compared to the distribution of an inheritance between joint owners.

     A similar situation arose three generations later, when Henry
V of England claimed the French throne and was recognized by the
Treaty of Troyes in 1420 as "heir of France". At the time, he married
Catherine of France, so their son Henry VI of England and France re-
presented two Capetian *Tochterstämme* at once: first through Isabelle
from the direct line; second through Catherine from the Valois line.
The fact that these two English claims to the French throne made the
Hundred Years War a war of succession is well known. But what has
been not been known is that Charles of Navarre's claim to the French
throne and the Burgundian claim to sovereignty can be explained in
the same way as the English claim: the closest representatives of
Tochterstämme could and did claim a part of the heritage of a dynasty
which died out in the direct male line, even if there were further
cousins in the agnate lines.

     The peculiarity of our case lies in the fact that the king of
Navarre and the duke of Burgundy also belonged to the dynasty of
Capet in the male line. Thus, they were at the same time both, agnate
Capetians and scions of Capetian *Tochterstämme*. As Capetian agnates, in
cadet lines, they ranked considerably lower than the lines of Valois,
Orleans, and Anjou in the right to succeed to the French throne. If,
however, the right of *Tochterstämme* to succeed had been accepted in
France, the lines of Evreux-Navarre and Burgundy would have ranked
much higher than their opponents in the pure male lines of Valois,
Orleans and Anjou.

     Hence, one of the results of our genealogical reconstruction is
an explanation of why the male lines of Valois, Orleans, and Anjou
were allied as one party in opposition to England, Burgundy, and
Navarre. Each party had a common interest: the agnates fought for a

purely male right of succession; the cognates sought for the recognition of the right to succession through female lines as well. Seen from this perspective, the Peace of Arras (1435) was a compromise which allowed the Burgundians, as both cognates and agnates of the Capetians, to change sides: the sovereignty of the duke of Burgundy in his own territories was recognized by the French king. In exchange, the Burgundians recognized the kingship of the Valois. The English party, thus weakened, could not permanently hold their possessions in France. Thus, the end of the Hundred-Years-War marked the victory of the purely agnate principle (the famous "Salic Law") in France.

But the fact that in other European dynasties successions took place through female lines can be illustrated by the somewhat more complicated example of Denmark. In 1375, the house of Sven Estridson died out in the male line with Valdemar Atterdag. The next five successions took place exclusively in the female line.

As can be seen on Table XIV, Valdemar had two daughters, Ingeborg and Margaret, each of whom had one son (Albert of Mecklenburg and Olaf of Norway). The older daughter, Ingeborg, was already dead when her father died; so she could not support the claim of her son, Albert, who was still a minor. Instead, the younger daughter of the deceased king, Margaret, titled herself *regina Daciae, filia et heres Valdemari*. She was successful in having her juvenile son Olaf elected king of Denmark under her wardship.

Olaf died at the age of seventeen without issue, so this Norwegian *Tochterstamm* of Denmark was not continued. His cousin Albert, who was about 22 at the time, tried once more to gain the Danish throne. But his claim was again rejected and he died the next year without issue. But still living was a seven-year old son of Albert's sister, Erik of Pomerania, whose wardship was seized by Queen Margaret. In 1396, Erik was elected king of Denmark.

Because his lineage from the old Danish dynasty was traced through two female generations, he is a representative of a secondary *Tochterstamm*. Erik was followed by the son of his sister, Christopher of Bavaria, who should be seen as coming from a tertiary *Tochterstamm* of the house of Sven Estridson.

All of these kings representing royal *Tochterstämme* were elected. But in all three cases, the choice fell upon the closest kinsman of the preceding king! When Erik tried to abrogate this principle, he lost his throne. In 1439, he was deposed on the explicit argument that he had attempted to constitute his cousin, Bogislaw of Pomerania, as his successor. As indicated at the bottom left of the table, within the house of Pomerania, Bogislaw was Erik's closest agnate cousin. But as the main table shows, within the Danish *stirps regia*, Bogislaw was related to Erik by a distance of ten degrees. The Danish *Riksrad* did not wish to override the claims of Erik's sister's son, Christopher of Bavaria, who was only three degrees removed. So Erik was deposed and Christopher elected.

When Christopher died in 1448 without issue, the *Riksrad* did not elect one of his many agnate cousins but again searched among the *Tochterstämme* of the the the old Danish kings. They had to go back no fewer than six generations to Erik Klipping and his daughter, Richiza of Werle, to find the next closest living relative (Table XIVa). By 1448 most of Richiza's descendents had died. All of the closest living kinsmen were eleven or twelve degrees removed from the deceased king: Albert of Lindau and Ruppin; Adolf of Schleswig-Holstein; Gerhard of Oldenburg; Ulrich of Mecklenburg. What is most remarkable is precisely that these four men were considered by the *Riksrad* as royal candidates. This identity between the closest kinsmen and the candidates to the throne is striking proof that even in royal elections fundamental principles of laws of heredity were taken into consideration although the degrees of kinship may have been remote. Thus, here too, the primary requirements for royal candidacy were descent from the first king, and the lowest possible degree of consanguinity to the deceased king.

Of the four candidates, Ulrich of Mecklenburg was rejected because he was twelve degrees removed, one further than either Albert of Lindau or Adolf of Schleswig. Of these two, the *Riksrad* preferred the latter, for as the duke of Schleswig, Adolf was landed within the Danish kingdom, while the count of Lindau was a foreigner. Since Adolf's only child had already died, he abdicated in favor of his nephew, Christian of Oldenburg, who was then elected king of Denmark. To be sure, Christian had first to acknowledge his indebtedness to the electoral process and concede that Denmark was a free electoral state *(frii korerighe)*. But in fact, he became founder of the Oldenburg dynasty which has ruled Denmark ever since.

Lack of space does not permit a similar detailed analysis of the successions in the other European kingdoms. These are summarized on the tables that serve as a basis for statistical and systematic observations. The single filiations are drawn from the best standard genealogical works.[62] Yet the concept and arrangement of the tables are original. While genealogies chart only the branches of individual dynasties, the following succession tables refer to individual countries. In contrast to works previously available, most of which considered male lines exclusively and female lines only partially, I have systematically investigated the lines stemming from royal daughters and the lines of maternal descent, which to my mind offer the key to understanding the practice of royal succession. It would be desirable to work out such succession tables for the entire course of European history, from Charlemagne to Napoleon. I have attempted to make the family and hereditary connections as clear as possible in the graphic arrangements of the tables, and I hope to have demonstrated my methodology in the two extreme examples: patrilinear France, with one prevailing dynasty; and matrilinear Denmark, with its continually changing dynasties.

2. *Statistical Analysis*

Exactly 100 successions took place in the eighteen European kingdoms between 1350 and 1450; hence, by coincidence all absolute figures represent percentages as well.

In only fifty-six of the one-hundred cases, did *agnates*, i.e. male relatives of the preceding ruler, succeed to the throne . Of these fifty-six, thirty-seven were the oldest living legitimate sons. Two were illegitimate sons. In one odd case, a father inherited from his predeceased son (Sicily, 1409). A younger brother followed in five instances. Twice, a grandson succeeded his grandfather. Agnate cousins succeeded nine times. It should be noted that the more distantly related relatives were only considered if the closer relatives were no longer alive, or were excluded for some other reason. Where cousins, who were only distantly related, succeeded, they were usually married to a female cousin who was herself more closely related by degree to the antecedent.

Women succeeded in a total of twelve cases: in seven instances, a daughter succeeded her father; a mother followed her son twice; once a female grandchild followed her grandfather; and twice sisters followed their childless brothers. The number of reigning women would rise considerably if one included regents,[63] women acting for minor kings, particularily mothers for sons. Naturally the number would become even higher if one also considered the spouses of reigning kings. This would produce valuable new insights, but would lead us too far away from the issue even if it would be profitable to investigate queenship in a pan-European context.

In almost one-third of the successions (thirty-one times), *cognates* followed as kings, that is, relatives on the distaff side. This surprising fact proves that, contrary to prevailing opinion, dynastic succession could also be traced through women; never, however, through spouses, but only through mothers and daughters; not by marriage but by descent. This was regularly the case with the extinction of dynasties, and often the case when individual male lines on the male side expired. In many instances when historians talk of royal elections or dynastic changes, they are actually witnessing the succession of a *Tochterstamm* of the old dynasty.

Cognates succeeded to the throne a total of sixteen times after the male lines of these various houses died out: for example, Bruce (Scotland, 1371); Sven Estridson (Denmark, 1375); Folkung (Sweden and Norway, 1387); Evreux (Navarre, 1425); Luxemburg (Germany, Hungary and Bohemia, 1437); Wittelsbach-Neumarkt (Denmark, Norway, and Sweden, 1448). In most of these cases, the closest kin of the late king succeeded. In the few exceptions, when a more distant cousin succeeded, he was married to the closest heiress.

In ten further instances, cognates claimed the throne even though distant members of the male line were still alive. Such situations produced conflicts within the rules themselves; usually close cognates prevailed over more distant agnates. Circumstances were similar for the five cases in which kings were deposed and replaced by cognates.

Thus, from a total of one-hundred successions, agnates succeeded fifty-six times, women twelve times, and cognates thirty-one (+1?) times. Thus nearly half of all the successions fell to women, or went through the distaff side.

Comparing the various kingdoms in the period between 1350 and 1450, one can notice a sharp distinction between agnate and cognate successions. This difference was above all dependent upon biological circumstances: some old dynasties continued to survive while others expired in their male lines. Agnate successions were typical in France and England (four successions), Castile and Portugal (five successions), where in all cases the same dynasty held power during the century in question. But on the other hand, frequent cognate successions (that is, dynastic changes) were typical for the three northern kingdoms. Here, five *Tochterstämme*, some of them common to all three realms, followed one another. The rest of Europe was characterized by an oscillation between agnate and cognate successions, and in each case the dynasty reigning in 1450 was not the same as the one which held power in 1350.

THE KINGDOMS OF EUROPA AROUND 1400
The numbers refer to the tables of successions I – XVII

ABBREVIATIONS		SIGNS	

ABBREVIATIONS

A	Austria
agn.	agnate
AR	Aragbn
b.	born
Bgd.	Burgundy
BO	Bohemia
Cand.	Candidate
capt.	captured
Cast.	Castile
Const.	Constantinople
CT.	crowned
Ct.	Count
d.	died
dep.	deposed
Dk.	Duke
DK	Denmark
E	England
el.	elected
Emp.	Emperor
exc.	excommunicated
F	France
H	Hungary
Imp.	Imperial
K.	King
K/R	King of the Romans
marr.(∞)	married
Mgv.	Margrave
murd.	murdered
N	Norway
NAP	Naples
NAV	Navarre
PL	Poland
posth.	posthumous
Pr.	Prince
pred.	predeceased
pret.	pretender
Q.	Queen
Reg.	Regent
S	Sweden
SIC	Sicily
Tit.	Titular
Yr	year

SIGNS

KINGS,   (QUEENS)
(Women)

<	descendant from
†	died
††	died without surviving male issue
†††	died without surviving issue
x	fell in battle
II 3	degrees of consanguinity according to canonical (II) and roman (3) calculation

Filiation

Filiation illegitimate

Filiation uncertain

----- Identity uncertain

Adoption

Blocks show kings
and royal candi-
dates in successions
between 1350 and
1450

Continuous, broken, and dotted
lines of the frame represent different dynasties.

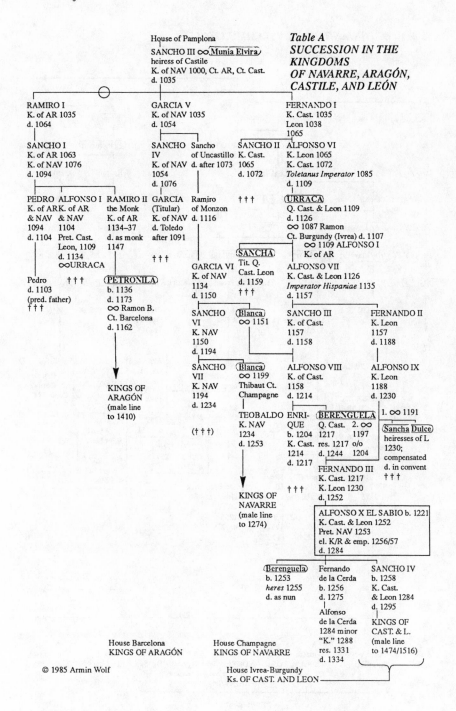

House of Pamplona
SANCHO III ∞ Munia Elvira
heiress of Castile
K. of NAV 1000, Ct. AR, Ct. Cast.
d. 1035

Table A
SUCCESSION IN THE
KINGDOMS
OF NAVARRE, ARAGÓN,
CASTILE, AND LEÓN

RAMIRO I
K. of AR 1035
d. 1064

GARCIA V
K. of NAV 1035
d. 1054

FERNANDO I
K. Cast. 1035
Leon 1038
1065

SANCHO I
K. of AR 1063
K. of NAV 1076
d. 1094

SANCHO
IV
K. of NAV
1054
d. 1076

Sancho
of Uncastillo
d. after 1073

SANCHO II
K. Cast.
1065
d. 1072

ALFONSO VI
K. Leon 1065
K. Cast. 1072
Toletanus Imperator 1085
d. 1109

PEDRO
K. of AR
& NAV
1094
d. 1104

ALFONSO I
the Monk
K. of AR
& NAV
1104
Pret. Cast.
Leon, 1109
d. 1134
∞URRACA

RAMIRO II
(Titular)
K. of AR
1134–37
d. as monk
1147

GARCIA
(Titular)
K. of NAV
d. Toledo
after 1091

Ramiro
of Monzon
d. 1116

† † †

URRACA
Q. Cast. & Leon 1109
d. 1126
∞ 1087 Ramon
Ct. Burgundy (Ivrea) d. 1107
∞ 1109 ALFONSO I
K. of AR

Pedro
d. 1103
(pred. father)
† † †

† † †

PETRONILA
b. 1136
d. 1173
∞ Ramon B.
Ct. Barcelona
d. 1162

† † †

GARCIA VI
K. of NAV
1134
d. 1150

SANCHA
Tit. Q.
Cast. Leon
d. 1159
† † †

ALFONSO VII
K. Cast & Leon 1126
Imperator Hispaniae 1135
d. 1157

SANCHO
VI
K. NAV
1150
d. 1194

Blanca
∞ 1151

SANCHO III
K. of Cast.
1157
d. 1158

FERNANDO II
K. Leon
1157
d. 1188

↓
KINGS OF
ARAGÓN
(male line
to 1410)

SANCHO
VII
K. NAV
1194
d. 1234

Blanca
∞ 1199
Thibaut Ct.
Champagne

ALFONSO VIII
K. of Cast.
1158
d. 1214

ALFONSO IX
K. Leon
1188
d. 1230

(† † †)

TEOBALDO
K. NAV
1234
d. 1253

ENRI-
QUE
b. 1204
K. Cast.
1214
d. 1217

BERENGUELA
Q. Cast. 2. ∞
1217   1197
res. 1217 o/o
d. 1244   1204

1. ∞ 1191

Sancha Dulce
heiresses of L
1230;
compensated
d. in convent
† † †

↓
KINGS OF
NAVARRE
(male line
to 1274)

† † †

FERNANDO III
K. Cast. 1217
K. Leon 1230
d. 1252

ALFONSO X EL SABIO b. 1221
K. Cast. & Leon 1252
Pret. NAV 1253
el. K/R & emp. 1256/57
d. 1284

Berenguela
b. 1253
heres 1255
d. as nun

Fernando
de la Cerda
b. 1256
d. 1275

Alfonso
de la Cerda
1284 minor
"K." 1288
res. 1331
d. 1334

SANCHO IV
b. 1258
K. Cast.
& Leon 1284
d. 1295

KINGS OF
CAST. & L.
(male line
to 1474/1516)

House Barcelona
KINGS OF ARAGÓN

House Champagne
KINGS OF NAVARRE

House Ivrea-Burgundy
Ks. OF CAST. AND LEON

Table B: OTTONIAN TOCHTERSTÄMME 1256/57

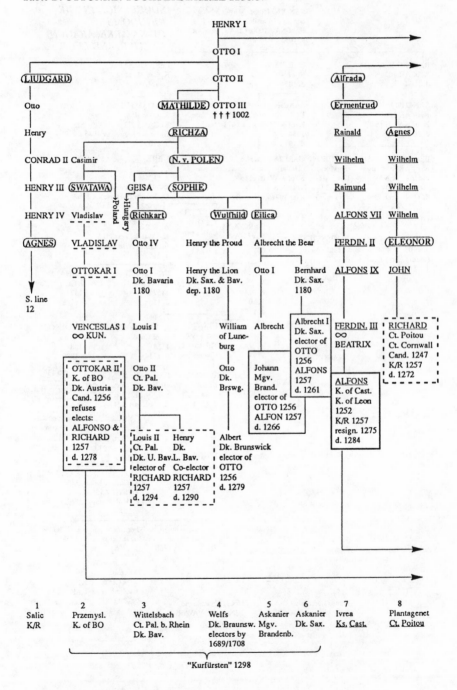

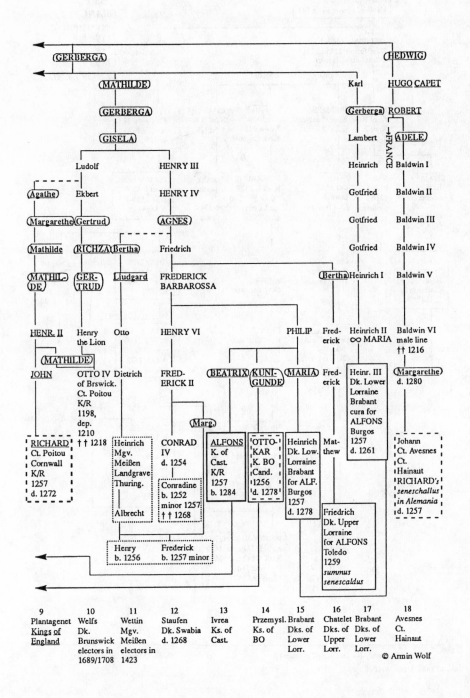

© Armin Wolf

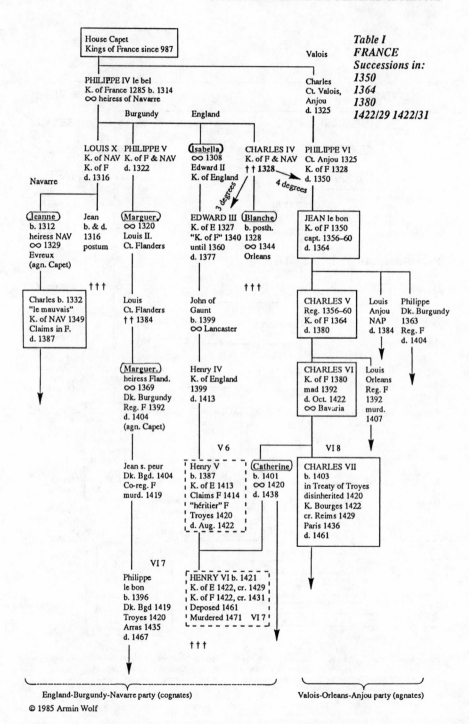

Table I
FRANCE
Successions in:
1350
1364
1380
1422/29 1422/31

England-Burgundy-Navarre party (cognates)

Valois-Orleans-Anjou party (agnates)

© 1985 Armin Wolf

Armin Wolf   229

Table II
ENGLAND
Successions in:
1377
1399
1413
1422/29

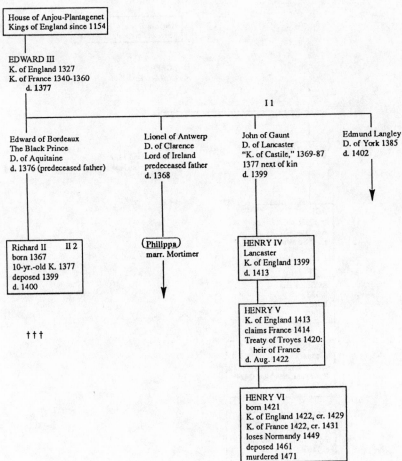

```
House of Anjou-Plantagenet
Kings of England since 1154
```

EDWARD III
K. of England 1327
K. of France 1340-1360
    d. 1377

                                                                I 1

Edward of Bordeaux   Lionel of Antwerp   John of Gaunt   Edmund Langley
The Black Prince   D. of Clarence   D. of Lancaster   D. of York 1385
D. of Aquitaine   Lord of Ireland   "K. of Castile," 1369-87   d. 1402
d. 1376 (predeceased father) predeceased father   1377 next of kin
                            d. 1368   d. 1399

```
Richard II      II 2
born 1367
10-yr.-old K. 1377
deposed 1399
d. 1400
```

Philippa
marr. Mortimer

```
HENRY IV
Lancaster
K. of England 1399
d. 1413
```

    † † †

```
HENRY V
K. of England 1413
claims France 1414
Treaty of Troyes 1420:
    heir of France
d. Aug. 1422
```

```
HENRY VI
born 1421
K. of England 1422, cr. 1429
K. of France 1422, cr. 1431
loses Normandy 1449
deposed 1461
murdered 1471
```

Table III
SCOTLAND
Successions in:
1371
1390
1406/24
1437

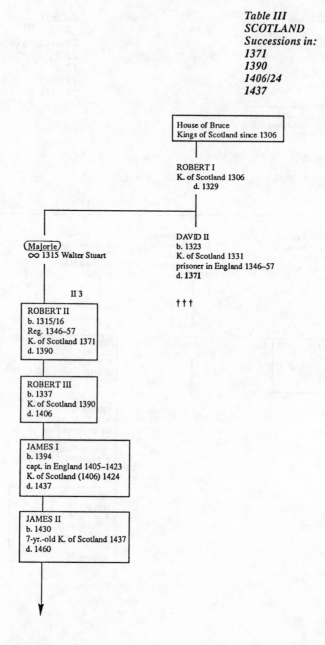

House of Bruce
Kings of Scotland since 1306

ROBERT I
K. of Scotland 1306
d. 1329

(Majorie)
∞ 1315 Walter Stuart

DAVID II
b. 1323
K. of Scotland 1331
prisoner in England 1346–57
d. 1371

††

II 3

ROBERT II
b. 1315/16
Reg. 1346–57
K. of Scotland 1371
d. 1390

ROBERT III
b. 1337
K. of Scotland 1390
d. 1406

JAMES I
b. 1394
capt. in England 1405–1423
K. of Scotland (1406) 1424
d. 1437

JAMES II
b. 1430
7-yr.-old K. of Scotland 1437
d. 1460

© 1986 Armin Wolf

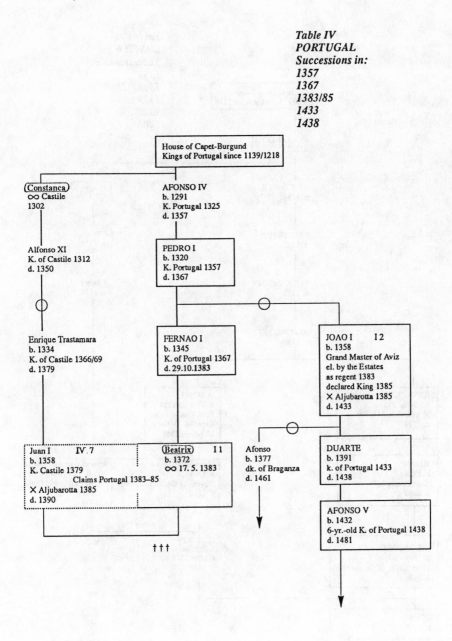

Table IV
PORTUGAL
Successions in:
1357
1367
1383/85
1433
1438

House of Capet-Burgund
Kings of Portugal since 1139/1218

Constanca
∞ Castile
1302

AFONSO IV
b. 1291
K. Portugal 1325
d. 1357

Alfonso XI
K. of Castile 1312
d. 1350

PEDRO I
b. 1320
K. Portugal 1357
d. 1367

Enrique Trastamara
b. 1334
K. of Castile 1366/69
d. 1379

FERNAO I
b. 1345
K. of Portugal 1367
d. 29.10.1383

JOAO I   I 2
b. 1358
Grand Master of Aviz
el. by the Estates
as regent 1383
declared King 1385
X Aljubarotta 1385
d. 1433

Juan I   IV.7
b. 1358
K. Castile 1379
    Claims Portugal 1383–85
X Aljubarotta 1385
d. 1390

Beatrix   I 1
b. 1372
∞ 17. 5. 1383

Afonso
b. 1377
dk. of Braganza
d. 1461

DUARTE
b. 1391
k. of Portugal 1433
d. 1438

AFONSO V
b. 1432
6-yr.-old K. of Portugal 1438
d. 1481

† † †

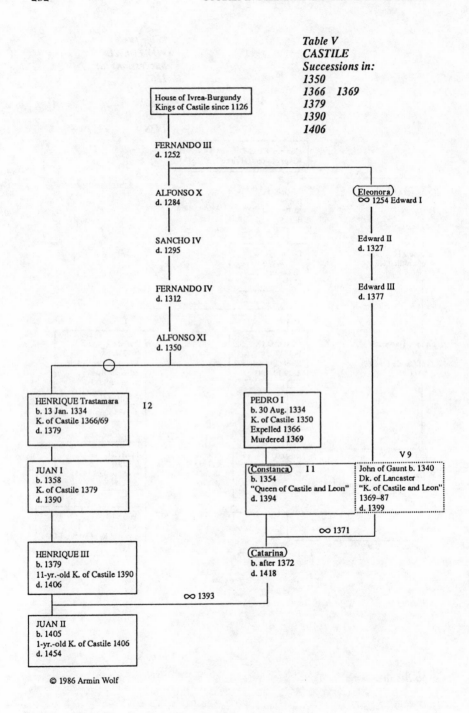

Table V
CASTILE
Successions in:
1350
1366   1369
1379
1390
1406

House of Ivrea-Burgundy
Kings of Castile since 1126

FERNANDO III
d. 1252

ALFONSO X
d. 1284

Eleonora
∞ 1254 Edward I

SANCHO IV
d. 1295

Edward II
d. 1327

FERNANDO IV
d. 1312

Edward III
d. 1377

ALFONSO XI
d. 1350

HENRIQUE Trastamara
b. 13 Jan. 1334
K. of Castile 1366/69
d. 1379

I 2

PEDRO I
b. 30 Aug. 1334
K. of Castile 1350
Expelled 1366
Murdered 1369

V 9

JUAN I
b. 1358
K. of Castile 1379
d. 1390

Constanca   I 1
b. 1354
"Queen of Castile and Leon"
d. 1394

John of Gaunt b. 1340
Dk. of Lancaster
"K. of Castile and Leon"
1369–87
d. 1399

∞ 1371

HENRIQUE III
b. 1379
11-yr.-old K. of Castile 1390
d. 1406

Catarina
b. after 1372
d. 1418

∞ 1393

JUAN II
b. 1405
1-yr.-old K. of Castile 1406
d. 1454

© 1986 Armin Wolf

Table VI
NAVARRE
Successions in:
1387
1425   1425

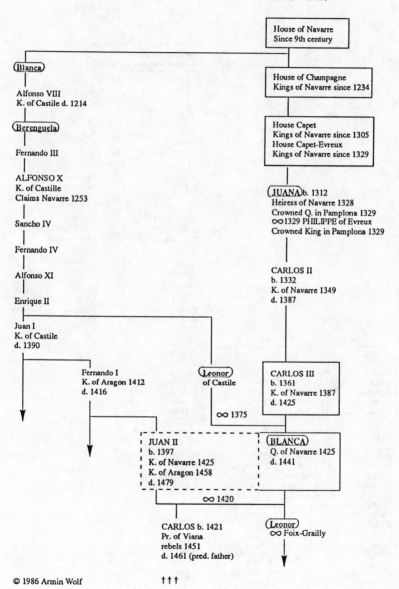

House of Navarre
Since 9th century

House of Champagne
Kings of Navarre since 1234

House Capet
Kings of Navarre since 1305
House Capet-Evreux
Kings of Navarre since 1329

(Blanca)

Alfonso VIII
K. of Castile d. 1214

(Berenguela)

Fernando III

ALFONSO X
K. of Castille
Claims Navarre 1253

Sancho IV

Fernando IV

Alfonso XI

Enrique II

Juan I
K. of Castile
d. 1390

(JUANA) b. 1312
Heiress of Navarre 1328
Crowned Q. in Pamplona 1329
∞ 1329 PHILIPPE of Evreux
Crowned King in Pamplona 1329

CARLOS II
b. 1332
K. of Navarre 1349
d. 1387

Fernando I
K. of Aragon 1412
d. 1416

(Leonor)
of Castile

CARLOS III
b. 1361
K. of Navarre 1387
d. 1425

∞ 1375

JUAN II
b. 1397
K. of Navarre 1425
K. of Aragon 1458
d. 1479

(BLANCA)
Q. of Navarre 1425
d. 1441

∞ 1420

CARLOS b. 1421
Pr. of Viana
rebels 1451
d. 1461 (pred. father)

(Leonor)
∞ Foix-Grailly

© 1986 Armin Wolf   † † †

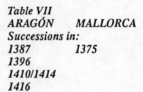

Table VII
ARAGÓN   MALLORCA
Successions in:
1387   1375
1396
1410/1414
1416

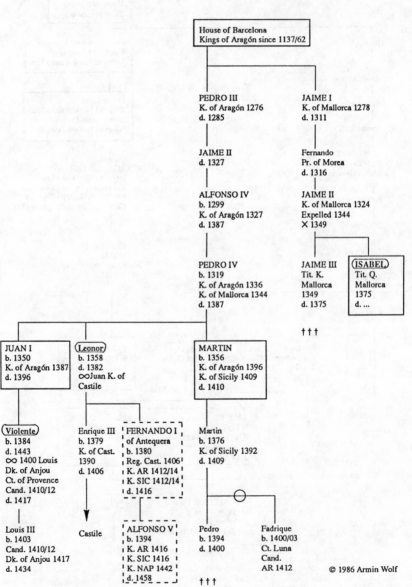

House of Barcelona
Kings of Aragón since 1137/62

PEDRO III
K. of Aragón 1276
d. 1285

JAIME I
K. of Mallorca 1278
d. 1311

JAIME II
d. 1327

Fernando
Pr. of Morea
d. 1316

ALFONSO IV
b. 1299
K. of Aragón 1327
d. 1387

JAIME II
K. of Mallorca 1324
Expelled 1344
X 1349

PEDRO IV
b. 1319
K. of Aragón 1336
K. of Mallorca 1344
d. 1387

JAIME III
Tit. K.
Mallorca
1349
d. 1375

ISABEL
Tit. Q.
Mallorca
1375
d. ...

† † †

JUAN I
b. 1350
K. of Aragón 1387
d. 1396

Leonor
b. 1358
d. 1382
∞Juan K. of
Castile

MARTIN
b. 1356
K. of Aragón 1396
K. of Sicily 1409
d. 1410

Violente
b. 1384
d. 1443
∞ 1400 Louis
Dk. of Anjou
Ct. of Provence
Cand. 1410/12
d. 1417

Enrique III
b. 1379
K. of Cast.
1390
d. 1406

FERNANDO I
of Antequera
b. 1380
Reg. Cast. 1406
K. AR 1412/14
K. SIC 1412/14
d. 1416

Martin
b. 1376
K. of Sicily 1392
d. 1409

Louis III
b. 1403
Cand. 1410/12
Dk. of Anjou 1417
d. 1434

Castile

ALFONSO V
b. 1394
K. AR 1416
K. SIC 1416
K. NAP 1442
d. 1458

Pedro
b. 1394
d. 1400

Fadrique
b. 1400/03
Ct. Luna
Cand.
AR 1412

† † †

© 1986 Armin Wolf

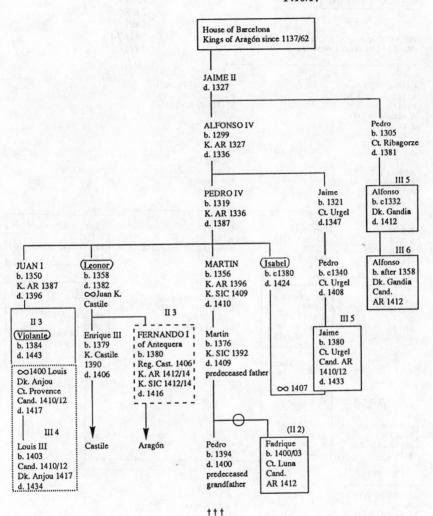

Table VIIa
ARAGÓN
Successions in:
1410/14

House of Barcelona
Kings of Aragón since 1137/62

JAIME II
d. 1327

ALFONSO IV
b. 1299
K. AR 1327
d. 1336

Pedro
b. 1305
Ct. Ribagorze
d. 1381

PEDRO IV
b. 1319
K. AR 1336
d. 1387

Jaime
b. 1321
Ct. Urgel
d.1347

III 5
Alfonso
b. c1332
Dk. Gandia
d. 1412

JUAN I
b. 1350
K. AR 1387
d. 1396

Leonor
b. 1358
d. 1382
∞Juan K.
Castile

MARTIN
b. 1356
K. AR 1396
K. SIC 1409
d. 1410

Isabel
b. c1380
d. 1424

Pedro
b. c1340
Ct. Urgel
d. 1408

III 6
Alfonso
b. after 1358
Dk. Gandia
Cand.
AR 1412

II 3
Violante
b. 1384
d. 1443

II 3

Enrique III
b. 1379
K. Castile
1390
d. 1406

FERNANDO I
of Antequera
b. 1380
Reg. Cast. 1406
K. AR 1412/14
K. SIC 1412/14
d. 1416

Martin
b. 1376
K. SIC 1392
d. 1409
predeceased father

III 5
Jaime
b. 1380
Ct. Urgel
Cand. AR
1410/12
d. 1433

∞1400 Louis
Dk. Anjou
Ct. Provence
Cand. 1410/12
d. 1417

∞ 1407

III 4
Louis III
b. 1403
Cand. 1410/12
Dk. Anjou 1417
d. 1434

Castile

Aragón

Pedro
b. 1394
d. 1400
predeceased
grandfather

(II 2)
Fadrique
b. 1400/03
Ct. Luna
Cand.
AR 1412

†††

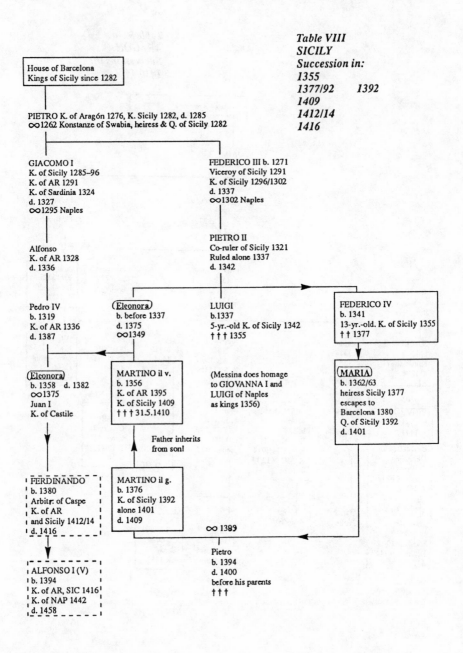

Table VIII
SICILY
Succession in:
1355
1377/92   *1392*
1409
1412/14
1416

House of Barcelona
Kings of Sicily since 1282

PIETRO K. of Aragón 1276, K. Sicily 1282, d. 1285
∞1262 Konstanze of Swabia, heiress & Q. of Sicily 1282

GIACOMO I
K. of Sicily 1285–96
K. of AR 1291
K. of Sardinia 1324
d. 1327
∞1295 Naples

FEDERICO III b. 1271
Viceroy of Sicily 1291
K. of Sicily 1296/1302
d. 1337
∞1302 Naples

Alfonso
K. of AR 1328
d. 1336

PIETRO II
Co-ruler of Sicily 1321
Ruled alone 1337
d. 1342

Pedro IV
b. 1319
K. of AR 1336
d. 1387

Eleonora
b. before 1337
d. 1375
∞1349

LUIGI
b.1337
5-yr.-old K. of Sicily 1342
††† 1355

FEDERICO IV
b. 1341
13-yr.-old K. of Sicily 1355
†† 1377

Eleonora
b. 1358   d. 1382
∞1375
Juan I
K. of Castile

MARTINO il v.
b. 1356
K. of AR 1395
K. of Sicily 1409
††† 31.5.1410

(Messina does homage
to GIOVANNA I and
LUIGI of Naples
as kings 1356)

MARIA
b. 1362/63
heiress Sicily 1377
escapes to
Barcelona 1380
Q. of Sitily 1392
d. 1401

Father inherits
from son!

FERDINANDO
b. 1380
Arbitr. of Caspe
K. of AR
and Sicily 1412/14
d. 1416

MARTINO il g.
b. 1376
K. of Sicily 1392
alone 1401
d. 1409

∞ 1389

ALFONSO I (V)
b. 1394
K. of AR, SIC 1416
K. of NAP 1442
d. 1458

Pietro
b. 1394
d. 1400
before his parents
†††

←↓↑→ Direction of inheritance

© 1986 Armin Wolf

Table IX
NAPLES
Succession in:
1343/52

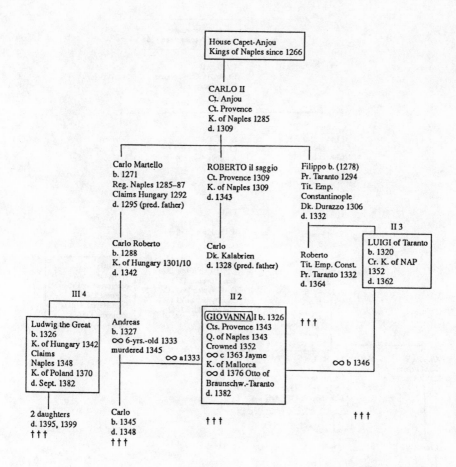

House Capet-Anjou
Kings of Naples since 1266

CARLO II
Ct. Anjou
Ct. Provence
K. of Naples 1285
d. 1309

Carlo Martello
b. 1271
Reg. Naples 1285–87
Claims Hungary 1292
d. 1295 (pred. father)

ROBERTO il saggio
Ct. Provence 1309
K. of Naples 1309
d. 1343

Filippo b. (1278)
Pr. Taranto 1294
Tit. Emp.
Constantinople
Dk. Durazzo 1306
d. 1332

Carlo Roberto
b. 1288
K. of Hungary 1301/10
d. 1342

Carlo
Dk. Kalabrien
d. 1328 (pred. father)

Roberto
Tit. Emp. Const.
Pr. Taranto 1332
d. 1364

II 3

LUIGI of Taranto
b. 1320
Cr. K. of NAP
1352
d. 1362

III 4

Ludwig the Great
b. 1326
K. of Hungary 1342
Claims
Naples 1348
K. of Poland 1370
d. Sept. 1382

Andreas
b. 1327
∞ 6-yrs.-old 1333
murdered 1345
                    ∞ a1333

II 2

GIOVANNA I b. 1326
Cts. Provence 1343
Q. of Naples 1343
Crowned 1352
∞ c 1363 Jayme
K. of Mallorca
∞ d 1376 Otto of
Braunschw.-Taranto
d. 1382

†††

∞ b 1346

2 daughters
d. 1395, 1399
†††

Carlo
b. 1345
d. 1348
†††

†††

†††

© 1986 Armin Wolf

Table IXa
NAPLES
Succession in:
1381   1382

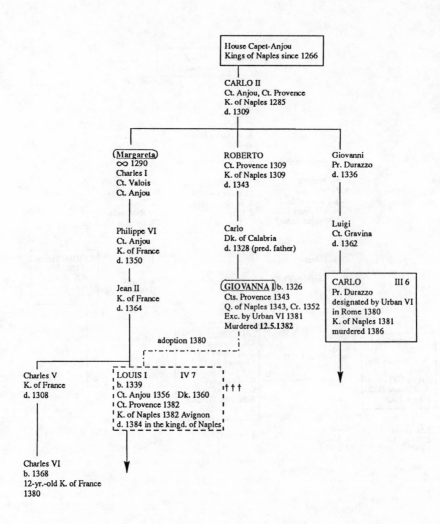

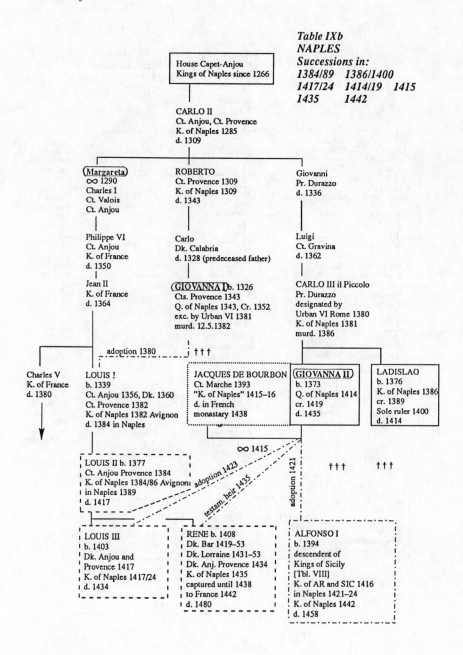

Table IXb
NAPLES
Successions in:
1384/89   1386/1400
1417/24   1414/19   1415
1435   1442

House Capet-Anjou
Kings of Naples since 1266

CARLO II
Ct. Anjou, Ct. Provence
K. of Naples 1285
d. 1309

Margareta
∞ 1290
Charles I
Ct. Valois
Ct. Anjou

ROBERTO
Ct. Provence 1309
K. of Naples 1309
d. 1343

Giovanni
Pr. Durazzo
d. 1336

Philippe VI
Ct. Anjou
K. of France
d. 1350

Carlo
Dk. Calabria
d. 1328 (predeceased father)

Luigi
Ct. Gravina
d. 1362

Jean II
K. of France
d. 1364

GIOVANNA I b. 1326
Cts. Provence 1343
Q. of Naples 1343, Cr. 1352
exc. by Urban VI 1381
murd. 12.5.1382

CARLO III il Piccolo
Pr. Durazzo
designated by
Urban VI Rome 1380
K. of Naples 1381
murd. 1386

adoption 1380   † † †

Charles V
K. of France
d. 1380

LOUIS I
b. 1339
Ct. Anjou 1356, Dk. 1360
Ct. Provence 1382
K. of Naples 1382 Avignon
d. 1384 in Naples

JACQUES DE BOURBON
Ct. Marche 1393
"K. of Naples" 1415–16
d. in French
monastary 1438

GIOVANNA II
b. 1373
Q. of Naples 1414
cr. 1419
d. 1435

LADISLAO
b. 1376
K. of Naples 1386
cr. 1389
Sole ruler 1400
d. 1414

∞ 1415

adoption 1423

testam. heir 1435

adoption 1421

† † †   † † †

LOUIS II b. 1377
Ct. Anjou Provence 1384
K. of Naples 1384/86 Avignon
in Naples 1389
d. 1417

LOUIS III
b. 1403
Dk. Anjou and
Provence 1417
K. of Naples 1417/24
d. 1434

RENE b. 1408
Dk. Bar 1419–53
Dk. Lorraine 1431–53
Dk. Anj. Provence 1434
K. of Naples 1435
captured until 1438
to France 1442
d. 1480

ALFONSO I
b. 1394
descendent of
Kings of Sicily
[Tbl. VIII]
K. of AR and SIC 1416
in Naples 1421–24
K. of Naples 1442
d. 1458

© 1986 Armin Wolf

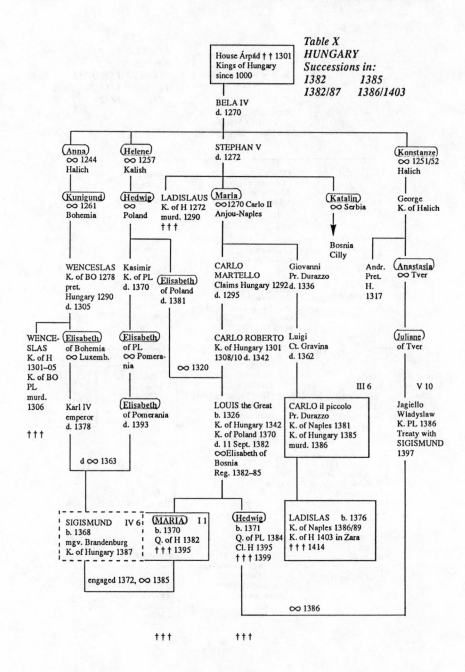

Table X
HUNGARY
Successions in:
1382   1385
1382/87   1386/1403

House Árpád † † 1301
Kings of Hungary
since 1000

BELA IV
d. 1270

STEPHAN V
d. 1272

Anna
∞ 1244
Halich

Helene
∞ 1257
Kalish

Konstanze
∞ 1251/52
Halich

Kunigund
∞ 1261
Bohemia

Hedwig
∞
Poland

LADISLAUS
K. of H 1272
murd. 1290
† † †

Maria
∞∞1270 Carlo II
Anjou-Naples

Katalin
∞ Serbia

George
K. of Halich

Bosnia
Cilly

WENCESLAS
K. of BO 1278
pret.
Hungary 1290
d. 1305

Kasimir
K. of PL
d. 1370

Elisabeth
of Poland
d. 1381

CARLO
MARTELLO
Claims Hungary 1292
d. 1295

Giovanni
Pr. Durazzo
d. 1336

Andr.
Pret.
H.
1317

Anastasia
∞ Tver

WENCE-
SLAS
K. of H
1301–05
K. of BO
PL
murd.
1306

† † †

Elisabeth
of Bohemia
∞ Luxemb.

Karl IV
emperor
d. 1378

Elisabeth
of PL
∞ Pomera-
nia

Elisabeth
of Pomerania
d. 1393

d ∞ 1363

CARLO ROBERTO
K. of Hungary 1301
1308/10 d. 1342

∞ 1320

LOUIS the Great
b. 1326
K. of Hungary 1342
K. of Poland 1370
d. 11 Sept. 1382
∞Elisabeth of
Bosnia
Reg. 1382–85

Luigi
Ct. Gravina
d. 1362

CARLO il piccolo
Pr. Durazzo
K. of Naples 1381
K. of Hungary 1385
murd. 1386

III 6

V 10

Juliane
of Tver

Jagiello
Wladyslaw
K. PL 1386
Treaty with
SIGISMUND
1397

SIGISMUND   IV 6
b. 1368
mgv. Brandenburg
K. of Hungary 1387

MARIA   I 1
b. 1370
Q. of H 1382
† † † 1395

Hedwig
b. 1371
Q. of PL 1384
Cl. H 1395
† † † 1399

LADISLAS   b. 1376
K. of Naples 1386/89
K. of H 1403 in Zara
† † † 1414

engaged 1372, ∞ 1385

∞ 1386

† † †   † † †

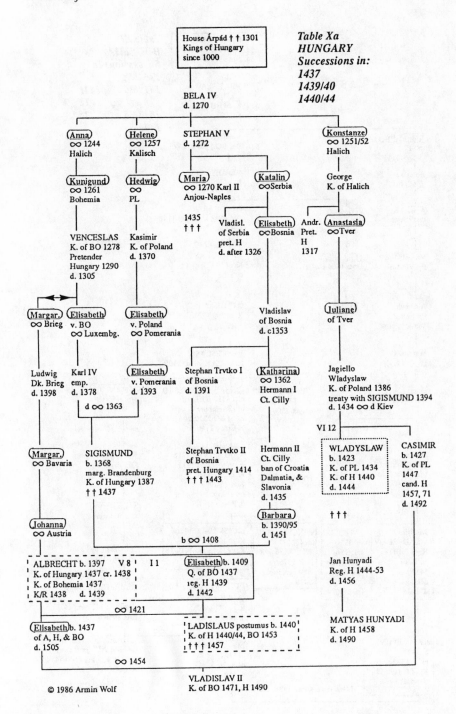

Table Xa
HUNGARY
Successions in:
1437
1439/40
1440/44

House Árpád † † 1301
Kings of Hungary
since 1000

BELA IV
d. 1270

Anna
∞ 1244
Halich

Helene
∞ 1257
Kalisch

STEPHAN V
d. 1272

Konstanze
∞ 1251/52
Halich

Kunigund
∞ 1261
Bohemia

Hedwig
∞
PL

Maria
∞ 1270 Karl II
Anjou-Naples

Katalin
∞ Serbia

George
K. of Halich

1435
† † †

Vladisl.
of Serbia
pret. H
d. after 1326

Elisabeth
∞ Bosnia

Andr.
Pret.
H
1317

Anastasia
∞ Tver

VENCESLAS
K. of BO 1278
Pretender
Hungary 1290
d. 1305

Kasimir
K. of Poland
d. 1370

Vladislav
of Bosnia
d. c1353

Juliane
of Tver

Margar.
∞ Brieg

Elisabeth
v. BO
∞ Luxembg.

Elisabeth
v. Poland
∞ Pomerania

Ludwig
Dk. Brieg
d. 1398

Karl IV
emp.
d. 1378

Elisabeth
v. Pomerania
d. 1393

Stephan Trvtko I
of Bosnia
d. 1391

Katharina
∞ 1362
Hermann I
Ct. Cilly

Jagiello
Wladyslaw
K. of Poland 1386
treaty with SIGISMUND 1394
d. 1434 ∞ d Kiev

d ∞ 1363

VI 12

Margar.
∞ Bavaria

SIGISMUND
b. 1368
marg. Brandenburg
K. of Hungary 1387
† † 1437

Stephan Trvtko II
of Bosnia
pret. Hungary 1414
† † † 1443

Hermann II
Ct. Cilly
ban of Croatia
Dalmatia, &
Slavonia
d. 1435

WLADYSLAW
b. 1423
K. of PL 1434
K. of H 1440
d. 1444

CASIMIR
b. 1427
K. of PL
1447
cand. H
1457, 71
d. 1492

Barbara
b. 1390/95
d. 1451

† † †

Johanna
∞ Austria

b ∞ 1408

ALBRECHT b. 1397   V 8 ¦ I 1
K. of Hungary 1437 cr. 1438
K. of Bohemia 1437
K/R 1438   d. 1439

Elisabeth b. 1409
Q. of BÖ 1437
reg. H 1439
d. 1442

Jan Hunyadi
Reg. H 1444-53
d. 1456

∞ 1421

Elisabeth b. 1437
of A, H, & BO
d. 1505

LADISLAUS postumus b. 1440
K. of H 1440/44, BO 1453
† † † 1457

MATYAS HUNYADI
K. of H 1458
d. 1490

∞ 1454

© 1986 Armin Wolf

VLADISLAV II
K. of BO 1471, H 1490

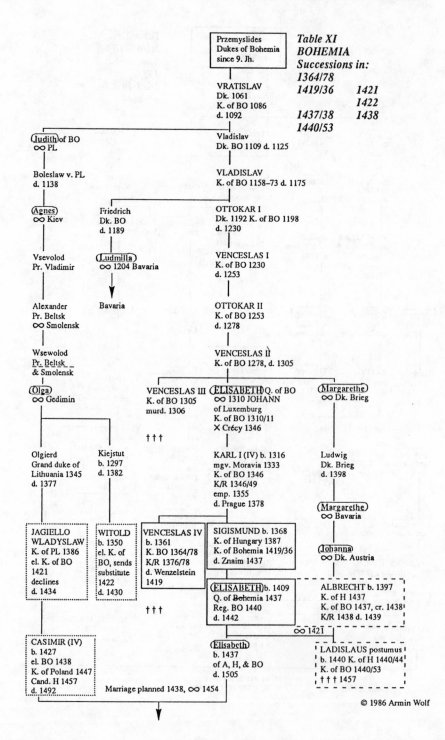

Przemyslides
Dukes of Bohemia
since 9. Jh.

Table XI
BOHEMIA
Successions in:
1364/78
1419/36   *1421*
           1422
1437/38   *1438*
1440/53

VRATISLAV
Dk. 1061
K. of BO 1086
d. 1092

(Judith) of BO
∞ PL

Vladislav
Dk. BO 1109 d. 1125

Boleslaw v. PL
d. 1138

VLADISLAV
K. of BO 1158–73 d. 1175

(Agnes)
∞ Kiev

Friedrich
Dk. BO
d. 1189

OTTOKAR I
Dk. 1192 K. of BO 1198
d. 1230

Vsevolod
Pr. Vladimir

(Ludmilla)
∞ 1204 Bavaria

VENCESLAS I
K. of BO 1230
d. 1253

Alexander
Pr. Beltsk
∞ Smolensk

Bavaria

OTTOKAR II
K. of BO 1253
d. 1278

Wsewolod
Pr. Beltsk
& Smolensk

VENCESLAS II
K. of BO 1278, d. 1305

(Olga)
∞ Gedimin

VENCESLAS III
K. of BO 1305
murd. 1306

(ELISABETH) Q. of BO
∞ 1310 JOHANN
of Luxemburg
K. of BO 1310/11
✗ Crécy 1346

(Margarethe)
∞ Dk. Brieg

† † †

Olgierd
Grand duke of
Lithuania 1345
d. 1377

Kiejstut
b. 1297
d. 1382

KARL I (IV) b. 1316
mgv. Moravia 1333
K. of BO 1346
K/R 1346/49
emp. 1355
d. Prague 1378

Ludwig
Dk. Brieg
d. 1398

(Margarethe)
∞ Bavaria

JAGIELLO
WLADYSLAW
K. of PL 1386
el. K. of BO
1421
declines
d. 1434

WITOLD
b. 1350
el. K. of
BO, sends
substitute
1422
d. 1430

VENCESLAS IV
b. 1361
K. BO 1364/78
K/R 1376/78
d. Wenzelstein
1419

SIGISMUND b. 1368
K. of Hungary 1387
K. of Bohemia 1419/36
d. Znaim 1437

(Johanna)
∞ Dk. Austria

(ELISABETH) b. 1409
Q. of Bohemia 1437
Reg. BO 1440
d. 1442

ALBRECHT b. 1397
K. of H 1437
K. of BO 1437, cr. 1438
K/R 1438 d. 1439

† † †

∞ 1421

CASIMIR (IV)
b. 1427
el. BO 1438
K. of Poland 1447
Cand. H 1457
d. 1492

(Elisabeth)
b. 1437
of A, H, & BO
d. 1505

LADISLAUS postumus
b. 1440 K. of H 1440/44
K. of BO 1440/53
† † † 1457

Marriage planned 1438, ∞ 1454

© 1986 Armin Wolf

Table XII
POLAND
Successions in:
1370   1373

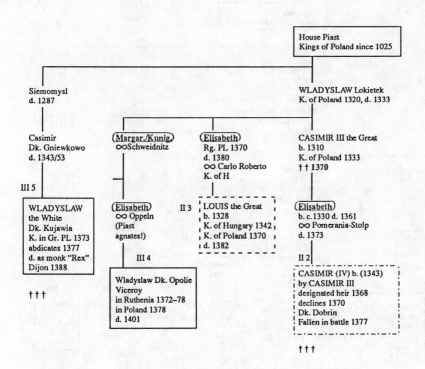

House Piast
Kings of Poland since 1025

Siemomysl
d. 1287

WLADYSLAW Lokietek
K. of Poland 1320, d. 1333

Casimir
Dk. Gniewkowo
d. 1343/53

III 5

(Margar./Kunig.)
∞Schweidnitz

(Elisabeth)
Rg. PL 1370
d. 1380
∞ Carlo Roberto
K. of H

CASIMIR III the Great
b. 1310
K. of Poland 1333
†† 1370

WLADYSLAW
the White
Dk. Kujawia
K. in Gr. PL 1373
abdicates 1377
d. as monk "Rex"
Dijon 1388

†††

(Elisabeth)
∞ Oppeln
(Piast
agnates!)

III 4

II 3

LOUIS the Great
b. 1328
K. of Hungary 1342
K. of Poland 1370
d. 1382

(Elisabeth)
b. c.1330 d. 1361
∞ Pomerania-Stolp
d. 1373

II 2

Wladyslaw Dk. Opolie
Viceroy
in Ruthenia 1372–78
in Poland 1378
d. 1401

CASIMIR (IV) b. (1343)
by CASIMIR III
designated heir 1368
declines 1370
Dk. Dobrin
Fallen in battle 1377

†††

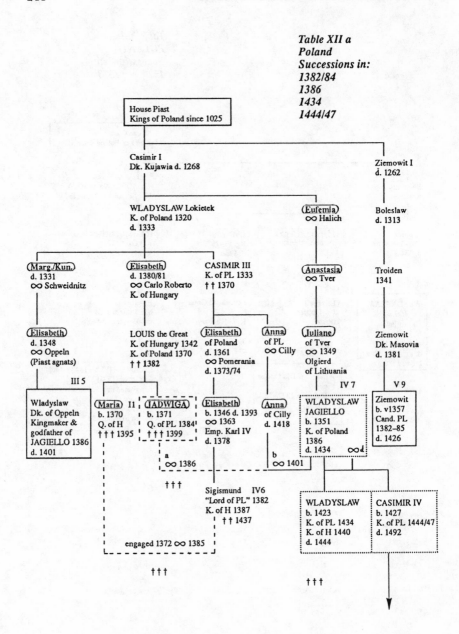

Table XII a
Poland
Successions in:
1382/84
1386
1434
1444/47

House Piast
Kings of Poland since 1025

Casimir I
Dk. Kujawia d. 1268

Ziemowit I
d. 1262

WLADYSLAW Lokietek
K. of Poland 1320
d. 1333

Eufemia
∞ Halich

Boleslaw
d. 1313

Marg./Kun.
d. 1331
∞ Schweidnitz

Elisabeth
d. 1380/81
∞ Carlo Roberto
K. of Hungary

CASIMIR III
K. of PL 1333
†† 1370

Anastasia
∞ Tver

Troiden
1341

Elisabeth
d. 1348
∞ Oppeln
(Piast agnats)

LOUIS the Great
K. of Hungary 1342
K. of Poland 1370
†† 1382

Elisabeth
of Poland
d. 1361
∞ Pomerania
d. 1373/74

Anna
of PL
∞ Cilly

Juliane
of Tver
∞ 1349
Olgierd
of Lithuania

Ziemowit
Dk. of Masovia
d. 1381

III 5

IV 7

V 9

Wladyslaw
Dk. of Oppeln
Kingmaker &
godfather of
JAGIELLO 1386
d. 1401

Maria II
b. 1370
Q. of H
††† 1395

JADWIGA
b. 1371
Q. of PL 1384
††† 1399

Elisabeth
b. 1346 d. 1393
∞ 1363
Emp. Karl IV
d. 1378

Anna
of Cilly
d. 1418

WLADYSLAW
JAGIELLO
b. 1351
K. of Poland
1386
d. 1434   ∞4

Ziemowit
b. v1357
Cand. PL
1382–85
d. 1426

a
∞ 1386

b
∞ 1401

†††

Sigismund   IV6
"Lord of PL" 1382
K. of H 1387
†† 1437

WLADYSLAW
b. 1423
K. of PL 1434
K. of H 1440
d. 1444

CASIMIR IV
b. 1427
K. of PL 1444/47
d. 1492

engaged 1372 ∞ 1385

†††

†††

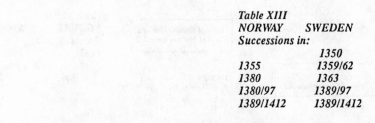

Table XIII
NORWAY   SWEDEN
Successions in:

	1350
1355	1359/62
1380	1363
1380/97	1389/97
1389/1412	1389/1412

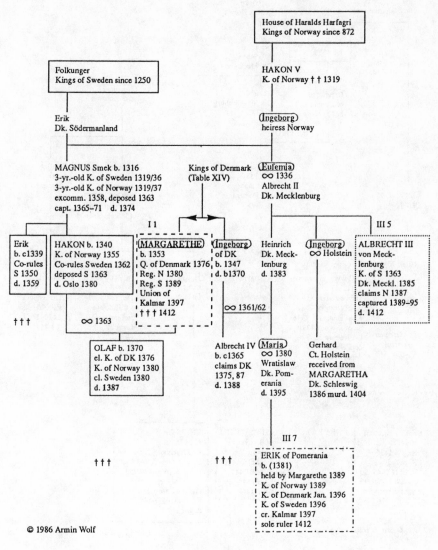

House of Haralds Hœrfagri
Kings of Norway since 872

HAKON V
K. of Norway † † 1319

Folkunger
Kings of Sweden since 1250

Erik
Dk. Södermanland

(Ingeborg)
heiress Norway

MAGNUS Smek b. 1316
3-yr.-old K. of Sweden 1319/36
3-yr.-old K. of Norway 1319/37
excomm. 1358, deposed 1363
capt. 1365-71   d. 1374

Kings of Denmark
(Table XIV)

(Eufemia)
∞ 1336
Albrecht II
Dk. Mecklenburg

I 1   III 5

Erik
b. c1339
Co-rules
S 1350
d. 1359

HAKON b. 1340
K. of Norway 1355
Co-rules Sweden 1362
deposed S 1363
d. Oslo 1380

(MARGARETHE)
b. 1353
Q. of Denmark 1376
Reg. N 1380
Reg. S 1389
Union of
Kalmar 1397
† † † 1412

(Ingeborg)
of DK
b. 1347
d. b1370

Heinrich
Dk. Meck-
lenburg
d. 1383

(Ingeborg)
∞ Holstein

ALBRECHT III
von Meck-
lenburg
K. of S 1363
Dk. Meckl. 1385
claims N 1387
captured 1389-95
d. 1412

†††

∞ 1363

∞ 1361/62

OLAF b. 1370
el. K. of DK 1376
K. of Norway 1380
cl. Sweden 1380
d. 1387

Albrecht IV
b. c1365
claims DK
1375, 87
d. 1388

(Maria)
∞ 1380
Wratislaw
Dk. Pom-
erania
d. 1395

Gerhard
Ct. Holstein
received from
MARGARETHA
Dk. Schleswig
1386 murd. 1404

†††

†††

III 7

ERIK of Pomerania
b. (1381)
held by Margarethe 1389
K. of Norway 1389
K. of Denmark Jan. 1396
K. of Sweden 1396
cr. Kalmar 1397
sole ruler 1412

© 1986 Armin Wolf

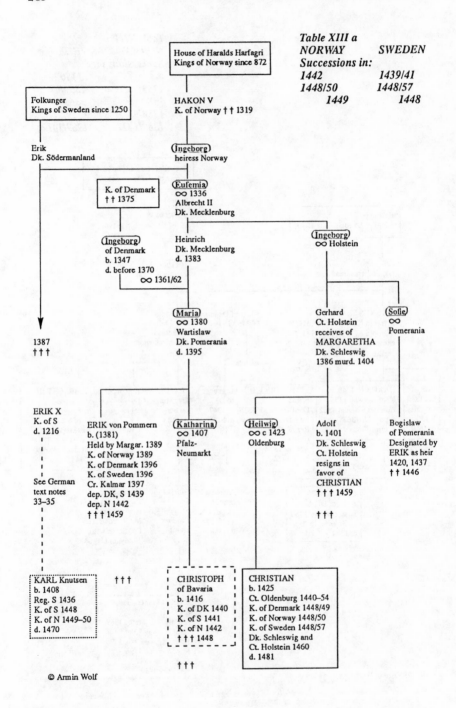

Table XIII a
NORWAY   SWEDEN
Successions in:
1442   1439/41
1448/50   1448/57
1449   1448

House of Haralds Harfagri
Kings of Norway since 872

HAKON V
K. of Norway †† 1319

Folkunger
Kings of Sweden since 1250

Erik
Dk. Södermanland

Ingeborg
heiress Norway

K. of Denmark
†† 1375

Eufemia
∞ 1336
Albrecht II
Dk. Mecklenburg

Ingeborg
of Denmark
b. 1347
d. before 1370
    ∞ 1361/62

Heinrich
Dk. Mecklenburg
d. 1383

Ingeborg
∞ Holstein

1387
†††

Maria
∞ 1380
Wartislaw
Dk. Pomerania
d. 1395

Gerhard
Ct. Holstein
receives of
MARGARETHA
Dk. Schleswig
1386 murd. 1404

Sofie
∞
Pomerania

ERIK X
K. of S
d. 1216
|
|
|
See German
text notes
33–35
|
|
|

ERIK von Pommern
b. (1381)
Held by Margar. 1389
K. of Norway 1389
K. of Denmark 1396
K. of Sweden 1396
Cr. Kalmar 1397
dep. DK, S 1439
dep. N 1442
††† 1459

Katharina
∞ 1407
Pfalz-
Neumarkt

Heilwig
∞ c 1423
Oldenburg

Adolf
b. 1401
Dk. Schleswig
Ct. Holstein
resigns in
favor of
CHRISTIAN
††† 1459

†††

Bogislaw
of Pomerania
Designated by
ERIK as heir
1420, 1437
†† 1446

KARL Knutsen
b. 1408
Reg. S 1436
K. of S 1448
K. of N 1449–50
d. 1470

†††

CHRISTOPH
of Bavaria
b. 1416
K. of DK 1440
K. of S 1441
K. of N 1442
††† 1448

†††

CHRISTIAN
b. 1425
Ct. Oldenburg 1440–54
K. of Denmark 1448/49
K. of Norway 1448/50
K. of Sweden 1448/57
Dk. Schleswig and
Ct. Holstein 1460
d. 1481

© Armin Wolf

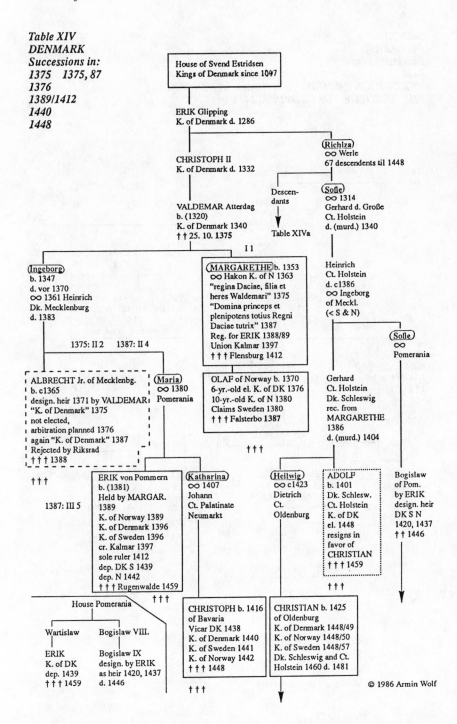

Table XIV
DENMARK
Successions in:
1375   1375, 87
1376
1389/1412
1440
1448

House of Svend Estridsen
Kings of Denmark since 1047

ERIK Glipping
K. of Denmark d. 1286

(Richiza)
∞ Werle
67 descendents til 1448

CHRISTOPH II
K. of Denmark d. 1332

Descen-
dants

(Sofie)
∞ 1314
Gerhard d. Große
Ct. Holstein
d. (murd.) 1340

VALDEMAR Atterdag
b. (1320)
K. of Denmark 1340
†† 25. 10. 1375

Table XIVa

I 1

(Ingeborg)
b. 1347
d. vor 1370
∞ 1361 Heinrich
Dk. Mecklenburg
d. 1383

(MARGARETHE) b. 1353
∞ Hakon K. of N 1363
"regina Daciae, filia et
heres Waldemari" 1375
"Domina princeps et
plenipotens totius Regni
Daciae tutrix" 1387
Reg. for ERIK 1388/89
Union Kalmar 1397
††† Flensburg 1412

Heinrich
Ct. Holstein
d. c1386
∞ Ingeborg
of Meckl.
(< S & N)

1375: II 2   1387: II 4

(Sofie)
∞
Pomerania

ALBRECHT Jr. of Mecklenbg.
b. c1365
design. heir 1371 by VALDEMAR
"K. of Denmark" 1375
not elected,
arbitration planned 1376
again "K. of Denmark" 1387
Rejected by Riksrad
††† 1388

(Maria)
∞ 1380
Pomerania

OLAF of Norway b. 1370
6-yr.-old el. K. of DK 1376
10-yr.-old K. of N 1380
Claims Sweden 1380
††† Falsterbo 1387

Gerhard
Ct. Holstein
Dk. Schleswig
rec. from
MARGARETHE
1386
d. (murd.) 1404

†††

†††

†††

1387: III 5

ERIK von Pommern
b. (1381)
Held by MARGAR.
1389
K. of Norway 1389
K. of Denmark 1396
K. of Sweden 1396
cr. Kalmar 1397
sole ruler 1412
dep. DK S 1439
dep. N 1442
††† Rugenwalde 1459

(Katharina)
∞ 1407
Johann
Ct. Palatinate
Neumarkt

(Heilwig)
∞ c1423
Dietrich
Ct.
Oldenburg

ADOLF
b. 1401
Dk. Schlesw.
Ct. Holstein
K. of DK
el. 1448
resigns in
favor of
CHRISTIAN
††† 1459

Bogislaw
of Pom.
by ERIK
design. heir
DK S N
1420, 1437
†† 1446

†††

†††

House Pomerania

Wartislaw

ERIK
K. of DK
dep. 1439
††† 1459

Bogislaw VIII.

Bogislaw IX
design. by ERIK
as heir 1420, 1437
d. 1446

CHRISTOPH b. 1416
of Bavaria
Vicar DK 1438
K. of Denmark 1440
K. of Sweden 1441
K. of Norway 1442
††† 1448

CHRISTIAN b. 1425
of Oldenburg
K. of Denmark 1448/49
K. of Norway 1448/50
K. of Sweden 1448/57
Dk. Schleswig and Ct.
Holstein 1460 d. 1481

†††

© 1986 Armin Wolf

Table XIVa
DENMARK
Successions in:
1448
NEXT OF KIN FROM DANISH ROYAL DYNASTY AT
THE DEATH OF CHRISTOPHER, 1448

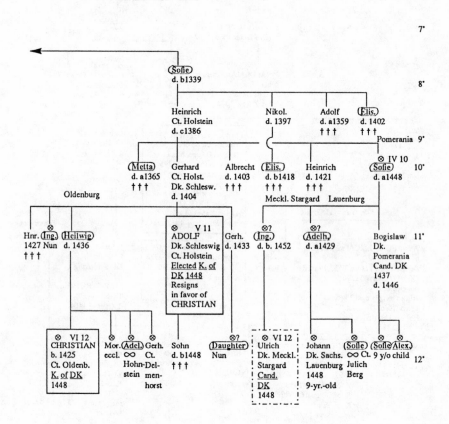

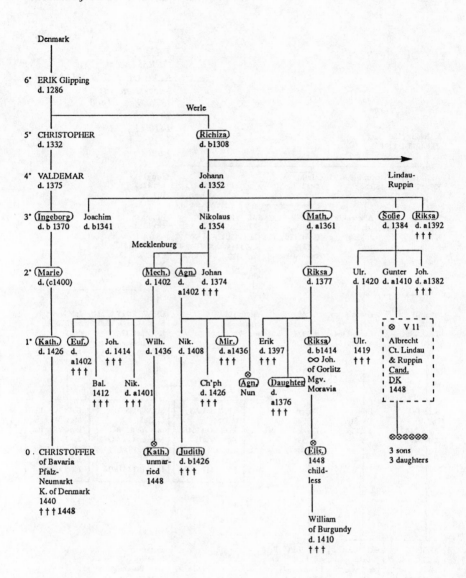

Denmark

6* ERIK Glipping
d. 1286

Werle

5* CHRISTOPHER   (Richlza)
d. 1332   d. b1308

4* VALDEMAR   Johann   Lindau-
d. 1375   d. 1352   Ruppin

3* (Ingeborg) Joachim   Nikolaus   (Math.)   (Sofie)   (Riksa)
d. b 1370 d. b1341   d. 1354   d. a1361   d. 1384   d. a1392
                                                         † † †
           Mecklenburg

2* (Marie)   (Mech.) (Agn.) Johan   (Riksa)   Ulr.   Gunter   Joh.
d. (c1400)   d. 1402 d.   d. 1374   d. 1377   d. 1420 d. a1410   d. a1382
                          a1402 † † †   † † †

1* (Kath.) (Euf.) Joh.   Wilh.   Nik.   (Mir.) Erik   (Riksa)   Ulr.   ⊗   V 11
d. 1426 d.   d. 1414 d. 1436 d. 1408 d. a1436 d. 1397 d. b1414 1419   Albrecht
         a1402   † † †   † † †   † † †   ∞ Joh.   † † †   Ct. Lindau
         † † †   of Gorlitz   & Ruppin
                 Bal.   Nik.   Ch'ph   ⊗   (Daughter) Mgv.   Cand.
                 1412   d. a1401   d. 1426 (Agn.) d.   Moravia DK
                 † † †   † † †   † † †   Nun   a1376   1448
                                                       † † †

0 . CHRISTOFFER   (Kath.) (Judith)   (Eils.)   ⊗⊗⊗⊗⊗⊗
of Bavaria   unmar- d. b1426   1448   3 sons
Pfalz-   ried   † † †   child-   3 daughters
Neumarkt   1448   less
K. of Denmark
1440   William
† † † 1448   of Burgundy
                                                 d. 1410
                                                 † † †

Legend: ⊗ = alive in 1448
         * = degrees of consanguinity (Roman)
         a = after
         b = before

© 1985 Armin Wolf

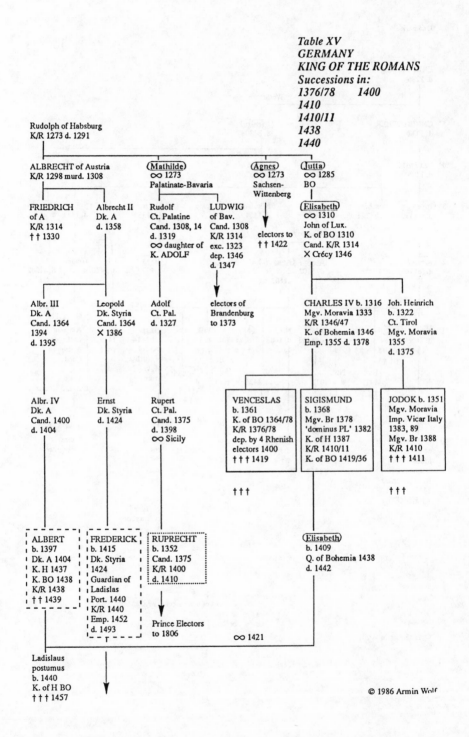

Table XV
GERMANY
KING OF THE ROMANS
Successions in:
1376/78   1400
1410
1410/11
1438
1440

Rudolph of Habsburg
K/R 1273 d. 1291

ALBRECHT of Austria
K/R 1298 murd. 1308

Mathilde
∞ 1273
Palatinate-Bavaria

Agnes
∞ 1273
Sachsen-Wittenberg

Jutta
∞ 1285
BO

FRIEDRICH
of A
K/R 1314
† † 1330

Albrecht II
Dk. A
d. 1358

Rudolf
Ct. Palatine
Cand. 1308, 14
d. 1319
∞ daughter of
K. ADOLF

LUDWIG
of Bav.
Cand. 1308
K/R 1314
exc. 1323
dep. 1346
d. 1347

electors to
† † 1422

Elisabeth
∞ 1310
John of Lux.
K. of BO 1310
Cand. K/R 1314
✕ Crécy 1346

Albr. III
Dk. A
Cand. 1364
1394
d. 1395

Leopold
Dk. Styria
Cand. 1364
✕ 1386

Adolf
Ct. Pal.
d. 1327

electors of
Brandenburg
to 1373

CHARLES IV b. 1316
Mgv. Moravia 1333
K/R 1346/47
K. of Bohemia 1346
Emp. 1355 d. 1378

Joh. Heinrich
b. 1322
Ct. Tirol
Mgv. Moravia
1355
d. 1375

Albr. IV
Dk. A
Cand. 1400
d. 1404

Ernst
Dk. Styria
d. 1424

Rupert
Ct. Pal.
Cand. 1375
d. 1398
∞ Sicily

VENCESLAS
b. 1361
K. of BO 1364/78
K/R 1376/78
dep. by 4 Rhenish
electors 1400
† † † 1419

SIGISMUND
b. 1368
Mgv. Br 1378
'dominus PL' 1382
K. of H 1387
K/R 1410/11
K. of BO 1419/36

JODOK b. 1351
Mgv. Moravia
Imp. Vicar Italy
1383, 89
Mgv. Br 1388
K/R 1410
† † † 1411

† † †   † † †

ALBERT
b. 1397
Dk. A 1404
K. H 1437
K. BO 1438
K/R 1438
† † 1439

FREDERICK
b. 1415
Dk. Styria
1424
Guardian of
Ladislas
Port. 1440
K/R 1440
Emp. 1452
d. 1493

RUPRECHT
b. 1352
Cand. 1375
K/R 1400
d. 1410

Elisabeth
b. 1409
Q. of Bohemia 1438
d. 1442

Prince Electors
to 1806

∞ 1421

Ladislaus
postumus
b. 1440
K. of H BO
† † † 1457

Table XVI
BURGUNDY-ARLES
Successions in:
1365
(1378)

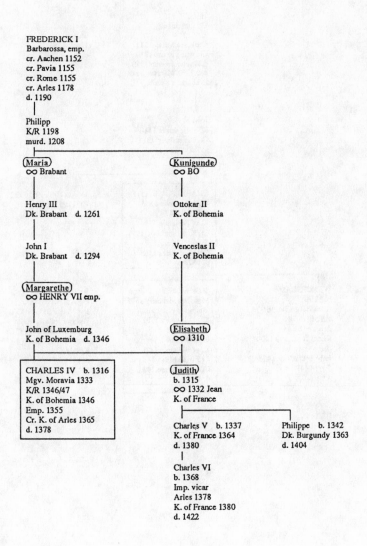

FREDERICK I
Barbarossa, emp.
cr. Aachen 1152
cr. Pavia 1155
cr. Rome 1155
cr. Arles 1178
d. 1190

Philipp
K/R 1198
murd. 1208

(Maria)
∞ Brabant

(Kunigunde)
∞ BO

Henry III
Dk. Brabant   d. 1261

Ottokar II
K. of Bohemia

John I
Dk. Brabant   d. 1294

Venceslas II
K. of Bohemia

(Margarethe)
∞ HENRY VII emp.

John of Luxemburg
K. of Bohemia   d. 1346

(Elisabeth)
∞ 1310

CHARLES IV   b. 1316
Mgv. Moravia 1333
K/R 1346/47
K. of Bohemia 1346
Emp. 1355
Cr. K. of Arles 1365
d. 1378

(Judith)
b. 1315
∞ 1332 Jean
K. of France

Charles V   b. 1337
K. of France 1364
d. 1380

Philippe   b. 1342
Dk. Burgundy 1363
d. 1404

Charles VI
b. 1368
Imp. vicar
Arles 1378
K. of France 1380
d. 1422

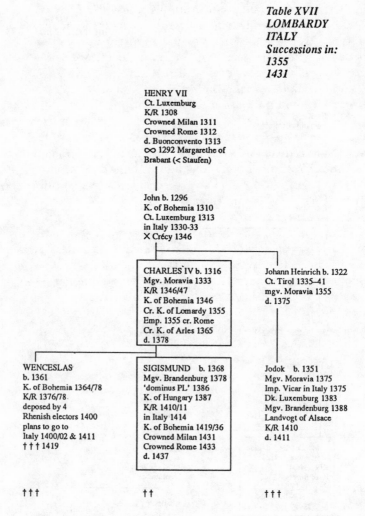

Table XVII
LOMBARDY
ITALY
Successions in:
1355
1431

HENRY VII
Ct. Luxemburg
K/R 1308
Crowned Milan 1311
Crowned Rome 1312
d. Buonconvento 1313
∞ 1292 Margarethe of
Brabant (< Staufen)

John b. 1296
K. of Bohemia 1310
Ct. Luxemburg 1313
in Italy 1330-33
✕ Crécy 1346

CHARLES IV b. 1316
Mgv. Moravia 1333
K/R 1346/47
K. of Bohemia 1346
Cr. K. of Lomardy 1355
Emp. 1355 cr. Rome
Cr. K. of Arles 1365
d. 1378

Johann Heinrich b. 1322
Ct. Tirol 1335–41
mgv. Moravia 1355
d. 1375

WENCESLAS
b. 1361
K. of Bohemia 1364/78
K/R 1376/78
deposed by 4
Rhenish electors 1400
plans to go to
Italy 1400/02 & 1411
† † † 1419

SIGISMUND   b. 1368
Mgv. Brandenburg 1378
'dominus PL' 1386
K. of Hungary 1387
K/R 1410/11
in Italy 1414
K. of Bohemia 1419/36
Crowned Milan 1431
Crowned Rome 1433
d. 1437

Jodok   b. 1351
Mgv. Moravia 1375
Imp. Vicar in Italy 1375
Dk. Luxemburg 1383
Mgv. Brandenburg 1388
Landvogt of Alsace
K/R 1410
d. 1411

† † †   † †   † † †

© 1986 Armin Wolf

We encounter personal unions in eighteen cases, where kings held or claimed to hold more than one kingdom. There were twelve such personal unions of two kingdoms, five of three kingdoms and once even a union of four kingdoms (Emperor Charles IV).

Five successions were connected with adoptions or testamentary appointments, all taking place in Naples and all within a circle of relatives. Nowhere was a stranger adopted or declared heir by testament.

3. Systematic Conclusions

As we have seen, there is no contradiction in principle between elective and hereditary kingdoms, because there were a number of essential principles of royal succession tacitly recognized in all eighteen European kingdoms, regardless of whether these kingdoms were called electoral or hereditary monarchies. With the exception of one or two cases in which the genealogy is not entirely clear, all successors were descended from the first ruler of the kingdom. Descendents of the first king living simultaneously formed a group of persons of common blood *(stirps regia)*, of whom one would become the new king. Who this was, depended on his ranking within the royal family, which included *Tochterstämme.*[64]

Let me explain the two exceptions. With our present genealogical knowledge, only a tenuous direct lineage in the ninth degree can be assumed between the first Bohemian king and the Gedyminides, who were elected kings by the Hussite party after the deposition of Sigmund of Luxemburg in 1421 (see Table XI). We do not know whether the Przemyslide lineage of the Lithuanian Grand Dukes was known at the time. In any case, Wladyslaw Jagiello rejected the Crown of St. Wenceslas. His cousin, Witold, who was thereupon offered the Bohemian throne, sent a nephew in 1422 as a governor. This nephew was imprisoned in 1424 and exiled three years later. Even the Jagiello, Kasimir IV, who was elected to the Bohemian throne by a faction opposed to Albert of Austria in 1438, did not assume power there. But in 1454 he married Elizabeth of Austria, who through her mother — a daughter of King Sigismund — was descended from more than one Bohemian king. Then in 1471, their son, Vladislav II, actually became king of Bohemia. Thus the first Jagiello on the throne of Bohemia was the first generation that in fact belonged to the consanguinity of the country's previous kings; hence, the exception becomes rather a confirmation of the rule.

The second possible exception is the succession of Karl Knutsson in 1448 in Sweden. Today, Karl is not considered a descendent of the old Swedish kings. But in his time it was argued that the grandfather of the new line of kings — through three explicitly named links — stemmed directly from King St. Erik. Whether this line of descent was merely a "propaganda trick" or contained a grain of truth is still to be investigated. Either way, the efforts to legitimize the kingship of Karl Knutsson with this propaganda testifies to the principle of tracing lineage to an earlier king of the land. Since we are less concerned with biological genealogy than with the reconstruction of concepts that were significant in the Middle Ages, even this case, a postulated genealogical lineage, confirms the principles discovered from actual royal successions.

The fundamental principle of the law of succession can be formulated thus: in order to become king one had to be a) a descendent of the first king of the land, and b) next of kin to the last king. In many cases, however, it was not clear who was next of kin. If there was more than one claimant to the throne, decisions had to made according to legal proceedings along the lines of election, arbitration, renunciation, distribution or compensation. And if no peaceful solution was found, recourse was had in duels or even war. The method of reconciliation was often an alliance by marriage; this was, so to speak, the medieval form of "make love, not war."

The descendents of the first king of a land living at the time of the succession formed a royal family from which the new king would emerge. The royal family of every kingdom had its own individual structure, even though these structures often overlapped because of marriage unions between kingdoms. Put another way, individuals could be members of more than one royal family. Whoever belonged to more than one family could accumulate candidacies in more than one kingdom, and in specific situations could even gain more than one throne. Through further marriage, new families were continuously grafted onto the royal family. The composition of the royal families changed almost constantly through birth and death. Thus, if one wants to understand the effective principles of royal successions, these royal families have to be reconstructed from succession to succession, or from election to election (see, for example, Table XIVa: Denmark 1448).

Such inquiries reveal that one's consideration for the royal throne depended upon one's ranking within the royal family, which was the result of various anthropologically determined factors and

juridically relevant criteria. Within the *stirps regia,* that is, the descendents of the first king, the following principles seem to have been
observed: the closest relative in degrees of consanguinity was preferred
to more distant relatives; males were preferred to females; agnates to
cognates; older individuals to younger ones; those of age to minors;
legitimate to illegitimate offspring; natural to adopted heirs; healthy to
handicapped or insane individuals; natives to foreigners.

The calculation of degrees of relationship had a special significance. Proximity could refer to either the first king of the respective
kingdom *(primus acquirens)* or the last preceding king *(ultimus defunc-
tus).* The number of degrees could be counted either in generations to
the first common ancestors, male or female (Canonical computation),
or in generations to the last deceased predecessor (Roman computation).

Opposed to this was the view that the actual decision in contested successions was based less on degrees of relationship than on the
outcome of the forces at work at a given moment. Of course, but this is
not a contradiction. Whence did power come in ca. 1400? Predominantly from inherited material! And the closest relatives of the king
had the greatest chances to inherit just such power bases or to provide
them for their descendents through marriage. In many cases it is possible to show that the number and strength of allies also depended upon
the circumstances of kinship. My research leads me to argue that a vital
link existed between circumstances of kinship and political interests,
and that a reconstruction of the context of active personalities' kinships
can explain the development of historically active interest groups, conflicts, and alliances.

The principles we have discussed are not derived from written
law but are clearly apparent from our observations of actual practise —
at least in the examples discussed from the thirteenth century and
those between 1350 and 1450. If, however, two or more of these principles were in mutual conflict, problems arose as to which of them was of
higher rank. For instance suppose a younger but legitimate son was
confronted by an older but illegitimate son (as with Pedro the Cruel
and Enrique Trastamara) — or an adult from a cadet line was faced by
a minor from a senior line (as with Fernando de Antequera and Louis
d'Anjou in Aragon and Sicily). In such cases each party could refer to a
principle favoring its own respective position. Many of the disputes in
that period can be explained in terms of the conflict between different
principles.

The danger of conflict was especially heightened when a distantly related agnate was opposed by a closer cognate, for the agnate or masculine principle stood against the principle of proximity in degrees to the previous ruler. If no agreement was found, and neither of the opponents resigned, died, or was murdered, the dispute had to be settled by arbitration or by generally accepted elections; or a decision had to be sought by combat. This was the classic constellation of European wars of succession.

Most of the time, the closest kinsman was accepted, even if he was a cognate. Apart from the biological existence of a widely ramified and long-lived dynasty, it took a Hudred Years War to enforce the exclusively agnate principle in France. Only then was this exception legitimized by calling upon the *Lex Salica*. Contrary to prevailing thought, the purely agnate principle of succession was not the rule, but the exception.

It was a tragedy of the dynastic world that it was unable to achieve a general agreement on a hierarchy of the aforementioned principles. Herein lies the explanation for why there were so many dynastic struggles and wars, lasting at times for generations, as with the wars for the crowns of France or Sicily-Naples, or with the Wars of the Roses in England.

Considering the face of warfare itself at that time — pillage and burn — this tragedy afflicted not only dynastic members but a considerable portion of the entire population, often in the most dreadful ways. But on the other hand, the principles mentioned indicate that even in those unruly times people by no means struck out randomly at one another but only in very specific situations; and in some situations they did not strike out at all.

The comparative analysis of the 100 successions between 1350 and 1450 shows that a considerable number of the royal successions proceeded peacefully in accordance with the principles mentioned above. Such peaceful successions occurred when the principles did not oppose each other, or if one individual could call upon more than one principle, or if there was nobody who could or wanted to call upon contradictory principles.

Because of the natural occurrence of death, it was necessary time and again to transfer the functions of one person to another. Every such transfer could entail a crisis, and were they not regulated by generally accepted principles, transfers of royal power might plunge an entire kingdom into crisis. In this respect the recognition of these principles served to maintain peace, a function which itself was good reason for their recognition. Nowadays, one likes to dismiss the fundamentals of hereditary power as belonging to another epoch. But if one seeks to understand the fundamental traditions of a predominantly agrarian world, then it must become clear that not only kings but most others as well, from those of social or economic prominence down to the rustic landowner, owed their positions largely to successionary law. Would it have been in their interests to reject the principles of inheritance? Of course not, and this seems to be the reason why these dynastic principles were tacitly acknowledged in so many countries.

Numerous dynastic disputes can be understood as wars of succession, not only in the Middle Ages, but right down to the eighteenth century. Seen from this perspective, the history of the dynastic world is not the history of class struggles but the history of struggles of classes of heirs.

NOTES

1.   *AHR* 82 (1977), 943.
2.   The following chapter is a revised version of an article published in parts in Spanish as "Derecho electivo y sucessión hereditaria en los reinos y en el imperio de Alfonso el Sabio," in: *España y Europa, un pasado jurídico común. Actas del I Simposio Internacional del Instituto de Derecho Común,* ed. A. Perez Martin (Murcia 1986) pp. 223–58, and in German "Wahlrecht und Erbfolge in den Reichen Alfons' des Weisen," *Zur Geschichte des Familien- und Erbrechts,* ed. H. Mohnhaupt [Studien zur Europäischen Rechtsgeschichte 32] (Frankfurt 1987), pp. 1–36, where additional references can also be found.
3.   Especulo Libro I, Titulo I, Ley XIII. Alfonso el Sabio, *Opúsculos legales, publ. por la Real Academia de la Historia* I (Madrid 1836), p. 7.
4.   Crónica Alfonso X, cap. 67; quoted from F. W. Schirrmacher, *Geschichte von Spanien* 4 (Gotha 1881) 580 with n. 2: *Señor, el árbol de los reyes non se pierde por postura, nin se deseereda por y al que viene por natura, é si el mayor que viene del árbol fallesce, debe fincar la rama de so él en somo; é tres cosas son que non son so postura, ley, ni rey, ni reino; é cosa que sea fecha contra cualquiera destas, non vale nin deve ser tenida nin guardada.*
5.   *Fuero Juzgo en latin y castellano cotedajo con los más antiguos y preciosos codices por la Real Academia Española* (Madrid 1815) Lib. IV, 2, 2 (pp. 50, 67).
6.   Especulo Libro II, Titulo XVI, Ley I, *Opúsculos* (as n. 3) 69; Ley III also lists the heirs in the sequence: son—daughter—grandson— granddaughter *(fijo o fija o nieto o nieta),* ibid. 70.
7.   *Las Siete Partidas* II tit. 15, ley 2, ed. Academia II, 2 (Madrid 1807) 133.
8.   Memorial hist. Esp. II, 112 (quoted after Schirrmacher, as n. 4) 581. R. A. MacDonald ("Problemas, Politicos y Derecho Alfonsino considerados desde tres puntos de vista", *Arch. Hist. Der. Esp.* 54 (1984) p. 42, n. 45) brings a section of the Latin text: *nos inspiciendo jus antiquam et legem rationis secundum forum Yspanie, conces-*

simus tunc quod donus Sancius alter noster filius secondogenitus nobis succederet in loco Fferandi, quia per rectam lineam propinquior nobis erat quam nostri pronepotes filii doni Fferandi....

9. J. F. Boehmer, J. Ficker, *Regesta Imperii* [henceforth: RI] V (Innsbruck, 1881–2) 4885e, p.919.

10. MGH Epp. saec. XIII, 3, No. 440.

11. RI V 5289a. MGH Const. 2, No. 428 XI, p. 587-8. Cf. Ann. Wormat. ad a. 1256: *Putabant plurimi marggravium Ottonem fuisse electum in regem; sed nihil actum est tempore illo, quia Richardus, Angliae regis frater, totis ad hoc instabat viribus ad suscipiendum regni Romani gubernacula* (MGH SS 17, 59).

12. RI V 5483e.

13. MGH Const. 2, No. 392, p. 491; RI 5484.

14. MGH Const. 2, No. 395, p. 498.

15. As n. 13, above.

16. As n. 14, above.

17. Cf. the style of Alfonso's son of 12 May 1266: ...*nos infans Fernandus, primogenitus et heres domini Alfonsi Dei gracia Romanorum regis semper augusti, Castelle, Toleti, Legionis, Galletie, Sibilie, Cordube, Murcie, Gienni et Algarbii regis illustris.* G. Daumet, *Mémoire sur les relations de la France et de la Castille de 1255 à 1320* (Paris, 1913) 149.

18. RI V 5492.

19. RI V 5526a, RI VI, 392.

20. MGH SS 25, 462. Cf. RI V 5488a.

21. MGH SS 24, 413.

22. Ibid., 412.

23. *Acta imperii inedita*, ed. Ed. Winkelmann I (Innsbruck, 1880, repr. Aalen, 1964), No. 579, p. 464.

24. *Mathei Parisiensis Chronica Majora*, ed. H.R. Luard, V (London 1880), p. 603. On the negotiations, *v* Ch. C. Bayley, "The Diplomatic Preliminaries of the Double Election of 1257 in Germany," *English Historical Review* 62 (1947) 457–83; Idem, *The Formation of the German College of Electors in the Mid-Thirteenth Century* (Toronto 1949); H.-E. Hilpert, "Richard of Cornwall's Candidature for the German Throne and the Christmas 1256 Parliament at Westminster," *Journal of Medieval History* 6 (1980), 185–98.

25. *Sanctae namque Margarethae mater, Agatha nomine, filia fuit germani Henrici, clarissimi imperatoris Roman(orum), v* Sz. de Vajay, "Agatha, Mother of Saint Margaret, Queen of Scotland," *Duquesne Review* 5 (1962), p. 73, 77-78 where additional source references can also be found.

26. RI V 5293 f.

27. RI V 5473a; cf. also Ann. Parmenses, MGH SS 18, 683, where Henry is described as *filius condam regis Ricardi de Anglia, qui iam fuerat electus in regem per ecclesiam Romanam.* On later English candidates for the Empire, *v* A. Wolf, "Das 'Kaiserliche Rechtbuch' Karls IV (sogenannte Goldene Bulle)," *Ius Commune* 2 (1969), p. 30, n. 101.

28. MGH SSrerG 18, 25.

29. MGH Const. 2, no. 385.

30. It has been pointed out that Richard had "the additional qualification that he could speak English. This may be regarded as an accomplishment still unusual amongst the earls and barons of England" (N. Denholm-Young, *Richard of Cornwall,* [Oxford, 1947], pp. 86 f.)

31. *V* n. 24.
32. Gesta episc. Leodiensium abbrev., MGH SS 25, 132. The oft-cited passage about the (later) seven electors, ibid. p. 130, is in contradiction to this statement; however, since this passage pretends to refer to the age of Charlemagne, it is spurious and may be an interpolation. Referring to the ruler of Bohemia as *dux* and not *rex*, suggests dependence on Hostiensis (v below, nn. 57, 59). The only extant manuscript (Brussels, BR 19627) is from the sixteenth century. Hence, the list cannot serve as proof for the existence of the seven electors "from the mid-thirteenth century".
33. Cf. A. Wolf, "Le deux Lorraines et l'origine des princes electeurs du Saint-Empire. L'impact de l'ascendence sur l'institution," *Francia* 11 (1984), 241–56, esp. the table on pp. 246 ff. The sixteenth vote may have been that of the dukes of Zähringen, who became extinct in the male line in 1218.
34. MGH Const. 2, no. 329, p. 440.
35. K. Bosl, in Gebhardt, *Handbuch der deutschen Geschichte* 9th ed. (Stuttgart 1970) 799.
36. K. Zeumer, "Die böhmische und die bayrische Kur im 13. Jahrundert," *Historische Zeitschrift* 94 (1905), 209-50, esp. p. 211 f.
37. Jofré de Loaysa, *Crónica de los Reyes de Castilla*, c. CCXIX, 6. Ed. A. Garcia Martines (Murcia 1982) 80.
38. MGH Const. 4, no. 8.
39. Memorias de D. Fernando IV de Castilla, I. Ed. Real Acad. de la hist. (Madrid 1860), pp. 447, 489.
40. Winkelmann (as n. 23), no 579, p. 464.
41. "...*el emperador, luego que es escogido de todos aquellos que han poder de lo esleer ó de la mayor parte,...* " Las Siete Partidas, II.tit. 1, ley 2; ed. Academia (Madrid 1807) II, p. 5.
42. Cronica Alfonso X, cap. 18.
43. Alfonso el Sabio, *Setenario*, ed. K.H. Vanderford (Buenos Aires 1945; repr. Barcelona 1984).
44. This also holds true for the *Litera missa de electione comitis Ricardi in regem Rom[anorum] magnatibus imperii*, first cited (without this title) by Zeumer *(v* n. 36), 216–7; cf. MGH Const. 2, no. 385. My comments on this matter are to be printed in one of the forthcoming issues of *Parliaments, Estates and Representation*, as "Observations on Mathew Paris's Lists of Electors."
45. Mathew Paris (as n. 24), V, pp. 694–95.
46. MGH Const. 2 no. 405.
47. A. Fanta, "Ein Bericht über die Ansprüche des Königs Alfons auf den deutschen Thron," MIÖG 6 (1885), p. 96.
48. MGH Const. 3, no. 83.
49. MGH Const. 4, no. 8.
50. According to Frank R. Lewis ("Ottokar II of Bohemia and the Double Election of 1257," *Speculum* 12 (1937), 513–5) it is "very doubtful" that Ottokar voted for both candidates: "Neither the English nor the German chronicler have a word about his support for Richard."
51. Hermann of Altaich, MGH SS 17, 397.
52. Salzburg Annals, MGH SS 9, 794.
53. RI V 5493
54. Chronica majora (as n. 24), 604.
55. Ibid., 617
56. MGH Const. 2, no. 379, 381–84; RI V 11768–71, 5289.

57. This sentence was recorded by Hostiensis who attended this meeting of the princes: *Sicut vidi in Alemania per principes iudicari* (Gl. ad X. 5. 40. 26. s.v. *imperatorum vel regum).*

58. K. G. Hugelmann, *Die deutsche Königswahl im corpus iuris canonici* (Breslau 1909, repr. Aalen 1966), pp. 28–31.

59. Hostiensis, *Lectura super V libris decretalium,* ad X. 5.40.26 s.v. *imperatorum vel regum.*

60. *Las Siete Partidas,* II tit. 1, ley 2, ed. Academia (Madrid 1807) II, pp. 5. The variants in the right column are from Escorial 1.4.

61. This part is a revised version of an article published in German as: "Prinzipien der Thronfolge in Europe um 1400. Vergleichende Betrachtungen zur Praxis des dynastischen Herrschaftssystems", in: *Das spätmittelterliche Königtum in europäischem Vergleich,* ed. R. Schneider [Vorträge und Forschungen 32] (Sigmaringen 1987) pp. 233–78.

62. W. K. Prinz von Isenburg, *Stammtafeln zur Geschichte der europäischen Staaten, I–II,* rev. ed., ed. F. Baron Freytag von Lothringen (Marburg 1960), now in: *Europäische Stammtafeln. Neue Folge,* ed. D. Schwennicke (ibid. 1984). Several other works on genealogy and the dynastic history of the single countries were also consulted.

63. On this topic, V my "Königtum Minderjähriger und das Institut der Regentschaft," in: *L'Enfant: Europe médievale et moderne* [Recueils de la Société Jean Bodin pour l'histoire des institutions 36] (Brussels 1976), pp. 97–106.

64. The Bible, the supreme authority of Christian Europe, also acknowledges female succession; e.g. in 4 Mos. 27, 8–11.

CHILDREN OF MEDIEVAL GERMAN JEWRY: A PERSPECTIVE ON ARIÈS FROM JEWISH SOURCES

Israel Ta-Shma
Hebrew University of Jerusalem

Children in Medieval Germanic Jewry: A Perspective on Ariès from Jewish Sources[1]

The last thirty years have witnessed a lively and steadily growing interest in the history of childhood. The point of departure was undoubtedly the appearance in 1960 of Phillipe Ariès's *Enfant et vie familiale sous l'ancien régime,* a work which has retained nearcanonical status in the profession,[2] but which has also been challenged by subsequent historians on numerous points.[3] What has characterized this new field of research from the outset is its interdisciplinary nature, use of historical, social, psychological, and purely biological and medical tools and data. Armed with these new resources, historians have re-read many well-known medieval texts with the resulting discovery of much interesting evidence, hitherto neglected by conservative and inattentive scholars. Besides helping to further the area of the history of childhood — the practical and openly declared goal of a major part of this research — these scholarly efforts have also lent considerable impetus to historical inquiry into the enigmatic medieval mentality, opening up entirely new vistas.

It is therefore somewhat surprising that few efforts have been made up to now to reexamine medieval and Renaissance Hebrew literature, with a view of extracting relevant information and evaluating its contribution to the history of childhood. Considerable research was done — mainly in the late 19th and first half of the 20th centuries, before any serious attention was given to our subject — on the history of Jewish education, which, though verging on the subject of childhood, is quite a different matter and actually has very little direct bearing upon it. The study of medieval Jewish education, which began at the average age of four to six, is concerned mainly with the curriculum

263

and the teacher, and touches upon the child only insofar as he was seated before his teacher and his books. The history of childhood, on the
other hand, takes a global interest in the totality of the adult-child relationship, with emphasis on early life and the more developed stages of
childhood, within the family unit and the larger communal framework.

In this paper I shall examine the thesis presented by Ariès
from the perspective of Hebrew legal and non-legal sources. More
specifically, I shall question whether the sources emanating from
medieval Ashkenazic Jewry support Ariès's thesis that the idea of a separate phase of human development, known as childhood, did not exist
in the Middle Ages, and to an extent children were not considered
entirely "human," and that as a result various practices associated with
medieval parenting, such as beatings, farming out children to wet-nurses, and even infanticide were a logical corollary. Two major critiques of
this thesis have already been articulated; on the one hand, some have
argued that there is strong evidence for an appreciation of childhood
on its own terms in the Middle Ages, and that Ariès has turned a blind
eye to the evidence of love for children. From an altogether different
beginning-point, scholars such as Lloyd deMause have argued that
exploitation, cruelty, and brutality constituted the backbone of child-
rearing in the Middle Ages. As a psycho-historian, deMause does not
perceive this brutality as an epiphenomenon, resulting from the image
of the child as a young adult. Instead, he argues, the brutality is at the
very heart of the parent-child relationship, with profound social impli-
cations. The importance of our inquiry into the Hebrew sources is its
possible contribution to a better understanding not only of Jewish family life and function — itself a much neglected subject — but also of the
history of childhood in general.

Special mention must be made of the pioneering work of
Ephraim Kanarfogel, who, in an excellent article,[4] follows the group of
scholars who attack Ariès by arguing that children were treated in the
Middle Ages and Renaissance with better understanding and more love
than Ariès would have us believe. Kanarfogel claims that his "study will
demonstrate that if the questions which Ariès raised are asked about
Jewish society in Western Europe in the Middle Ages, the answers will
not always be the same as those of Ariès" — with which statement I
readily agree. Kanarfogel adduces interesting evidence for "an appreciation of childhood for its own sake among medieval European Jewry,"
and he is of course well aware that there is much more evidence to that
effect. But it should be borne in mind that this is true not only on the

basis of Jewish sources, but also on the testimony of European sources in general, as has been amply demonstrated by many scholars, cited by Kanarfogel himself. Moreover, the undoubted truth of this argument in no way detracts from the cogency of the evidence produced in support of the other side of the coin, that children were treated in a curious and frigid manner, which Ariès has depicted so sharply and convincingly. Both descriptions are valid, and probably coexisted simultaneously within the same society and the same families. The novel element of Ariès's picture relates to the strange, unfamiliar, frigid aspect of the parent-child relationship; love for children is, of course, common knowledge and taken for granted, even though Ariès seems to have ignored it altogether.

On the other hand, notwithstanding Kanarfogel's evidence, it would seem that much of the information to be gleaned from Jewish sources tends to corroborate Ariès's description. In fact, it can be shown that many of the central phenomena of attitudes towards children described by Ariès existed within the framework of the medieval Jewish family, although, as we shall soon see, they fulfilled fundamentally different social roles. In Kanarfogel's article itself I could find one example of this type,[5] where he points out that the terms for small child, young child, adolescent, etc., were often interchanged in Jewish as in medieval French literature. Kanarfogel admits that "this interchangeability does show, to some extent, that the ages and stages of childhood were not as fixed then as they are today." But there is far more to be said in this respect.

It is a plain fact that children were far more assured of their personal safety in the Franco-German Jewish family than in the homes of their gentile neighbours. We know of no Jewish child who was ever sold willingly into slavery, delivered to foreign servitude or offered as an oblation to an outside institution. Neither were Jewish children sent away to study under advanced scholars until coming of age.[6] Jewish children were exposed — as were other children, and perhaps more so — to the dangers of abduction, captivity and forced apostasy, but they were never surrendered willingly by their parents, although the latter were legally permitted to do so. Cases of infanticide of any variety were so rare in Jewish society as to be hardly detectable in the voluminous corpus of medieval Hebrew literature. Nevertheless, a few such cases are recorded, one of them in *Sefer Hasidim* (#173), which tells of a widow who indirectly caused the death of her children — of whom there were at least two — by a magic spell, because her prospective new

husband refused to marry a woman with children.[7] Presumably, moreover, the bleak stories of child-devouring witches recounted in *Sefer
Hasidim* indicate unexplained disappearances or straightforward infanticide, but of course one cannot be sure.

Another ancient type of silent infanticide is apparently accidental smothering of children in their sleep, known as crib death,
which has long been suspected of possibly masking intentional and
semi-intentional cases. The subject has been treated by many scholarly
students of infanticide, who seem to eye this poorly understood but
widely known phenomenon with deep suspicion. It is interesting to
note that the earliest rabbinical testimony for crib death comes from
the second half of the thirteenth century, from a responsum by R. Meir
of Rothenburg, and only very few other cases are mentioned in fourteenth-century rabbinic literature.[8] These rare incidents, however, are
only exceptions to the rule.

The protection afforded the child in the Jewish tradition has
indeed been mentioned in passing by some scholars. William Langer[9]
has emphasized the influence of ancient Jewish traditions on the firm,
though inefficient, official Christian stand against all forms of infanticide and cruel estrangement of children. Another interesting point has
been made by Magdalene Schultz,[10] who suggests that this very difference of attitudes toward small children — harsh neglect on the gentile
side compared with caring responsibility on the Jewish — produced
guilt feelings that had to be warded off, "through projection upon the
minority in relation to which one feels inferior in this respect" — therefore affecting mainly small children, as demonstrated so well by the sanguinary history of the blood libel. I cannot form an opinion of any
value on the psychological plausibility of this theory, but we can safely
accept the basic assumption of both Langer and Schultz as to the substantially different treatment accorded small children in Jewish and
gentile families, though neither of them has systematically analyzed the
subject on the basis of contemporaneous source material.[11]

There is a twofold reason for this difference between Jewish
and the gentile attitudes in regard to children under one's control.
First and foremost, one has the unequivocal halakhic concept of
pikkuah nefesh, which permeates every nook and cranny of Jewish existence and is the major and absolute consideration governing each and
every circumstance, with the three exceptions of adultery, idolatry, and
homicide. To be precise: under no conditions is a Jew allowed to com-

mit one of these three transgressions. He is instructed to give up his life rather than agree — even under duress — to rape his fellow man's wife, act against his own God, or take someone else's life. The Jews of Germany stretched this principle to its extreme; not content to let themselves be killed by their oppressors, rather than superficially and temporarily adopt Christianity, they went much further, slaying their wives and children with their own hands lest they fail the difficult test and surrender their faith rather than their lives. This is one of the most tragic and famous chapters of Ashkenazi experience.[12] It is also, incidentally, a rare manifestation of Jewish infanticide — if it can really be called that. With these three exceptions, preservation of Jewish life was the ultimate desideratum of Jewish law, and responsibility for its destruction, even second-degree responsibility, was the gravest possible crime. This very deep-rooted sense of the sanctity of Jewish life is the major reason for the specifically Jewish attitude to children within the family, as children themselves are unaware of the dangers of life and unable to care for themselves.

The contrast between the traditional Jewish approach to life, which derives from the religious stratum of the personality and is related to the primary idea of the holy, and the pagan attitude, which derives from the social stratum and is related to the sophisticated idea of utility, has been described, explained, and copiously demonstrated by Moshe Weinfeld in an outstanding article dealing with Jewish attitudes towards abortion.[13] My point will be clarified by a few sentences from the English summary of Weinfeld's Hebrew article:

In comparison with the Jewish–Hellenistic and Christian view concerning abortion, the Biblical and Rabbinic outlook in this matter is more lenient and more tolerant.... The difference between the Jewish and Hellenistic views of abortion seems to lie in their different attitude towards the life of an individual as a value. Abortion in the pagan world is mainly a sin against state and society (loss of manpower and the strength of the community), whereas the Jewish legislator cares about the religious-moral meaning of murder: the term murder applies to a living creature and not to a foetus which is part of its mother's body. The view of the pagans concerning infanticide may be learned from their attitude towards exposure of children. Contrary to the rigid approach towards abortion, we encounter complete lawlessness in respect to exposure and especially the exposure of crippled children. This shows that the motive force concerning abortion and infanticide was mainly social-political and not religious-moral, as it was amongst the Jews and later among the Christians.[14]

Before I proceed to the second reason for the protection of the Jewish child, there is one more aspect of Jewish child-rearing which derived from the traditional principle of *pikkuah nefesh* which must be addressed. There is a long-standing and strictly observed injunction among the Ashkenazim against marrying a widowed mother who is still nursing her child, for a period commonly agreed to be twenty-four months. The reason is the fear that the new husband might force the mother to neglect her child, since breast–feeding was an onerous task — it was then considered the mother's duty to feed the baby whenever it cried and could not be pacified, day and night. As nursing was the sole technique of effectively feeding a baby, concern for such an orphaned child is readily understood. The matter is discussed at length in the Talmud (Ketubbot 60a-b) and Shemuel, the great first-generation amora, rules that such a marriage is forbidden even if the baby dies within the twenty-four month period, lest the mother kill the child intentionally to clear the way for an expected marriage. The Talmud rejects this seemingly repulsive idea, adding that the incident quoted by Shemuel as evidence for such inhuman behaviour concerned an insane woman, whereas normal, healthy women do not strangle their sons. The Jerusalem Talmud (Sotah 4:3) accepts Shemuel's position, though without mentioning his name, and rules against such marriages. Another important difference between the two Talmuds concerns the acceptability of various safeguards against possible neglect on the part of the mother, such as arranging for an alternative prepaid wet-nurse. The Babylonian Talmud seems to sanction such legal solutions, provided they are really reliable, but the Jerusalem Talmud makes no mention of them and on the whole treats the matter with excessive stringency. Other early Palestinian sources stress the prohibition even more explicitly, mentioning the fear of deliberate murder.[15]

There is no need here to enter into a full analysis of the talmudic material. Medieval Ashkenazi Jewry adhered fanatically to this injunction, inclining heavily to the Jerusalem Talmud and absolutely rejecting any alternative arrangements suggested by the couple. Indeed, following the relevant discussion in the Babylonian Talmud, it was further ruled that all such marriages must be terminated by a formal divorce, to be re-wed after the twenty-four month period by a full-fledged marriage ceremony.

A case in point — a *cause célèbre* at the time — occurred in the city of Krakow, Poland, some time during the first quarter of the thirteenth century, i.e., in the earliest stages of Jewish settlement in that country. A certain scholar, R. Jacob Ha-Kohen, wedded a nursing widow within the forbidden twenty-four months, contrary to all accepted rules and norms. However, he took extraordinary measures to safeguard the baby's interests. He contacted two different wet-nurses, paid them in advance and enjoined them under pledge and an oath in God's name not to forsake their post. The most interesting point is R. Jacob himself was a great rabbinic scholar and authority, recognized as such by first-rank German rabbis such as R. Isaac Or Zarua', who actually headed R. Jacob's opponents.

We do not know too much about the whole affair, and none of the Polish rabbis involved are known to us by name. All we know is that R. Isaac Or Zarua' and his colleagues in Germany took an intransigent stand and employed very strong language, threatening to excommunicate R. Jacob if he did not immediately divorce his wife — a very unusual procedure when dealing with a colleague. But R. Jacob was a kohen, and according to Jewish law, if he divorced his wife he would not be able to remarry after the twenty-four month period, nor indeed at any other time! This did not deter the German rabbis, however. R. Isaac Or Zarua' expresses in his letter a profound concern that if R. Jacob were allowed to keep his wife, the ban on such marriages would be completely violated, to the detriment of many other orphaned children, for people would remember R. Jacob's precedent but not his pledges, details of which would be unknown or forgotten in remote localities and at distant times.

The desperate R. Jacob appealed to numerous rabbinic authorities, in various and far-off countries, to help him in his anguish, and to approve of his halakhic position; we also know that R. Tobias of Vienne, a well-known French tosafist, actually approved of the marriage and ruled that it was permissible a priori, given the special provisions made by R. Jacob. All these letters — and there were certainly many of them — are now lost, and there can be little doubt that they were censored by the Ashkenazi rabbis, who even forbade them to be copied.[16]

Comparing the situation described here with the general practice of wet-nursing, which was extremely common in twelfth- and thir-

teenth-century France and Germany and was mostly tantamount to getting rid of the baby for good, one clearly perceives the fundamental difference between the two cultures, and at the same time fully understands the significance of this notable rabbinic controversy. On a personal note: when I first encountered the material relating to this affair,
I was utterly unable to understand the obstinacy of R. Isaac Or Zarua'
and his group, especially under the unusual circumstances associated
with the case from the start. True, German Jewry is known to have been
under relatively strong Palestinian influence from the Early Middle
Ages on, as I myself have pointed out on other occasions.[17] And this is a
clear instance of a Palestinian tradition exerting its hidden power on
the German rabbis. There is no other example, however, of such strong
feelings being expressed under similar circumstances. A true understanding of this strange case can be achieved only on the background
of actual wet-nursing practices and their true significance in the
Germany of those times.

In addition to the protection of *pikkuah nefesh,* the second reason why the child was protected has to do with the specifically
Ashkenazi concept of the religious duty of *hinnukh,* i.e., the obligation
to educate children for full and informed participation in their traditional communal life. The primary mission of the Jew in this world was
to study Torah and instruct his children in Torah, *mitzvot,* and the fear
of heaven. By thus ensuring the continuity of absolutely orthodox,
devout, meticulous and pedantic halakhic practice and Torah study,
the individual fulfilled his mission in the best possible way; his offspring
would do the same in his turn, guaranteeing that the eternal chain
would never be broken. Such was the responsibility that lay on a Jewish
parent's shoulders. And one should always remember that normative
Jewish practice consisted to a considerable extent of local customs, *min-
hagim,* which were not set out in any written book but were current in
daily practice, and the younger generation was expected to learn them
in the family and in the synagogue.[18]

These two major reasons — the absolute sanctity of life and
the supreme educational responsibility of the parent — created a major
difference between Jewish and gentile families, saving the Jewish child
from many of the hardships that befell his Christian counterpart.
Analysis of the contemporary Hebrew sources, therefore, makes it possible to examine Ariès's thesis regarding the frigidity of adult-childhood
relations without the background of physical danger. And, in fact, there
are many similarities between the Jewish and non-Jewish family on this

score, and thus these phenomena indeed developed from deeply-rooted family practices, as Ariès claims, and have little to do with other external factors and sectors of the social complex.

It must be borne in mind that, although there was very much in common between Franco-German Jewish practices and gentile behaviour — this is common knowledge today and was in fact admitted by our ancestors too — Jews were kept apart from their neighbors by a not inconsiderable barrier, due to the existence of the unavoidable, omnipresent, ubiquitous Halakhah, which completely dominated Jewish private and community life. Sometimes of little significance, the gap could at other times be of major and decisive importance. One simple example — which, incidentally, has a direct bearing on our subject — will help clarify my meaning. The ideal of extreme religious piety coupled with social sectarianism, so fundamental to the ideology of Hasidei Ashkenaz, had its striking parallel in the contemporaneous European monastic ideal. Yizhak Baer elaborated on this equation in a famous paper on *Sefer Hasidim*,[19] demonstrating many of the less prominent aspects of the similarity. It should be remembered, however, that Hasidei Ashkenaz did not — indeed, could not — adopt celibacy, a crucial element of monasticism, since Halakhah postulates marriage — and procreation — as one of its central and most significant demands; and the attitude of Hasidei Ashkenaz to family life as a religious duty was most enthusiastic, to say the least. Hence they were absolutely convinced, in the face of the Christian *consensus omnium,* that religious piety did not involve abstinence from marital life; in consequence, they never withdrew from society into remote seclusion, and moulded their conception of the sexual impulse and its ambivalent nature in a different way. Thus, the Christian and Jewish brands of pietism both reflect the deep religious spirit of the age and similar attitudes toward God and human society, and indeed have many features in common; but a clear realization of the differences and their underlying reasons is necessary to set proper limits, and permits better delineation of the true frontier lines between the two cultures, which had so much in common and yet were so different.

Having stated this, we can now return to the issue of the attitudes expressed towards children. Even a partial survey of the medieval Hebrew material relating to Aries's thesis concerning the attitude to children would be beyond the scope of this article, but I would like to present a few examples gleaned from the inexhaustible *Sefer Hasidim* in order to press my point.

The first issue one notices is the rarity of any direct reference to children in Hebrew literature from the eleventh to the thirteenth centuries, including *Sefer Hasidim*. Moreover, even when children are mentioned no age is given, the age terms — na'*ar, yeled, tinok, bahur* and the like — being vague, ambiguous, and inconsistent. Most important of all, nothing positive is ever said about them, nor are they ever described as engaged in some praiseworthy activity. What is described is merely their innocent — or, more often, noxious — presence, in situations that call for a halakhic or moral decision by the rabbi, which is the only reason they are mentioned at all. To the best of my knowledge, toys are never mentioned in early medieval Hebrew literature; children are always playing adult games or imitating the daily routine of adults. This is all typical of medieval literature, as observed and described by Ariès. At first sight this would seem to present an insurmountable obstacle to research, but actually that is far from being the case. On the contrary, it implies that we now have at our disposal a set of candid snapshots, so to speak, taken in situ and without any distortions.

Small children — that is to say, children under the age of five to six years, which was considered early for standard schooling — were the direct responsibility of their mother. The father was usually not at home; according to *Sefer Hasidim*, fondling one's children and going out for a walk with them, was a major — if not the major — delight and recreation for the busy and usually absent father. *Sefer Hasidim* holds that the pious, who avoid such amusement even when their children are crying and their hearts go out to them, because they will not interrupt their holy studies for such mundane and egoistic ends, will not exchange divine love for fatherly love; such pious souls will therefore leave the crying child to his mother's care, and will be fully rewarded in the world to come. The domestic scene of the father embracing and, especially, kissing his children, crops up here and there in *Sefer Hasidim*. Attraction to children and women, playing with friends and idle walk and talk are the main causes of *bittul torah*, neglect of the study of Torah (#815). Renouncing these pleasures is a taxing demand, certainly something hard to expect and difficult to achieve.

The crying baby was a notorious nuisance in antiquity. A baby was usually expected to be crying day and night, wreaking havoc with its parents' nerves, most probably because it was constantly in a state of semi-hunger, the outcome of ineffective and inordinate nursing and the total lack of alternate baby food. Incidentally, babies' physical development was nevertheless not hindered, as we learn from the laconic statement in *Sefer Hasidim* (#944). "Children are not strong enough to hold something in their hands until they are six months old" — a figure somewhat lower than contemporary averages. Another important factor was the already mentioned absence of toys, which were unknown at the time; even dolls were apparently unknown in the Jewish home, probably because they contravened the injunction against three-dimensional human images. The prescribed remedy for a crying baby was to breast-feed it again, and when that did not help lullabies were sung — *Sefer Hasidim* warns against the use of gentile melodies or even synagogal-liturgical songs (!) — for the purpose. As a last resort one appealed to magic, which certain women knew how to perform, in order to counteract the effects of the evil spell that had evidently been cast by some witch, anonymous or otherwise, who was always held responsible for constant, incessant weeping (#174).

Children used to roam about with their noses filthy and dripping. This was the norm and to be expected: "Small children are customarily filthy around their noses"; there was nothing amiss in children appearing thus before guests and strangers visiting their homes. But small children accompanying their father when he was visiting another household were expected to have clean noses; otherwise the father was considered responsible and was even liable to be sued for damages (#104). However, the main significance of this piece of information lies in the field of medieval paediatrics, which needs separate treatment.

As stated, children were normally under their mother's care. An unusual case is described in *Sefer Hasidim* (#569). The text may be rendered approximately as follows:

> The wise man heard somebody say his Grace after Meals hurriedly. He said to him, when you ate you did not hurry, why are you in a hurry now? The man answered, when my little children are near me I always make haste, lest they ease nature on me. So the sage said to him, then remove them from you! But the man answered, I am not the ruler of the house and its inhabitants, and the maidservants do not heed me, and my wife governs the money and from her hand do I eat.

As we have already encountered the unclean child, we may well understand the father's distress. But this man was not master of the situation in his own house. The mother regularly sent her dirty children to nag their pious father while he was at his meals and leave her alone. And the poor man could do nothing about it, not even call in the maids for help! Though this story seems to draw a topsy-turvy picture of the situation, it nevertheless brings out very vividly the same principle of complete — though ineffective — maternal responsibility, temporarily let loose on the good-for-nothing father while he was at home.

A very amusing instruction advises a person who cannot help meditating on the Torah even when he is in the lavatory to take his small children there with him, in order to distract his mind. But, the text adds, "if he is afraid lest they become accustomed to being near him and distracting his mind when he is studying Torah," then it is better that he should not take them with him, but perhaps try to think about other matters in the privy...! (#771)

The fact that children were completely under their mother's care was no guarantee of their good conduct. Undisciplined children appear quite often in our sources, which tell us that unruly, even wild, behaviour was normally expected from them. We learn again from *Sefer Hasidim* (#600):

A person was told, many people hang pretty decorations in their *sukkah*,[20] why do you not do so? But he said: What is the use? The children will disconnect the fruits and the threads on the Sabbath, so I had better not be the cause of their sins.

The children would do so any time, of course, but the pious man was worried only on account of the Sabbath. It did not occur to him simply to forbid them, on pain of punishment, to touch the decorations, thus enabling him to beautify his *sukkah*, as befitted his piety — and as his pious friends though fit. For if he did, most probably only his wife could see to it that his instructions were observed, and she was always busy indoors. At any rate, no one seems to have believed that issuing the necessary instructions and ensuring that they were carried out was an essential part of education and child rearing.

A similar situation is described and pictured in vivid colors in another interesting passage (*Sefer Hasidim* #684):

A boy stood on a table upon which his father was accustomed to put his books. But the table was not reserved for books only, as he would place food on it too when he wished to eat. Books were always on the table, but when he ate he put them elsewhere. So the boy stood on the table, and as he let himself down he cut his foot on a knife that was lying on the table. And the father said, I am to blame. Why did I allow him to tread on a table which usually has holy books on it?

The moral of this story for its readers is quite clear, as is its significance for our inquiry: Neither father nor mother thought it necessary to prevent the child from climbing the furniture. The pious father understood — too late, admittedly — that holy books were a different matter, but that is all. A much more interesting point is that the father's conscience actually troubled him — it troubled him that he was responsible for his son's accident; but he understood his guilt as directed against the holy books, not against the child himself, whom he could easily have trained never to climb tables (provided of course, that his wife co-operated). As already pointed out, these passages capture for us minute snapshots of domestic scenes, complete with soundtrack, recording the actual voices of the protagonists. The same scene could be encountered in any household; the unique feature in this case was the pious father's reaction, in taking the blame upon himself and admitting that holy books demand special care. Ordinary fathers would never have such sentiments, even if they happened to have holy books regularly lying upon their tables.

Harsh disciplinary measures were considered a necessity in school, that is, before a teacher, but nowhere else. Elsewhere children were known — and expected — to act as they pleased, as long as they did not encroach upon someone else's rights; this was understood as part of their underdeveloped nature. The solution was to have them seated before a teacher as early as possible and for as long a time as possible. However, this is beyond the scope of this article, as we are interested only in pre-school years.

Children's games, on the testimony of *Sefer Hasidim*, were all of a social type. Children old enough to walk and talk always played in the company of other children, mainly imitating adult activity or playing their games. There is no telling how younger infants occupied themselves when not crying; I have already stated that, to the best of my knowledge, toys, dolls, and puppets are never mentioned. Table games and open-air games alike are mentioned mostly in connection with adults, and it is clear that recreation of any variety was mainly an adult occupation, children imitating them in this respect as they did — and still do — in all other fields of behaviour. Jewish boys played together with their gentile coevals, and no one seemed to mind. For example (#1243):

> If children brought stone weights and scales which gentile children had calibrated according to their father's, whose measures were considered more or less exact, and Jewish boys played with them and calibrated their stones accordingly....

The writer seems to be concerned with the stones, ignoring the children's behaviour.

Children under schooling age were considered incapable of coping with academic material of any level. Even later, when they attended school, they were allowed to progress only very slowly and under strict supervision. As I have discussed this principle at length elsewhere,[21] I shall not dwell on it here. The reason for this distrust, which is an inheritance from time immemorial and still lingers today, is rooted in the ancient belief that wisdom literature conveys more than its superficial content and is always concealing deeper matters between the lines. Neither does Nature, or Holy Script, speak to us in an unambiguous, direct manner; a real and thorough understanding of their true inner meaning — which is always there — can be achieved only through able intermediaries, who interpret their message to us. Interpretation, mostly professional and often counter to the simple sense of the text, is unavoidable if we are to understand the sayings and teachings of old; otherwise we might easily be misled into gross errors by the superficial meaning. I mention this in passing as a mere digression.[22]

Returning now to our main inquiry, it would be particularly interesting to see what individuals in the Middle Ages thought of the general abilities and inclinations of young children, and how they assessed their talents, which they do not seem to have noticed at all. Unfortunately, direct evidence to that effect is most rare in medieval Hebrew literature, and I shall now proceed to cite the sparse information I have been able to cull from *Sefer Hasidim.*

The melammed, who teaches the youngsters, is instructed to point to the sky with his finger, to show his pupils where God is.

> Later on the teacher should explain to the boy the existence of paradise and hell, because a child's intellect is like that of an adult in his

sleep, believing everything to be true. In the same manner children believe everything you tell them is true, before bad friends accustom them [to wrong opinions]. (#820)

This naiveté, considered here to be the best shortcut to correct beliefs, is only one side of the child's immature personality. The other side may be found in his straightforward commonsense and healthy critical attitude:

One should not reveal to children strange legends, lest they say there is nothing to them, they are not true, and since they are not true other things [that the children have been told] are also not true. (#811)

Being naive, the small child will easily accept the existence of God, paradise, and hell, but he will not give credit to apparent absurdities and will be quick enough to reject prior information of the same type or quality, previously accepted on a *bona fide* basis and now recognized as false and rejected — quite a realistic assessment of juvenile reasoning.

The emphatically social nature of childhood was perfectly understood: *Sefer Hasidim* says that "small children, before they get married, cannot do without friends" (#1084), and therefore advises the father to ensure that the child has worthy friends. It also warns against permitting the child to eat in other homes, lest he adopt evil ways and come under the influence of bad friends.

In apparent disagreement with talmudic conceptions, *Sefer Hasidim* is of the opinion that young boys under the age of thirteen are responsible, under certain conditions, for their deeds, though they are not punishable or answerable to the law before reaching that age. After achieving maturity at the age of thirteen, they may be required to rectify some of their past misdeeds. This idea is worthy of a detailed scrutiny, which is beyond the scope of this article. Suffice it to quote *Sefer Hasidim* on this intriguing point:

A person came before the rabbi and said to him, I remember that when I was a child I used to steal from people and commit other sins. And he said, presumably I need not repent, because at the time I was not yet thirteen, and as I was still young why should I repent or repay my thefts? But the rabbi said to him, All the sins that you remember and everything that you stole you must repay.... But if a person was told by others that he used to steal when he was a child and he does not remember this himself, he need not repay [or repent]. (#216)

Religious responsibility depends on intelligence, while legal liability depends on age. Intelligent boys are answerable for their actions, as can be proved from the Bible (II Kings chap. 22). People who recall negative personal involvement in events from their younger days are therefore fully responsible, once they grow up, for their misdeeds. The very fact that the events in question were recorded in their memory as negative or forbidden acts is proof positive that at the time they possessed sufficient understanding and were fully conscious of their wrongdoing.[23] That is why they are held responsible after reaching maturity.

I cannot enter here into an inquiry concerning the opinion of professional halakhists on this very moot point. Suffice it to say that we have here a very elegant "Ariès motif", identifying the adult male with his younger version, the child, and postulating a purely quantitative difference between them regarding physical maturity and intellectual level. In other words, we once again have evidence of a very interesting point: that despite the special physical treatment accorded the Jewish child, ultimately the child was not treated as a distinct entity, but as in the non-Jewish world, an adult-in-miniature. The edifice of parent-child interrelationships, though quite similar to that described by Ariès was built on a completely different infrastructure. The implication is that medieval concepts of childhood, as delineated and characterized by Ariès, stemmed from medieval mental and social attitudes and were not connected with — certainly not a result of — the cruel treatment accorded to medieval children, as argued by some of Ariès's detractors.

These conclusions must not be extrapolated to all of medieval Jewry. They represent one attempt to re-examine Jewish sources, and focus only on medieval Germanic Jewry. New studies of other times and places will undoubtedly yield variations on the thesis presented above. But the importance of other studies, which carefully examine the legal and non-legal literature of the Jews, and are sensitive to historiographic debates of medievalists, will hopefully be amply demonstrated in the above study.

NOTES

1. In November 1988, the Committee for Medieval Studies at the University of British Columbia hosted its eighteenth annual workshop, on the theme "Education in Medieval Jewish Society." Scholars from Canada, France, the United States and Israel presented papers on a variety of issues in the history of Jewish Education. The heterogeneous nature of medieval Jewish culture became apparent in the papers on curriculum, the battle–ground of the argument over what should be the subjects included in the curriculum of medieval Jewry, and which should occupy place of priority (Bible, Talmud, mysticism, philosophy). Other scholars discussed a variety of underexplored issues such as education and sectarianism, education and medical training among the Jews, late medieval *Yeshivot,* and education and women. Behind all of these discussions, however, must lie the issue of just how the Jewish child was perceived in the Middle Ages, and it is this topic which Israel Ta-Shma, of the Hebrew University of Jerusalem addressed in his keynote address, now revised for publication. The particular value of this paper is not just that it sheds light on Jewish society, but by confronting the thesis of Ariès, Ta-Shma enhances our understanding of the Middle Ages as a whole. Ta-Shma displays his mastery of both the legal and non-legal literature of medieval Jewry, and of contemporary historiographical issues, thus broadening our understanding of medieval society.

   The Social Sciences and Humanities Research Council of Canada has provided funding for the conference in general and this publication in specific. Their generous assistance is gratefully acknowledged. —Richard Menkis (co–ordinator, XVIII Medieval Workshop, "Education in Medieval Jewish Society," November 17-18, 1988).
2. Philippe Ariès, *L'enfant et la vie familiale sous l'ancien régime* (Paris, 1960).
3. A particularly powerful challenge was articulated by Lloyd deMause in his impressive article, "The Evolution of Childhood," *The History of Childhood Quarterly* 1 (1973): 503–575. The critiques of Ariès will be outlined briefly below.
4. Ephraim Kanarfogel, "Attitudes toward Childhood and Children in Medieval Jewish Society," *Approaches to Judaism in Medieval Times* 2 (1985), 1–34.
5. Kanarfogel, "Attitudes toward Childhood," p. 25, n. 43.
6. *V Sefer Hasidim,* #554. *Sefer Hasidim* is a book of exempla emanating from a group of pietists (known as Hasidei Ashkenaz) in mid-twelfth century Germany. References to some of the secondary literature are provided below. I have followed the second edition of Jehuda Wistinezki (Frankfurt, 1924).
7. We shall have occasion to refer to this story below, p. 281.
8. This has been amply demonstrated by E.E. Urbach, who has collected all the relevant material and added interesting insights on the subject of Jewish infanticide, in his "On Manslaughter and Crib Death," *Asupot* 1 (1987): 319–332 (in Hebrew).
9. William Langer, "Infanticide: A Historical Survey," *History of Childhood Quarterly* 1 (1973): 353–365.
10. Magdalene Schultz, "The Blood Libel — A Motif in the History of Childhood," *Proceedings of the Ninth World Congress of Jewish Studies* Div.B. I, (Jerusalem, 1986), pp. 55–60.
11. In fact, the subject has not been analyzed by anyone, nor has its importance in our context been properly understood. As already indicated, it is not my intention to undertake such analysis here, though I shall presently produce some interesting supportive evidence.
12. It has been studied at length by Haym Soloveitchik, in an as yet unpublished article.
13. Moshe Weinfeld, "The Genuine Jewish Attitudes towards Abortion," *Zion* 42 (1977): 129–142 (in Hebrew).
14. Ibid., from the English summary. For further interesting material see I. Jakobovits, "Jewish Views

on Infanticide," Marvin Kohl, ed. *Infanticide and the Value of Life* (London, 1978), pp. 23–31.

15. *Sefer ha-hillukim she-beyn benei mizrah u-veney erets-yisrael* (Jerusalem, 1983), p. 95 and *Sefer ha-ma'asim li-veney erets-yisrael,* as cited by B.M. Levin in *Tarbiz* 1,1 (1930): 94 (in Hebrew).

16. The unusual affair was described by Ephraim Kupfer in his "From far and near," *N.M. Gelber Jubilee Volume,* ed. Y. Klausner et al., (Tel-Aviv, 1963), p. 218 (in Hebrew) and later by E.E. Urbach in his introduction to *Arugat Ha-Bosem* (Jerusalem, 1963) (in Hebrew). For a more detailed account, *v* my article, based upon manuscript material, "On the History of Polish Jewry in the 12th–13th Centuries," *Zion* 53 (1978): 353–359 (in Hebrew). I must add here that far–reaching inner censorship was certainly not rare in medieval Ashkenazi literature, though the subject has never been discussed by modern scholars.

17 *V* Israel Ta-Shma, "Law, Custom and Tradition in 11-12th century German Jewry," *Sidra* 3 (1987): 85–161(in Hebrew)

18 On this weighty and complex topic, *v* my article "Law, Custom and Tradition in 11–12th century German Jewry."

19 Y. Baer, "The Religious and Social Tendency of *Sefer Hasidim,*" *Zion* 3 (1938): 1–50 (in Hebrew).

20 A Jew is enjoined by law to construct a *sukkah*, or tabernacle, during the festival of Sukkot, in commemoration of the tabernacles that the children of Israel inhabited in the wilderness after the Exodus from Egypt.

21 Ibid., pp. 136-140.

22 Interesting material on this topic has been assembled by Jane Chance Nitzsche, *The Genius Figure in Antiquity and the Middle Ages* (New York, 1975), esp. pp. 56–64. On the famous Book of Nature and its significance for a true understanding of *Sefer Hasidim*, v Haym Soloveitchik, "Three Themes in *Sefer Hasidim,*" *AJS Review* 1 (1976): 311–325.

23 Or consider the following passage (#1774): "A person having a fruit tree in his garden should have a thornbush fence, so that children should not break through, climb the tree and pluck its fruit on the Sabbath. The owner cannot say, 'Let the wicked gorge themselves and die' [Babylonian Talmud, Bava Kama 69b], because they are still children," and therefore not responsible for themselves.

Review Essay

THE GOTHIC IDOL AND MEDIEVAL ART

Carol Knicely

University of British Columbia
Vancouver, Canada

Review Essay
The Gothic Idol And
Medieval Art

Anyone casually familiar with Gothic art and its presentation in the literature, indeed, even those professionals whose business it is "to know" Medieval art, might be a little surprised to find a book devoted to the subject of "the Gothic idol."* It is not that the discussion of a theme is not a respected genre of Medieval art history. One has seen or can imagine books on, "the Virgin Mary in Gothic art," "the King in Gothic Art," "the Saints...," "the Devil...," "the Peasant...," "the Virtues and Vices...," or to be more probing, "the imagery of women in art," or, "the imagery of work...", etc. What might seem incongruous though, is the choice of this particular theme — the idol, or even the broader issue, idol–worship. While we would agree that idol–worship, particularly image worship, was a critical issue during the Iconoclastic controversy in the eighth and early ninth century, can it be said this was such an important one in the thirteenth and fourteenth? From what kind of perspective would the theme of the idol be deserving of study in Gothic art? The reader might therefore be disappointed to find that Camille does little at the outset to provide a rationale for dealing with the idol or to clarify his conception of this theme, except for a personal anecdote where he says the book began when he became "fascinated by the demonic leer of the rude little idol in a Parisian Psalter leaf in Blackburn City Art Gallery" (xxxi, fig. 1 in the book). I would accuse Camille of a certain amount of "mauvaise foi" in not revealing his full intentions, because *The Gothic Idol* is much more ambitious than the

---

*Michael Camille, *The Gothic Idol, Ideology and Image-Making in Medieval Art,* (Cambridge New Art History and Criticism, ed. Norman Bryson). Cambridge: Cambridge University Press, 1989. Pp. xxxii, 407, 181 halftones.

pursuit of a personal whim or curiosity. Although, by traditional standards, the imagery of idols and idol-worshipping can be seen only as marginal in the thirteenth and fourteenth centuries, Camille has nonetheless uncovered hundreds of images and texts that deal with ramifications of this theme, employing a provocative interdisciplinary approach which I will detail below. The book is wonderfully illustrated with 181 pictures, (perhaps explaining the hefty price), neatly accompanying the text at every step, many of which are little known — or perhaps it would be better said, little noticed until Camille's encompassing analysis. One of the benefits of Camille's study will have been to sensitize us to the range of significations that can be deposited in marginal details, thereby encouraging us to look closely at all aspects of a work. Therefore it is an important feature of the book that it is well illustrated.

It does not appear, however, to be Camille's intent to prove that art historians have somehow missed an important central theme until now, the idol. Rather, Camille has chosen this marginal image, because it is a propitious site from which to attempt to weave an analysis that addresses the very issue of representation itself. What seems to have appealed to Camille is that a representation of an idol is an image within an image; the discourse on idolatry is at the same time a discussion of image making; hence, the sub-title of the book, "Ideology and image-making in the Middle Ages." Since we have few direct statements about making images in the Middle Ages, this focus has provided Camille with a handhold on an area where artists might be more self-conscious about the making and viewing of representations or at least have to deal with the problem of distinguishing licit from illicit images, thereby revealing their own ideas of representation (pp. 71–72). This theoretical concern places Camille within a growing group of what can be called the new philosophers of art history. While this seems to be the fascination that has driven Camille's pursuit of the idol in its many forms, it is not so simple a matter to judge the results of the inquiry, even though his observations are almost always intriguing and thought-provoking.

This is really only one side of Camille's concern; the other deals with questions about how art historians today should be analyzing representation. In *The Gothic Idol* Camille is stressing the inadequacy of an iconographic approach that focuses narrowly on a pictorial image whose meaning is then explicated through its relationship to particular texts. Camille's work does encompass the actual imagery of idols based on texts — for example, the imagery of the "The Fall of Idols" in "The Flight into Egypt"; "The Vice of Idolatry"; Old Testament images of idol worship; the imagery of Saints destroying idols, etc., but he generally ignores the direct textual references. Instead Camille seems to suggest that the way to get a clearer perspective on the significance of idol imagery in any one particular instance is by seeing it in the context of a much broader discourse on idolatry — a discourse which would necessarily have informed both producers and beholders of the artworks — one that is not restricted to the traditional modes and compartmental divisions of the art historical discipline. For example, apart from the focus on the more obvious images of idolatry, Camille includes the question of idolatry in Biblical and theological texts, the concept of idols in society, relevant topical history, and idol-worship in literary and dramatic texts. There are interesting reflections about the differences between words and images and how they work in his discussion of aspects of a manuscript of the *Roman de la Rose,* and Camille should also be praised for his intriguing find and analysis of the play, *Jeu de Saint Nicolas,* where he has shown that an actual "idol" was constructed for a prop and inhabited by an actor to make it come to life. Camille examines the medieval conception of this "foreign" idol and how it is differentiated from the true and correct image of St. Nicolas, which also features in the play. Furthermore, the range of images brought to bear in Camille's process of analysis is much broader than usual (dauntingly so), purposely addressing different genres: a wide range of religious imagery (cathedral sculpture and stained glass, saints' lives, *Bibles Moralisées*), and secular imagery (statues, chronicles, epics, romances, tales and even a doodle on an Exchequer roll). Camille's pursuit of the discourse of idolatry encompasses not only idolatry in the negative Christian sense but also forms of idolatry that were more acceptable in certain sectors of this society, as in the theme of "Woman on a Pedestal" in Courtly Love. Camille also addresses the ambiguous problematic of how contemporaries as well as modern day interpreters of this period can differentiate the growing popularity in the Gothic West of idol-like Virgin statues from what in other contexts would be considered idolatry in the negative sense.

Thus, Camille has identified a number of themes within the discourse on idolatry which form the various chapters of his book, arranged roughly according to their chronological importance, focusing mainly on thirteenth and fourteenth century France and England. In the process we learn that images are not simple, innocent reflections of texts: images can even subvert texts. Relationships can be intervisual rather than image/textual. Images are often misrepresentations, obfuscations as well as promoters of ideas and ideologies that have little to do with idolatry at all, as in the racist and politically motivated attribution of idolatry to Jews and Muslims, peoples of aniconic cultures. On the other hand, Camille makes us aware of the importance of paying attention to particular contexts and genres of works: the same image in another context can have a radically different meaning, or different contexts might demand a varying treatment of a similar theme. These are all excellent observations from the point of view of methodology. Camille's book will be assured a place in forums where these issues are debated, and this was surely one of his aims.

There is, in fact, such a high level of methodological self-awareness in Camille's book that at times one suspects certain examples have been chosen precisely to demonstrate a methodological point. Camille must have thought this rather belabored expository approach was necessary because so much in his method of analysis might appear unconventional to traditional art historians. Camille seems to have directed his book towards a conservative audience, while expecting congratulations from those who are methodologically more sophisticated. After all, he is not the first art historian to take into account theories of Walter Benjamin, Michel Foucault, Ferdinand de Saussure, Clifford Geertz, Umberto Eco, Frederick Jameson, Jean Baudrillard, Guy Debord, Pierre Macherey, and Edward Said to name only some of the influential modern thinkers cited rather gratuitously in the text. Camille could only have been speaking to the most conservative group of medieval art historians when he made this surprisingly naive confession: "...I have been struck by one of the difficulties facing the historian of medieval art. It is the problem of privileging these objects as 'works of art.' ...When we discuss the majestic colors and superbly detailed designs of the *Bible Moralisée,* how conscious are we that its luminous pages reek with poisonous untruths? How can we explicate its ideological aims and its purposeful misrepresentation if we are misrepresenting it to ourselves in the twentieth century as an important work of art, with all the overtones of disinterested contemplation that such 'aesthetic' status carries?" (pp. 189–190) One can hardly question the importance of this thought, but one can object to the posturing that elicited such, hopefully, false naivete.

The Gothic Idol: Ideology and Image-Making in Medieval Art is one of the first books to be published in a new series edited by Norman

Bryson under the rubric, "Cambridge New Art History and Criticism."
Michael Camille's work may thus be seen as a response to the challenge
of Norman Bryson's lament in 1983, as he was then Director of English
Studies at King's College, Cambridge:

> It is a sad fact: art history lags behind the study of other arts... while
> the last three or so decades have witnessed extraordinary and fertile
> change in the study of literature, of history, of anthropology, in the
> discipline of art history there has reigned a stagnant peace; (art his-
> torical work has continued to be produced:) but produced at an
> increasingly remote margin of the humanities, and almost in the
> leisure sector of intellectual life.

Bryson went on to say:

> What is equally certain is that little can change without radical re-
> examination of the methods art history uses — the tacit assumptions
> that guide the normal activity of the art historian.[1]

Michael Camille had this re-examining attitude fully at heart
when he wrote *The Gothic Idol;* we can find him taking on, among others, such paragons of art history as Erwin Panofsky and Ernst Kitzinger
(p. 102). Moreover, Camille tells us that the title of the book, *The Gothic
Idol,* alludes to "one of the most important studies of medieval art,"
Émile Mâle's, *The Gothic Image,* for whose author the cathedral appealed
as a "coherent 'summa' in stone." Focusing on a minor theme, rather
than setting forth to describe a general view of Gothic art or to get at its
"essence," Camille is aiming to chip "away at the neatly organized foundations of Mâle's cathedral (to) reveal ambiguous gaps, inconsistencies,
and contradictory cracks in what (Mâle) saw as a supremely codified
whole." (p. xxvii) This breaking away from the pretensions of a totaliz-
ing vision is a common theme in much contemporary cultural theory,
and the concomitant interest in marginal detail is something that was
already stressed in the work of Walter Benjamin and Aby Warburg,[2] and
in a related manner, in the *Annales* school of history and the writing of
Foucault. Foucault's stress on the methodological importance of focusing on marginal elements because they can be actually more revealing
and symptomatic than the central one is an idea that Camille is trying
to put in evidence in his book. Foucault's statement in 1976 about
methodological aspects of his research parallels the approach of

Camille's work: "It seemed important to accept that the analysis in question should not concern itself with the regulated and legitimate forms of power in their central locations... On the contrary, it should be concerned with power at its extremities, in its ultimate destinations, with those points where it becomes capillary, that is in its more regional and local forms and institutions."[3] With his treatment of the theme, Camille hopes to show, in his words, "how that society's perception of the Other (a concept which he explains in his preface was important for his study), and necessarily of itself, was articulated in the duplicitous and dangerous body of the idol." (p. xxx) It is likely that Camille's conscious positioning against aspects of the traditional discipline of art history will help gain him a certain amount of notoriety and go part way towards altering the unwarranted perception of medieval art history as a complete backwater in the area of methodological concerns. It is therefore heartening to see a book on medieval art placed in the ranks of "New Art History", and Camille and Bryson deserve thanks for this. That is why *The Gothic Idol* should be read closely by art historians of all fields and, as Camille suggests, should be of interest to the "multidisciplinary medievalist" as well as "anyone concerned with the history and theory of representation" (p. xxvii).

Camille has structured his book around two major parts with an introduction and an epilogue. The first part called, "The Gothic Anti-image," deals with what would normally be associated with idolatry proper — images of non-Christian idols and idol-worshippers, including a section on images of pagan idols and also a discussion of the depiction of Jews and Moslems as idolators. These chapters are prefaced by a somewhat loosely formulated one on the "literature" of idolatry and idol making taken from a range of theological writings, and the original prescriptions against idol worship and image-making in the Bible. In the second part of the book, "Gothic Idols," Camille explores the discourse on idolatry and image-making within the contexts of the ecclesiastical institutions, on the one hand, and within lay society, on the other, focusing on images that in a certain light could have been considered idols, but which were nontheless made and appreciated. In the chapter, "Idols in the Church," for example, Camille discusses how idol-image constructs were sometimes appropriated for positive Christian use, as in images of Christ (the good idol) set up upon a column, and other examples of "Latria;" that is, the kinds of sacred figuration (Christ on the Cross, the Host) which were properly worshipped. The most contentious of these was the proliferation of Virgin statues, which in the manner they were displayed and the way they were seen to "come to life" were almost indistinguishable from contemporary concepts of pagan idols.

The last two chapters of Camille's book deal with "idols" in secular society. He alerts us to the aristocratic fascination with automata, that is, mechanical image devices, which were considered by the church to be nothing other than devilish idols. Following this is a section on the adorers of "Nummus: God of Gold," a new notion constructed in response to the changing social and economic developments of the thirteenth and fourteenth century whereby successful dealers in money were portrayed as worshippers of gold. Camille next includes an interesting historical account of Philip the Fair's political use of the accusation of idolatry as a weapon to bring down his enemies, the Templars and Pope Bonaface VIII. "Status and Statutes: Allegorical Idols and the Body Politic" contains some interesting text and depictions from Deguileville's poem, "The Pilgrimage of the Soule," that comment on the making of public images of rulers and on Idolatry, which Camille uses to make some otherwise rather obvious observations about the political function of ruler imagery.

One could question here the supposition that ruler imagery ought to be considered idolotrous. There is a problem in this section that is sometimes evident, as we shall see, in other parts of Camille's book. With respect to the issue of idolatry, Camille does not distinguish carefully between the making of an image (something that can be sanctioned) and the worshipping of the image (which usually could not). Further remarks will be made on this issue below. The final chapter, "Idols in the Mind," treats the themes of the "idolization" of women in Courtly love, and the Pygmalion myth in Medieval art. Going against traditional art historical interpretations which want to interpret all art with the moralizing tone of religious art, Camille stresses the different inflection of the theme of idolatry in these works of profane art, which can be playful, often subverting the religious formulas, and increasingly ironic, rather than moralistic.

Michael Camille has an interesting hypothesis in *The Gothic Idol,* one that should have been given more extensive treatment, particularly in its historical grounding. This is the suggestion that the peculiar anxiety about idolatry in this period, indicated by the proliferation of visual references to it and the increase in the discourse about idols in general, was a result of the uneasiness created by the "image explosion" of the later Middle Ages.[4] In other words, it was the medieval society of the thirteenth and fourteenth centuries that was itself becoming idolatrous; it was being already criticized for this from within and, of course,

290 STUDIES IN MEDIEVAL AND RENAISSANCE HISTORY

this was a major charge in the Reformation which responded with a new iconoclasm. Thus in this period we see both a love and fascination for "idols" of all sorts, as well as a defensive attitude which attempted to foist the accusation of idolatry onto enemies, onto the bad "Other," — heretics, Muslims, Jews, political enemies, homosexuals, usurers, etc. — in a process which was invariably exaggerated, unjust, and thoroughly hypocritical.

The major points of the "Introduction" and the "Epilogue" of Camille's book are actually two sides of a basic theme that runs throughout the text. This is a stress on the powerful sense of reality that images of idols conveyed to the medieval audience. This was an impression of the real that has "little to do with our modern notions of what constitutes an illusionistic or a naturalistic image"(p. 23). The image could be dangerous in an instrumental way. The most dramatic proof of this, cited by Camille in his chapter on "Nummus," is the story about a usurer from Dijon who was killed on his wedding day before he could enter the church by a falling piece of portal sculpture, the very one that depicted a usurer being carried off to hell by a demon. This so frightened the bourgeois of the town that "by dint of bribes" they managed to get all the portal sculpture destroyed(p. 264). This was an example of a very literal fear of the power of images, but this fear is also expressed in more subtle ways. It is part of the reason why idols were so often shown in a position of defeat or in other ways depicted as ugly, base, or devilish. This may also be why, as Camille has discovered, representations of idols have sometimes even been defaced after the making, or erased altogether, or never even completed in the first place. Since a representation of an idol is an image of an image, this sort of fear of the idol image should alert us to the powerful impact all imagery must have had on the medieval audience. For this audience, Camille explains, images are almost magically potent "sites of power, vehicles of appropriation and instrumentality"(339). This attitude, in his view, is fundamentally different from our modern notions that have developed since the Renaissance.

In the Epilogue, presumably in an effort to make the issue of idolatry relevant to us today, Camille has tried to chart general changes in attitudes toward "the idol" since the Middle Ages. Following some notions of Walter Benjamin, he suggests that in the Renaissance there was a loss of the medieval sense of the real, of the demonic, in idol imagery; hence the idols of the ancients could be studied without any qualms for they were not worshipped as idols but as objects of beauty. Concern was now with the producer, the named artist, not the audience or function. Camille is treading on dangerous ground here. There may be a change in the sense of the demonic (in some areas), but it is hard to imagine any contemporary Renaissance art historian who would agree that audience and function are no longer a concern, even if it is true there is more of an interest in the producers and in aesthetic contemplation. On the other hand, Camille suggests that during the Reformation and during periods of Protestant iconoclasm, one can witness again the medieval sense of the power of images which in this case needs to be crushed in favor of the word. Finally, in "Idols of Postmodernity," Camille brings his historical reflections on idol imagery up to date with observations about our own postmodern era that has discarded the modernist disengagement and fetishization of the object (as "idol"), and where (this could only pertain to "critical" thinkers), "idolatry is once again a vital theoretical issue in today's Western culture supersaturated with representations"(p. 150).

It is unfortunate that after the complexities of the main text in the book, Camille has been willing to fall back on gross generalities that even seem to imply a cyclical notion of history. What is worse, we are left with an uneasy feeling about the whole concept of "the idol," if it can be applied so indiscriminately. These are methodological problems that will be further addressed towards the end of this review.

Clearly, there is an incredible range of imagery and issues brought under purview in Camille's book. Perhaps even too much, because within each section, the discussion seems to mushroom at an incredible pace into related issues: A mention that a frequent idol type had demonic features, revealing the medieval interpretation of pagan gods as demons, develops into a lengthy discussion of Devil imagery in general (p. 62ff). Later, pursuing the fact that the idol was most frequently depicted as a nude statue, Camille moves from nude idols, to the nudity of Adam and Eve in the Fall, then to the issue of sexuality, to a discussion of homosexuality as a despised sin (in images though, homosexuals are fully clothed). This might strike the reader as pure "stream of consciousness writing." Nor is one completely reassured by the evidence Camille proffers to establish the connection between idolatry and homosexuality. Quoting from the Epistle of Paul to the Romans (1:23–7) and a statement by a fourteenth-century commentator on Canon Law, which associate the unclean and unnatural sins of idolatry and homosexuality, Camille reaches the general conclusion: "What one did with actual as well as represented bodies could be described as idolatry." (p. 92).

This is a sweeping statement. One cannot quarrel with the

observation that homosexuality could be associated with idolatry; but the question remains, just how useful is this observation. How far does it take us along the road to a better social and historical understanding of the strategies of the representation of idolatry? Camille has done a good job in sensitizing us to possible ways in which undesirable sectors in society could be set up as scapegoats by this means of stigmatizing them with idolatry. But to get any sense of the effectiveness or even the meaning of such attacks, we need to know a lot more. How frequently was this tactic used? In what circumstances; why at this time, in this place, and so on. The historical questions still loom large. The fear is that we might even begin "to chip away" at the perspicacity of the model, "subject = idolatry/scapegoatism," if we begin to search out the historical circumstances that Camille has only touched upon in the most superficial manner. It is worth remembering that idolatry and homosexuality (together with loose sex of any kind) were the two mores of ancient pagan society that Christians most abhorred from the beginning, for reasons that have their own complex history. It was through their refusal to practice idolatry and their insistence on sexual restraint, even more than their positive love of and belief in Christ, that ancient pagans came to be aware that Christians were different. In other words, the association of idolatry and homosexuality has a very clear historical origin and basis in Early Christian society.[5] One could not say, then, that homosexuality was defamed by its association with idolatry; both were equally abhorrent. It is of course likely that the association of these two behaviors had a different inflection in the thirteenth-century, even if the pattern of their association might have been taken over from the earlier period. In the least, it will take a lot more complex historical questioning and research to sort out these issues.

These comments lead to two general questions about Camille's method of interpretation. One is both a theoretical question, and a practical one for anyone who would like to emulate Camille's approach while dealing with a different topic: How should one go about establishing a discourse? The other concerns the difficulty of striking a balance between the formulation of a broad discourse and the necessity for historical specificity.

One of the most admirable features of Camille's book is the breadth and interdisciplinary nature of the material he has been willing to include in order to pursue the study of the Gothic idol. One must wonder, however, on the practical level, how he went about finding all of this, and on the theoretical level, what criteria he used to determine, define, or recognize whether "that something" was indeed part of the discourse on idolatry. Camille seems to have used a number of criteria. The most basic appears to derive from the images of idols contained in depictions of Biblical texts dealing with idols. These were generally images, frequently nude, set up on top of free-standing columns. Camille never poses the question of why this particular form of idol image was so predominant, nor does he speak of the origin of this sort of image as a means of understanding it better, nor comment on the fact that this was not the only way ancient pagans displayed their idols. On the other hand, Camille feels free then to extend the appellation of idol — or the aura of idol — to any image that sits on top of a column or pedestal, such as Gothic saints' columns and Donatello's "David." Is this justifiable? Almost any image of a pagan god is, for Camille, a potential idol. Equestrian statues of kings, because they refer back to Roman prototypes, are brought into the discourse of idolatry. Presumably this was because in certain circumstances in the Roman era images of Roman emperors were venerated, although this was probably not true of the equestrian statue, which is more commemorative in nature. Camille provides us with none of this history, nor do we learn whether this was ever the case with the Gothic images. There are really no grounds, at least as presented in this text, for associating images of rulers with idolatry.

This haphazard approach to the issue of idolatry is most blatant in the chapter which addresses the literary sources on idolatry, "Fallen Fabrication." It speaks much more about comments on the making of images, taken from a whole variety of sources, than it does about idolatry. Camille should have taken greater care in this section, because it is here that the whole problematic of idolatry and image making has its grounds. There is an inherent ambiguity in the biblical First and Second Commandment (Exodos 20:1–5), not adequately analyzed by Camille, that tends to confuse these issues. Does God mean, "Thou shalt have no strange gods before me, *therefore* thou shall not make graven images and adore them," or does he say, "Thou shalt have no strange gods before me, *and neither* shall thou make graven images [of any sort]"? It is precisely this ambiguity that has allowed for radically different interpretations in the Judaic, Christian, and Islamic traditions, and within Christianity surprisingly divergent opinions depending on the historical moment or circumstances. One result of this continuing debate is that for Protestants, the command to worship no other god is the First Commandment and the stricture against graven images is the

Second, while the Roman Catholic Church, in a less iconoclastic manner, combines the two notions into the First Commandment. Camille's random citations of various prouncements about idolatry and image-making are objectionable because virtually no attempt has been made to clarify the positions upheld or the contexts in which they were made or later maintained or transformed.

Most surprising, however, in spite of Camille's claims, is the real difficulty we have in getting any clear sense of what the notion of idolatry could have meant to the medieval society Camille purports to study. It is true, his point is that notions were forever shifting. But one might suspect that much of the confusion derives from Camille's lack of conceptual rigor in distinguishing his modern and very fluid notions of what seems like an idol or idolatry from that which was in effect in the period under consideration. The establishment of a discourse should be more carefully constituted. There is also the sense that Camille has little patience for the work of historical investigation. The point is not that art historical interpretation must be restricted to concepts that were current at the time, but it is certainly important to know what they were, and to be able to distinguish them from one's own.

The other problem that admittedly faces anyone attempting to outline a broad structural discourse is the limitations that necessarily have to be placed on the depth of discussion of specific cases. Camille's book is already over four hundred pages long; it would be hard to recommend adding more. Nevertheless, in the interpretations in *The Gothic Idol* we seem to be missing important parts of the equation, on the one hand, with respect to individual works and on the other, to the historical context.

There is a real breathlessness in Camille's text because we move so quickly from example to example, situation to situation, each with its own set of problems and peculiarities. We never have time to "get to know" anything in depth; we never really understand what was at stake in any particular case. Camille's is the diachronic account, the broad overview. Because it is self-consciously not a traditional overview which attempts to "organize" history along a trajectory of a few easily remembered principles or "trends," but instead more like a series of shooting stars going out in all directions, it is hard to come away with the satisfied feeling, "I really understand the Middle Ages better now." In the end, even more surprisingly, one cannot feel confident he or she fully understands the issue of idolatry and image-making in this period, although Camille's book certainly has the virtue of making us see it as an issue. Indeed, anyone who has read this book will probably forever be on the look-out for idols and idolatry, and strategies to contain or appropriate them. There remains, however, the nagging question, "was it really so important?".

This is because we do not learn enough in Camille's text about how the particular strategies for dealing with the "idol issue" operate. How do they act upon or within the context of a single work and what do they signify in a particular historical case and moment? Almost all of Camille's examples of idol imagery are details from a larger collection of images, about which we hear very little. It is true that Camille in his preface acknowledges the fact that he does not do justice to the contexts of his examples, but still, we are left wanting. Situations of patronage, purpose, and audience are most often dealt with, if at all, in the broadest possible terms: ecclesiastical (secular; moralistic) playful entertainment, etc. We hardly ever learn how the idol image fit into, or informed, the rest of the imagery in which it is inscribed. Camille might argue that what he saw in the treatment of these idol images, were symptoms on a level that were never meant to be consciously part of a programmatic whole; that he was trying to analyze a broad discourse on idolatry that carries certain significations apart from the semantic value of the particular inscription. But for all of Camille's talk of ideology and the "terrible tyranny" of these beautiful images (351), the impact of these notions would be much better served if there were greater specificity in the account.

Historians and art historians who take history seriously will be disappointed to learn there is a similar lack of specification about the historical conditions of the works as well. To his credit, Camille has "left room" for history in his methodology, and he does refer generally to some historical factors pertinent to images in question: the Crusades, effects of the Fourth Lateran Council, the rise in lay piety, economic transformations of the thirteenth and fourteenth centuries, etc. But he has shown a decided lack of curiosity and effort to pursue any of the historical questions further. Camille's strength lies in his reformulation of the questions and his ability to come up with novel interpretations even when using commonly known sources. He has done a very impressive job of accumulating the materials and "laying out" the imagery of idols, but there is really no new research in connection with them. Indeed, with respect to historical information, there is little here beyond what could be found in an introductory "Western Civilization" text. For this reason, the sense of urgency and relevance that might otherwise have attached to Camille's analyses is too frequently lost, and at times, as was suggested above, one might begin to wonder about the adequacy of even the general interpretation.

On the other hand, there is a real value in breaking away from a myopic approach to provide an intensive look at a single issue on a broad scale. There is no denying the general interest of the fascinating material that has come to light through Camille's novel look at Gothic art through the body of the idol. In an ideal world, what we ought to be able to see is a series of synchronic studies of individual cases, intersecting the broader range of Camille's account. We could then alternate between zooming in and stepping back in a process that would impact on each argument. To some extent, what is necessarily expressed here is the sense of frustration and the dilemma faced by all art historians who have any pretensions of being up–to–date and serious. The more we become aware of the necessity to interpret the visual image within the nexus of a myriad of associative factors, and the more we want to evaluate the feasibility of new theoretical models, and the more sophisticated become our abilities in historical analysis, and the more we break down the false boundary of disciplinary divisions; the less and less confident we become of ever "doing justice" to the study that we know is needed.

NOTES

1. Normon Bryson, *Vision and Painting: The Logic of the Gaze* (New Haven, 1983) p.xi. It would appear that Bryson, having observed and been part of 'the advent of theory" into the field of art history, and hopefully taken better cognizance of the revisionism that had in fact been well under way in 1983, has of late become much more confident about the state of art history: "Art history, so far from being in parlous shape, is in fact one of the most buoyant and energetic fields within the humanities today.: *Art Bulletin* 71–4 (Dec. 1989) 707. Significantly, Norman Bryson is now a professor in the Department of Fine Arts at Harvard University.

2. Camille has made this point himself in "Walter Benjamin and Durer's Melencolia I: The Dialectics of Allegory and the Limits of Iconology," *Ideas and Production, A Journal of the History of Ideas* (5:1985) 58-73. 5 (1985), 58–73.

3. Colin Gorden, ed. *Power/Knowledge: selected interviews and other writings 1972–1977* (New York, 1980) 96.

4. W.T.J. Mitchell in *Iconology: Image, Text, Ideology* (Chicago, 1986), pp. 90–91 presents a similar structural argument, in reference to our modern era, when he suggests that "the Western idolatry of the natural sign disguises its own nature under cover of a ritual iconoclasm, a claim that 'our' images, unlike 'theirs,' are constituted by a critical principle...." Camille has acknowledged the importance of Mitchell's work to the formulation of his own ideas.

5. Elaine Pagels convincingly argues that these were seen as the two distinguishing features of Christians, even though Stoic philosophers also advocated sexual restraint but without refusing to honor the gods. *Adam, Eve, and the Serpent* (New York, 1988).

BOOK REVIEWS

Book Reviews

Hans-Joachim Reischmann ed. And trans., *Willibrord — Apostel der Friesen: Seine Vita nach Alkuin und Thiofrid, Lateinisch-Deutsch.* Sigmaringendorf: Verlag Glock and Lutz, 1989. Pp. 128, DM 38.

This handsomely produced monograph was published to commemorate the 1250th anniversary of Willibrord's death. Reischmann provides an introduction for both *Vitae,* translates the text of Alcuin's *Life of Willibrord* completely and selections (chapters 1, 6, 9, 11, and 22) of Thiofrid's, and adds a commentary wherever necessary. The introduction to Alcuin's *Life of Willibrord* (pp. 11–42) deals briefly with the lack of recognition given to Willibrord, especially when he is compared to his contemporary Boniface, with biographical data for Alcuin, and generic observations on hagiography, as well as with a structural analysis of the *Vita.* The considerably shorter introduction to Thiofrid's *Life of Willibrord* (pp. 92–103, of which four pages are illustrations) concerns itself with the different historical context in which this later *Life* was composed, and biographical data for Thiofrid, as well as with a stylistic analysis of his work.

Reischmann is entirely convincing when he argues that more attention should be paid to Willibrord. His polemic beginning, however, that Willibrord deserves the title "apostle of the Frisians" without contradiction, while Boniface's claim to the title "apostle of the Germans" needs to be modified (p. 11), undercuts his argument because it seems to suggest that Willibrord was as great, if not greater than, Boniface. Willibrord founded the bishopric of Utrecht as well as the monastery Echternach and he certainly worked hard at converting the Frisians; Boniface, on the other hand, founded the bishoprics Salzburg, Regensburg, Passau, Freising, Würzburg, Erfurt, Büraburg, and Eichstätt, as well as several monasteries. Thus, his sphere of activity was much larger than Willibrord's. Moreover, Boniface's death at the

hands of Frisians throws doubt on the effectiveness of Willibrord's conversion of them. Reischmann also complains that Boniface's role in the
conversion of Germany is given ample space in the history books of
high schools while Willibrord is hardly mentioned at all (p.11).
Geography may have something to do with that: Boniface worked in the
area that is now Germany, while Willibrord achieved his major successes outside modern Germany's borders, in the Netherlands and
Luxembourg. I do not mean to suggest that Willibrord does not
deserve more attention than he gets, but merely that he will always,
deservedly, be on the losing end in a comparison with Boniface.

Reischmann's biographical data of Alcuin, his generic observations on hagiography, and his structural analysis of Alcuin's *Vita* are
sound, though he appears to be innocent of much English literature
written on the subject. To give an example: speaking about the fact that
Alcuin wrote the *Life of Willibrord* twice, once in prose and once in verse,
i.e., that he composed an "opus geminatum," he cites Curtius's
Europäische Literatur und lateinisches Mittelalter (1967) as well as Klopsch's
"Prosa und Vers in der mittellateinischen Literatur" (1966), but not the
much more recent works by P. Godman, "The Anglo-Latin *opus geminatum* from Aldhelm to Alcuin," *Medium Aevum* 50 (1981), pp. 215–29 or
the present author's "*Geminus Stilus:* Studies in Anglo-Latin
Hagiography," *Insular Latin Studies,* ed. Michael Herren, *Papers in
Mediaeval Studies* 1 (Toronto 1981), pp. 113–33. A more thorough
knowledge of the recent (and non-German) literature on Alcuin would
certainly improve the book.

Reischmann's strength lies in his translations. The various sections of both Alcuin's and Thiofrid's *Lives* which I examined are not
only correctly, but also elegantly translated. This is especially praiseworthy for Thiofrid's *Life* where Reischmann manages to retain the Latin's
bombastic style in his German translation, and at the same time never
sacrifices clarity. The difficulties in Thiofrid's text (and in Alcuin's, but
then Alcuin's is not as difficult), whether they be caused by his
Grecisms, his periodic sentences, or simply the amount of verbiage in
any given sentence, never overwhelm Reischmann. The result is a clear,
readable, and easily intelligible German text.

Critics must cavil, and, where this critic greatly admires
Reischmann's translations, he is less happy with the Latin texts, especially that of Alcuin's Life, that are being translated. Alcuin's *Vita
Willibrordi* exists in two editions (one in the *Patrologia Latina,* the other
in the *Monumenta Germaniae Historica, Scriptores Rerum Merovingicarum*),

both mentioned in the bibliography (p. 127), but Reischmann does not indicate which forms the basis of his translation. A comparison of his text with that of the two editions suggests that he chose the MGH edition, but then he sometimes quietly, and for no apparent reason, changes some readings, while he leaves other, possibly incorrect ones, as they are and comments at length on them. To give an example of the latter: on p. 44 Alcuin apparently uses the form *servienti* in an ablative absolute construction (I say "apparently" because one would have to decide the extent to which scribes are responsible for this incorrect form) and Reischmann takes this opportunity to castigate Alcuin because "die Ablativbildung auf "i" zu [seinen] Marotten zählt." Would it not have been fairer simply to change *servienti* to *serviente?* Reischmann's "Marotten" (=quirks) in the Preface and the first chapter of Alcuin's Life include *mae* instead of *meae* (p. 44, 1. 8), *Piero* instead of *Piereo* (p. 44, 1. 13), *elegiacum* instead of *heleiacum* (p. 46, 1. 1), *cursu* instead of *versu* (p. 46, 1. 5), *curente* instead of *currente* (p. 46, 1. 5), *omni sua* instead of *omni domu sua* (p. 46, 1. 12), *Andrae* instead of *Andreae* (p. 465, 1. 17), and the constant, unexplained, change of the name *Wilgils* to *Wilgis* (e.g. p. 46, 1. 1–2, or 1. 11). Some of these are surely just typographical errors, possibly caused by a secretary — but then, cannot Alcuin use the same defence? The change of the name *Wilgils* to *Wilgis*, however, needs some explanation, especially in view of the fact that the manuscript which is reproduced on the cover of the book has the reading *uuilgils*, though a later hand using darker ink tampered with that spelling. Reischmann should have indicated which text he used as the basis of his translation and should have commented on all changes made to that text. (In all fairness it should be mentioned that the Latin of the later chapters is not as sloppily reproduced as that of the Preface and the first chapter).

In a similar vein (more cavilling, I am afraid): Reischmann provides us with only selected passages from Thiofrid's *Life,* but never gives us a reason for his selections. Did he wish to avoid translating too much of Thiofrid's difficult Latin? Do the omitted chapters follow Alcuin's Latin too closely? Are there not enough stylistic differences in the omitted chapters to warrant inclusion? Reischmann's Latin text and translation do not give a complete impression of Thiofrid's achievement since the reader does not know how many additional classical authors are hidden in the omitted portions. I understand that Reischmann did not want to include all of Thiofrid's *Life,* but I do not understand on what principle the chosen passages were included.

Reischmann wished to set Willibrord a worthy monument, wished to bring him out of the shadows of obscurity: he certainly achieves his aim in his excellent translation which will make Willibrord's *Life* available to the ever-growing number of those who cannot read Latin. Unfortunately, the monument is not flawless: the scholarship on which it is based is too narrow, the editorial principles used in arriving at the Latin texts are not enunciated, and the Latin text itself is at times sloppily reproduced. But then, maybe Willibrord would have preferred a flawed monument to none at all.

Gernot Wieland
University of British Columbia

Martha A. Malamud, *A Poetics of Transformation: Prudentius and Classical Mythology.* (Ithaca and London: Cornell University Press, 1989.). Pp. xiii, 192. $ 24.95

Ms. Malamud's book takes up a matter of great interest to both historians and literary critics in that she tries to determine Prudentius' place at the intersection of classical Antiquity and early Christianity. Her first chapter, "Backgrounds," contains an historical examination of the time of the Emperor Theodosius under whom Prudentius presumably served (though Malamud's statement on p. 22 "he [i.e., Prudentius] ascribes his successful career to Theodosius in his preface" is incorrect; Theodosius' name is *not* mentioned in the preface; Cynegius, who is mentioned on p. 21, was not "praetorian prefect of the East from 284–288," but from 384–388). In chapter 2, "Word Games," she traces Prudentius' debt to authors such as Lucretius, Virgil, Ausonius, and Optatian for a tendency towards puns, anagrams, and etymologies. Chapter 3, "Words at War," predictably examines the *Psychomachia*, specifically the fight between Concordia and Discordia, and attempts to show that in defeating Discordia, Concordia takes on attributes of the Vice. Chapter 4, "A Mythical Martyr," seeks parallels between the Hippolytus of classical myth and the Hippolytus of *Peristephanon* 11. Chapter 5, "Dubious Distinctions," examines St. Cyprian of *Peristephanon* 13 and concludes that the man who was a seducer before he converted to Christianity also was a seducer after his conversion. Chapter 6, entitled "Saint Agnes and the Chaste Tree," finds that the Christian virgin "oscillates wildly between sexual extremes" (p. 179).

This short synopsis of course does not do justice to Malamud's more sophisticated arguments but only hints at the direction in which the book is going. Malamud herself states that she undertakes a "close reading of several of his [i.e., Prudentius'] texts" (p.2), and the "close reading" cannot be duplicated here, nor can all the arguments by which *Discordia* is made a parallel to Rufinus, the Christian Hippolytus to his mythological counterpart as well as to Rufinus, Cyprian to Venus, Adonis and Ganymede, and Agnes to Arachne, Medusa, Atalanta, and the Amazons. Suffice it to say that many of these parallels are interesting and certainly deserve to be examined.

Malamud's primary critical tool is an examination of etymologies, word plays, anagrams, allusions, and similarity in plot. She relies heavily on that strand of modern critical theory that likes to find the opposite meaning of the writer's stated intentions (cf. her comment on p. 79: "The more closely his martyrs are examined, the less Christian they seem") and hence discovers that Concordia is as vicious as Discordia, that Agnes, though a virgin, shares characteristics usually attributed to prostitutes, that the martyr Hippolytus is not only torn apart for his faith but as schismatic also tears apart the faith, and that Cyprian remains a dangerous seducer even after he had converted to Christianity. Personally I have always wondered why a poet would wish to undercut his purported intentions: Malamud gives a partial answer here in that she argues that Prudentius could not tear himself away from his classical upbringing; for her "there is a radical disjunction... between Prudentius' belief in Christ and his intellectual understanding of the world" (p. 10), and this disjunction makes itself manifest in the texts she examines.

Malamud's arguments might be more persuasive if she would really do what she says she wants to do: to provide a close reading of the text. On more than one occasion she takes liberties; to give a few examples: on pp. 76–77 she translates the Latin lines

> septimus insuper
> annum cardo rotat, dum fruimur sole volubili.
> instat terminus, et diem
> vicinum senio iam Deus adplicat *(Praefatio,* 1–5)

as "the turning world spins a seventh year, while I enjoy the swift sun. The end presses upon me, and the day God weaves now is close to old age." She then proceeds to speak about the "spinning and weaving" imagery in these lines. Unfortunately, the spinning and weaving imagery is Malamud's, not Prudentius'. *Rotare* means "to turn" (and here it is the hinge, *cardo,* that turns; a hinge "spinning" [cloth] would be a rare sight indeed), and the root of *adplicare* means "to fold," not "to weave," essentially depriving Malamud of an argument. On p. 176 she comments on the lines "nostrum si iecur inpleas" *(Peristephanon* 14. 131) with these words: "Prudentius... ends this poem... by asking rather illogically for the renewal of his *iecur,* " and goes on to claim that therefore Prudentius casts himself as a Promethean figure because Prometheus' *iecur* also was in need of "renewal." *Inplere* does not mean the same thing as *replere;* it does not mean "to renew," but "to fill up," presumably with bile. These few examples could be multiplied. Malamud's "close reading" often seems to be a "distant approximation," and an approximation at that which bears the weight of the argument.

Malamud experiments with a different form of "approximation" on p. 45 where she attempts to explain the crux in *Hamartigenia* 966 ("me poena levis clementer adurat") by claiming that the line (leaving out the *me)* is an anagram for "Aurelio Prudente se clamante", and what seemed to be a prayer to be spared in Purgatory actually turns out to be a boast by the poet ("Aurelius the Prudent proclaiming himself"). This is intriguing, so intriguing in fact that I tried to see what other anagrams could be hidden in this line. How about "Prudens levi mente coela arat" ("Prudens ploughs the heavens with a light mind") or "ater clemens durat levi poena" ("black Clemens endures by [suffering] light punishment"), or, including the *me* and seeking an anagram that does not contain Prudentius' name, "deus poenam lenem terra celavit" ("God hid a gentle punishment on the earth")? How does Malamud know that her anagram is the correct one? She does not, since she did not consider the other possibilities, and yet she makes her anagram carry the burden of an argument, it is ill prepared to carry.

Malamud also fails in a "close reading" of her own text; on more than one occasion she presents an interesting parallel between an event of classical mythology or history and an event in Prudentius' poems and argues that Prudentius *might* have been influenced by the parallel. What at first is seen as a possibility, suddenly becomes a certainty; consider the following two sentences: "It is unlikely that any of Prudentius' contemporaries would have missed an allusion to a recent event as important and as well publicized as Rufinus' spectacular assassination. There is at the very least a heavy irony in Prudentius' decision to use Rufinus' death as the model for the death of Discordia" (p. 66). The first sentence operates in the realm of possibility ("it is unlikely"), while the second one turns that possibility into a certainty ("Prudentius' decision to use Rufinus' death"). Is it not possible that Prudentius never thought of Rufinus when he wrote of Discordia's death, but that he was guided instead by the desire to have the vices killed in exactly the same way as they spread their poison among the faithful (Christian Gnilka calls this the "Talionsprinzip")? If Malamud wished to prove that Prudentius consciously used Rufinus' death as the model for Discordia's, then she would have to bring stronger arguments than a mere possibility. Are there, for instance, verbal echoes of Claudian's *In Rufinum* in the *Psychomachia,* or does Prudentius elsewhere speak about Rufinus? These questions, however, which might have brought certainty are not answered.

In her "close reading" Malamud pays special attention to the "golden line," in which nouns and adjectives are symmetrically arranged around a central verb, as in *Psychomachia,* 688: *ostentans festis respondet laeta choraeis,* which according to Malamud "achieves apparent harmony" (p. 61). She similarly comments on *Psychomachia,* 718: *pollutam rigida transfigens cuspide linguam,* where the "effort to achieve clarity... is in vain" (p. 65). Since neither of these "golden lines" seem to achieve their goal, one wonders whether they should be mentioned at all. Her concern with "golden lines," however, approaches the absurd when she argues on pp. 75–76 that Prudentius' failure to provide another "golden line" after *Hamartigenia,* 235 shows "a disintegration of Prudentius' own verse" or "the collapse of the poet's verse." If absence of a "golden line" argues for a "collapse of the poet's verse," how often does Prudentius' poetry actually get off the ground? Malamud herself seems to have recognized the untenable nature of her statement; at least she does not comment on the "golden line" *dissociata putrem laxent tabulata carinam (Peristephanon* 11, 73), which she translates as "the rotten hull's timbers will disintegrate" (p. 96), and which seems to show that "golden lines" can deal as well with disintegration as with harmony.

"Close reading" can often lead to the problem that the author ignores or seems to ignore passages in the larger context of the poem or the culture of the time. Malamud, who brings a large array of texts from classical mythology to bear on Prudentius' poems at first does not seem to fall into this class of critics. Nonetheless, there are some curious omissions in her work. On p. 59 she mentions that Discordia "is a master of disguise," ignoring that Avaritia, too, *inque habitum sese trans-*

format honestum (Psychomachia, 552) and that she wreaks much greater damage than Discordia ever does. On p. 69 Malamud says that "the final battle of the *Psychomachia* ends in a Pyrrhic victory for the Virtues," and that "the stage is set for the battle in the soul to continue at a new level of intensity," ignoring, or neglecting to mention, that Prudentius himself in the concluding passage of the *Psychomachia,* 888–915 refers to the cyclical nature of the fight against the Vices. There, however, he also indicates how Christians can escape from any further harm from the Vices. An example of ignoring the cultural context appears on p. 125, where Cyprian's loss of *caesaries* is seen as a loss of his "young masculinity:" it may be no more than a reference to tonsure. On p. 136 Malamud claims that "Prudentius shows the passion that inspires his erotic saint [=Cyprian] and his followers to be a kind of madness, leading not to oneness with God, but to self-destruction and sterility." This, to me, seems to ignore Christianity's paradoxical attitude which celebrates the death of a martyr as his birthday. What the world sees as death, "self-destruction and sterility," the Christians see as life, resurrection and increase in the number of saints. If the individuals of the *Candida Massa* (why is that translated as "Glowing Mass" instead of "White Mass" on p. 141? — lime is white and not glowing) wanted rather to commit mass suicide in the lime pit than to sacrifice to the pagan gods, then their action is seen as heroic by their fellow-Christians, though it may seem madness to non-Christians. And if Cyprian inspired them to persevere in the faith by his seductive words, then he has seduced them into heaven and not into "self-destruction."

If I seem to have ignored some of the larger issues of Malamud's book in this review, then I have done so quite intentionally. Her book rises or falls with her stated intention that she wishes to provide a "close reading." When the "close reading" is not close, as it often is not in this book, then the argument rests on spindly foundations and ultimately collapses. The book presents fascinating material, but it does so by often riding roughshod over the fine points of the text it examines. Ironically, Malamud's book turns its underlying theory into practice: to paraphrase her sentence on the martyrs ("the more closely his martyrs are examined, the less Christian they seem," p. 79): the more closely her book is examined, the less it turns out to be a close reading.

Gernot Wieland
University of British Columbia

Susan Ashbrook Harvey, *Asceticism and Society in Crisis. John of Ephesus and The Lives of the Eastern Saints*. Berkeley and London, The University of California Press. Pp. xvi. 226. $35.00.

In A.D. 502. according to the chronicle of "Joshua the Stylite". Kawad, king of Sassanid Persia, attacked Amida *(mod.* Diyarbekr) and besieged it with no success until 10 January of the next year when some guards, having drunk wine too liberally, fell asleep, while others deserted their posts because of rain, and the Persians climbed over the walls with scaling ladders. A version of the story, which Joshua did not repeat, had it that the negligent guards were monks from the abbey of Mar John Urtaya nearby, for the ascetic community at Amida chose its sites for monasteries close by the city defenses and sought shelter within them when the Persians attacked. Susan Ashbrook Harvey, who refers to the incident in the book under review, considers the charge of drunkenness slanderous, and probably it is, though it is not in the least improbable that the monks helped man the walls during the siege. The event happened some four years before John of Ephesus was born, and some twenty years or so before he entered the monastery of Mar John Urtaya.

The Persian sack, followed by the equally costly counter-offensive of the Roman army which recovered Amida in 504/5, was only one of a series of disasters that overtook Amida. The century had begun with plague. The years that followed brought worse: incursions by Persians and White Huns, wild beasts with a taste for human flesh which terrified the peasants, locusts, finally the pandemic of bubonic plague on 542, and in its trail, famine; and along with all these, the persecution of the Monophysites that began with the death of Anastasius and the accession of the emperor Justin I in 518. In 560, the trauma proved too much: the whole city gave way to outright hysteria upon hearing a false rumour that the Persians were attacking. People foamed at the mouth, barked like dogs and bleated like sheep. The mass madness lasted for perhaps as long as a year and is evidence, as Harvey puts it (p. 65), that society, like the individual, has a breaking point.

This was the world of the eastern ascetic into which John was born. One of Harvey's chapter headings is "Amida: The Measure of Madness." John's description of the Amidan monasteries at night, after the daytime ministries of the monks were completed, is revealing, all the more so because John so clearly admires it. Some of the monks spent the night singing psalms or genuflecting, others stood on standing-posts, or tied themselves to the wall or ceiling of the room with ropes or vine branches, while still others sat out the night on seats without falling over. These were men who would not break easily under stress. For them, the worst of their travails was the imposition of the creed of Chalcedon. The deposition of Severus, the Monophysite patriarch of Antioch, followed the accession of Justin. Severus' immediate successor was Paul "the Jew" who began a string of persecutions during which the chief villain of John's story. Abraham bar Kaili, secured the metropolitan seat of Amida. Paul's less rigorous successor died in the earthquake of 526 at Antioch, which struck the Monophysites as only just, but his successor, Ephrem, with Abraham's help, stoked the conflagration even more. The ascetic community at Amida, no less than one thousand men in all, was forced to abandon their monasteries three times; twice the monks returned and rebuilt them, but at the end of Justinian's reign, they were back in exile, though still unbowed.

For these events, John is an important witness. Bilingual in Greek and Syriac, a loyal subject of the emperors in Constantinople in spite of everything, and a friend of the empress Theodora whom he nonetheless noted came from the brothel, thereby providing our only independent affirmation for the story in Procopius' *Secret History,* John lived on into the reign of the emperor Maurice to see the Monophysites persecuted again and split by Christological dispute. As an infant, his parents brought him to their local stylite saint, one Maro who had just inherited his brother's pillar at the monastery of Ar'a Rabtha, and prayed for a cure for the congenital illness that otherwise would certainly have claimed John's life. The saint prescribed lentils, and asked to have the boy brought back to him after two years, to be brought up as his son. Thus John entered the monastic life. After Maro died, John left Maro's abbey of Ar'a Rabtha and joined the monastery of Mar John Urtaya at Amida. It was with it that he felt the closest bond during his life, and it is a chapter on it that concludes his *Lives of the Eastern Saints,* which was written shortly after Justinian's death while John himself was living in a monastery in Constantinople.

Justinian was not unfriendly. He may always have had some covert sympathy for Monophysite theology, which was his wife's creed, for at the end of his life he adopted a Monophysite position which differed little from that of Julian of Halicarnassus. At any rate, Justinian commissioned John to convert the remaining pagans in Asia Minor, and John carried out the mission with great success. In the *Lives,* John expresses the hope that Justinian's nephew and successor Justin II might accomplish the peace of the church.

It was not to be. John wrote his *Ecclesiastical History* in prison. With the accession of Maurice in 582, the attempt to accomodate the Monophysites ceased. John, who remained loyal to the "God-loving emperor" nonetheless, went to jail, and from there his *Ecclesiastical History* was smuggled out. The third part survives and substantial fragments of the first two parts lie behind later authors.

Harvey's interest lies in the *Lives* as a sociological document and a witness to its times. Most of John's ascetics were men, but there were a few women, and Harvey looks at them with especial interest. Harvey has already published, with Sebastian Brock, a translation from Syriac of female saints' lives, *Holy Women of the Syrian Orient*,[1] where two of John's biographical sketches are included. These women are, as Harvey remarks, an "arresting group."

The sisters Mary and Euphemia represent the two types of female saint that we find in the *Lives*. Mary went to Golgotha and remained there before it for three years in tears and ecstasy, passing for a foolish old dame until some people who had known her blameless past came by, and recognized her. Her secret was out, and Mary became known as a holy woman. Mary, however, dreaded fame, and fled, but once a year, she would return to Golgotha.

Her younger sister chose a different path. Euphemia was married in childhood and had a daughter. After her husband's death, Euphemia adopted the religious life. She learned the psalms by heart and taught them to her daughter. Mother and daughter made a living by receiving goat wool yarn from the great ladies of the city, and weaving it at two pounds for one denarius. Half their income they gave to the poor. When the Monophysite monks were driven from their abbeys by persecution. Euphemia arranged places of refuge. She rented rooms for them, and when her own resources proved inadequate, she harassed imperial officials until they helped. She rebuked the well-to-do fearlessly if they failed to assist as she thought they should. John writes that the upper crust was afraid of her.

These two represent the two types of the Monophysite female saint as they appear in John of Ephesus. There are no transvestites, and no struggles with the demon sex torment them, whether they be men or women. Mary was a votary; like her also was another Mary, known as the Anchorite, who protested the persecutions by vigils that lasted a week or ten days. Euphemia was the practical saint, assuming a leadership role in a man's world. One might without whimsy compare her (though Harvey does not) with the empress Theodora herself. Both were women thrust into a crisis situation and both acted effectively to promote the interests to which they were committed.

Theodora's role was crucial. The palace of Hormisdas in Constantinople became a refugee center for Monophysite monks. John says that it held no less than five hundred of them: hermits, stylites forced off their pillars and heads of convents from all over the east. Theodora backed both John of Hephaestopolis and James Burd'aya who continued where John of Tella left off, ordaining Monophysite bishops and priests: it was Jacob who consecrated John of Ephesus bishop. By the mid-century, there was a separate Monophysite hierarchy in place. It could not have happened without the shrewd and dedicated support of the empress.

Harvey's book is a splendid study of this world which analyzes the human aspects of the Monophysite schism, and complements Frend's *The Rise of the Monophysite Movement*. Harvey has recognized the value of John's Lives for the sociology of eastern Christianity. Place John beside Procopius and we seem to have two separate worlds, though they were not. This is a book well worth reading by any student of the medieval eastern churches.

J.A.S. Evans
The University of British Columbia

1. Berkeley, University of California Press, 1987.

Giovanni Tabacco, trans. Rosalind Brown Jensen, *The Struggle for Power in Medieval Italy: Structures of Political Rule*. Cambridge: Cambridge University Press, 1989. pp. vi 353, cloth, $49.50; paper $14.95

This book originally appeared as one of the long chapters comprising the multi-volume, momumental *Storia d'Italia* published in Turin by Einaudi.[1] With the prodigious reading of a lifetime in both archival and secondary sources, Tabacco traces the development of political dominance throughout the Italian peninsula, the fragmentations and consolidations of power from the fall of the Roman Empire in the fourth century through the invasions of the Ostrogoths and Hungarians, the Lombard expansion, Italy's incorporation into the Frankish Empire of Charlemagne, the political anarchy of the tenth and eleventh centuries and the gradual growth of stable political institutions centered around the cities of central and northern Italy. This book, however, does not simply chronicle the rise and fall of political regimes but rather places questions of political structure and power within the framework of social relations and social classes. Moreover, unlike many recent texts on Italy which purport to span the peninsula but end by concentrating on the north between Rome and Milan, Tabacco's survey stretches to the northern borders — to regions such as Istria and to alpine passes controlled by the Piedmontese — and devotes more than a passing glance at the Mezzogiorno. It traces the history of the Kingdom of Sicily from the late Roman period through the Norman conquest, the development of feudal and bureaucratic unity under the Hohenstaufen, the region's political fragmentation after the Sicilian Vespers of 1282, and the beginnings of its economic dependence on the north after the financial incursions of the principle banking houses of Florence in the fourteenth century.

Despite a myriad of political details scanning not only the major power bases of Italy but touching places as obscure as Gazzo and Caresana, several bold conclusions arise. Tabacco argues that the German invasions of the fourth and fifth centuries hardly disturbed the administrative structures of the Roman Empire; nor did they disrupt the landowning dominance of the old senatorial and equestrian elites or diminish their social prestige. Instead, the decisive rupture with the Roman past came with the Lombard expansion of the seventh century; the old Roman elites then vanish completely from the records as landowners and the Roman senate finally lost its political and social functions.

Tabacco, moreover, reopens the old debate on the thirteenth-century conflict between the *popolo* and the *magnati*.[2] While the consensus of the past two generations of historians has favored Nicola Ottokar's contention that these parties were only political factions indiscriminantly composed of merchant guildsmen and feudal landlords, Tabacco argues that these forces represented class and economic interests: "But how can it be seriously argued that class was not a significant element in this conflict?... a constant point of reference in the conflict throughout the thirteenth century was the ostentatious and repeatedly-denounced arrogance of the 'nobles and great men'..." (p. 231). Against the arguments that the anti-magnate legislation in Florence was applied not only to old aristocratic families but also extended to the principle merchant families of the Arte di Calimala between 1293 and 1295, Tabacco reasons that the enactment of these laws "only demonstrates that the concept of 'magnate' was also being extended to the most overbearing elements of the *popolo*... And so the legislation against the magnates was truly part of a class conflict, and included under the designation political groups which in social terms certainly qualified, through the solidarity which bound them to magnates..." (p. 234).

In addition, Tabacco goes against tendencies in recent historiography which hold that the Guelf and Ghibelline factions were nothing more than names applied to political groups of noblemen in a city or province. He suggests instead that they reflect cultures and communities yet to be explored by scholars: "types of behavior which tended to persist over time and to be transmitted from one generation to the next with a progressive enrichment of language and myth..." (p. 257)

Other conclusions — that Frankish institutions of benefice and vassalage cannot be accurately labelled "feudal," that the Frankish system of vassalage did not create a uniform hierarchy of control across the geography of Italy or provide the structure for all relations between landowners and rural laborers, and that feudal language and its particular ceremonies and reciprocal relations of power come into northern Italy only with the development of the communes in the thirteenth century — will not strike the reader as novel or controversial. The central problem with this text, however, is the difficulty it will pose for the student in ferreting out its principle arguments and following its narrative. This difficulty arises first from the density of the presentation — the text's numerous topics, place-names (without the assistance of any maps) and the sheer weight of Tabacco's immense learning. But the atrocious translation of Tabacco's complex prose redoubles these problems. This insensitive and literal translation leaves the reader with a tangle of sentences in which subjects are separated from objects with contortions of multiple dependent clauses, some sentences stringing out to comprise entire paragraphs. Not only is the translation lacking in grace; in places it is incomprehensible and misleading. "Arte", the word for guild, is translated as "Arts" rendering confusing phrases such as "Arts of salaried workers" and "the precapitalist Arts" (p. 283), and "scienza", meaning scholarship, is translated as "science" (p. 22) misleading the reader into perceiving Tabacco as a 19th-century positivist. In conclusion, Tabacco's grand synthesis is a valuable tool for scholars of medieval Italy, but because of its complexity and density, coupled with this regrettable translation, it does not serve the purposes of its series, "Cambridge Medieval Textbooks." I, for one, would never dare to assign it to my undergraduates.

Samuel Cohn, Jr.
Brandeis University

1. *Storia d'Italia,* Vol 2: *Dalla caduta dell'Impero romano al secolo XVIII,* pt. 1, pp. 5–274. To this text has been added an historiographical introduction and a essay called "The Institutional Synthesis of Bishop and City In Italy."
2. Gaetano Salvemini, *Magnati e popolani in Firenze dal 1280 al 1295* (Florence, 1899); and Ottokar, *Il Comune di Firenze alla fine del dugento* (Florence, 1926).

Renée Giménez, ed., with Ch. Lauvergnat-Gagnière and P. Gondret, *La Tragédie Françoise du Bon Kanut, Roy de Dannemarch* (1575). Saint-Étienne: Publications de l'Université de Saint-Étienne: (Institut d'Études de la Renaissance et de l'Âge classique). Pp. 140, 1989.

This carefully prepared critical edition is based on two extant manuscripts, one in the Biblothèque Nationale, *fonds* Rothschild (manuscript "R"), the other in the Biblothèque de l'Arsenal (manuscript "A"). It seems impossible to affirm that one manuscript is a copy of the other; the editor presents the hypothesis of a third manuscript of which these are copies. Both "R" and "A" are very corrupt; rather than choosing one of them as the basis of her edition, the editor offers a conflation of both, with variant readings given in the footnotes. In manuscript "R" the final line of the text is followed by eight pen-and-ink sketches depicting the characters in the play. These drawings are reproduced on the cover of the present edition, and I shall refer to them later. An unusual feature appears in both manuscripts: a list of proper names, probably those of actors, accompanies the list of characters.

For the historian, perhaps the most interesting feature of the manuscript are the abbreviations JHS and MRA (for Jesus/Marie) which also occur on the final page of "R". As the editor points out, these initials seems to indicate that the play was written for, and presented at, one of the Jesuit colleges. Now the role of the Jesuits in the development of humanist tragedy is well known. Equally well known is the use of dramatised versions of episodes from Roman and biblical history to reflect the political and religious struggle raging in France at this time. What is particularly interesting about this play is that the author has chosen to dramatise an episode, albeit familiar to contemporary scholars, from early medieval Danish history. Some excellent research has led the editor to conclude that the topical reference for this play is a dispute between Henri III and his brother, the Duc d'Alençon. Two written documents signed by the latter, dated March, 1574, and September, 1575, in which he proclaims his loyalty to the king, but states clearly the basis for their dispute, are reprinted in an appendix to this volume. The thesis is convincing, all the more so since the rebels in the play, whose cause resembles that of d'Alençon, are shown to have justice on their side. That the Jesuits should stage such a play, the nub of which is the assassination of a king, is understandable, if one considers the involvement of the Society of Jesus with the Guise family and the Catholic League.

The play itself is representative of humanist tragedy. The action is based on Senecan models; the language is rhetorical and lyrical; only occasionally does a truly dramatic conflict arise. Choral odes repeating Stoic platitudes occur between acts, and the catastrophe is reported by a Messenger. The tone is generally one of foreboding before the king's murder, and of lamentation after. The characters are presented as types rather than individuals, and the psychology is rudimentary. On his first appearance in Act Two, the king conforms to the type of the Senecan tyrant, only rather less violent in word and deed than many. The traitor alone shows any psychological complexity in the doubts and hesitations he expresses before deciding to support the rebels, but such mental conflict is typical of this role in humanist tragedy. In other words, in many respects this play is no better and no worse than the majority of tragedies being written at this time.

For the theater historian, the interest of this edition is to be found in the details of the manuscripts themselves. As was noted above, a list of what appear to be actors' names accompanies the list of characters. Could these manuscripts in fact be actor's copies, transcribed, or possibly taken down from dictation, from a master script? Then there is the matter of the sketches at the end of manuscript "R". The editor states that they represent the characters of the play *"en costume et porteurs de divers attributs"* (p.8). So they do; but may they not indicate rather more than this? In discussing the theatrical qualities of the play, C. Lauvergnat-Gagnière notes that the two groups of rebels — the "Wandales" and the "Lutiens" — are each represented on stage by a single spokesman (pp. 28–29), a conclusion which is supported by the fact that the name of a single actor is given opposite each of these groups in the list of characters. Now, the reproduction of the sketches on the cover of the present edition shows, not a single actor, but groups of several armed men above the caption "Les Wandales" and "Les Lutiens," and the details of their "costume et attributs" are unclear to say the least. As a hypothesis, I would suggest that we have here an indication of the stage set for this play. A multiple set ("décor simultané") was commonly employed in stage performances at this time, and, indeed, survived until much later: Corneille's *Cid* and even *Cinna* could have been conceived only for a modified multiple set. The medieval mysteries were also produced on a form of multiple set, where the principal locales of the action (Paradise, Hell, Calvary) and the "mansions" of the main characters were represented simultaneously on a vast stage. Renaissance translations and adaptations of Terentian comedy seem to have been performed on a multiple set with mansions.1 Might not therefore the sketches in manuscript "R" also represent the arrangement of mansions for a production of this tragedy? There would be eight of them, the king and the queen, as the principal characters, occupying the two in the center of the set, with those of the two groups of insurgents and of the traitor to the (spectator's) left, and those of the three loyalists to the right. If this hypothesis is accepted, the actor's movements across the stage become very clear, and there would be no confusion in the spectator's mind when the action shifts from the territory of the rebels to the royal court and to Flanders.

If these inferences be correct, the *Tragédie du Roy Kanut* is a precious document for our understanding of the conditions of theatrical performances in Jesuit colleges in sixteenth-century France. Whatever the merits of the play itself, we must indeed be grateful to Renée Giménez and her collaborators for their careful scholarship in preparing this edition.

James Panter
University of British Columbia

1 Cf. T.E. Lawrenson and Helen Purkis, "Les éditions illustrées de Térence dans l'historie du théâtre", *Le Lieu théatral à la Renaissance,* p. p. J. Jacquot. CNRS. (1964), pp. 1–22.

Books Received

Listing of a book here does not preclude a review in a later issue of Studies in Medieval and Renaissance History.

— Stephen Bann. *The True Vine. On Visual Representation and the Western Tradition.* Cambridge, Cambridge University Press, 1989. Pp. xv, 286. $55.00.

— Bernald Bischoff, trans. Dáibhi ó Cróinin and David Ganz, *Latin Paleography. Antiquity and the Middle Ages.* Cambridge Medieval Textbooks. Cambridge: Cambridge University Press. pp. 291, illustrated, cloth $59.50. paper $22.95.

— Mary Carruthers. *The Book of Memory. A Study of Memory in Medieval Culture.* Cambridge Studies in Medieval Literature, 10. Cambridge: Cambridge University Press, 1990. Pp. xvii, 342. $54.50.

— Pierre Chuvin, trans. B.A. Archer, *A Chronicle of the Last Pagans.* Cambridge, Mass: Harvard University Press, 1990. Pp. 188.

— Graeme Clarke, ed. with Brian Croke, Raoul Mortley and Alanna Emmett Nobbs, *Reading the Past in Late Antiquity.* Rushcutters Bay. NSW. Australia: Pergamon Press, 1990. Pp. xv, 370.

— R.R. Davies, *Domination and Conquest. The Experience of Ireland. Scotland and Wales, 1100–1300.* Cambridge: Cambridge University Press, 1990. Pp. XVII, 134, $29.95.

— Elizabeth Ewan. *Townlife in Fourteenth-Century Scotland.* Edinburgh: Edinburgh University Press, 1990. Pp. ix, 201. £25.00.

— William V. Harris, *Ancient Literacy.* Cambridge, Mass: Harvard University Press, 1989. Pp. xv, 383. $35.00.

— Alan Harvey, *Economic Expansion in the Byzantine Empire, 900–1200.* Cambridge: Cambridge University Press. 1990. Pp. xvi, 298, 3 maps. $49.50.

— Thomas Head, *Hagiography and the Cult of Saints. The Diocese of Orleans, 800–1200.* Cambridge Studies in Medieval Life and Thought. Cambridge: Cambridge University Press, 1990. Pp. xvii, 342, $59.50.

— R.H. Helmholz, *Roman Canon Law in Reformation England.* Cambridge: Cambridge University Press. 1990. Pp. xxiv. 209, $44.50.

— Ann Kussmaul. *A General View of the Rural Economy of England, 1538–1840.* Cambridge Studies in Population. Economy and Society in Past Time. Cambridge: Cambridge University Press, 1990. Pp. xiv, 345. $39.50.

— Andrew Palmer, *Monk and Mason on the Tigris Frontier. The Early History of Tur'Abdin.* The University of Cambridge Oriental Publications, 39. Cambridge: Cambridge University Press, 1990. Pp. xxiv. 265. $65.00.

— David Sven Reher, *Town and Country in Pre-Industrial Spain: Cuenca. 1550–1870.* Cambridge Studies in Population, Economy and Society in Past Time. Cambridge: Cambridge University Press, 1990. Pp. xiv, 337.

— I.S. Robinson. *The Papacy. 1073–1198. Continuity and Innovation.* Cambridge Medieval textbooks. Cambridge: Cambridge University Press. 1990. Pp. xvi, 555. cloth $59.50, paper, $16.95.

— Peter-Johannes Schuler. *Grundibliographie Mittelalterliche Geschichte.* Historische Grundwissenschaften in Einzeldarstellungen, Bd. 1. Stuttgart: Franz Steiner Verlag, 1990. paper. DM 20.

- Denis Sinor, ed., *The Cambridge History of Early Inner Asia*. Cambridge Medieval Textbooks. Cambridge: Cambridge University Press, 1990. Pp. x, 518. $79.50.
- James D. Tracy, ed., *The Rise of Merchant Empires. Long-Distance Trade in the Early Modern World*. Studies in Comparative Early Modern History. Cambridge: Cambridge University Press, 1990. Pp. xviii, 442, $44.50.
- David Walker, *Medieval Wales*. Cambridge Medieval Textbooks. Cambridge: Cambridge University Press, 1990. Pp. x, 235. cloth $39.50; paper $14.95.
- Lee Palmer Wandel, *Always Among Us. Images of the Poor in Zwingli's Zurich*. Cambridge; Cambridge University Press, 1990. pp. vii, 199. $29.95.
- Kozo Yamamura, ed., *The Cambridge History of Japan, Volume 3: Medieval Japan*. Cambridge: Cambridge University Press, 1990. Pp. xviii, 712, $99.50.

CONTENTS OF
PREVIOUS VOLUMES

VOLUME I (1978)
ROSLYN PESMAN COOPER
Pier Soderini: Aspiring Prince or Civic Leader?

BERNARD F. REILLY
On Getting To Be a Bishop in Leon-Castile: The "Emperor"
Alfonso VII and the Post-Gregorian Church.

MICHAEL M. SHEEHAN
Choice of Marriage Partner in the Middle Ages: Development and
Mode of Application of Theory of Marriage.

RICHARD C. TREXLER
The Magi Enter Florence: The Uhriachi of Florence and Venice
INDEX, Volume IX (Old Series).

VOLUME II (1979)
JERRY H. BENTLEY
New Testament Scholarship at Louvain in the Early Sixteenth
Century.

LEROY DRESBECK
Techne, Labor et Natura: Ideas and Active Life in the Medieval
Winter.

M. PATRICIA HOGAN
Medieval Villainy: A Study in the Meaning and Control of Crime
in an English Village.

BERNHARD SCHIMMELPFENNIG
Ex Foriiicatione Nuti: Studies on the Position of Priests' Sons from
the Twelfth to The Fourteenth Century.

VOLUME II (1980)
ERIC FÜGEDI
Coronation in Medieval Hungary.

ARCHIBALD LEWIS
Patterns of Economic Development in Southern France,
1050–1271 A.D.

MARY STROLL
Calixtus II: A Reinterpretation of His Election and the End of the
Investiture Contest.

M.F. VAUGHAN
The Liturgical Perspectives of Piers Plowman.

VOLUME IV (1981)
MARC GLASSER
Marriage in Medieval Hagiography.

ALBERT L. ROSSI
"A L'Ultimo Suo": *Paradiso* XXX and Its Virgilian Context.

RICHARD C. TREXLER
and MARY ELIZABETH LEWIS
Two Captains and Three Kings: New Light on the Medici Chapel.

VOLUME V (1982)
ALAN E. BERNSTEIN
Theology Between Heresy and Folklore: William of Auvergne on
Punishment after Death.

ROBERT D. STEVICK
A Formal Analog of *Elene.*

ARON JA. GUREVICH
On Heroes, Things, Gods and Laughter in Germanic Poetry.

PAUL C. BURNS
Beneventan Interest in Vergil.

VOLUME VI (1983)
RICHARD C. HOFFMANN
Outsiders by Birth and Blood: Racist Ideologies and Realities around the Periphery of Medieval European Culture.

KATHRYN L. REYERSON
Land, Houses and Real Estate Investment in Montpellier: A Study of the Notarial Property Transactions, 1293–1345.

D.L. FARMER
Crop Yields, Prices and Wages in Medieval England.

VOLUME VII (1986)
BERNARD S. BACHRACH
Geoffrey Greymantle, Count of the Angevins 960–987: A Study in French Politics.

ROSLYN PESMAN COOPER
The Florentine Ruling Group under the "governo populare," 1494–1512.

JENNIFER L. O'REILLY
The Double Martyrdom of Thomas Becket: Hagiography or History?

VOLUME VIII (1987)
MAVIS MATE
The Estates of Canterbury Prior before The Black Death, 1315–1348.

SHARON L. JANSEN JAECH
"The Marvels of Merlin" and the Authority of Tradition.

M. PATRICIA HOGAN
The Labor of their Days: Work in the Medieval Village.

MARY ERLER and NANCY GUTIERREZ
Print into Manuscript: A Flodden Field News Pamphlet.

JAMES D. ALSOP and WESLEY M. STEVENS
William Lambarde and Elizabethan Policy.

VOLUME IX (1988)
CAROLA M. SMALL
    Medieval Settlement in Basilicata

QUENTIN GRIFFITHS
    The Capetian Kings and St. Martin of Tours

ROSALIND KENT BARLOW
    The Rebels of Vézelay

CLAIRE WHEELER SOLT
    Romanesque French Reliquaries

VOLUME X (1989)
BERNARD S. BACHRACH
    The Angevin Economy, 960–1060: Ancient or Feudal?

PAUL F. GRENDLER
    Chivalric Romances in the Italian Renaissance

JANET L. NELSON
    A Tale of Two Princes: Politics, Text, and Ideology in a
    Carolingian Annal

VOLUME XI (1990)
THEODORE JOHN RIVERS
    The Meaning of Alodis in the Merovingian Age

RUDOLF BIEDERSTEDT
    The Material Situation of the Working Population in the Towns
    of West Pomerania in the Era of the "Price Revolution."

GUNARD FREIBERGS
    The Knowledge of Greek In Western Europe In the Fourteenth
    Century

WILLIAM SAYERS
    Warrior Initiation and Some Short Celtic Spears in the Irish and
    Learned Latin Traditions

JOHN FREED
    The Crisis of the Salzburg Ministerlalage, 1270–1343

INDEX

Abbots Ripton, village of, 6, 16–22, 25, 27–28, 34, 38–41
Abbott, William, 15
Abraham bar Kaili, Bishop of Amida, 310
ad Pontem, Thomas, 14
ad Portam, John, 13–14
ad Portam, William, father of John, 15
Adam and Eve, 291
Adams, Paul, 5
Adolf of Schleswig–Holstein, 220
Adonis, 305
Agnes, Saint, 304
Agnes, wife of John Pege, 10
Agnes of Poitou, 206
Albert of Austria, 253
Albert of Brunswick–Lüneburg, Duke, 211
Albert of Lindau and Ruppin, 220
Albert of Meckleburg, 219
Albrecht of Austria, 209–10
Alcuin's Life of *Willibrord*, 301–02
Alesia, Roman siege of, 134
Alexander IV, Pope, 200–01, 209
Aleyn, William, 15
Alfonso I of Aragon, 195
Alfonso VII, first Castilian king of house of Ivrea, 195
Alfonso IX of León, 195
Alfonso X, the Wise, 193–95, 207–14
Allegrin, Jacques (II), 52
Amazons, 305
Amelot, Jean, 62
Amida, (mod. Diyarbekr), 309–10
Amitia, wife of Simon, son of Richard, 16
Amussen, Susan D., 15, 24
Anastasius, Emperor, 309
Andrew, Mariota, 19
Anjou–Plantagenet, House of, *vide*

Plantagenet Dynasty.
Annales de France of Belleforest, 73
Anonimalle Chronicle, 144
Arachne, 305
Ariès, Phillipe, 263–65
Aristotle, 4, 32, 83
    Politics, 83
Arnold of Isenburg, Archbishop of Trier, 203
Arnold, Thomas, son of Thomas, 19, 30
Arpâds, Hungarian Dynasty, 187
Arras, Peace of (1435), 219
Arte di Calimala, 313
Ashkenazic Jewry, 264, 267–71
Askania, House of, 211
Aspelon Thomas, 15, 25
Atalanta, 305
Attebrok, Robert, 16
Attebroke, Roger, 29–30
Attehalle, Sarra, 18
Attelane, Agnes, 16
Atterdag, Valdemar, last of the male line of the house of Sven Estridson of Denmark, 219; House of, 221
Ausonius, 304
Aylmar, John, 18, 30

Baer, Yizhak, 271
Bailey, F. G., 30–31
Baker, Geoffrey le, 140, 152
Balduin of Avesnes, younger brother of John of Avesnes, 203
Ballard, John, 12–13
Balle, Margaret, 17, 19
Barker, Juliet, 107
Barnavi, Elie, author of *Le Parti de Dieu*, 55
Baroun, Robert, 16
Bartholomew of Brescia, 214

Baudrillard, Jean, 286
Beatrix of Swabia, mother of Alfonso
    X, 201
Bele, Katherine, 11, 13
Beneyt, John, 9, 11, 17
Benjamin, Walter, 286–87, 290
Berenger, Richard, 23
Berenguela, mother of Ferdinand
    III, 194
Bergeron, David M., 127
Berges, Wilhelm, 202
Berman, Harold J., 5
Bible Moralisée, 286
Biblioteca Ambrosiana (Milan), 46,
    65
Biblioteca Apostolica Vaticana, 46,
    102
Bibliothèque de l'Arsenal, 315
Bibliothèque Nationale (Paris),
    45–46, 315
Bindoni, Gaspare, 78
Black Death, 163
Blaxter, Lorraine, 30
Bodin, Jean, 90, 260
    Six Livres de la République, 90–91
Bogislaw of Pomerania, 219
Bole, Agnes, 38
Bole, Alice, 16, 18
Boncompagni, Ugo, *vide* Gregory
    XIII
Boniface, "Apostle of the Germans",
    301–02
Bonaface VIII, Pope, 289
Bornstein, Diane, 108, 123
Brabant, Count Henry II of, 200
Brabantse yeesten, 138
Bretigny, Treaty of, 218
Breve chronicon Flandriae, 139, 169,
Brewester, Robert, 25, 28
Brid, Simon, 20, 26, 30, 42
Bridlington, John of, 153, 156
Brisson, Barnabé, 61, 63
British Library, 34, 46
Brives–Cazes, E., 56–58
Brock, Sebastian, 311
Broughton, John of, 12–13
Broughton, Thomas of, 16
Broughton household, 13

Broughton, village of, 6–7, 13, 16,
    21, 22, 26, 28
Bruce, David, Scottish king, 133, 141
Bruce, Scottish house of, 222
Brun, Adam, 22
Brut, The, chronicle, 144, 176
Bryd, Richard, 26
Bryson, Norman, 283, 287, 296
Bugge, Matilda, 17, 23
Bugge, Nicholas, 29
Burne, Colonel Alfred H., 136
Burton, Thomas of, 138;
    his *Chronica monasterii de Melsa*,
    138, 150, 154–55, 169

Cade, Jack, 114
    his 1450 uprising, 114
Calais, burghers of, 142, 144
Calais, seige of, 129, 131–42
Camille, Michael, 283, 287, 289
Campbell, J. K., 3
Capetian dynasty, 187, 217;
Capetian–Valois line, 217;
Capetian daughters,
    Jeanne, 217;
    Marguerite, 217;
    Isabelle, 217–18
Capilupi, Camillo, 68
Carpenter, Elias, 11
Carpenter, John, 25, 28
Carpenter, Roger, 25
Castile, House of, 195
Castle of Perseverance, 109, 124
Catherine de Médicis, 72
Catherine of France, wife of Henry
    V of England, 218
Catholic League, 45, 60–63
Catullus, 46
Caxton, William, 123
    his *Game and Playe of Chesse*, 114
Champagne, House of, 195
Chandos, John, 140;
    his *Life of the Black Prince*, 140,
    141, 151
Charlemagne, 186, 221, 259, 312
Charles IV, Emperor, 216, 253
Charles IV, King of France 217–18
Charles of Navarre, 218

Charpentier, Jacques, 82
Chickering, Howell, 107
Christian of Oldenburg, 220
Christina of London, 10
Christopher of Bavaria, King of
   Denmark, 219–20
Chronicle of "Joshua the Stylite,"
   309
Chronicon anonymi Cantuariensis, 139
Chronicon comitum Flandriae, 146,
   148, 154, 165
Chronicon Hanoniense, 203
Chronique de Pays–Bas, 146, 149, 151
Chronique des quatre premiers Valois,
   161–62, 164
Chronique Liegeoise de 1402, 138
Chronique Normande, 159–60
Chronographia regum Francorum, 160,
   162
Cicero, 71, 90
Clairvaux, Joan, 18
Claremont, Lord of, 148
Clark, Elaine, 19, 21, 26
Claudian's *In Rufinum*, 307
Claudii Puteani Tumulus, 45
Claudius Puteanus, *vide* Dupuy,
   Claude
Clement VI, Pope, 146
Clerk, Thomas, 13
Clerke, William, 23
Coligny, Admiral de, 68
Colliard, L. 61
Conrad IV, Hohenstaufen, 199–201,
   204, 208;
   his son, Conradin, 199–200, 211
Constantine, Roman Emperor, 98,
Contarini, Gasparo, 76,
Continuatio chronici of Adam of
   Murimuth, 155
Corbinelli, Jacopo, 68
Cordeliers, convent of, 51–52, 54
Corneille's *Cid*, 317
   his *Cinna*, 317
Count of Palatine, 206, 208–10, 214
Couper, Christina, 10, 14
Couper, William, 13
Crane, John, of Wistow, 23, 29–30,
   39

Crane, John, son of Simon, 11
Crane, Robert, 13
Crane, Walter, 11
Crécy, Battle of, 131, 136, 151, 166
Crónica de Los Reyes de Castilla of
   Jofré de Loaisa, 208
Crónica del rey Don Alfonso X, 209
Cujas, Jacques, 48
Cursor Mundi, 114
Curtys, Robert, 10
Cuvelier, author of *Chronique de
   Bertrand de Guesclin*, 157, 160
Cyprian, Saint, 308–09, 312
Cyril, 88

David, image of, 153
Davis, J., 4
De antiquo iure populi Romani by
   Sigonio, 82–83
de Dynter, Edmond, 138
   his *Chronicon ducem Brabantiae*,
   138
De Hocsem, Jean, 138
   his *Liegeois Chronique*, 138
de la Cerda, Alfonso, grandson of
   Alfonso X, the Wise, 195
de la Cerda, Enrique, (Henry),
   brother of Alfonso X, 201
de la Cerda, Fadrique, (Frederick),
   brother of Alfonso X, 201
de la Cerda, Felipe, (Philip), brother of Alfonso X, 201
de la Cerda, Ferdinand, eldest son
   of Alfonso X, 194–95
de la Cerda, Fernando, brother of
   Alfonso X, 196–97
de la Cerda, Manuel, (Emmanuel),
   younger brother of Alfonso X,
   195–96, 201
de la Cerda, Sancho, brother of
   Alfonso X, 201
de la Cerda, Sancho, second son of
   Alfonso X, 195–97
De la Roncière, Charles, 134
De Manny, Walter, 144
de Rada, Rodrigo Ximénes,
   Archbishop of Toledo, 202
De Thou family, 48

De Thou, Augustin, father of Barbe de Thou, 55, 60
De Thou, Barbe, 47, 55
De Thou, Christophe, brother of Barbe De Thou, 47, 55
De Thou, Jacques–Auguste, 47–48, 50–55, 84–86, 89
De Thou, Potier, 60
De Tournes of Lyon, printing firm, 83
de Vienne, Jean, French leader within Calais, 141–42, 144
De Winterthur, Jean, 137
Debord, Guy, 286
Del Bene, Pietro, 61, 64
Delbrück, Hans, 136
della Torre, Michele, Bishop of Ceneda, 77
deMause, Lloyd, 264
Denifle, Henri, 134
Derlyng, Roger, 16, 25, 28
Diefendorf, Barbara, 55
Domesday Inquest, 6
Don Fernando, *vide* Alfonso the Wise
Don Juan (Manuel), nephew of Alfonso the Wise, 209
Donatello's "David," 293
Donzellini, Girolamo, 79
Dorat, Jean, 48
Du Boulay, Juliet, 5
du Mesnil, Marie, wife of Jacques Sanguin the younger, 55
du Muiseau, Jean Morelet, 52
Du Puys, Jacques, 75, 82–83, 99–100
Du Voësin, Lancelot, (La Popelinière), 69
Duke of York, *vide* Henry VII
Dulcia, half–sister of Ferdinand III of Castile, 195
Dunbar, William, 127
  his "Ane Blak Moir," 118
  his "Sowtar and the Tailoris War," 112
Duncans, Scots dynasty, 187
Dupuy, Christophe, son of Claude Dupuy, 53
Dupuy, Claude, 45–91

Dupuy, Clémente, father of Claude Dupuy, 47
Dupuy, Clémente, S.J., brother of Claude Dupuy, 47
Dupuy, Clémente, son of Claude Dupuy, 59
Dupuy, Jacques, son of Claude Dupuy, 48, 50
Dupuy, Judith, sister of Claude Dupuy, 47
Dupuy, Pierre, son of Claude Dupuy, 48, 50, 59
Duval, Denis, bookseller and publisher, 64, 76, 82

Echternach, monastery, 301
Eco, Umberto, 286
Edward, the Black Prince, 141
Edward III, 123–68, 217–18
Egbert, King, 186
Eleanor, heiress of Aquitaine, 206
Elizabeth I of England, 109
Elizabeth II of England, 185, 188
Elizabeth of Austria, married Kasimir IV in 1451, 253
Enfant et vie familiale sous l'ancien régime by Phillipe Ariès, 263
Ephrem, Patriarch of Antioch, 310
Epistle of Paul to the Romans, 291
Erhith, John, 15
Erik of Pomerania, elected king of Denmark in 1396, 219
Espléchin, Treaty of, 132
Estienne, Robert, 83
Eulogium historiarum, 152
Eunapius of Sardis, 84, 90
Euphemia, Monophysite Saint, 311
Everard, Ralph, 9, 13
Evreux, House of, 222

Fanta, Adolf, 210
Favier, Jean, 136
Ferdinand III of Castile, father of Alfonso X the Wise 194–195, 200, 208
Fernando de Antequera, 255
Fine, William, 20
Fisher, James, 115–117, 122

Foire St. –Germain, 54
Foix, Paul de (Foxius), 85–86
Folkung, House of, 222
Folyot, Matilda, 17
Foster, George, 20
Foucault, Michel, 286, 287
Fourth Lateran Council, 295
Francesco I, Grand Duke of
    Tuscany, 86
Frankfurt, semi–annual book fair at,
    74–78, 80, 82, 83
Frederick Barbarossa, 202;
    bethrothal of his son Conrad to
        Berenguela of Castile, 202
Frederick II, Emperor, 200–01, 204,
    208
Frederick of Upper Lorraine, Duke,
    211
French Valloire villagers, 4
Frisians, 301–02
Froissart, Jean, 138–39, 141–42,
    144–45, 148, 151, 155–56,

Ganymede, 305
Gardiner, Richard and Geoffrey, 25
Gedyminides, elected kings of
    Bohemia by Hussite party, 253
Geertz, Clifford, 108, 123
Geoffrey, Bedel of Upwood, 24
Geoffrey of Swynford, Bailiff, 10
George I, 188
Gerberga, sister of Otto I of
    Germany, 198
Gerhard of Oldenburg, 220
Gernoun, Andrew, 28
Gernoun, John, 22
Gernoun, Margaret, 18
Gerold, Simon, 16
Gesner, Konrad, author of *Bibliotheca
    Universalis*, 78
Gesta of Liège, 208
Gesta Treverorum, 203–04
Ghibelline faction, 314
Ghislieri, Michele, *vide* Pius V, Pope
Girard (du Haillan), 69
Gisela, Empress, mother of Ludolf
    of Brunswick, 205
Gluckman, Max, 3, 8, 13, 26, 29

Gnilka, Christian, 307
Goffman, Erving, 29
Goldsmith, James C., 186
Gore, John, 11, 36
Gore, Thomas, 11–13
Grafton, A., author of *Joseph Scaliger*,
    46
Grandes chroniques de France, 157, 178
Greenblatt, S., 112, 118
Gregory X, Pope, 202
Gregory XIII, Pope, 58, 84
Gregory, William, his *Chronicle*, 115,
    126–28
Grendler, Marcella, 65
Grendler, Paul F., 78–80
Gualdo, Paolo, 65
Guelf faction, 314
Guise, Duc de, 60
Guise family, 316

Habsburg Dynasty, 187
Hamartigenia, 306–07
Hanecock, William, 12
Hannibal, Lord, 148
Hanover royal family, 188
Harlay, Achille de, 47, 59–61, 64
Harvey, Susan Ashbrook, 309–310,
    312
Harying, Matilda, 25
Hasidei Ashkenaz, 271, 279
Haugate, Alan, 26
Haukyn, John, 19, 21
Haukyn, Sarra, 18
Haukyn, Thomas, 26
Haviland, John Beard, 22
Hedwig, sister of Otto I of Germany,
    198
Heilman, Samuel, 29
Henri III, 60, 62, 316;
    his brother, Duc d'Alençon, 316
Henri IV, 45, 52, 60, 62–64
Henri of Navarre *vide* Henri IV
Henry, Duke of Lancaster, 153–154
Henry I of Germany, 198, 200–01,
    205–06
Henry II of England, 205–06
    his daughter, Matilda, 205–06
Henry III of England, 27, 205, 213

Henry V of England, 218
Henry VI of England, 218
Henry VII of England, 107, 110
Henry VIII of England, formerly
    Prince Henry, Duke of York, 108,
    110, 111, 120
Henry of Bavaria, brother of Duke
    Ludwig of Bavaria, 210
Henry of Brabant, Duke, 211
Henry the Lion, 211
Heryng, Richard, 24
Higgeneye, John, 20, 30
Higgeneye, William, 20–21
Hippolytus, 304–05
Hobbe, Catherine, 12
Hobbe, John, 10
Hobbe, William, 10
Hobbes, John, 12
Hobbes, Thomas, 4
Hobbes, William, brother of John,
    13, 14
Hoffman, Bonnie, 112
Hogar, Spanish villagers of, 5
Hohenstaufen Dynasty, 187,
    197–201, 211–12, 313
Holy Women of the Syrian Orient,
    311
Homans, George C., 30
Horseman, William, 22
Hostiensis, 214–15
Hotman family, 51
Hotman, François, 70, 71, 93;
    his *Francogallia*, 70–71
Houllier, Jacques (Jacobus
    Hollerius), father of Jacques
    Houllier, 48
Houllier, Jacques, 48, 51–52
House of Wittelsbach, *vide*
    Wittelsbach Dynasty.
Huguenots, 54, 56–58, 63, 68, 70–71,
    91
Hundred Years War, 131, 134, 135,
    163, 218

Imperial Electors, College of, 185,
    208
Index Librorum Prohibitorum, 84
Ingeborg, elder daughter of

Valdemar Estridson, 219
Inquisition, 78–79
Isaac Or Zarua', Rabbi, 269–70
Isabel, daughter of Edward III, 134,
    156
Isabella, sister of Richard of
    Cornwall, wife of Emperor
    Frederick II, 204
Istoria Pistolensi, 137
Ivrea–Castile, Dynasty, 187, 202

Jacob, Ha–Kohen, Rabbi, 269
Jacob, story of, told by Welsh chroni-
    cle, 156
Jagiello, Wladyslaw, 253; his cousin,
    Witold, 253
James Burd'aya, 312
James IV of Scotland, 108, 118
Jameson, Frederick, 286
Jean III, duke of Brabant, 156;
    Margaret, his daughter, 156
Jesuits, 315–16
Jeu de Saint Nicolas, 285
Johann, Margrave of Brandenburg,
    200, 210
Johannes Teutonicus, 214
John II, son of Philip VI, 146
John of Avesnes, 203
John of Ephesus, 309–12;
    his *Lives of the Eastern Saints*, 310;
    his *Ecclesiastical History*, 311
John of Hephaestopolis, 312
John of Reading, 143
John of Tella, 312
John the Couper, 13
John the Pondere, butcher, 17
Jones, George, 113
Jonson, Ben, 119;
    his *Masque of Blackness*, 119
Julian of Halicarnassus, 310
Julian, 88
Julio–Claudian emperors, 72
Justes of the Moneths of Maye and June,
    110, 120
Justin I, Emperor, 309
Justin II, Emperor, 310
Justinian, Emperor, 310
Justus Lipsius, author of commen-

tary on Tacitus, 72

Kanarfogel, Ephraim, 264–65
Kasimir IV, elected king of Bohemia, 253
Kawad, King of Sassanid Persia, 309
Keen, Maurice, 107
Kitzinger, Ernst, 287
Klipping, Erik, 220
his daughter, Richiza of Werle, 220
Knighton, Henry, 138, 141–42, 144, 146–47, 150, 153, 169
Knutsson, Karl, King of Sweden, 254
Knyghthode and Bataile, 114
Knyt, Margaret, 14, family 15
Kronyk van Vlaenderen, 145, 155
Kyng, Robert, 30, 40

l'Estoile, Louis de, 60
l'Estoile, Pierre de, 60–61
Lacy, Agnes, 18
Lambin, Denis, 48
Lanerok, Thomas, 16
Langer, William, 279
Latin Panegyrics, 45
Lauvergnat–Gagnière, C., 316
le Bel, Jean, 138, 141, 142, 144–46, 149, 151
Le Bon, John, 9, 13
le Bon, Petronilla, 13
le Bon, Simon, 10, 11, 13
le Bond, Agnes, 22
le Bond, John, 22
le Bond, William, 22
Le Bonds, family, 28
Le Bons, family, 23
Le Fèvre, Nicolas, 51–52
le Palmer, Michael, 16
le Pondere, John, 23–25
le Stake, John, 14, 15
Leclerc, Bussy, 59, 60, 63
Lenot, Anabile, 16
Lenot, Robert, 12, 16, 26
Lescot, Richard, 157, 159–60
Leunclavius (Johannes Löwenklau), 84, 88–89
Leunye, William, 18

li Muisit, Gilles, 138, 143, 148;
his Chronicon from Tournai, 138,
Liechtenstein, Ulrich von, 108
Life of the Black Prince, by the Herald of John Chandos, 140–41, 151
Liudgard, sister of Otto II of Germany, 198–99
Loisel, Antoine, 51, 56–58;
his Guyenne, 56
Lolgi, Guido, Italian letterato living in Paris, 77
Longo, Pietro, 75, 78, 82;
put to death by the Holy Office, 79
Louis d'Anjou, 255
Louis of Male, Count of Flanders, 134, 156, 162, 165
Louis of Nevers, Count of Flanders, 132
Lucas, Henry Stephen, 135
Lucian, 88
Lucretius, 304
Ludolf of Brunswick, brother of Emperor Henry III, 205;
his daughter, Agatha of Brunswick, 205
Luillier family, moneylenders, 54
Luxemburg Dynasty, 187, 222
Luyeres, Monsieur de, *vide* Pithou, Francois
Lydgate, John, 153
Lyon, John, 30

Macherey, Pierre, 286
Makah Indians, 22
Malamud, Martha A., 304–08
Mâle, Emile, 287
Manilius, Scaliger's edition of, 73
Manuel, Byzantine Emperor, 201
Manuzio, Aldo, 77
Mar John Urtaya, monastery of, 309–10
Margaret, Countess of Kent, 145–46
Margaret, daughter of Valdemar Estridson, 219
Margaret, Queen, wife of Henry VI of England, 110, 118

Margaret, Saint, daughter of Agatha
   of Brunswick and Edward the
   Exiled, 205
Margaret, wife of Hugh Knyt, 9
Maro, Stylite Saint, 310
Marshall, William of Wistow, 23
Martyn, Andrew, 17
Martyn, John, 15
Mary, Monophysite Saint, 311
Mary of Anchorite, Monophysite
   Saint, 311
Matilda, sister of Otto III of
   Germany, 198
Matilda of Upwood, 19
Maugis, Edouard, 61–63
Maurice, Emperor, 310
Mayenne, Duc de, 61
Mead, G. H., 29
Médici, Catherine de, 72
Medici, Marco, OP, Inquisitor,
   76–78
Medusa, 305
Meir of Rothenburg, Rabbi, 266
Mercuriale, Girolamo, professor of
   medicine at Padua, 78
Mesmes, Henri de, Sieur de Roissy,
   66, 67
Miller, William, 26
Minot, Laurence, English poet, 141,
   143, 147, 150, 153
Mohaut, Thomas, 11
Monophysites, 309–11
Montaigne, Michel de, 57
Montaillou, 28
Montbrison, 47
Morin, F., author of *Dialogue d'entre
   le maheustre et le manant*, 63
Muret, Marc–Antoine, 50, 64, 84–86,
   88, 89
Murimuth, Adam, *vide Continuatio
   chronici*

Nangis, Guillaume de, 206
Napoleon, 221
Navarre, Henri de *vide* Henri IV
Nero, 72
Neville's Cross, Battle of, 134
Nicolas, son of Richard of

Broughton, 10
Numatian, 88
Nummus, God of Gold, 289
Nunne, Dionysia, 18

Olaf of Norway, 219
Onufre, *vide* Onofrio Panvinio.
Optatian, 304
Order of the Garter, 135
Orgel, Stephen, 111, 124
Orsini, Fulvio, 50, 86, 92
Otto I of Germany, 198
Otto II of Germany, 198
Otto III of Germany, 198
Otto IV of Brunswick, Emperor, 204,
   206
Otto of Brandenburg, 200, 211, 213
Ottokar, Nicola, 313
Ottokar of Bohemia, 200, 210
Ottonians, Imperial House of,
   198–200, 204, 206–07, 214, 216
Outy, Andrew, 13, 29
   John, servant of, 29
Outy, John, 15

P. Servilius Rullus, 90
Pacatus Drepanius, 64
Paine, Robert, 4, 26
Pakeral, Henry, 30
Paleotti, Gabriele, Cardinal, 86
Pamplona, House of, 195, 198, 216
Panofsky, Erwin, 287
Panvinio, Onofrio, 84, 85
Paris, Matthew, 205, 207, 212–13
   his *Chronica maiora*, 212
Parlement de Paris, 50, 52, 56,
   59–60, 91, 93–95
Parys, Juliana, 17
Paul "the Jew", Patriarch of Antioch,
   310
Pedro the Cruel, 255
Pege, Agnes, wife of John Pege, 14
Pege, William, 10, 14
Peristephanon, 304
Peristiany, J. G., 3
Perna, Pietro, 78, 79
Perroy, Edouard, 136
Philip, King, 199;

his grandsons by his daughters,
the Duke of Brabant, the King
of Bohemia, King Alfonso of
Castile, 199–200
Philip VI of Valois–Anjou, 136,
140–43, 145, 153, 155–57, 160,
163–65, 218
Philip the Fair, 289
Philippa of Hainault, wife of Edward
III, 145
Piasts, Polish dynasty, 187
Pikeler, John, 21
Pilche, John, 20, 26
Pinelli, Gian Vincenzo, of Padua, 46,
48,50 53, 59, 63, 67, 69, 73–84,
83, 84, 86, 88, 90, 91
Pithou, François, 51, 88–89, 101
Pithou, Pierre, 51, 57–58, 89
Pitscottie, Robert Lindesay of, 119,
120
Pitt–Rivers, Julian, 3
Pius V, Pope, 84, 85
Plantagenet Dynasty, 187, 18
Plantin polyglot Bible, 73
Politian, 84, 85
Politiques, 59, 61, 71–72, 91
Pollock and Maitland, 5, 6, 27
Pomerania, House of, 220
Pontcarré, Geoffroy Camus de, 63
Postan, Michael M., 19
Prepositus, Geoffrey of Caldecote,
17
Previté–Orton, C. W., 136
Prince Henry, Duke of York *vide*
Henry VIII
Procopius' *Secret History*, 310
Prometheus, 306
Propertius, 46
Prudentius, 304–08
Psychomachia, 304, 307–08
Pygmalion myth, 289

Ralph, brother of Nicolas, son of
Richard of Broughton, 9–10
Ralph, reeve of Broughton, 23
Ramsey Abbey, 6
Ramus, Petrus, 90
Randolf, John, 11

Raugei, A. M., 65
Récits d'un bourgeois de Valenciennes,
139
Reeve, Joan, 28
Reischmann, Hans Joachim, 301–04
René of Anjou, 110
Reve, Agnes, 19
Revison, Richard, 22
Riccoboni, Antonio, professor of
humanity at Padua, 78
Richard of Cornwall, 185, 193, 197,
200–01, 204–14
Richard of Hyrst, 10
Rigault, Nicolas, 48, 64
Rivolta, Adolfo, 65
Robbe, Nicolas, 20
Robert of Avesbury, 144, 147, 151,
153, 155;
his *De gestis mirabilibus regis
Edwardi III*, 155
Robert the Dyker, 24
Robert the Swineherd, 10
Roger the Miller of Houghton, 10
Roman de la Rose, 285
Rose, John, custodian of the light at
Abbots Ripton, 20
Rostaing, Jean de, 58
Rotondò, Antonio, 79
Rudolf of Habsburg, King, 203, 210
Rufinus, 305–07

Sabyn, Matilda, widow of Andrew, 18
Said, Edward, 286
St. Bartholomew Massacre, 68, 82,
90
St. Erik of Sweden, King, 254
St. Galmier, town of, 47
St. John, Sir John, 28
Salian kings, 198–99
Agnes, Salian daughter, 199
Salic Law, 219
Salviati, Cardinal, 85, 88
Salviati, Signor Jacopo, 88
Sancha, half–sister of Ferdinand III
of Castile, 195
Sancho, second son and heir of
Alfonso X (the Wise), 195–97,
Sancho III, founder of house of

Pamplona, 195–97, 201
Sanguin, Christophe, canon of Notre–Dame, 55, 63
Sanguin, Claude, wife of Claude Dupuy, 47, 53, 55, 59
Sanguin, Jacques, father of Claude Sanguin, 47
Sanguin, Jacques, the younger, 55, 63
Sanguin family, moneylenders, 55,
Sarakatsani shepherds, 4, 13
Saussure, Ferdinand de, 286
Saxe–Coburg–Gotha, royal family, 188
Scaliger, Joseph, (de la Scala), 46, 48, 51, 61
Schnur, Roman, 56
Schultz, Magdalene, 266, 279
Schwarzburg Dynasty, 187
Scut, Elena, 16
Sefer Hasidim, 265–66, 271–77, 279–80
Segeley, Robert, 29
Séguier, Claude, Sieur de Verrière, 47
Séguier, Pierre (II), 57
Seize, leaders of the Ligue in Paris, 60
Servin, Louis, 51
Severus, Patriarch of Antioch, 310
Sharpe, J. A., 4, 14, 27
Shemuel, 268
Shepherd, Ivo, 26
Shepherd, Philippa, 16
Shepherd, Roger, 16, 26
Shepherd, Simon the, 16, 26; Richard, father of Simon, 26
Shrovetide, 113
Sicilian Vespers of 1282, 313
Sicily, Kingdom of, 313
Sigmund of Luxemburg, deposed as king of Bohemia in 1421, 253
Sigonio, Carlo, author of *De regno Italiae*, 47, 78, 82, 86
Sirleto, Guglielmo, Cardinal, 84, 87, 88
Sixtus V, Pope, 58
Sluys, Battle of, 131

Smith, Agnes, 12
Smith, Stephen, 12
Snape, William atte, 28
Solente, Suzanne, 47, 53
Spacks, P., 29
Stenkils, Swedish dynasty, 187
Stephen of Burton, 13
Storia d'Italia, published by Einaudi, 312
Stratford, John, Archbishop, 152
Strazel, Jean, 48
Strong, Roy, 123–24
Stuart dynasty, 188
Suetonius, 88
Sutor, Agnes, 26
Sven Estridson, House of, 219
Sylburgius, Fridericus, collaborator of the Wechel heirs, 89

Tabacco, Giovanni, 312–15
Tacitus, 64, 72
Talmud, Babylonian, 268
Talmud, Jerusalem, 268
Templars, 289
Ternour, Thomas, 25, 28
Theodora, Empress, 310–11
Theodosius, Roman Emperor, 64, 304
Thevet, André, 70
Thiofrid's Life of Willibrord, 301–02
Tiberius, Roman emperor, 72
Tibullus, 46
Titus Livius, 59
Tobias of Vienne, Rabbi, 269
Torah, 270, 272, 274
Tournai, seige of, 131–32
"Tournament of Tottenham," 114–15, 117–19, 123
Tragédie Françoise du Bon Kanut, Roy de Dannemarch, 315–17
Trastamara, Enrique, 255
Tudor, Mary, 135
Tudor Dynasty, 188
Turnèbe, Adrien (Turnebus), 48, 93
Tyb, the Reeve's daughter, 113 Perkin, Tyb's father, 113

Ulrich of Mecklenburg, 220

Underdown, David E., 24, 27
Upwood, village of, 6, 17, 19–21, 23–25, 27
Urban IV, Pope, 210
Urraca, Queen, mother of Alfonso VII, 195

Vale, Malcolm, 107
Valois, Henri de, 60
van Berchem, Willem, 137
Vegetius, 114
    De re militari, 114
Velleius Paterculus, 64
Venette, Jean de, 157–62
Venus, 305
Vernoun, John, 17
Verres, Sieur de, 57
Verses on the Kings of England, 153, 176
Vettori, Pier, 83
Victoria, Queen of England, 188
Villani, Giovanni, 137
Ville-à-Neuve, town of, 133, 139
Virgil, 304
Vladislav II, King of Bohemia, 253
von Nuwenberg, Mathias, 137
von Rebdorf, Heinrich, 137

Wake, Juliana, 16, 28, 38
Walsingham, Thomas, 135, 146, 148, 151
Walter Ivo, 26, 30
Warboys, village of, 6, 7, 16–26, 29–30
Warburg, Aby, 287

Warde, Johanna, 18
Wars of the Roses, 256
Webester, Agnes, 18
Webester, John the, 23, 24
Wechel, Andreas, publisher of Paris and Frankfurt, 76, 81, 82
Weinfeld, Moshe, 267
West, Alice, 19, 21
Wettin, House of, 211
Whithorn, Thomas, 115–16, 122
Wickham, G., 107, 109
Wilkes, Richard, 18
William, Count of Burgandy, 202
William, the Smith of Warboys, 23
William of Holland, nephew of Count Henry II of Brabant, 200–01, 203, 214
Willibrord, "Apostle of the Frisians," 301–02, 304
Wilson, Peter J., 4
Windsor, House of, 188
Wistow, village of, 6, 16–27
Wittelsbach Dynasty, 187, 210–11
Wittelsbach–Neumarkt, House of, 222
Wymar, Agnes, 19, 23

Ynglings, Norwegian dynasty, 187
York Psalter, 114

Zetzner, Lazarus, 80
Zeumer, Karl, 208
Ziletti, Giordano, Venetian printer, 78
Zosimus, Greek historian, 84–89